THE WORD

A PHILOSOPHY OF WORDS

THE WORD

A PHILOSOPHY OF WORDS

A literology or science of literate characters; a psychology or logic of The Logos (Soul); a word analysis or word treatise.

By

EDNA SARAH BEARDSLEY

FOREWORD

The purpose of this book is to set forth The Logos as Root of all radically literate words, and to point out the more grossly illiterate nature of words that only usurp the rights and the places of good words.

A good word is treated as a literate idea made up of highly literate characters immediately derived from its Root. Each gross one is treated as an illiterate, illogical and illegitimate word, and other words are either relatively literate or relatively illiterate. In this way the words may classify themselves as to their degrees of literacy by means of their own letter construction, because some of the letters of the alphabet are fully literate, some are relatively so and some are illiterate. Thus an illiterate one becomes the antonym of the true word, or of the truly literate idea.

This book is a philology or a *literology* setting forth the unique principles of The Logos as The Word.

Philology, in this treatise, means love word; loving the logos; fond of the word; love of the word. It is the Greek *phileo-logos,* love and word.

This word book does not pertain to languages as applied to peoples of the Earth. It does not apply or pertain to races or to their literate cultures. It pertains only to words and to their letter constituents or literate construction, and to their relationship or lack of relationship to The Logos.

The purpose of this book is to make plain to those who love The Word or The Logos-Root many pertinent facts concerning words which the world of books may not have treated. It may appear to be a religious work, because it bases its logical and literate premises upon The Logos, but it is rather in disregard of orthodox religious usage, and of popular human doctrines, established theories and theologies.

Each word is made up of literate characters including at least one vowel, one vocal sound, or one vocable letter. Each letter has individual character, whether spoken or written. Each vowel has the power of speech as a literate idea or entity, which entity must have expression. Each good word may be a speaker, an advocate or an agent presenting an idea. Each word speaks with the authority of its Root, which Root gives it its power of verbal iteration or vocal expression. A true word may be an idea, a compound entity, or an assemblage of literate, ideate characters. Thus they identify, classify, and define themselves, or they speak for themselves as to their origin.

This book is intended to serve the true philologist as a further word analysis or as a further reference book elaborating noteworthy words found in the dictionaries. It leaves the dictionaries to fulfill their own purposes, while this book deals with the literate characters, and with words as characters, entities or individuals (individual characters); deals with a few score of selected words.

This book is a word philosophy or a philosophy of words. It deals with the word itself as independent of human usage, humanly assigned character, classification and reputation.

An wholly literate word may not have a true synonym or a duplicate. It is absolute in character and it is definable or soluble only through its Root-Logos. This Word or Logos is The beginning Principle and Premise in which all sound words originate; The Root, The self-existent, all-existent Supreme Being, known to our Earth as the Greek *Theos,* the Latin *Deus* (*Divinus, Dei, Deite*) or Divinity, and the Anglo Saxon God or Good.

An illiterate or unsound word is fathered and mothered by the human intellect. Many words have been humanized, literalized, materialized or physicalized in order to meet the demand of human utility, or to conform to human knowledge. Thus they are applied, so they are adopted, and so they are humanly assumed to be, and thus this treatise has had to disregard human parlance where necessary to preserve and to cherish the literacy and the legitimacy of a word which is fathered and mothered by The divine creative Word (Logos-Root). This Word is Root of divine literology; Source and Soul of philology, and The Speaker—via conscience—of divine soliloquy.

The writer has sexed many nouns by showing their verbal action or function. These words are identified by their masculine or feminine functions or coordinate agencies. They are living words, at work, forever propagating, multiplying and presenting their literate and logical ideas to the thinker. There are three masculine and three feminine forms of verbal action, making six (or sex) altogether; and this is one of the purposes of this book—to make plain the spiritual logic of the sexes and the literacy of word-gender; to make plain the six or sex or sextette of processes of realization, ideation or word life.

A literately constituted or truly ideated word must be constituted or composed of letters, and an idea must be worded, whether thought, spoken or written. Each letter of each word and each word in a statement, phrase, or sentence must have its individual power of address; its own peculiar ingenuity. Each must be invested or endowed with its own rudimental substance and literate essence, and be assigned to its own literate office as assignee possessing its own peculiar properties, which properties are properly derived from its own creative

Root. Each one of these ideas or words has the state, condition, position, disposition, and quality-constitution peculiar to its Word-Root. This Root, being altogether wise, divinely intelligent, spiritually excellent or supreme, substantially beneficent, essentially good, positively true, actually existent, perpetually and forever articulate (via conscience), is of infinitely literate continuity. Therefore, ideas or words springing from this Word or Logos-Root are divinely confirmed, verified and substantiated; are sublimely perfect or perfected. They must be letter perfect. They must be completely and entirely coherent, universally applicable or relevant. They must be fully equipped and thoroughly qualified to perform the literate functions or ideations to which they are assigned, and for which they are created.

The thinker could not form a thought without words. They are the ideate forms; the letter figures; logical entities; legitimate images; radically rooted identities, or rudimentally constructive agencies. They are the whole elements of holy realization and ideate demonstration. They are didactic or instructive; self interpretative, luminous or illustrious in their illustrations and manifestations. They are masterful in their explanations or verbal expositions—whether spoken, written or thought. They are specific or precise in description and in specification, because they are sent or set forth by their own tutelary Spirit, which is The Logos Spirit. They speak in their own divine idiom. They speak of their Root and by means of the urge, erg or energy (inspiration, aspiration or animation) of their Root. They speak with the authority of their Root.

Human usage (human nature, human intellect and its mode of teaching) has humanized or finitized many infinitely literate words. Many words have been stolen, misappropriated or assumed, and have been demoted to human degree, because they were presumed to be of human caste or degree.

The author has undertaken to restore such words to their literate and legitimate lofts or realms by means of tables such as this:

REALM   I   DIVINITY: The Logos or The Word-Root;
                           The Origin, Source or Beginning or crea-
                           tive Principle of words or ideas.

REALM   II   SPIRITUALITY: the logician; the radically
                           literate and fundamentally legitimate ideas
                           of The Logos.

REALM   III   MORALITY: the highest human concepts
                           of Realms I and II; the conscientious be-
                           liefs or the honest human convictions of

right; the moral instincts, intuitions, sentiments and motivations; the humanly and morally practicable virtues.

REALM IV   PHYSICALITY: human   nature,   human knowledge or physical knowledge.

REALM V   IMMORALITY: amorality; nonmorality and all of the antonyms of good and of morality; all of the curses and vices resulting from Realm IV — its presumptive premises which, as physics or natural science, is knowledge of a finite sort or of the physical sort and nature.

This realm pertains to the sub-animal nature, the unduly indulgent nature, or the morally unrestrained sub-animal, or unnatural habits and phases of human existence. It pertains to all that is hurtful, hateful, proud, wilful, deceitful, revengeful, aggressive, self-justified, inhumanly acquisitive, selfishly and murderously possessive.

This Realm V is used to compare the con-*science* or the conscientious manifestations of Realm III with the utter and total lack of conscience and its science in Realm V.

Realm II pertains to that which is comparable to and related to Realm I.

Realm III pertains to that which *con*-science (the science or scientific intuition within oneself) dictates as comparable to Realm II.

Realm IV is used for the sake of comparison. It does not treat of physical science, but, as used in this treatise, it serves to compare the physically literal with the metaphysically figurative. It serves to show by way of comparison the vast difference between the physically natural sciences and the spiritually natural science manifested in conscience as moral-spiritual intuition, and known to the human race as conscience and as intuition.

The purpose of this treatise is to bring The Logos law, literacy and logic down to Realm III where it may meet the conscientious thinker's moral-spiritual desire, but to leave Realm IV to its own kind of knowledge.

CONTENTS

[ix]

THE WORD, Abortion

The word *abortion* comes from the word abort, meaning to arrest the development of; to make to become useless, vain or unsuccessful.

The prefix *ab-* means from, off, or away.

The root is the Latin *orior,* meaning I rise or become visible; I grow.

Literal meaning: away from growth or from growing; off or away from natural and *original* state, position or condition. *Original* is from *origo, orior,* rise.

Common meaning of abortion: failure in anything during progress and before maturity; an untimely birth; miscarriage.

The word *orient* pertains to the East or to the sunrise. It is called the land of the rising sun. The word origin is from the same root. It is that which gives rise to anything; that which is the commencement, source, cause or beginning of anything, or of the existence of a thing.

The word abortion is a noun of action or condition. It pertains to the unnatural expulsion of a conception—physical or metaphysical—or of the rudimentary fetus before it is viable, or capable of maintaining *vita.*

In the lowest realm of inhuman and criminal or immoral affairs, it may be said that a scheme or conspiracy is abortive when it is arrested by the law element and thus fails to mature or to be carried out.

In the physical realm an abortion pertains to the casting off of the embryonic growth or fetal formation; pertains to its being cast away from its natural place of lodgment. Thus a physical conception is aborted. It never rises, grows, matures or becomes visible, viable, vital, valid or veritable.

In the metaphysical human realm a plan, a project or a perception (outlined) may be heartily conceived and entertained for a while —even sustained for a while. Then this conception may be aborted; may fail to mature when the hope has failed or when the plan is off. This conception may be said to be thrown out of the human mentality or to be cast away, off or from the attentive thought when the plan or project is abandoned. When this happens it means that the male and female mental faculties have ceased to coordinate. Hope (moral prosperity) and faith (fidelity, confidence and expectancy) have failed when they do not unite, harmonize or unify their action. Sentiment

[1]

must be mutual. Honesty, veracity, affection, loyalty, sincerity and all of the moral forces are involved in making this conception manifest, or in making this hope to prosper.

When one plants grain in the spring one does not neglect to cultivate or to attend the plants from the time of their germination to the time of fruition. If human intellect knows all things then humanly instituted knowledge embraces all things within its finite horizons.

When faith fails to adhere to her concept, and fails to cohere with hope, and when the masculine and feminine elements fail to combine their comprehensive and apprehensive abilities or their sentimetal capabilities, then the conception is soulless, lifeless, without feeling, senseless, not cherished, not nourished. For instance, a successful career may be only an attempt—an unsuccessful attempt—or a mere hope or contemplation of a harvest time without the faithful application of mental energies that make the harvest possible.

Hope must be a worthy quality; an element of moral stamina; a condition of moral courage; a state of virile purpose, or a virtuous resolution. It must have moral promise and valid anticipation. The conceiver of this kind of hope must have the fertile element of patience, piety, equity, chastity, moral clarity, sentimental splendor and all of the feminine graces and glories if she is to carry this hope out to a realization or to its full fruition. Thus faith and hope keep their troth. They concur. They cannot fail.

In the realm of human conception it is common to hear that there has been a miscarriage of plans, or that the things hoped for and prayed for, have not materialized; have not arisen or become visible. This is commonly called bad luck, even though it is humanly possible of achievement, or probable of attainment. It is seldom remembered that things conceived are in the metaphysical human matrix, and that it is there that they must be sustained while they are being heartily and conscientiously maintained by their perceiver. It is seldom remembered that the male perceiver cannot gestate his own rudimental (potential) plans, since he has no natural mental matrix or place of lodgment for embryonic issues. He furnishes only the pater, pattern, plan, outlined specification or the rudimentary vital element (germ) as patron of these issues. He can morally support his conceiver, but she it is who can substantiate his worth or confirm his merit and his virility.

The well established issues in the human social world today exist as such because those issues were agreeable to the conceptual thinkers. The instituted moral, civil, and industrial affairs which exist today were once at issue; were once unsettled or unestablished issues; but they exist today because of the concipient thinkers who were sentimentally, morally and affectionately interested in them.

Public sentiment or human sentiment is a tremendous power exist-ing within womanhood. It is a deciding factor. Public opinion is a masculine thing, and it is only a potential thing. Woman's power of conception carries with it her power of contraception. She is quick to detect the fraud. She is quick and thorough in changing her mind concerning the virile element when she finds him to be dishonest and unworthy of her confidence. Human sentiment is constantly at work, aborting and defeating many unworthy issues. If public sentiment does not sustain an issue it fails. If she does not conceive it, it is because she does not believe in it. She is veracity, the lover of honesty. She honors him and obeys his principles. This is woman's intuition; a spiritual gift; one of the sexual (*sixual*) functions. (See page 370.)

Metaphysical and world-wide marriage is established in the human realm today. This marriage functions by means of six spiritual agen-cies; by the law of *sixual* conjunction. The male element advocates his opinions. The female element silently conceives or silently contra-ceives his opinions, according to whether or not her sentiments are with them. Thus it is in public life. In private life the male element confides in his conceiver. He whispers his hopes and aims in her ear, and trusts them to her care.

The sixual elements, agencies or faculties consist of six specifically different but precisely cooperative mental functions, acting in turn, and acting in their naturally, morally and mentally constructive way. The constructive and virtuous perceptions (virile precepts) destroy or sup-plant the worthless, wrong or bad perceptions that speculate in schemes detrimental or destructive (in human affairs).

There is no virtue in destruction or in its seed. There being both virtue and constructiveness in morally virile perceptions, they stand as first of the six mental actions. The second mental action is feminine fertility acting as charity, affection or the compassion which cherishes all masculine perceptions worthy of her consideration.

The third functioning agent is the power of speech emitting his honest convictions with enthusiasm; with moral energy. The fourth functioning agent is the power of conception. The fifth functioning agency is masculine wisdom fathering and maintaining what he has advocated.

The sixth functioning agency is feminine vitality, quickening, moth-ering and sustaining or nurturing what she has conceived, and what she has gestated, developed and brought forth; what she has acted upon and brought to issue or brought to sturdy maturity in human affairs.

Thus are all wise issues established in human affairs. The mascu-line (three) elements perceive, present and father the issues. The feminine (three) elements love and conceive by intuition, verify or prove the legitimacy of, and bring forth and mother the issues.

The masculine perceiver may be said to furnish the *pater-ial,* not the *mater-ial,* for the issue. The mater or mother furnishes the *mater-ial* out of which an issue is composed, or is constructed. If, therefore, the male or fertilizing element fails to live up to honest precept in practice, he is not giving his conceiver his moral support and the embryonic issue may become invalidated or devitalized. His very trustworthy conceiver may lose her sentimental faith in his worthiness, and his issue may be sentimentally aborted, because of lack of sentimental coordination.

Destructive thinking and constructive thinking are always at war within. The virile thinker must stand by his moral standards, his principles and his conscience. The fertile thinker brings forth his perceptions spontaneously, intuitively and naturally, if they stand together in sentiment. There must be a collaboration of veracious effort; a cooperation of reasoning; a correlation of rational qualities, appreciation and affection. The conception must be cherished. A concept or a conception is that which has been conceived; and to conceive means to take with (the perceiver), or to take jointly; to take wholly, or to take together as an whole. A metaphysical conception or concept is like the physical human one. It is an embryonic thing combining, uniting or joining together the fertilizing element and the ovum or egg element. Thus it is an whole element; a compound of all essential properties.

It is the female mentality that feeds, nourishes and nurtures an unborn hope. Nothing unfavorable should interrupt, interpose, interfere, intercept or intervene to disrupt or to disturb by faction or by friction.

It has been said that it is a woman's prerogative or privilege to change her mind. This means that it is her moral right to be exercised; her peculiar feminine privilege to change her concept. If it were not possible for her to abort a conception, she would be compelled to gestate and sustain that which she does not love, belove, give lief, give leave or believe. If she could not abort a conception that she had believed to be *with* her own familiar sentiments (and later found to be against her sentiments), if she could not correct her mistake when she learned of her mistake, there would be no hope beyond contraception.

A mental conception must go through the same several processes of development as a physical one:
1. She must conceive or contraceive.
2. She must gestate or abort.
3. She must quicken or refuse to act upon the concept.
4. She must give it of her sentiments to sustain it, or she must let it perish for lack of sentimental nutriment.

A conceptual or concipient thinker must cast out, cast off or arrest the development of a germ of error in some way, or she must allow that germ to develop into greater embryonic proportions. She must *not* mold or cast it in her mind. She must not bear it, carry it, gestate it or bear it out, else she will be untrue to herself. She will be in conflict with her own ideals and sentiments, and she will be untrue also to the advocates of truth and right whose germs counteract a germ of error.

If the concipient thinker's intuition, her conscience, her finer sensibilities and her highest sentiments do not sustain a rudimental issue, it is unsustained. She cannot sustain it when once her sentiments have turned against it and its advocates. She cannot honor that which she does not feel sentimentally inclined toward. Dishonor and disbelief constitute either contraception or complete abortion. Miscarriage of a mental monstrosity is more honorable than mental war and infanticide when it does what abortion failed to do, or what contraception did not do in the first place. The mental anguish, labor, pain and contest is very similar to the physical kind of danger and extreme desperation that accompany miscarriage. It is the necessity to wrest oneself free from something that tenaciously adheres to one, as identified *with* one, while in reality it is *not with* one but against one, and is quite foreign to one. It means that she must wrest herself free from something that is not her own peculiar metaphysical property; something that she can no longer nourish or mother, conscientiously and rightly.

The masculine thinker can change his mind without inflicting trouble on anyone. His mentality is a pouch full of potential germs of perceptions to be advocated, and until they *are* advocated, uttered, emitted, or set forth for conception, they are of no concern to anyone. He may reject, eject, spend, destroy, or cast out his preconceived opinions, or he may eliminate them easily and naturally to make room for new and better perceptions or opinions, or points of view, as he gets a closer view of the precept or premise from which he deduced them.

A perception is like a seed ready to be sown and ready to be germinated by means of the processes of vegetation. It is also like the blue prints, plans and specifications of a house, which house is to be made of certain materials, which materials are the mater or mother elements, goods or constituents (*mater-ials*); materials pertaining to and of the mater element. She furnishes or supplies the material. The perceiver furnishes the outline and specifications which are often changed or corrected.

A conception involves the sentiments or the mother instincts, which are the strongest of all human instincts. The conceiver does not abort that which she cherishes, but the perceiver may discharge or dismiss an element of a theory which he does not cherish.

A conception lodges in the confident heart (or mental matrix) of the feminine thinker. Her powers of appreciation, comprehension, cohesion, contemplation and amplification are tremendous, but contrary to popular belief.

A wise perceiver confides in, and leaves his most highly esteemed treasures with, the morally-spiritually teeming or productive intelligence, which intelligence is not human intellect, but is a spiritual gift, or an intuitive sense. She is his confidant, his metaphysical mate, his inspiration and incentive. She stimulates his mentality and lends courage to hearten his undertakings. She carries or conveys his convictions — his wholehearted convictions, visions, and perceptions — through from premise to conclusion.

When the male fraud's clay feet appear under him to convince her of his insincerity, forfeiture, failure, fault or spurious nature, the veracious woman (true conceiver) must abort. A sentimental abortion of this sort is painful, sad, laborious, anguishing and heartfelt. It is commonly called the condition of being disappointed in love.

The untrue and insincere woman usually aborts her conceptions, because of lack of constancy or faithfulness to stay with an unformed and unmanifested project.

The human mental matrix is exposed to fraudulent perceptions, evil knowledge and its vile forces at all times. It is vulnerable and pregnable to the male forces. Hence the practice of mental abortion is her defense, and is a defense and a benefit to the human race.

Mental crime prospers when it is not stayed, checked, aborted or miscarried. The feminine mentality must either multiply crime or must contraceive of it, abort it, miscarry it, commit infanticide upon its issues, and cease to suckle them or to mother them.

The mental matrix and the mental mammal with her mammary glands, is equipped to nurture the criminal's offspring (at her mental breast) or to betray the male criminal and his scheme. This kind of abortion is usually vital to the female involved. It means being involved in working with or against the law or the outlaw, as traitress or as accomplice since the human mentality is capable of baneful intrigue and vilest intent. It means having no protection, but being victimized, enlisted and subordinated to the schemer.

The power of conception and fruition is woman's reason for existing. The capacity (matrix) to hold and to form or to mold human thought should be a sacred trust.

THE WORD, Adam

The word *Adam* is made up of four letters, two of which are vowels. This *a* vowel is the least literate of all the vowels. This initial *a* in the name Adam gives it a most illiterate introduction. The other *a* vowel doubles, repeats, and emphasizes the fact and state of this illiteracy.

Adam is commonly defined as "unregenerate or depraved human nature." He is considered to be progenitor of the human nature, the human (humus-man) kind or the human race, human clan, kin, family, tribe or people; the male parent, pater or pattern of humanity, human nature, or the humus-kind collectively.

Adam is symbolically defined or characterized as of the red earth; (Latin *terra rubra* or *ruber*) or *humanus* or human impulse; as earthy, earthly, worldly, mundane, temporal, unspiritual or profane; as pertaining to humanity which is of the *humus* or ground; is of the human (humus-man) nature; is of the nature of the soil or ruddy dust. He is of the red sand or stuff; is of a red color, or bloody hue. This blood or bloody color is suggestive of strain, stock, or lineage. This lineage makes Adam the ancestor of the human family or the Adamic kind; makes him blood relative in the ancestral line; means consanguinity (Latin *sanguis*, blood), of the same blood, affinity or kin or kind.

This lineage is adam-ant or hard against any other kind or affinity. It is a dam (A-dam) serving as obstruction or dam to shut out all but the Adamic human impulses, human nature or the unrestrained, cursed human characteristics.

Adam is typical of that character which fathers the criminal instincts in human nature. He himself is unrestrained human impulse, and thus his son Cain typifies the criminal instinct of fratricide, or the unrestrained impulse to kill his brother Abel.

Adam is typical of the dramatic physicist. The serpent plays the part of the melodramatic metaphysicist. Abel is simply typical as the victim of these circumstances, before which he was as vapor (breath; transitoriness), and unable to protect himself. He may be the unsuspecting, unwary character who is unguarded and unshielded from spear and lance of the acquisitive Cain character which typifies envy and unrepressed covetousness, or possessiveness.

Adam is the fool, the egotist who knows nothing beyond his own physical consciousness; nothing beyond his own flesh and bones horizon. He is the husband of flesh and bones—feminine—and the product of the god of physical finity, humanity or mortality. He is the husbandman of the delightful garden which he cannot keep, and he is resident of the Eden (flesh and bones body) in which the bodily physical pleasures or pleasurable impulses reside. This Eden means *voluptas,* pleasure; voluptuous; full of sensuous delight or pleasure; given to sensual gratification. This characterizes Adam as first resident of the sensuous and sensual human nature, material physique or mortal (dust) body.

Adam's existence is a dream and he the dreamer, and a person or character created by the human imagination, sensual impression, and sensuous animal, chemical manipulation.

This fantastic Adam character is a dreamer (fantast), a fantasy, phantasy, or a product of the capricious, human imagination. The word phantom is from Greek *phainein,* meaning to show. The word phenomenon comes from the same form. Thus Adam is a thing of fancy to show, or that shows the whimsical nature of the character, and the extravagant imagination of his damning, dooming god, or phantastic maker.

Moses uses the character Adam to dam up or to stop the flow of divinely logical ideas abruptly and completely; to be the adamant god—or the *Adam-ant,* hard against reality.

Thus human imagination — manipulated by this agent or god — creates this puppet-like character, which character in turn outlines an image of female form to match himself which he called woman. But before this, it was necessary for a deeper sleep to befall Adam. He was to become more deeply hypnotized or affected by excited and unrestrained imagination, or he was to become more thoroughly manipulated, and more deeply impressed with the phantoms and images in his consciousness, such as the luscious Eve.

Adam is, again, a dam which confines the human conception of the human race to this Adam and Eve realm of phantasy and mythology, and finity, and human nature, with its dust make-believe; with its proud regalia—the human physique—or as Adam puts it, flesh and bones, or the product of his god's sentient physical, or physically sensual imagination.

The Adam doctrine is to this day a fantastic mental dam, or a doctrinal barrier, that restrains the flow of liberated and free moral agency; that dams the four rivers of infinite metaphysics, and turns the mental waters into physical, animal channels; into carnal courses impelled by Adamic impulses and concepts.

Adam and his perception of woman constitute the clearest definition of what man *is not;* the best illustration of what the rational faculties of the human race *is not* and are not, and what reason is not.

Adam is father of all damage. The word damage, being related to the word dam. Damage is the sum or total of that which is damned; the collection and recollection of the various penalties self-inflicted by moral ignorance and ignorance of moral law, or by moral insensibility.

The root of the word damage is the Latin *damnum,* loss or penalty, harm or injury; *demnere, damnatum,* to condemn. Literally damage is the condition of the condemned; the aggregate of that which is without virtue or reason for its existence; that which is illiterate—not under the moral law; illogical—not lettered and not reading the science which con-science presents and teaches; not legitimate, but illegitimate —not born of the marriage of virtue and veracity, or of honesty and honor for verity.

Adam and Eve portray all that marriage is not meant to be. They father and mother all damage and all of the curses of the wandering human imagination excited by the legendary serpent. They bring forth all that is doomed or damned; all that hinders moral prosperity, spiritual liberty or freedom and divine security.

Moses uses the Adam character to dam, to turn, or to stop the flow (influence) of the legitimate substance and essence of ideas, and to turn the reader's attention to the shocking story; to change the mood abruptly to the illegitimate or humus-man or humus kind of man, for the sake of contrast with the *mon* or man not made out of the organic matters of the humus (ground); on the ground or basis of the soil. This humous or human mammal derived from the soil (the humorous —*humeo* person) or the humorous human imagination is called Adam, the character who is used facetiously as sub-animal in nature and in character, used by way of comparison.

Adam is actor *A* in this great drama of human nature. Moses intended it to be a witty or capricious story, to show perhaps by immediate and direct comparison, the vast difference between the dreamer— Adam—and the thinker or man of the preceding chapter. It is meant to be humorous, freakish or fanciful. It is indeed a great story or legend; an allegory or a very striking burlesque; a masterfully written parody, travesty, or a mockery of his first chapter which is a most elegantly concise piece of divine literature.

By the use of metaphor Moses brings the spiritually pure literate substance down to moral evaluation. But the amoral human nature may read only what it gathers.

This parody caricatures marriage and it physicalizes all things, and reduces all human character (and nature) to the sub-animal position —lower and less moral than the animal or mammal nature. This contrast is striking.

And so it is to this day that humanity chooses the Adamic perception of woman, preferring not to wake out of that "deep sleep" or the excited human imagination; ignoring the fact that the Adam character presents the antithesis of every logical, literate and legitimate idea; the malediction and antonym of God's benedictions.

Adam is the phenomenon of officious human nature; the impertinent human ego character, characterizing human impulse; the state of consciousness created by human knowledge; the hypnotic condition —being asleep to reality; the cursed creature that the evil god made; the effect of suggestive manipulation.

Moses is one of the greatest of writers. He wrote the first five books of the Holy Bible. He succeeded in writing that which no other writer, prophet, seer or sage undertook. He gave us his vision and version of the true, divine creation of man, and of all of the substances, realities and properties peculiar to man's divine Heaven and Earth; all that is under the reign or the jurisdiction of The Logos-Spirit; all that is therefore wholly and purely spiritual and divinely logical. Thus Moses introduced the character Adam to show by means of direct comparison, the vast difference between the spiritual image recorded in the Genesis, first chapter, and the actor-character Adam, presented as legendary evil.

Moses must have introduced Adam as a character-actor just as Shakespeare and other writers have introduced characters, humanly impulsive actors, agents and representatives.

Adam first enters into the scene as a most illiterate character, because of his name. Then as being derived from the dust, which is the lowest form of stuff or matter. Then as the subject for manipulation, imagination, hypnotism or the deep sleep. Then as having no dominion or spiritual domain. Also as having no feminine mate, as half of the compound man. In fact every contrast and comparison to the real man is definitely followed out in the Adam satire.

Moses must be the only writer who had the moral courage to tell the world that natural human impulse (portrayed by the character actor Adam) is the direct opposite of the spiritual nature of which man is born; that Adam, in his human pride make-believe, is the illegitimate fancier, the mimicker, the would-be man. Thus he illustrates what dust or clay can do to dam the flow of divinely legitimate ideas coming to the reader.

Adam is the *pater,* pattern, perceiver, outliner and advocate of materialism; pater of all curses, suppositions and false knowledge; god of illusion, idolatry, mortality and misapprehension; *pater* and patron of mythology and all that is adverse or opposed to the real and true *-ologies,* or the spiritual logic, or the science such as *con*-science.

THE WORD, AFFECTION

The word *affection* is built upon the word affect, which is a verb meaning to do to, to make to do, or to make to feel.

The prefix *af-* is *ad-*, meaning to.
The root *fect* is *facio* (*facere, factus*), I make; *facio* (*factum*), to do or make.
The suffix *-ion* means act of. It forms the word affect (a verb) into a noun of action or condition.
Literal meaning: the result of having been affected or made to do; the state or condition of having been acted upon or made do.

Affection is a noun denoting that one's feelings or one's emotions have been affected; that one has been made to feel sentimentally moved or emoted; that an exterior force has affected one by acting upon one. It may be a feeling of fondness for another or toward another, or it may be another's feeling affecting one. It may be a mutual fondness impelling both or many.

Affection understood thus becomes an entity or a human mental state of being and of metaphysical feeling. It is an element of sentiment (*sentio-mentis*). Affection says: "I am influenced or affected or made to feel fond. I make you to be fond." It is friendship itself making contact with another or with others. It is a tender attachment making itself felt as a quick or vital mental feeling. Thus one feels the fondness expressed by another, and in turn expresses or is impelled to express fondness or favor for the same sentiments or standards of human excellence.

The word *affect* is a verb meaning to do. It embodies the essence of doing unto others as one's highest sentiments dictate. Affection is a strong and tender attachment, a warm regard or a sentimental emotion affecting one.

The word *affection* is not a synonym for the word love. The following table classifies both love and affection:

REALM   I   DIVINITY: Love, The noumenal Logos-Love.

REALM   II   SPIRITUALITY: love, the phenomenon of Love.

REALM III HUMANITY: human affection, friendship, charity; a natural human liking for moral sentiments.

REALM IV PHYSICALITY: human nature and its affection for self. Here human impulses act and react in favor of self, affecting others by magnetic, hypnotic or electric forces; by personality influencing, possessing and controlling.

REALM V IMMORALITY: moral ignorance or unmorality; hatred or disaffection. Here one may be affected with envy, malice, revenge and such miasmal infections as dishonesty.

Affection is a morally stable quality or character which stands by or with friendship, against human and inhuman animosities. It is a feeling of good will; a settled or firm sentiment with a bent or inclination toward virtue and wisdom. It is a living sentiment or zeal of good will for all humanhood. It is a virtue that rises and stands above the human nature vices. It is a sentiment entertained for one's neighbor. It functions and lives in its native realm of human ethics (Realm III in this treatise).

This Latin root *facio* takes the form *fec* or *fect* in the words fecundate (to make fruitful), confection (made with sugar), and perfect (thoroughly made). It takes the form of *fac* in factotum (to do all), and facsimile (made like), and facile (easily done). Affection is morally fecund.

Affection is a noun of action or condition; the action, the actor, character, quality or agent in action. It is the friend-hood or sentiment-hood or sentimental condition of being subject to morally metaphysical fecundation.

Affection is a condition of being which is peculiar to the whole human race or the whole of human kind. It stands as a mature or well developed virtue with the ability to withstand the immoral forces of disaffection, within and without. One may be affected by exterior forces or by his own interior forces which respond spontaneously to these immoral forces. These exterior forces may be good forces presenting themselves through the influence of conscience, or they may be bad forces presenting themselves through the influence of human nature.

The foregoing analyses show that affection is a spontaneous will within one; a voluntary good will, counteracting ill will, discontent, disloyalty and estrangement. Humanly it is a natural and spontaneous response of any kind. It may be the action and impulse of the human nature (the animal or the mammal) or it may be that the human individual is greatly affected (attacked, concerned, diseased or made to be ill at ease, ill-humored or immorally emoted) by adverse influences. For this reason affection must be morally, ethically and conscientiously emoted or energized and forever at work if she would countraceive and counteract disaffection, disloyalty, discontent or the lack of good will.

The human magnetic personality would affect the morally and truly affectionate individual, if it could, by controlling, counteracting, crossing, frustrating and defeating him in his attempt and intent to be affectionate and to act affectionately. He would affect others with his disaffection.

The human nature, its mentality, and its impulses are never affectionate. Human nature is devoted to self. It gives out nothing.

THE WORD, AFFINITY

The word *affinity* analyzes thus:

Prefix *af-* means to.
Latin root *finis* means end or limit.
Suffix *-ity* means state, quality or condition of being.
Literal meaning: state, quality or condition of existing to
finis or to end; state of being to limit and thoroughly.
Common meaning: kinship, alliance or agreement.
Common antonyms: antipathy, aversion, antagonism or dis-
like.

The word affinity lends itself to many uses and it may apply to
the chemical world, the world of natural sciences, or to the world of
sentiment, specifically. In this world of human sentiment it is a moral
quality, attribute or thing. It may be defined as the moral, metaphysical relationship existing in conscience, or existing between the masculine and feminine qualities of conscience or consciousness:

Honesty is the affinity of veracity. She honors him.
Moral courage is akin to moral heartiness or health. She
heartens or befriends him.
Moral stamina is akin to constancy. She stands by and with
him, in his principles.
Moral steadfastness or steadiness is the affinity of feminine
troth. She keeps troth with him. She (veracity) keeps her
word to him.
Fidelity is the affinity of faith. He confides in her. She promotes his confidence.
Moral virility is the affinity of feminine fertility. All of the
mental-moral virile abilities match the feminine capabilities or conceptual capacities.
Integrity is the affinity of chastity or trustworthiness. They
cherish each other.
Temperance is akin to compassion, serenity, contentment
or moral tranquillity. Sobriety, modesty, piety, meekness
and obscurity are the unselfish virtues. Patience and
peace, loyalty and sincerity are unobtrusive.
Masculine eminence (or loftiness in the human affairs of
promoting morality or of moralizing human kind) is the

[14]

husband of her who conceives and nurtures his potential
moral issues designed to promote moralization. She is
humble, silent, obscure or unassuming, while he is prominent and outspoken, or conspicuously vehement.

Masculine eminence is the complement or affinity of feminine
modesty or obscurity. There is a gravid attraction, affection or avidity between these similar but different characters.

Masculine hope is the affinity of feminine expectancy; the
husband of her, and the pater of moral prosperity.

The rational power of honest and accurate perception is the
affinity of morally chaste power of conception (of right).

Compassion is the affinity of patience and sentiment. Compassion has a passion for affection or patient sentiment.

Sobriety or temperance has an affinity for moral zeal and
fervor.

Piety has an affinity for the bliss or joy of devoutness or for
the expression of honest devotion and loyalty in human
affairs.

In the realm of spiritual literacy and logic, sentiment and intelligence, the virile thinker is the affinity of the fertile, concipient, or
conceptual thinker:

Wisdom, the spiritual seer (acting, speaking, and thinking
in the wise way, mode or manner), is the affinity of spiritual, universal sentiment or love.

The virile power of speech, address or presentation is the
affinity of the ear of fertile understanding or spiritual
reception. The power to perceive and to set forth is the
affinity of the power to conceive and to bring forth.

Virile integrity or masculine virtue, or holiness, or wholeness of the spiritual sort, is the affinity of her who is spiritually wholesome, sound, healthy or alive; of her who
is fecund, fruitful or productive of wisdom's issues.

There must be a mental and sentimental agreement between the
male and female faculties. There must be harmony, kinship, alliance
or understanding—that state of standing, together, under the same
precepts and principles. There must be a union but not a fusion of
these virile and fertile faculties and characters, to the end that they
produce their mental, sentimental or spiritual kind. Thus affinity is
the basic and underlying science of marriage. It is that which makes
two individual thinkers metaphysically marriageable. It is the premise

of marriage, and matrimony (*mother-mony*) is the conclusion and the fruition, for wisdom is potential. His virile perceptions must be conceived and his issues must be brought forth and must be sustained by feminine sentiment. His affinity must make his issues actual and apparent, or veritable to other thinkers.

The word affinity may mean from beginning to end, or it may mean having no end. The word finite means having the quality of coming to an end, hence limited in degree. The word infinite means having no limit, unlimited, limitless, not finite; not having the quality of coming to an end. The word affinity means to the end, and without an element of limitation, or interruption, or with continuity; to agree to the end; the state of having no finish. In this sense spiritual affinities form a coalition, or an eternal compact; form a wedlock of qualified powers or powerful qualities. Wisdom and his conceiver (in limitless and close spiritual, universal agreement) constitute a compound of intelligence or intelligent force. She loves and honors him, and she loves, honors and obeys his principles or Principle.

The law and rule of affinity is complete freedom and unlimited action, carrying out and sustaining wise issues. This law of affinity holds in balance the active and the passive elements of ideation, the similar but different individual powers of demonstration, fruition and realization, and it brings into evidence the essence of speech and the substance of understanding (the speech) which is a complete process.

The word family means affinity or kin. Thus in marriage two individuals may become one, twain one, of one family, or of the same family. This pertains to physical relationship.

The word family means affinity in a metaphysical relationship when two become familiar or thoroughly versed in the same kin or kind of incorporeal things, principles or subjects. This metaphysical familiarity marries or weds them. It is an intuitive or natural mental bond.

Two individuals interested in, concerned in and considering the same classification, kin or kind of moral and spiritual precepts, become familiar, become affinities, become kin, become of kindred or family likes and dislikes and of a likeness, excepting the female thinker or conceiver never usurps the male thinker's sphere of perception (and presentation) but stays in her sphere of conception and verification and is intuitively and intelligently passive to his vision, wisdom and oracle.

THE WORD, ANGEL

The word *angel* comes from the Greek *angello* (*angellein*), I bring tidings; *angelos,* messenger; *angellos* (angel), an holy messenger. Thus an angel is a purely spiritual entity I, or identity bringing tidings or word (divine words or messages) from The Word (Logos or God).

An archangel is of highest order, chief, head, leader and foremost in authority. They are authorized, appointed and sent out to man—the purely spiritual thinker—to convey divine intelligence, information or tidings. They are a means of communication by way of worded thoughts. They function as divine impartations from The Logos to the wholly (holy) spiritual logician; from The Word, in worded form, to the divinely literate, attentive, intuitive and devoted ones.

In the realm of human imagination, angels are usually portrayed as babes, maidens, or virgins having white wings to symbolize purity and innocence; as heavenly or ethereal things out of this world (this unspiritual world). Humanity may believe angels to be idle, decorative things or creatures that do little else than to sit in heaven, where they play golden harps. Humanity may believe that angels are imaginary forms flying through the ether in an effortless fashion, wearing long, filmy, flowing robes. They are the rational and spiritual faculties ever at work, ever moved and energized or spirited, even as consciousness is ever at work. They are elements of intuition and wisdom offsetting human nature's sensuality. They are immortal, immutable, universal elements of The Logos-Mynde supplanting the finite elements of the human intellect.

Angels are the evangelists, ever at work, ever bringing good tidings, ever proclaiming the good story, or The story of Good or God; ever evangelizing, through conscience, and thus ever speaking to the human ear. This is the work of ministering angels. In this work *con*-science is preacher or speaker addressing himself to human perception.

Angels do not communicate with humanity directly. Conscience does. Humanity is familiar with conscience and its moral science, while it is not familiar with the angels who bring divine messages, divinely worded tidings or angelic communications. Humanity is familiar with moral instincts and intuitions as presented by con-science, but humanity is unfamiliar with angelic, spiritual or divine instincts and intuitions. Humanity can understand the messages as they are iterated, reiterated, translated and interpreted by con-science, and thus the angels minister.

[17]

The angels may be symbolized by the sunbeams that bring light and warmth from the sol (sun). Angels bring word, light, love, warmth, and enlightenment from Soul.

An angel is as near and as dear to one as one's tutelar spirit. It is one's spiritual genius acting as tutor; one's own intuition; one's guardian sent from Divinity. The thinker who adores and obeys the angels is adoring and worshipping or serving his own deific Principle as disciple or as offspring, under the parental discipline of his Creator. He is following the recipes brought to him by the angels. He is the recipient of these beneficial recipes, remedies or directions (direct messages). He understands these divinely worded directions.

Angels are not fragile things. They are able or capable tutors; leaders in all fields of Divine Logic, literacy and law (the infinite, universal sphere of The Logos). They convey and present all of the divine, immutable graces which conquer the transcient and mundane conceptions of grace. They teach love, beauty and dignity of speech in harmony with The Logos excellence or quality. They convey these graces to Realm II or to the sphere of divine reality or spirituality. Then in turn they are reconveyed to Realm III by means of the faculties of conscience, as the following table will indicate:

REALM   I   DIVINITY: The Logos; The Word.

REALM   II   SPIRITUALITY: wisdom, the logician; the divinely literate and legitimate man; the wholly intelligent thinker.

_____*

REALM III   MORALITY: humanity; human ethics; the realm of orthodox human precepts and practices; human intellect.

REALM IV   PHYSICALITY: the realm of the physical sciences; the world of human nature and human impulse.

Realm III is tempered, restrained and tutored by conscience, while Realm IV is untouched by conscience. It stands on its own physical feet or foundations, and observes only its own sciences. Angels, having no physical form or significance, are believed to be spirits, ghosts, fantoms or ghastly specters visiting the physical Earth to bring messages of portentous significance.

_____

* The line in the foregoing table marks the extent of the angel's direct activities, because con-science begins its activities, or conscience takes over the indirect activities of the angels, at the line, as representative of the angel.

Angels signify and constitute the all-pervading and all-prevailing divine influence speaking or dictating the God-sent word or messages to the spiritual mentality or to the spiritually minded. Conscience and its spiritual sciences constitute the all-pervading influence of wisdom dictating to the morally minded, or teaching the rules of rightness.

The angel's didactic nature or spiritual abilities are too logically harmonious or heavenly to be acceptable to the human intellect of Realm III. Con-science is also didactic but has the human sense of directness, and the moral sense of commandment or mandatory nature as well.

The angels have a gentle aptness to teach. The human intellect is obstinate and, therefore, the angels method or manner of teaching is too gentle to be effective in Realm III. Conscience is a more compelling force; an irresistible, incessant, dogmatic and doctrinal urge or force that is well equipped to teach, influence, command and control in the realm of the moral instincts, where human nature and its natural sciences attract attention, and where human intellect claims to have authority.

The angel conveys thought from its Root or Source to the thinker who is attribute derived from this radical Source, which is Source of all true and absolute logic. This logic is the spiritual or divine science of correct and accurate thinking, which accurate thinking makes cured, makes accured, or makes accurate and maintains the state and condition of spiritual correctness or perfection. Conscience makes morally accurate or accured and maintains the condition of moral order.

So it is that angels are industrious and prosperous; that they are energetic—spiritual energy itself—working with conscience to promote moralization in Realm III, and working with wisdom to promote spiritualization which follows moralization; working by contraceiving fiction.

Angels are—in their office—agents of intelligence. Their function is to convey or to carry purely logical thoughts from The Logos to the logician, from The Word to the literate reader or intelligent thinker, and from the Logos-Principle to the true thinker who entertains and who practices this precept or Logos-Principle.

Angels are no less real and no more ethereal, spiritual or heavenly than wisdom and his ideas, because angels are elements and agents of wisdom's realm of complete understanding, which understanding is also the whole sub-*stance* (*understance* and *understancing*) which The Logos substantiates.

Angels bring word from The Word. They bring ideas or elements of logic from The Logos. They bring instructions, specifications, directions and outlines for perfect concepts. They bring the divine design to the thinker who is demonstrating what he is perceiving and conceiving.

Angels are composed of angelic qualities such as spiritual or infinite, divine or universal purity (with no taint of humanly sensual sentiment). They are the ideate consequence of The divine creative Word —beneficence or Love. They are spiritual wisdom and perfection in action. They are ever living, ever acting goodness sent to the realm of Good's heaven or haven to bring thoughts of Good.

THE WORD, Animal

The word *animal* comes from the Latin root *animus, anima, animos* or *anim,* to which radical *anim* the suffix *-al* is affixed.

The suffix *-al* means relating to or that which, making the noun animal, or making it (the *anima*) that which breathes other than plants —literally, something having life; relating to this *anim;* pertaining to life (other than plant life); a sentient living organism or creature other than a plant.

Common meaning: the animal nature as distinguished from rational or spiritual nature.

A sentient living organism has physical sense-perception, sensation or feeling which is natural or physical. The feeling is not mental, neither is it other than the action of the sensitive nerves and brain, but remains in its physical (animal) organism. This physique is animated by the animal instincts or impulses—not by the *anima* (life) or the *animus* (mind) or the feeling of mind (sentiment) which is peculiar to the *animus* (soul), who is not merely a physique.

The common belief is that this *anim* (animal) is a mixture of all things; that this animal is the animus or soul; that it embodies the animus or mind, and the spirit or breath which is called *animo* (*anima*). But this is not true according to literology, because the initial *a* vowel classifies it (*anima* or animal) in the spiritually illiterate, physical, or mundane realm of rationality; in the realm of the natural or physical sensibility or sentient organism. *Literately* the Latin *spiro* is spirit; the Latin *mens* (*mentis*) is mind; the Latin *vita* is life; the Latin *sentio* (*sentire, sensum*) means to feel or to think.

The Latin *animus* is used as root of the word courage, but the word courage comes from the Latin *cor* (*cordis*), meaning heart.

The word passion is given as animosity, being full of passion; full of courage, intent, purpose or temper to feud or to be hostile (active ill will; vehement enmity or hatred, hating), but the word passion (also compassion) comes from the Latin *pati* (*patior, passus*), meaning to bear or to suffer; meaning patience or to be patient.

The Latin animus, as in the word magnanimous, means great soul. This animus may be ascribed to soul, in spite of its illiterate composition, for it is the only one of the Latin forms (radicals) that is not otherwise named. It has no relation to the animal, for it means elevated in soul or elevated (lifted up) above what is low, mean or base. It means to be honorable, noble and generous. This is the opposite of being full

[21]

of animal human impulses, intents, impatience or temper. Yet the word soul in its Anglo Saxon form is *sawl* or *sawel*. It is defined as that animating principle of individual being; the entity, the incorporeal, mental or spiritual nature of man. Here again this is the opposite of the human animal or mammal instincts, senses, agencies, animosities and activities or unspiritual animations.

It would seem that the word soul is more difficult to isolate or to separate from the other animations, or that it is least understood, because it is the *re* (*realis*) or *res*, the thing, or of the thing itself, or of Soul—The creative Logos or Principle itself. It is the entity, as a living reality in continuity or in spirituality which is two realms above the animal or mammal thing.

The following table will classify the word animal and will elevate the word soul, lifting it out of the mammal human being or the human physique:

REALM I

DIVINITY: The Logos-Soul; The divine creative Root, Source, Origin and sustaining Principle of creature and creation.

REALM II

SPIRITUALITY: the logician, soul, entity, expression, thinker or spiritual being; the reflection, attribute, offspring, representation, complete idea or compound concept of The Logos-Soul; the truly magnanimous perceiver; the whole integer animated by Soul.

REALM III

MORALITY: moral courage, stamina, sentiment and honor being animated by conscience; honesty, veracity, compassion, charity, affection, modesty, faith, moral prosperity, humanity, profundity, piety, sobriety and all moral dignity.

REALM IV

PHYSICALITY: the physical animal or mammal human being or the human conception of it; the humanly perceived, humanly constructed and humanly objectified animal which humanity has invested with a soul and in which natural science has encoffined a soul, a mind, a life and other spiritual properties which may not properly be confined in the human physique, and may not be known to this realm—animated by physical knowledge.

REALM V

IMMORALITY: sub-animality; the sub-animal nature more sensual than the brute or beast or the so-called lower animals. Here is animosity, dishonesty, vice or that which is vicious, that which is soulless, heartless, lustful and morally depraved.

THE WORD, Appreciation

The word *appreciation* comes from the Latin form *pretius,* meaning price or value. The words precious and depreciate come of this same form, *pretius.*

The word appreciate analyses thus:

Prefix *ap-* (*ad-*) means to.

Root *pretius* (*pretium*) means price or value; *pretio* means prize or praise.

Suffix *-ate* means to perform the act of.

Literal meaning of the verb appreciate: to price, to praise or to prize; to perform the act of pricing; to cause praise; to esteem adequately; to raise or increase in value.

Suffix *-ation, -ion,* or *-tion,* forms the verb appreciate into a noun of action or condition, denotes verbal action; means resulting state.

Literal meaning of the word appreciation: true estimation; adequate valuation or adequate recognition of value, price, praise or prize.

Common antonyms of the verb appreciate: depreciate, despise, flout, misjudge, scorn, undervalue, disparage, asperse, belittle, and discredit.

The foregoing antonyms teach the positive nature of appreciation as the act of mentally weighing, measuring, valuing or judging fully. These antonyms teach, by way of comparison, that appreciation is the direct opposite or is directly opposed to them, and that they (the antonyms) exist only as negatives of a positive, intelligent force. They exist only by way of contrast with the positive faculty or ability to esteem, price, prize, praise or perceive distinctly.

Each individual thinker appreciates according to his own sense of values. Each one praises that which he deems worthy of praise, or that which he perceives to be praiseworthy.

Praise is the forerunner of hope. Praise or appreciation leads on moral prosperity, because hope *is* moral prosperity. High, higher and highest hope is the urge, the energy or the activity and agency leading humanhood higher. The high hope of the individual is the anticipation leading his sense of appreciation higher, and urging or leading on to highest and fullest praise, price and appreciation.

The thing hoped for is the prize. Hope is an active or animate element of the masculine mentality, while faith (the silent partner of hope) is the passive substance of the feminine mentality that sustains masculine hope, by sustaining the potential issue hoped for. Thus are the moral sentiments able to understand, subsist, sustain and be sustained, because they are appreciated, praised or prized by the compound mental unit, before the issue appears.

Appreciation is a rational function; a full or complete ratio of cognition; an action or expression of intelligence; a manifestation of keen and clear perception; a positive and correct recognition of a prize, an award, a reward, a moral or spiritual gift or thing of highest metaphysical substance or divine nature. Appreciation and comprehension are alike since comprehension may mean to grasp, to understand or to perceive fully. Appreciation is essentially a state or quality of degree —high, higher and highest. It is essentially the correlative of intelligence.

In human affairs, and to human apprehension, faith is the substantiality of the potential thing hoped for. Faith is the judge of the validity of the thing prized or valued because faith bases her estimation upon things which may be spiritually classified and morally evaluated.

The following table shows the classifications of the word appreciation:

REALM I DIVINITY: Intelligence—highest.

REALM II SPIRITUALITY: intelligence or wisdom; higher appreciation of The Omniscient Divinity; spiritual sentiment, verity, validity or the holy and wholly immaculate powers of perception, conception or appreciation. Here understanding is substance and it is intelligent appreciation.

REALM III MORALITY: conscience and its truth or science constitutes faith and urges hope to rise up. Here moral appreciation is high— as high as hope and as strong as it is valiant or valid. Here the thinker is appreciating, praising, and prizing and honoring the substance of Realm II.

REALM IV PHYSICALITY: physical objects may be appreciated as things worthy of praise, only in so far as they serve as phenomena of their higher noumenon; only as they stand as symbols of higher understanding, be-

cause they are, of themselves, finite, having
no degree of value excepting the regard
and import that human knowledge and
utility attributes to them at the time or season.

Realm   V   UNMORALITY OR IMMORALITY: the
zero of human metaphysicality; the minus
sign of human normalcy; the ignorance in
human nature; the finity, vanity, invalidity
and worthless nature of human knowledge.

These two lower and lowest realms despise, disparage, discredit
and depreciate all things pertaining to the realms of intelligence, reason, wisdom or judgment.

Realm V is that human sense from which all true sense, good sense,
right sense or moral sense of things has been subtracted.

Realm V has no appreciation for anything beyond Realm IV. The
human mammal, the inhuman character, or the sub-animal mentality
of Realm V takes pride only in himself, praises and prizes self, glorifies self and hates the intelligence which, by comparison, makes him
feel obscure or inglorious.

His total ignorance of morally, spiritually and divinely glorious
ideas holds him in Realm V under physicality and its knowledge,
which knowledge is appreciable to him because of its physical appar-
ency and pertinency—so familiar to him.

Realm IV consists of human impulse, human nature or the human
animal (mammal) physique, physics and such matters.

Realm III depreciates Realm V completely. It has some appreciation for Realm II, but it finds much in Realm IV to appreciate
also. The moral thinker appreciates the moral virtues such as veracity,
chastity, affection, loyalty, humanity, sincerity, compassion, modesty,
sobriety or the ability to restrain human nature impulses such as pride,
self-pride, self-deceit, self-conceit or vanity, self-justification, disaffection, disloyalty, revenge, ill will, envy, malice, animosity and all of
the other vices.

The Realm II thinker has charity for Realm III, but his love and
appreciation is for Realm I. He worships, prizes and praises The
divine creative Logos (Word), intelligently. He finds his environment
to be spiritual and altogether praiseworthy, or holy and wholly understandable, divinely appreciable and infinitely glorious. This thinker
is wisdom, spiritual sentiment (love), immaculacy, divine accuracy
and highest powers of realization via perception and conception. He
has the infinite capacity to appreciate Realm I.

THE WORD, Art

The word *art* belongs to the world of material knowledge. It is of mundanely literate character, because of its initial *a* vowel, which is only humanly literate, and because of its lack of other vowels which might lift the word up and out of its illiterate classification and mundane characterization.

The word art comes from the old French and Latin *ars, artis*. Its synonyms are given as aptitude, calling, cleverness, ingenuity, dexterity, address, skill, tact, artifice, esthetics, knack, science, adroitness, profession, trade, duplicity, cunning and many others.

In order to analyse, define and classify the word art one must first classify its synonyms which belong to the various fields of human knowledge, learning, culture and humanity's esthetic sense. All of these synonyms pertain to the human intellect and its appreciation of all things, excepting the words science and ingenuity, which two may pertain to moral sense, *con*-science, instinct or intuition; may pertain to the science begotten of con-science or the ingenuity engendered by moral precepts and propagated under the first principles or spiritual premises of wisdom.

The following table classifies art:

Realm I

DIVINITY: The Logos—Root which is Father-Principle of all logic, literacy and law.

Realm II

SPIRITUALITY: the logician; wisdom—the correct and accurate thinker; the compound legitimate idea of The Logos Root-Principle; the literate image of The Word or Logos.

Realm III

MORALITY: the realm in which conscience takes the preponderant place over human intellect, human knowledge, human nature, and the humanly established arts; the realm in which science is engendered by conscience or moral ingenuity, instinct or intuition and in which ingenuity is not a thing of human invention or dexterity, but is a thing of conscientious moral originality or one's innate moral sensibility.

Realms IV and V (pernicious trickery)
PHYSICALITY: human nature; human knowledge; human artifice or craftiness; human esthetics of Realm V, acted upon.

In the realm of human knowledge, skill and esthetic professions, art may become the artificial semblance of the natural or the naturally beautiful physical thing; or it may symbolize a metaphysical thing; or it may be a human attempt to imitate or to duplicate a divinely natural thing, or a spiritually substantial thing.

The word science is of higher metaphysical classification and of higher literate classification, of higher moral worth or virtue, of higher legitimate status, and of higher logical character than the word art. The same may be said of the word ingenuity, derived from genius (one's tutelar spirit or spiritual intuition, intelligence or power).

Art is a thing of human accomplishment, not a thing of moral-spiritual inheritance. It is a humanly acquired skill or profession or occupation which occupies the human mental faculties and affirms physical dexterity, expertness, maneuver, machination or culture. It pleases human nature and it absorbs human interest. It entertains and occupies humanity physically as well as metaphysically.

The word art cannot be used as a synonym for ingenuity or for science. It is in a lower classification than either one. Science is directly derived or deduced from the logic of The Logos. It reaches Realm III in the form of con-science. Ingenuity originates or has its origin in the same science, which science is derived from the same logic, and which logic originates in The Logos.

One may speak of the science and art of moral thinking, perceiving, conceiving, reasoning or discerning, but this kind of art depends upon conscience, not upon humanity's metaphysical hypothesis or humanity's kind of reasoning.

Art may deviate from the precepts of conscience and may be prompted by that which is physically patent. It may present and represent mere human speculation; an artificial play upon that which is physically or humanly natural.

The word science has a more literate and logical construction. It begins with *sc* (breath letters), it embodies the very literate vowel *i* and it ends with the suffix *-ence,* which gives it literate and logical entity, virtue and power.

The word art uses the most illiterate vowel *a* as its only, its first, and its initial vowel. Art could not exist without the physical, literal or mundane sense of things, or without the metaphysical chemistry of human impulses and actions that act and react, or without human nature to appreciate its kind of facility. Art, in its broad sense, is dependent upon physical pattern for its arrangement and for its attainment, since physicality neither thinks nor produces metaphysical pattern. Ingenuity depends upon metaphysical, moral and conscientious pattern.

Art must be divided into several realms. This analysis leaves its humanly established technical phases to the scholars of art and their teachers.

The lowest form of art is artifice of the kind that makes an art of evading and avoiding personal accusation and of self-preservation, physically and metaphysically. The physical preservation is an attempt to preserve the physique from bodily harm at any cost to others. The metaphysical practice is to preserve, by artifice, guile, skillful evasion and artful deception, not physical existence, but smart reputation, or proud personality.

The moral form of art is the art of meeting the challenge of immorality, dishonesty, personal pride, active envy, human knowledge (with all of its arts and dexterity), human nature, human indulgences in hatred, vengeance, animosities, and its unrestrained will. This art is taught and directed by conscience and its science and art of reasoning.

The word art leaves off where the science of conscience begins to teach. This is Realm III. The moral qualities counteract the action of the artful hostilities, the artful presentations of self-justification and such, simply by being themselves and by holding their ground. There is no art that can prevail over science, right, or high ethics.

The art of being deceitful, unreasonable, incorrect, inhuman, impatient, pitiless, relentless, ruthless (and the other harsh and cruel characteristics), certainly does not constitute a victory for this deceptive art over the science and art of reasoning, or the science and art of correct and accurate thinking.

THE WORD, BEING

The word *being* is derived from the Anglo Saxon *beon,* be. The suffix *-ing* changes the verb be or to be into a verbal noun having state, quality, condition and character of being, and having being in the present tense, as an existing thing being considered. This suffix gives it existence in the present tense, or presents some classification of being.

The word being is a dependent word. It must be classified, defined, or set (by context) under its kind of being.

The function, action, or utility of this verbal noun being, reveals its kind or classification of being. Every kind of being must have its kind of premise, precept or noumenal principle from which it derives its existence or its being, as phenomenon. Every kind of thing that is in evidence as existing thing, must have been deduced from its self-existent and preexistent premise as conclusion or as conclusive evidence of the existence of its premise.

An existing premise is the cause of its conclusion. An existing precept is the source of its formulated concepts. An existing principle or a noumenal being is the origin of the highly principled concepts which rise up or become evident to the thinker. Thus a concept is a conception taken at its inception from that which rises or springs up, or becomes visible as being; as an existing presentation or representation of its self-existent premise and principle.

The following table classifies the word being in five classifications, three of which are humanly tangible or conceivable:

REALM I
DIVINITY: The Supreme Being; The noumenal Principle of all intelligent being; the Logos-premise.

REALM II
SPIRITUALITY: that which is being because The Logos is causing it to be, is sustaining and is maintaining its being; that which is, and is so because The Logos-intelligence makes it so; that which is conceived to be phenomenon of The noumenal Principle of Realm I.

REALM III
MORALITY: that which is the moral deduction, conclusion and concept taken from humanhood's understanding of Realm II; those conclusions and concepts over which conscience presides; moral consciousness, of which hon-

esty, piety, validity, veracity, faithfulness, chastity and all of the human virtues are the essential substance, or the essence of being moral.

Realm IV
PHYSICALITY: an human being; all physically tangible being.

Realm V
IMMORALITY: an inhuman and morally depraved being; a depraved human being or immoral person; an inhuman being. This is the pit into which all human beings fall (clinging to their Realm IV premises, in the absence of conscience) with their broken human idols, ideals or personalities or images (once praised). It is the pit of disintegrated hopes and trusted beliefs; the end of false conclusions.

The three humanly tangible realms are the three lower ones. The two upper ones penetrate or shine through and into the moral realm as the sun shines through every non-opaque place or open space, and into a room. Realm III is the state, quality, and condition of being moral or of being conscious of moral existence, moral being, or the existence of morality, or of the existence of one's being moral, or of one being a well established moral character.

THE WORD, Belief

The noun *belief* and the verb *believe* use the letters *f* and *v* interchangeably, as do the words life and live. This word belief is of Anglo Saxon radicals *leof, laefan,* and *lyfan.* These forms serve to express willingness, leave, permission, or allowing, as believing or as letting pass as something accepted, permitted or believed. They express sentiment also, as lief, *luf* or love; as dear and as pleasing. Belief is *beleafa* or *geleafa.* It is a noun of action giving lief or leave. Belief is *belefan, belifan.* It is a verb meaning to think, credit, trust or judge; to hold to be true.

The prefix *be-* may mean by, thoroughly, or to be willing or to be passive to.

The Latin *credo* means believe or I believe. This root is found in the words credit, creed, credulous, credential and others.

In common parlance or human usage, belief may be anything cherished, adhered to, trusted or willingly accepted as being according to one's conviction of right; anything to which one gives leave, lief, license, permission, intellectual assent, or sensible credence. It may be anything that one trusts, supports, patronizes or maintains to be true and trustworthy; anything that one believes or beloves for its mental and *senti-mental* character. Thus humanity's best judgment stands as its beliefs; stands as the aggregate of its best sentiments or the embodiment of its loftiest faiths, doctrines and concepts.

Belief leaves off where understanding (of the substantial spiritual sort) begins. Belief leaves off where the spiritual stance begins; where wisdom and his powers of infinite perception begin; where the thinker trusts Truth, directly and absolutely; where verity or truth herself verifies her conceptions of The Logos.

The following table classifies firm beloving as understanding, and firm believing as confidence born of conscience, and belief as that which the human race believes:

Realm I

DIVINITY: Love; The Logos-Truth; The Word of all true
literacy; Mother and Quickener of all logic and of the logician—wisdom.

Realm II

SPIRITUALITY: love; truth, the understander of The
Word. Here is *mon* (man, *monn, mann, munan,* mind,

[32]

mynd, and *mynde*), the absolute thinker who understands Realm I thoroughly; who is inseparable from and entirely passive to The Word; who is standing under Realm I as the understanding of The Logos-Truth and as lover of the Logos-Love.

Realm III

MORALITY: human affection, patience, compassion, moral assent, sincerity, confidence in, or faith in that which humanity honestly believes, or that which is conscientiously believed to be morally firm and spiritually promising.

Here the beliefs are morally radical. Honesty believes in being fundamentally honest and trustworthy, He believes in honoring verity, veracity, or truth, or in being veracious, and here all of the moral qualities and characters believe in their moral principles, precepts, and premises.

Realm IV

PHYSICALITY: human nature with all of its beliefs.

Realm V

UNMORALITY: human and inhuman activity and impulse giving credence to those beliefs which humanity has set up without benefit of conscience or of wisdom.

To believe is to belove. One does not love that which is not believable, neither does one believe that which is not lovable or belovable, or that *to* which one does not feel passive, or that which one feels is not worthy of trust. To believe is to take to one's heart; to adopt as one's own; to feel akin to or toward; to feel metaphysically or morally related to, and to give both *luf* (love) and *lief* (be-lief) or leave to—even to conceive of, and to carry (bear) as one's own concept.

Mother love is best understood by humanity, as being constant, true, most believable and most lovable. Thus Love Herself—The divine creative Word, Love—is The Mother of all love and all that is divinely believable.

The table shows again that which one believes and beloves to be the same:

REALM   I   DIVINITY: Love, Herself.

REALM   II   SPIRITUALITY: love, herself who worships, loves, and firmly believes in Love, who trusts Love's doctrine, Her literacy,

Her logic, or Her science, and who realizes or brings into evidence all proof of that firm belief.

REALM III   MORALITY: love as human reason understands it to be; constancy, charity, devoutness and human kindness as humanity practices or finds them practicable.

Here the moral instincts, sentiments and high intuitions govern beliefs or humanity's believing.

REALM IV   PHYSICALITY: Here love is completely physicalized, and belief is *in* the physical sciences which give proof of their own physical existence.

There being no spiritual wisdom and no moral science here, physicality claims all believers; physical knowledge claims all science.

THE WORD, BODY

The word *body* comes from the Anglo Saxon *bodig*. It has many meanings and many applications and classifications. A body may be anything that is formed, shaped, made or compounded into a unit; a collective whole or main part of anything. This thing or this body, in physical form, may be anything composed or compounded of physicality or anything of physical organism, organic matter or matters. It may be a vegetable, animal, or mineral body or thing. It may be the human physique—living or dead. It may be a mass of material, a body, a corpse, or a corporeal thing or unit. It may be anything that the human intellect perceives as a body that is organized into a unit, which unit may be animated as an animal, may be breathing as a vegetable, may be operating as mechanical, or may be an artificial thing without a natural or physical body.

The human race limits itself to the human animal body; to the *corpus* or corporeal unit which is a human mammal. It confines itself to the humanly incorporated or humanly organized material body, to that which consists of, is of the nature of, or pertains to matter (that of which any physical object is composed). It makes the person, the human physique or the body one; makes or creates its own conception, which conception embodies person and personality; embodies the mammal or physical instincts and sensibilities; embodies physical consciousness or corporeal mindedness; embodies all that is carnal or is composed of flesh and bones; all that embraces the fleshly states and customs or the physically dictated beliefs and rules.

The Anglo Saxon *bodig* gives little analytical material. The word bode or bide (abode or abide) concerns *bodian* to announce, or *bidan,* to dwell, to remain in a place.

Body may pertain to anything from the lowest human misconception to the highest concept; from the lowest form of stuff, material or matter (as place of abode) to highest formed concept of incorporeal embodiment.

Body may pertain to that which is without a unit of energy (*erg, ergon*), or that which is at work (in work) or is in force as an embodiment of working units or parts.

The following table classifies and compares five different concepts of body:

[35]

REALM   I   DIVINITY: The   Logos-Soul;   The   vital
              Principle of soul.

REALM   II   SPIRITUALITY: the logician, soul; the em-
              bodiment of the living idea or concept
              which The vital Principle sustains and em-
              bodies as soul, as body, or as spiritual
              temple; that divinely legitimate and literate
              thinker (or soul) who abides in the un-
              broken relationship peculiar to Soul which
              is soul continuity. This soul is conscious-
              ness. It pertains to the temple of divine
              contemplation where man, *mon* or mind
              or soul temples, consciously or contem-
              plates continually and realizes, under-
              stands and discerns or ideates perfectly.

REALM III   MORALITY: that conscience which is ener-
              gized by soul and is in the work of morali-
              zation and works as honesty, veracity,
              hope, chastity, humility, piety, equity and
              such; works as conscience—the science of
              soul.

REALM IV   PHYSICALITY: that human knowledge or
              intellect obtained from physics which
              places body in this realm.

REALM   V   IMMORALITY: that   knowledge   which
              places the person, the human physique, the
              body (and all that pertains to a humanly
              condemned or bad person) in this realm.

The temple of contemplation in which the thinker dwells is intelligence itself, forever vital, valid, energized or empowered; forever motivated and forever expressing Intelligence, or forever thinking. He
temples in Realm II.

This place or embodiment, this thinking temple, this home or this
thinker's abode, embraces or embodies all logic, all literacy, and all
of the principles of correct and accurate thinking. It embraces all rational power and all legitimate thought. This place, body or consciousness is at highest or most intelligent point of view; at highest degree of
contemplation or consideration. Thus he has or embodies all things
and all thoughts, needing nothing more than or other than what he has
in his abode. This abode, body, or temple of infinite contemplation is
forever quick, at work, in work or energized by Intelligence as a unit

or idea at work; as a thinker perceiving, conceiving, reflecting, receiving messages from Intelligence and sending intelligent, wise, and well thought out messages to such thinkers as depend upon him for intelligence or for intelligent ideas.

This body is sound in understanding, whole and wholly substantial or holy. It is universally substantiated and enjoys infinite continuity, constancy and substantiality or understanding. This body or this thinker is attribute of his Source—Intelligence. In this condition this soul, self, temple, entity or contemplator, ego, idea and wisdom are one—one body; are one animus, unanimous or one soul.

The word body ends in the suffix -y, which might mean the same as in the word stony (from stone), or mean to add the quality of possession or of likeness. Thus, *like bodig.*

The initial letter *b* in the word body is relatively illiterate. It may therefore be used and understood as applicable in the lower realms as well as in the higher ones. Its meanings run from high to lowest forms and its synonyms apply to many common uses.

The word embody may be used as the word embrace, encompass or contain. That which is embraced or embodied may be any kind or sort of body formed in or into one concrete idea or complete embodiment of functioning ideas of highest metaphysical quality; or it may be formed into corporeal or physical body of functioning organs.

The *o* vowel in the word body shows its capacity to embody, its capacity to contain or its capability to embrace or to encompass. That which the word body embraces or embodies is supplied by context, by science or by the subject or thing spoken of.

In this treatise Realm II embodies the elements, the qualities, states, conditions and characteristics of logic, literacy and law directly deduced from The Logos.

Realm III embodies, embraces or encompasses and possesses the moral virtues and qualities of science, literacy and law as derived from *con-science* (which is a further deduction from logic).

Realm IV embodies whatever is physically or humanly possible and whatever human nature possesses, and whatever human impulse demands, and whatever physical science outlines or embraces, and whatever human knowledge originates and acknowledges or appreciates as body.

THE WORD, Character

The word *character* comes from a Greek form meaning to engrave, to make sharp (pointed, decisive, keen, incisive, acute, well defined or fine pointed).

There was a time when records were engraved upon stone, with sharp instruments. These records or these writings were made by the use of graphic symbols or characters or letters or literate characters engraved, infixed, marked or indelibly imprinted upon or into the stone slab or tablet or table, or even upon stone walls.

The Anglo Saxon *grafan* means to dig, as in the words engrave, groove, graver, graft, grave and grub, and *graf* which means grove (a small wood).

Literal meaning: that which is engraved, stamped, inscribed, written, marked or imprinted; an engraved mark.

Common meaning: a sign, symbol or graphic token; a signal or insignia, emblem or distinguishing feature that identifies, classifies or indicates origin; a graphic symbol of any sort; quality or distinguishing feature.

The root of each word establishes its character, for it is of the same nature, temper, constitution or genius. The root is an independent entity. The character is a dependent entity; a manifestation of its root. It is of like nature or of peculiar constitution attributable to its root. The properties of a character must agree with its word root, as a property of that word root and as offspring expressing it by its noticeable likeness to it. The word speaks. The literate characters give the sound and substance.

The numeral characters speak of quantity, while the literate characters speak of quality. Both are ideate beings—component parts of ideas speaking for themselves.

As the keys on the piano key-board speak for themselves, as the middle c, the d, the f-sharp, the b and the b-flat have their places, and their tones, and their specific characters in the music world, so do literate and numeral characters have their power to speak for themselves.

In the realm of *literology* we find that letters speak for themselves, and that they dictate their own specific places in a word; that they give tone, sound, and euphony, while in the realm of mathematics we find that place is evenly as vital.

There is another relationship existing between the letters that indicate tones (in music) and the letters that indicate sound in words, or the figures that indicate quantity in mathematics. It is the fact that harmony is produced when tone, key, place and positive rules are observed, and that when such rules are disregarded, discord and mistakes are produced.

Words may be called compound characters made up of literate characters. Numeral characters (figures or symbols) have their places in columns (as in a ledger) and their positions give them degree as to value.

Words have degrees, positions or classifications which give them literacy according to their vowels, their other letter construction, or according to the adjectives that qualify them. Thus a sentence, a row of figures, or a row of notes upon their staff speak for themselves. The sentence speaks by means of literate characters, words, phrases, or literate composition of words. The row of figures speaks by means of position based upon the unit. The character 1 is highly important. It signifies the whole unit. The zero is important, not because of its amount or high value import, but because of its essential position in relation to the unit. The figure zero (0) is neither zero plus nor zero minus, but simply the character that denotes naught, nothing, the cipher or that which is empty; denotes the absence of quantity. Yet when the zero appears at the left or at the right of a numeral character it has meaning, according to its position in the column or in relation to the unit or units, which units do have degree, quantity, value or specific amount of plus value. For instance, the zero placed on the right of the unit forms 10—the sum next greater than nine. This cipher indicates no degree of and no fraction of a unit, yet when it is placed in certain position it occupies that column position to indicate nothing (in that column) and thus it is dependent upon the units for its position and it is altogether dependent upon them for its utility.

It may be said that there are ten numeral characters, figures, tokens, signs, symbols or marks and that there are twenty-six alphabetic characters with which to spell all English words. These words must be classified into positively literate, positively illiterate or negative, and relatively literate groups. They must be classified as to quality, as the following sequences show:

i   The most literate characters; those of highest degree of
        literacy.
ii   The literate characters.
iii The relatively literate characters.
iv   The relatively illiterate characters.

    v   The illiterate characters; those of lowest degree of literacy.

The most literate vowels are *i, o, ou,* and *u.*

The most illiterate vowel is *a.*

The most literate consonants and aspirates are *m, n, d, s, p, r, t, l, c,* and *f* or *v* (used interchangeably).

The vowel *i* typifies light, sight, wisdom, discernment, great vision or highest degree of enlightenment.

The vowel *o* typifies greatest capacity. It symbolizes infinity or endlessness. It characterizes eternity or divinely literate continuity.

The *u* vowel opens toward heaven (as does the *v*). It does not depend upon a wide earthly basis or earthy stance as does the illiterate *a* vowel (A).

The *ou* combination of vowels carries both the element or quality of continuity and the element of heavenly or highest intake capacity (as in the word soul).

REALM   I   DIVINITY: The self-existent Word; The divine creative Root and Origin of all words and literate characters; The infinite Logos; The Source of all logic and science of numeral characters; The Soul of literacy.

REALM   II   SPIRITUALITY: the divinely worded ideas, verities, qualities, realities and characters; the substance and the essence of The Word; the literate similitude or image of The Word; the divinely graphic words.

REALM III   MORALITY: the relatively literate words and characters; the humanly and morally worded sentences, axioms, sentiments and opinions; that which pertains to humanity as to its qualities, characters and conditions, or to that which partakes of moral substance and may be morally substantiated.

REALM IV   PHYSICALITY: that which must have physical form and character, rather than metaphysical form and character in order to exist as a word, a sign, a property or an essential thing; that which must have physical and humanly tangible objectification in order to exist as having character; that

> which substantiates the physical or natural sciences, characterizes human nature, or is that which human nature characterizes; that which signifies physicality.
>
> REALM V IMMORALITY, unmorality or social, civil and ethical depravity; that which has no value, virtue or worth.

In these lower realms there must be a character of human sort. There must be a human physique of familiar pattern to constitute a character. Flesh and bones constitute his prominent and distinguishing features, since he has no moral or spiritual constitution. He characterizes human nature in action; characterizes human impulse; begets blood-ego that carries the mark of fratricide; bears flesh-ego with the mark or stamp of transitoriness (breath in the nostrils). These cursed signs or marks are so deeply engraved upon the human intellect that they hold the whole human race (the *humus-man*) in this cursed character.

The human intellect is actuated by human impulse. It is audient to human meanings. Human knowledge dictates, designs and creates the human nature or tangible character because the *humus-man* physique or the human person (with all of its curses and misfortunes) is most conceivable to humanity as itself.

Spiritual intelligence or wisdom dictates an altogether impersonal, metaphysical character, and three spiritual persons. For instance the Latin *oro* (*orare, oratus*) means I speak, utter, pray. This *I* is the first person or speaker. The Latin *audio* (*audire, auditus*) means I hear. This *I* is the second person; the person or audient character spoken to; the hearer hearing, or understanding, receiving and conceiving. This is the ego (understanding) in action. This is the audient entity functioning as a living (quick) thinker; identifying herself as power of conception, understanding or spiritual audiency. These two persons are present and in action.

The third person is the person spoken of. This person is potential; the idea to be acted upon, realized or brought forth as that which has been set forth by the speaker.

These persons are not people. They are not human creatures, mammals, animals or physical objects. They are spiritual and individual characters, acting as the agents of Speech and of Reason (The Logos; The spoken or written Word).

These persons are animated by Soul, spirited or motivated by Spirit (The Spirit of The Word) and vivified by The vital Principle and Premise of all living characters. They speak with a divinely inspired eloquence. They speak of divine logic, literacy and law. They speak to those characters whose mental matrices are susceptible to divinely logical impressions; those characters whose holy dignity and sentiments stand with and understand The Logos-Speech.

The word constancy means I stand together, with, or wholly. Here constancy is a spiritual character or quality; a fixed, invariable and continually loyal or stable quality or character. Moral stamina carries the same mark among the moral qualities and thus character is engraved upon the heart, the soul, and sentiments. Stamina and constancy take their stance together.

The Greek *grapho* (*graphein*) means I write. This I is the character or quality, moral courage who understands and has learned by heart (by sentiment), and who can give a graphic account, or a vivid record of what he has learned concerning that which is right and equitable for the human race. This character has the ability to judge and the human affection to write what he has demonstrated to be right; has the benevolence to tell or to admonish. These individual characters are wisdom, the power of conception, substance, understanding, reception and fruition standing under or taking stance (spiritual-moral stance) under, and exercising their stamina under that Word and Logos-Soul of which they write. They are the agencies or faculties representing and presenting the logic, the literacy and the law of The Logos.

Words (spoken or written) are entities. Words (thought) are things of a metaphysical, moral or spiritual character. In order to think intelligently one must do so by means of words. Thoughts not put into words are not composed; not put together; not engraved or sharply defined in the individual consciousness or conscience; not stamped upon the tablet of the understanding. Words (spoken or written) are made up of literate characters which have literate, living roots that carry, bear or convey meanings. They speak for one's intuitions. They carry the enthusiasm of The Theos or the logic of true theology (*Soulology*). They put the spiritual and moral instincts into worded form. They record, write, engrave or set forth. They also hear, read, understand and bring forth the substance, essence and character of their Root or of The Logos-Spirit which inspired or gave breath or power of speech.

One of the simplest illustrations of literacy and illiteracy may be found by comparing the word bad to the word good. The letter *b* in bad is illiterate, and the *a* vowel is the most illiterate of the vowels. The letter *g* or *G* as in the word good is highly literate and the double *o* speaks of greatest literate and logical capacity, compounded or doubled.

The word good may not be deformed or degraded. There is no

2

such word as ungood, ingood, disgood or misgood, and no such word as goodless. It stands fully or completely or perfectly good, because it is the most literate or literately capacious name for The Deity—God, Good, or The Logos. There is no better word than Good to contradict it, to deny it, to mutilate its literacy, to dispute its logic or to equal its infinite goodness.

The word intelligence is more literate than the word intellect. The root *lig* is more literate than the root *lect* in the word intellect, since the *i* vowel is of highest literacy while the *e* vowel is relatively illiterate and pertains to human lecture, selection or election. The word intelligence is the logic of Soul and pertains to The Logos.

The word mother may change its form to lowest illiteracy which is matter, by doubling the *t* and substituting the *a* vowel. It goes from motor (to move), mother, miter, measure, meter and then to mater and to matter.

Many words have five degrees of literacy and illiteracy or of classification. The word mother is a universal word. It may be represented in five letter classifications by changing the vowel and doubling the *t*. The mother quickens, motivates, prompts and sustains in every realm from good to bad; from highest to lowest lettered form; from highest Mother to lowest matter.

In the physical realm the animal pater is the pattern character to be engraved upon his offspring. Each animal and each human mammal carries the decisive and well defined pattern of its pater, and the nature or physical mater-ial of its mater.

In the lowest metaphysical or mental realm these patterns, designs, characters, marks or engravings show themselves in patterns and in materials; in that which begets and that mater-ial which bears or carries out or brings forth her mental characteristics. For instance, revenge is engraved upon the mentality or in human memory, or in the inhuman and irrational mentality which is the irrational sense tablet.

Vengeance, envy, animosity and such are the materials out of which revenge, hatred, malice and personal vanity or pride are made. They beget their kind. Physicality begets the human mammal which begets personality or materiality, which begets mortality known as humanity and which is synonymous with humanity—state of being human, mortal or subject to death.

In the moral realm honesty begets his kind and veracity bears out or carries out his kind and her kind, since she is verity, moral intuition or conscience, herself. Here the pater and pattern is moral precept and the mater and material is moral concept. These precepts and concepts are engraved upon the heart or moral sentiment.

In the spiritual realm wisdom is the preceptial (instructive) element. Purity, as the power of true conception (and construction), constitutes the conceptual element. Wisdom marks his own offspring. Spiritual sentiment, intuition or love is the material (substance) out of which they are made.

One may be a man of letters, a man or woman of highest human literacy or degree of literacy, and still be a human character, a person highly educated. He may be a master of one, many or all of the languages spoken by human beings, and still be a human person.

A literate character is not a person. An idea made up of spiritually literate characters is not a person, not a human being. The idea speaks for itself, yet it has no human tongue and is not at all dependent upon the human being (or mammal) for expression. This idea is a *mon* (man) of letters, a *mon* of divine letters, or an expression of spiritual literacy. This idea has its existence in The self-existent and ever-existent Word or Logos.

A morally literate character is not a person. He is an entity identified by his moral integrity, his moral quality, or his conscientious, honest, sincere and veracious character. A morally literate character may not be broken down or caused to disintegrate. His integrity is untouched and unbroken by the illiterate, the morally ignorant, or the human kind of characteristics which do not pertain to moral innateness.

The moral character occupies a realm of his own. He is not literate enough to live in Realm II, but he is too logically and literately minded to live in Realm IV. In his realm (Morality) he has a voice, a value, a power, a place, and a reason for his existence there. In Realm IV there is no place for him, since the physique does not think either morally or immorally, and has no voice in moral and spiritual affairs. It is like the cipher character symbolizing the absence of quantity, yet having neither voice nor value as the following reading will explain: Seven thousand one hundred (7,100). There are two ciphers in the reading, yet they have no voice—no vocal recognition. They occupy space and place, yet they neither speak nor sound forth as literate or as logical characters. Their only use is to occupy a column so as to indicate that nothing (zero, nought) or a cipher—not a unit—is there; so as to indicate the absence of a unit or units.

The character of the *o* vowel is unique. It indicates or it characterizes continuity and infinity. The double *o* vowel in the word good or The Word Good (meaning God) doubles the goodness, emphasizes its continuity and its infinity, and expresses the character of The Deity.

The character of the aspirate *s* is singularly spiritual. And so it is that as a numeral character (such as the zero that means continuity of nothing or infinitely nothing and positively nothing) the cipher or circle means zero, and as a literate character the same character, figure or symbol means something else (such as the vowels in the word good).

The proportion of vowels (highly literate vowels) as in the word spirit, makes the word of highest literacy as though it were double *i*. If we capitalize the word spirit (thus, Spirit) we indicate The Word or The Spirit or The Deity which indicates The Logos—Origin of all literacy; Doctor of all letters; creative Root of all literately perfect, complete, whole or (holy) wholly spiritual words such as soul-wisdom (the wisdom born of Soul); such as soul-sentiment (the sentiment born of Love); such as understanding or the power of divine realization (the power born of The motivating Spirit—Good).

THE WORD, CHARITY

The word *charity* comes from the French *charite* and Latin *caritas* and *carus,* which are variations of dear, dearness, love, loved and beloved.

The word cherish comes from the same radical root. It means to hold dear. Its suffix *-ish* gives infinite action to the cherisher. Cherish is the verb form, while charity is the noun of state or quality; the condition, state or quality of being benevolence itself.

In the humanly orthodox world charity means many things, because humanity cherishes many things, treasures and holds dear many finite and relatively finite things. This humanly traditional and conventional concept of charity mixes love, charity and all qualities in one human comprehension. Love, however, is altogether spiritual in metaphysical ratio, while charity is a human concept of that love. Charity belongs in a less literate degree; in a lower ratio of comprehension. It may be a human readiness to overlook faults. It may be a civil generosity. It may be a moral affection, a patient, compassionate or benignly liberal action, but it can never be a synonym for love.

Charity is a humanly practical word. Its only vowel *a* is the most illiterate of all of the vowels, while the vowel *o* in the word love, is both literate and capacious, and symbolizes constancy or continuity.

Charity is a good moral word; a human virtue; a moral quality; a kindly equitable sentiment that lifts thought beyond and above the confinements of the orthodox world. Charity differs greatly from love, in that love is purely spiritual, having within it the properties that heal (that supply all good, well being or spiritual benevolence), and that eliminate the necessity for charity, while charity has not the power to heal or to supply spiritual goods. It supplies human sympathy, human mercy, consideration and good will—all human kindnesses—in the humanly charitable way.

Love loves, nourishes, nurtures or makes to flourish; promotes, establishes and sustains all joy, bliss or joyousness. In Realm II therefore there is no sorrow with which to sympathize; no misfortune with which to cope or to distribute or to deal charitably; no lack of anything good to call out benevolence (human) because all good properties are supplied in divine abundance in this realm.

The following table classifies charity:

[46]

REALM I

DIVINITY: Love; The Logos-Soul.

REALM II

SPIRITUALITY: love; the logician, soul, or self understanding Soul, and receiving the beneficence of The Logos
or Love.

REALM III

MORALITY: humanity, human charity, compassion or
kindly affection, cherishing and being charitable to the
persons in need of both physical and metaphysical charity; practicing charity, equity and human, civil and moral
generosity.

REALM IV

PHYSICALITY: physical property and moneys or financial aid considered to be charity in itself; a literal sense
of charity.

Charity is akin to humanity. It wishes well and does well or beneficently under all circumstances. The antonyms of charity work in the
human realm to exercise their revenge, pride, relentlessness, inhumanity, mercilessness, malice, deceitfulness and such. Human nature
is likely to be malevolent or to wish bad or ill to come to a neighbor.
Human nature has a physical sense or a literal sense of things; entertains the physical aspect and sense of values. Human nature has a
natural affinity for physical, personal treasures.

Charity is one of the more moral graces; a metaphysical property;
a high human impulse of unselfishness. It helps to counteract envy,
covetousness, vengeance and such. It may touch conscience and learn
to counteract feud, animosity, enmity and moral nakedness; learn not
to harbor grudges.

Charity is a quality that lives, grows, thrives and prospers and
becomes more substantial in the moral environment as it is practiced
under the direction of conscience. It stagnates under the human manner or the customary, traditional, conventional kind of charity. Human
nature and human orthodoxy tend to suppress the spontaneous moral
instincts, one of which is charity.

Charity suffers or lets, bears or undergoes, permits, allows or endures—with patience—those human injuries inflicted by hypocrisy,
intolerance, lust, bitterness and all of the human, mammal instincts;
endures—with compassion—those sharp or critical experiences which
spiritual-moral ignorance inflicts. She is that character who does not
indulge in pride, in self exaltation, justification or aggrandizement.

Charity suffers with, sympathizes with, feels with, or entertains sympathy and pity for, those who suffer any kind of pain, reverses, loss or wretchedness. She has a passion for helping those in distress, because she can suffer and sympathize without allowing the wretchedness to assume greater proportions than her charity offsets or relieves. Her gracious presence alleviates by bringing more charity, compassion, affection, grace, harmony and consolation to bear upon the human suffering; by bringing in those higher graces which tend to exempt or absolve, or bring a solution. Charity, being able to let the uncharitable elements of human nature strike at her, without feeling hurt or injured, can demonstrate this science and art of reasoning charitably.

Charity is didactic by example. Charity is the antonym of greed, envy, self esteem and all of the personal self or selves. She is generous, in a moral and metaphysical sense. Her generosity is super human—not human. Charity is that lovely quality that sustains hope and nourishes faith; that loving character who bends the knee—meekly and humbly—only before that greater charity which is love herself—the offspring of The Love who is God.

Charity has a passion for gentle equity, since she *is* compassion and patience. She has the gentle kindness that nurtures the infant moral thinker and causes him to grow into moral courage, stamina and that manhood which advocates the firmness of masculine honesty and the gentleness of feminine charity; the potency of masculine moral honor (integrity, fidelity) and the validity of feminine comfort and fondness.

THE WORD, CHASTITY

The word *chastity* comes from the Latin *castus*. This form is used in the words chaste and caste. It means pure.

> The suffix -*ity* gives it state or quality of being.
> Literal meaning: state of being pure; quality of being chaste or pure or of unmixed race.
> Common synonyms: continence, virginity, celibacy, purity, virtue, cleanness, innocence and many others.

The word continence is not a true synonym for chastity, because it savors of self-restraint or of abstinence from something desirable, as an act of self-denial, whereas chastity is a morally natural, spontaneous instinct; a state of being chaste by reason of highest moral parentage. She does not need to make an effort to be chaste. She could not experience moral restraint of any kind, for chastity, like honesty, is a fixed moral virtue, unmixed and unadulterated with an opposite element; unweakened by unmoral elements. Chastity embodies no unchaste influences which must be restrained, but functions as an intuition— conscientious, pious, innocent and clothed in innocence.

The word virginity is not a true synonym for chastity, since it belongs to spirituality, while chastity belongs to morality. Virginity is of higher spiritual, literate and logical substance. Its two *i* vowels are much more literate than the *a* vowel in the word chastity or chaste. Purity is a synonym for spiritual virginity or immaculacy. It is not a true synonym for chastity, since chastity may apply to human moral principles and standards or mere ethics.

The word chastity or chaste has six letters or literate characters, that is five letters other than the sounding vowel *a*. The final *e* is not important in either the word chaste or pure. The *u* vowel in pure is literate and capacious, and it is one of four literate characters, which is a better proportion of literacy than the word chaste exhibits.

The word celibacy pertains to physicality and to its immediate figurative nature, or figurative sense, or metaphysical sense of marriage. It pertains to the unmarried state.

Many spiritual virtues may be celebrated humanly.

Chastity does not struggle against a tendency to be unchaste, or with the temptation to be impure in thought or in act, but functions as a moral force counteracting and nullifying such tendencies. She is morally radical and radically moral by nature and in character. Honesty does not need to struggle in order to be honest. A numeral character such as a 3 (III) does not have to struggle in order to hold its position, its quantity, its identity or its value. So chastity being scientifically and radically fixed in character and in quality maintains her position as a major element of the moral virtues or human virtues in the moral realm. She is set apart from moral taint.

Chastity associates with her moral kind where she is honestly honored, genuinely appreciated, sincerely respected, heartily cherished and thoroughly understood. This does not mean that chastity is a person associating with people or human beings. She is a quality identifying herself with her associates who are of equal rank in the moral kingdom, or she is peer, a noble woman standing in honor as of royal birth.

Chastity is not spiritual purity but the phenomenon of it. Her associates are collaborators of high moral caste, which caste is not too highly refined, too sacred, too holy or too spiritually excellent for human utility. She is purity in its humanly ethical sense. She is humanity's best concept of purity. Some of her collaborators are loyalty, fidelity, integrity, veracity, moral stamina, firmness and soundness. They are untouched, unsoiled and unprofaned by that which is morally carious, spotted with moral rot, decay or disintegration. Her associates abide in the realm of moral integration, health, growth, thrift or prosperity; in the metaphysical kingdom of strict morality where there is no unchaste fiber to mentally ulcerate, but where the moral fiber is impervious to contamination, corruption and such adulteration or weakness.

Chastity keeps faith, keeps her word, keeps her troth or promise; is trustworthy or keeps her trust. She is serene, sublime and innately modest or radically prudent. Her office is not humanly defined but morally assigned as gentle rectitude, womanly dignity and moral sentiment.

There is a social caste which is morally unchaste or is popularly and pleasingly immoral. It is designed to suit human nature and human society or popular opinion. It is good or chaste enough, yet it is low enough in standard to suit and satisfy human society and to delight human nature. It finds chastity and her radical associates unreasonable, rabid, extreme or fanatical and unsociable. Hence chastity and her associates do not associate with the immoral, the unmoral or the relatively unmoral.

Purity is a spiritual creature, a spiritually pure entity, an wholly (holy) spiritual character and quality which identifies the thinker by the purity of his logic, literacy and precept or rule; by the purity of his ideation, and by the nature of his deductions.

Chastity is the elementary form, the lesser form, or the relatively spiritual form of purity. It is as the first lessons in purity, even as the first lessons in mathematics are purely mathematical, yet very elementary. It is adapted to the relatively logical and literate thinker, or to the morally legitimate thinker. However, the moral lessons are fundamental, and thus chastity is fundamental as a moral rule.

Human nature is adverse to chastity. Human impulse is the opposite of the leadings of chastity. Human nature's impulses lead to humanity's educated sense of itself (the human physique) or physical self which self demands notice; demands that its desires be known or duly regarded; demands attention whether this sense is enjoying itself or is suffering.

Human nature and its impulses, its characteristics and its humanly natural sense of itself, belongs to the physical caste. This is the most finite caste or classification. The physique does not and cannot think. It cannot reason. If therefore the morally substantiated mentality does not superintend and supervise it, it becomes weak as a caste. If chastity, veracity, modesty and such qualities do not have jurisdiction or some dominion over this physique, it is left to the mercy of the unchaste nature. It may be hypocritically so (not openly unchaste or chaste), but chastity is one of the genuine virtues. She is begotten of highest moral purpose, instinct or intent.

THE WORD, CHRIST

The word Christ is an holy and wholly spiritual title coming from the Greek *chrio* (*chriein*), I anoint; to anoint. *Chrio* (*Christos*), anoint or anointed. Chrism (*chrisma*), that oil, ointment or unguent with which one is anointed, or that chrism used for anointing.

The word anoint is of Latin origin. It partakes of the root *unguo* or *ungo* (*unguere* or *ungere, unctus*), I anoint. The prefix *an-* means in or on, and *ungo* means smear. Hence to pour, apply, smear, put or rub on that unguent or chrism which signifies consecration or to consecrate; to pour oil on or upon in loving gesture or sign of spiritual or divine consecration or sanctification; to spread over with oil as a symbol of being dedicated or set apart for sacred uses.

This I (First Person; Speaker) is The divine creative Logos, Speech or Word. I anoint means I dedicate (*dico,* declare); I christen or name The Messiah, The Anointed, The Christ or The Anointed One.

This title Messiah is Hebrew *Mashiach,* meaning anointed, and *mashah,* meaning to anoint. Messias means the Christ.

A christian is one who grants the Christhood to Jesus, and thus christianity is the christian's religion. Christendom pertains to the christian's world, or to Christians collectively. This title, the Christ, is given to Jesus.

The following table will classify and specify the divine title Christ, and The I who anoints, appoints or decrees:

REALM I
DIVINITY: The Logos; The divine creative Word God or Good; the I or Ego who anoints; The Speech, Speaker and I Principle who declares, christens, designates, names, dedicates and appoints the Christ.

REALM II
SPIRITUALITY: the logician or divine creature fully understanding The Word; the I or ego Christ whom The Word or Logos anoints, specifies, consecrates, sends, delegates, authorizes, directs and dispatches as messenger to purvey the doctrine of The Word, and to convey the logic of The Logos to all positive thinkers, or all spiritually minded.

REALM III
MORALITY: the realm of human theologies and humanly

[52]

established orthodoxies, religions or any of the humanly instituted systems of worship; the human concept of God and of that which God anoints; the individual conscience of the morally minded, acting as dictator and purveyor of spiritual messages.

REALM IV

PHYSICALITY: the realm of human nature; the home of the physically minded.

The positive thinker and logician of Realm II is the anointed one; the Messiah (Hebrew); the Christ (Greek); Immanuel (Hebrew word meaning God with us); the God or Good (Anglo Saxon form for God) with us or at hand; the divine representation, expression, simile, ideation, formation, signification or munificent manifestation at hand or with us, displaying, teaching, presenting, disclosing or making evident to the understanding, that which Good would have revealed; that which Soul advocates; that which the logic of The Logos decrees; that which The Spirit (of Good or God) would have breathed forth, set forth and brought forth.

Immanuel or Emmanuel is a masculine name. His function is to bring The Word down to the moral realm; to simplify the logic of The Logos and to teach it in morally simple terms; in elementary lessons; in especially selected lectures and legends which will interest humanity. This Emmanuel or Christ, or divine logician, teaches by means of purely spiritual agents.

Con-science is the doctor of moral sciences. He is the agency, the agent, the seer, the sage, and the saint among human-kind. He is the great preacher, dictator, prophet and leader of the people. He presents the science of soul. He is science itself, within oneself. He presents the science of righteousness. He preaches to the natural moral instinct or intuition, or communicates with the human heart.

Con-science ministers to the soul-self and administers his science, which science is reduced from the absolute logic of Realm II. Thus he teaches, preaches, instructs, illustrates, advocates, educates, indoctrinates, substantiates, and demonstrates his science for all thinkers who have an avidity for it. These thinkers constitute the members of what may be called The Religion of Con-science. They are moral stamina and courage, meekness or modesty, honesty or veracity, charity, affection, or compassion, patience, temperance, sobriety or moderation, virtue, constancy, loyalty, fidelity, confidence, trustfulness or faith, tenderness, kindness, gentleness or humanity, moral prosperity or living hope—these constitute the great congregation of worshippers over which conscience presides. They constitute one form of worship which con-science conducts. They trust and believe in one Theos or have one universal theology.

Emmanuel or Immanuel (*nobiscum Deus*) means God with us. The Christ is the omnipresent Immanuel teaching and demonstrating God with us, or teaching the logic of The Logos as being present with us, or teaching and demonstrating and illustrating the literacy of The Word with us, or teaching the recipes of The Principle (divine law) with us, or teaching the sacredness of the law and word of God.

The Christ typifies the center, central pivot, pivot and principle of logic; the power of divine reality or understanding; that under-*stancing* which substantiates the doctrine of The forever Logos. The Christ is the doctor of this forever doctrine or logic; the verifier of all truths; the witness to all wisdom; The divine advocate of The Logos Speech, reiterating and repeating what The Logos has in Mynde.

The Christ is divine perception or is divinely perceptive; is the power of perception, as masculine, while the feminine element is the power of conception and is divinely conceptive.

These elements are divinely united, compounded, or wedded and anointed. They present the compound function of the compound Christ. They illustrate the God blessed speaker and the God blessed hearer—the male setting forth The Word to be conceived and demonstrated, and the female (of Genesis i:27) bringing forth The Word in its divine literacy.

The Christ is the ever-living, ever acting logician, wedded to The divine creative Word as the divinely created idea which idea is compounded or wedded so as to multiply.

THE WORD, CIVILIZATION

The word *civilization* comes from the Latin *civis, civilis,* meaning citizen. The radical root *civ* adds the suffix *-ic* to form the word civic which means relating to a citizen, to a city, or to civil affairs; relating to the honors of a city. Civil means belonging to a citizen. The suffix *-ize,* added to the word civil, forms the word civilize, which means to make a savage people into a community having a government, or political organization; to reclaim from a barbarous state; to instruct in the customs of civilization. The last suffix is *-ion, -tion,* or *-ation,* which forms the word into a noun of action or condition or result of verbal action, meaning the state of being civilized, or the act of civilizing or the condition of having been (or result of being) politically organized.

The common meanings of civilization pertain to the citizen and pertain to his having been educated in the courtly policies or polite conduct prescribed by the city, the community, or the organized citizenry (government) or political organization of that city or community.

A citizen owes allegiance to citizens collectively, and to civilization itself. He is entitled to civil protection from that which is savage or barbarous, since to civilize means to reclaim from savagery or from a barbarous state. Yet literally civilization can never reclaim humanity from its own human nature, its savagery or its barbarity. The human animal or mammal (nature) *is* out of the woods or out of the forest— physically and bodily—but its nature is still unrestrained and still morally unrefined, for all that.

An undomesticated beast may be less beastly than the domesticated human animal.

The definition of the word savage is based upon the Latin *silva,* meaning wood or forest. The name Silvanus is *silvanatus,* in silva *natus,* or born in a wood.

A domestic animal is housed or domiciled or provided with a house other than the wood, but that domestic animal's natural instincts and impulses, characteristics and requirements, remain somewhat unchanged. Wildness may mean state of living in the wood physically, while the domesticated and highly civilized human mammal may be metaphysically somewhat inclined to be (at times) wild with bitterness, envy, or savage impulses; savage, or wild, or rude, or untamed, as when he is angry or impelled by animosity and revenge.

The human animal or person may fulfill all of the requirements of civilization, with all of its required civil and social proprieties, its blandness, politeness, and its prescribed courtliness and elegance of manner, or polished manners, and yet be more fierce or violent in his premeditated savagery than the so-called savage beast, and certainly more filthy, more sensually lewd, foul or morally debased than the wild horse, the ox, the deer, the moose or other beasts. Hence civilization in itself can only promote physical and literal cleanness, order and manner, while metaphysical zeal of moralization must lead on and on before the human nature will be subdued and mastered by the moral nature or temper. Human manners may be civilized. Humanity's mode of living may be reclaimed from brutish, animal, or mammal mode of living or manner of living in the forest, but only the moral conscience can reclaim insincerity, dishonesty, civil affectation, formal hypocrisy and such from metaphysical barbarity; only moral instinct can reclaim humanhood from human nature, from humanly orthodox craftiness or from humanly conventional artifice and finesse, for such art is traditional or humanly natural. Human nature is expected to perform in such manner, and it is so allowed, permitted or licensed by human society and by civilization.

Civil law preserves civil order. Moral law insists upon moral order, rule, and ordinance which depend upon conscience to dictate or to decree the right manner. Thus conscience becomes leading authority on the right manner in the moralized realm, and thus the moral law is gradually advancing under its leading authority or its right leadership, carrying on where civilization leaves off. Indeed civilization, the civil law and its administrators, look to moral instinct, law and conscience to make civil law effective.

The word barbarity, or a barbarous state, simply refers to brutish, brutal or brute-like people, who, compared to the early Greek and Roman culture, were barbarians, foreigners, or an uncivilized people. Civil means urbane as opposed to the rustic. It means city and community (civil) as opposed to uncivil or incivil manner that lacks the Roman culture. Thus to bring a people into or under this system of government and of culture, meant to civilize or to reclaim them from a barbarous state or from a *silva* state of living (in a grove or a wood or a forest). It does not mean that barbarity is altogether synonymous with inhumanity, cruelty or animal brutality, peculiar to the animal or mammal, since animality is as natural to the human mammal as to other animals, and since human nature is as warlike and as adverse to the restraint and refinements of peace, and love and spiritual equity, as any other animal, be it domesticated or not.

The animal instinct, called self-preservation, shows itself in the human nature or the human mammal. It calls that instinct war. The wild animal savagery usually shows itself in a single slaughter, while the domestic human animal can cunningly trap, capture, maim, scathe or slay its many. Thus one may conclude that the human animal's intellect is as savage as the human nature, or that human savagery is natural to the human animal. One may conclude that the beast or the brute in its forest, is governed by its own instincts, and is self-governed, while the human animal (civilized) may be only artificially and superficially civilized, and thus one may find, here, a civilized barbarity; a mental savagery; a cruelly refined and cultured manner that only feigns humaneness. One may find a barbaric occultness; a vicious person or an artful intellect full of criminal, unmoral, hostile or hateful devices. These devices are far more effective than the natural weapons of the animals—horns, fangs, heels, hoofs, tusks, teeth and such. These inhumanly designed weapons are only the mental noumenon or thing which the human fist would wield if it were deadly enough and occult enough, but the human fist or hand has long since been replaced by weapons having every advantage.

The social codes of the wild animal or brute are no more animal-like, its moral standards and habits are no more animal-like, and its mating instinct or its marriage relation is no more brute-like or mammal-like, than the same relation of the civilized and domesticated human mammal, since the animal or brute performs its function of mating in whole accord with its specific nature (or according to its natural species or according to its animal nature), while the human animal violates or profanes the temple (vestibule) of motherhood unnaturally, but in accord with popular social and civil usage and culture.

The beast, the brute or the animal, whose period of gestation is nearly equal to that of the human animal, is more orderly and more temperate, more natural and less sensual in its mating relation than the common practice of the human animal, since the civilized animal (human mammal) actually exploits, fosters, cultivates and even commercializes and legalizes that common practice.

The sub-animal human nature may be covered with layer after layer of social and civil veneer, but until morality and spirituality remove the veneer, or until the moral nature predominates over the lower untempered nature, the fruits of civilization will not be evident. Until the human being is disciplined, and until the human impulses are restrained or tamed or civilized, and until the human imaginations and sensations are replaced by moral realities and sentiments, the true purpose of civilization will be unapparent because it (the civil and moral law) only drives the crafty human animals into a realm of more subtle, wary, sly or politic practices; only drives them under cover.

Civilization depends upon moralization, and moralization depends upon conscience, and conscience depends upon spiritualization. Civilization is only a human formality. Moralization is a conscientious victory. Spiritualization is a rich inheritance of verity; a beneficent and glorious reality; a state of being pure, wholly refined or spiritually and fully cultured.

The following table classifies civility, morality and spirituality or civilization, moralization and spiritualization:

REALM I

DIVINITY: The Logos-Principle governing all mode, manner or way of procedure; The divine creative Logos-Precept designing the practice of that which is most highly refined, cultured, cultivated, enlightened or developed.

REALM II

SPIRITUALITY: the most highly cultured, most understanding, most wise, most pure and most loving compound entity, idea or representation of The Logos-Principle.

REALM III

MORALITY: the morally refined; the frank, candid, sincere, honest and conscientious thinker who may find himself unfit or unfitted and unfitting for orthodox formalities, or the civilly fitting courtesies of civil society. Thus the thinker of this realm must compromise with civil formalism and its courtly politeness; with its insincerity, vainglory and such.

REALM IV

PHYSICALITY: the human nature; the human physique or mammal who cultivates personal charm, pride, self-esteem, vanity, physical magnetism or finesse (the fine essence or esse of the most subtle and occult mental artifice); the unrestrained human and inhuman imagination; that manner or mode of living which is physically generated by physical mindedness; that realm in which courtesy is enough and in which social codes or common customs or practices are sub-animal, but popular; are dishonest and unconscientious, but urbane, affable, polite or civil.

THE WORD, CONCEPTION

The word *conception* is made up of three parts:

The prefix *con-* means with, together, wholly, jointly.
The Latin root *capio* (*capere, captus*), I take, seize, hold; *captum*, to take.
The suffix *-ion* makes it into a noun of action or condition, or a state of being.
Literally it means that the conceiver takes, jointly, with the perceiver. She holds to be true that which he also holds to be true or conceivable. She comprehends that which he has apprehended and has presented for the conceiver to seize, take or grasp. She receives wholly.

This same root *capio* is found in the words capacity (ability to receive, carry or contain), capture (to seize and hold), capable (qualified to do), anticipate (take before), participate (to take part), principle (take first), recipe (take thou), receptive (able to take in or hold), and it is found in many other words.

This word conception, being a noun of action, is a doer, an actor or the entity who acts as an agent, empowered by that power which she represents, manifests or expresses.

This word has many classifications, even as the precept of which she conceives has many. The following table will show precept, perception, concept and conception:

REALM   I   DIVINITY: Omnipotent Intelligence; the Logos-Precept, Principle or Premise.

REALM   II   SPIRITUALITY: the power of intelligent conception and logical perception and the power of speech derived from The omnipotent Principle. Here a concept is an idea.

REALM III   MORALITY: the human capacity to reason; the human capacity to receive and carry out (act upon) a concept or a moral precept seized and held as moral axiom.

REALM IV   PHYSICALITY: the physical ability to conceive, gestate (carry), quicken (act upon), and bring forth.

[59]

In Realm IV the conceiver has a physical matrix in which to hold that which she has taken or conceived. She has also the mammary or sustaining (nurturing) organs or the nutritive organs, all of which are essentially feminine.

In Realm III the conceiver is recognized as having a metaphysical matrix upon which rudiments of a precept may be impressed, and she has also the faith, patience, and expectancy to sustain that which she holds to be dear, true, right or good.

The foregoing table shows Intelligence or Verity as The power of infinite conception. It shows intelligence or the ideas of Verity to be the realities and verities existing in Realm II. These are purely, holy and wholly spiritual forms, ideas, images or concepts, verified and sustained by Verity; these are wholly logical, literate and legitimate manifestations such as wisdom and his patterns of realization or perfect demonstration.

In Realm III a conception consists of the elements of *con-science* and its science, its verities and veracious precepts. It is the deduction of universal logic of Realm II to Realm III; to human, moral utility. Here a concept is a mental image of moral significance, genius and excellence. It embodies the feminine moral sentiments, and is a thing of mutual moral interest. It embodies sound, virile perceptions impressed upon the fertile matrix; instructive precepts to be constructed. There must be moral stamina and virility in the male thinker. There must be a high degree of integrity in the perceiver, and there must be moral fertility, veracity, validity and vitality in the conceiver; there must be virtue in both thinkers if the issue is to take its stable place in human affairs.

A perception is something apprehended by the male thinker. A conception is that specific apprehension conceived or comprehended by the female thinker; that same potential issue after it has been uttered, emitted, expressed or set forth for conception. A conception matured in the mental matrix comes forth in such form as to be perceptibly manifest to wakeful, vital thinkers and right thinkers.

A didactic male thinker perceives in certain ratio of power. A coherent female thinker conceives in the same ratio, or in the same degree of reason. A perception is an outline or a prediction of fact; a form of solid conviction, individually embraced in the male mentality. The male enthusiasm or zeal causes him to put his perception into words and to voice it. The female furnishes the rational material out of which it is composed. Her rational and sentimental capacity, which is her mental matrix, instinctively enwombs and embosoms the potential issue.

Only the power of conception can conduce or can reproduce, or can procreate a concretely evident element of fact; can prove a theory; can verify and thoroughly demonstrate a verity before the face of a world of sleepers; can bring forth a perceived issue for a world of thinkers to inspect. Only the power of conception can bring forth the quick elements of logic; can bring forth, for human contemplation, those things not yet veritable to or conceivable to humanity. Only the female thinker can conceive and make evident those verities which are not yet parading, as such, in human consciousness. Only she can make conspicuous those elements of fact or verity which are not yet appearing as the phenomena of verity.

In the realm of human contemplation there is much instruction going on, but not all of that which is perceived and advocated is practiced or conceived, gestated, nurtured or constructed, and then sustained as the virile thinker has maintained or is maintaining, because the world of popular beliefs believes that woman is after the design of Eve; that she is physically made to be a mate for the Adam physique. Metaphysically she conceived of the serpent and carried out his conspiracies. Physically she conceived of Adam and brought forth war (fratricide). Thus human nature and human impulse unite to bring forth curse and destruction. This consensus of human belief does woman a great injustice. It holds her in physicality, by popular opinion.

The moral-spiritual woman's powers of conception and fruition are tremendous. Eve is the antonym of true womanhood. She is the contraceiver of all virtues and verities. She is the accomplice of the notorious talking serpent.

The true type of womanhood conceives directly of wisdom, and brings forth and sustains his infinite precepts in the Earth. Wisdom himself is helpless to conceive of himself. He must have a conceiver to demonstrate or to verify his wisdom, because it is rudimental and potential. Wisdom is not superior to verity—his conceiver. Both are of the same degree of intelligence. Wisdom is sterile (not fertile) to himself. He embodies only the germs, rudiments, or potential elements of a wise issue or a potent fact.

A perception is a thought germ embodying all of the essential, rudimental, and potential elements of a concept; all of the masculine mental factors which develop into a concept. This concept is a more concrete element or factor of a fact; a representative of a verity.

A concept or a metaphysical conception combines both the thought germ and the feminine mental factors which sustain it. A concept embodies the primal compound elements of the two dependent factors or the two sixual substances. It is an aggregation of the two mental factors. It is a mental compound of the two complementary essentials, or the two mental elements, which elements, like a seed, embody the concentrated or epitomized properties of reproduction.

The word conception is simply analysed as a noun of action or condition. It is the concrete result of having taken, embraced, conceived, comprehended, embodied, enwombed, enclosed, enveloped or taken and put together, and held together, the two rudimental parts of a fact to be developed. It is the quality or state of having been taken with, taken wholly or jointly with the masculine perception, or the state of having been joined or compounded with the primary masculine perception.

The first or primal action of the processes of development is germination. Then the other processes follow, as they do in the vegetable kingdom, by growth, vegetation, quickening, ripening or fruition.

The action and function of conception is to take, seize, grasp, accept, contain or hold together, the radical elements of that thing which is to be formed and made evident.

To illustrate the important function of the mental matrix, let us dramatize the historical fact: *The Earth is Round.* Let Christopher Columbus be Actor A, and let Queen Isabella be Actor B. When she heard that Columbus advocated his plan to sail across the great uncharted ocean to prove to the world that his perception was true, she joined mental forces with him. She was of equal awareness and alertness. She knew *that* he knew. She did not know *what* he knew, for he was a navigator, a forthright character, virile stamina itself, while she was simply an intelligent woman. She conceived *what* he knew, knowing *that* he knew, and *that* he was right. Thus his perception became her conception or concept. There was an impersonal, metaphysical bond formed as a marital bond is formed between two persons. She honored his perception or his honest conviction, and she sustained his hope. He was the seer. She presented woman's intuition.

Woman's sentiments or mental feelings are the elements of reason. They come to her from the metaphysical heights. She conceives spontaneously that which she believes, beloves, beluffs, belofts or holds to be aloft. She holds aloft. She lifts, inspires, encourages, lends hope, and she sustains his belief in fact, by proving his fact to be actual rather than potential. She realizes his hope for him, since the male cannot realize, bring forth, or materialize (mater-ize) his own perceptions. He can only perceive and set forth or proclaim. He can only testify, avow or advocate that his perception (his element of a precept) be conceived heartily, and that it be brought to issue. He can only declare it to be a fact. He can specify, outline, or describe, but he cannot test his own potency or effect its result.

The power of conception works silently and without display. It functions under the rule and regulation of infinite logic, conceiving and nurturing the spiritual issues of wisdom, to fill the Earth with spiritually and universally substantial issues, verities, sentiments, integers, concepts, realities, entities, energies, wholesome offspring and that which is pure and whole. Thus true and wise conception counteracts the human nature impulses that would draw, magnetize or turn attention to that low realm which is without reason for its existence—that low realm of Eve.

In the realm of geology this power of conception did function, according to history, more than four centuries ago. This power (if you please) enabled Columbus to do what he did in the way of carrying out that which he had proposed to do, had advocated as being true and had presented to the world in his name (that of being a wise and alert and courageous navigator; an enthusiastic citizen, with a potential issue to prove).

The power of conception seemed to have no part in this historical note. Only the male, the perceiver, was in the human picture. The conceiver who had conceived and had vigilantly, faithfully, carefully and constantly sustained his discovery—gestating, holding to this issue, enwombing, embracing and mentally embodying it—was unnoticed or unapparent in the human picture, because the world has not yet halfway guessed the magnanimity of conception, neither guessed the constructive ability, nor the sustaining capacity, with which the intelligent conceiver is endowed. The male of the thinking species has been given credit for many things, whereas the secret of his success was not within himself. Every element of fact that has been perceived thoroughly, correctly, precisely and logically, has also been immediately conceived and concisely (but fully) brought forth into evidence, in spite of ignorance, prejudice and intolerances and orthodoxies of whatever cruel nature. No great and wise idea has ever been delayed in coming to the ear of Earth because of a lack of conceptual power to receive it. Wisdom's mate is verity herself.

As conscience is science within oneself so the power of conception and verification is science or verity within. It is intuition. It is a *senti-mental* thing. It is the sense of feeling within oneself that a perception (presented for conception) is true and veritable. Thus intuition or woman's sentimental nature causes her to feel sure within herself. It is a power that senses a truth when she hears it. She finds these issues (advocated) either conceivable to herself, or utterly inconceivable as being contrary to her sentiments.

The power of true conception carries with it the power and tenacity of expectation. This is more than human faith, more than human belief or hope in something. It is solid conviction within herself. It is not

a technical or an intellectual thing, character or quality. It is her spiritual intelligence; her power of cognition for wisdom. It is hearty,
vital, valid, adhesive and cohesive. It is her reason for existing; her
innate rational existence. It is comprehension itself, ever at work,
encompassing, enwombing, enveloping and developing untested or
unconfirmed presentations.

THE WORD, CONSCIENCE

The word *conscience* is the word science, carrying the prefix *con-*, which means with, together, wholly or jointly. Literally science with or with science. It is about the same as conscious, which means know with. Thus to analyse the word con-science in two parts gives it less character than to analyse it in three parts:

Prefix *con-*, with or together.

Root *scio* means know; *scire*, to know; *sciens, scientis,* I know.

Suffix *-ence* gives esse or identity. It is *entia, antis,* meaning I, esse or ego. It gives entity, *entitas,* am or being.

Literal meaning: I know with, within, jointly or wholly; I know within myself; science within oneself; to know within oneself; science within one, or one with science, or the ego and science together, and wholly in agreement.

Common meaning: an abiding consciousness of right; one's own power of moral discrimination; that reasoning faculty which is wholly conscious of right as the moral essence of his own entity or character.

Consciousness is a noun; a state of being conscious, in which state the thinker finds himself to be the agent or the actor; the knower, the perceiver or the individual who is wholly aware, or altogether mindful of the science commonly called moral science. Here conscience is a peculiarly moral sensibility; a particularly well balanced (wholly balanced) sense of right; and it is also that moral consciousness which is quick, astute, acute or keen in detecting that which is immoral or unmoral or wrong.

Conscience pertains to moral science or highest human ethic, but its source is spiritual. It is the state of being humanly (fully and wholly) aware of one's state or moral stand or status. It is moral cognizance of one's standard of excellence. It is moral stamina standing by, with, together with and for, and under that highest humanly conceivable standard of moral excellence. It is understanding or moral substance supporting and sustaining moral science, but it is a spiritual agent or agency teaching, dictating and enforcing (making humanly practicable) the science of soul or the essence of the logic of The Logos-Soul.

[65]

The following table classifies science:

REALM I

DIVINITY: The Logos-Soul—Principle of all wholly logical ideas; Precept and Premise of all science; Intelligence.

REALM II   (logic)

SPIRITUALITY: the logician; intelligence; the wholly logical thinker; the realm where soul understands The Logos-Soul; where wisdom is divinely empowered.

REALM III   (moral science)

MORALITY: the moral scientist or ego who knows within himself what is right; the human reason (or precept) which picks, chooses and gathers and utilizes the moral qualities such as invincible moral stamina; confident faith in the conscientious convictions; positive hope or moral prosperity that never gives up hope or becomes desperate; honesty that always honors human veracity; moral courage and intuition, under the tutelage of Realm II.

REALM IV   (physical knowledge)

PHYSICALITY: humanly acquired and physically verified knowledge; human nature and its unrestrained human impulses; spiritual ignorance, depravity, vacuity.

REALM V

IMMORALITY: moral ignorance or depravity; moral insensibility; the vice element of every moral virtue.

The foregoing table has classified *con*-science and the *con-scioentis* or conscientious entity, and has compared it with the logic of Realm II and with the knowledge of Realm IV, which knowledge is without moral figure or fiber, but is based upon physically evident or patent premises.

Conscience, as it exists in Realm III, may be said to be the human moral phenomenon of Realm II logic; the moral translation or interpretation of the science of soul; the sagacity of wisdom, or the philosophy of understanding Soul as wisdom teaches it.

Conscience functions through moral axioms, truths or verities, by constantly presenting these to the human consciousness; by constantly dictating or repeating them in their maximum essence or essential value to humanity; and then conscience stands by to counsel and to support a high morale. Thus conscience is a great element of power and authority. It is like a great, good, wise king who is always right, yet this king is oneself, one's fidelity, nobility, honesty, loyalty, humanity, sobriety, piety, dignity and moral integrity always in action.

The lecture of conscience is soul inspired. It is the address, sermon or speech of soul, admonishing and teaching in the conscientious thinker's mental auditorium; teaching the science of soul; teaching spiritually and morally correct and accurate thinking; tutoring the higher intuitions, and developing the highest instincts.

Conscience is one of the greatest words in the human world. It is greater than veracity, honesty, loyalty, fidelity and constancy, of themselves, because it embraces all of the greatest moral virtues. It is familiar to the human world, even as honesty and loyalty are familiar.

Conscience is not greater than the virtues, qualities, and characters of Realm II, but it partakes of their great powers of perception and conception. The soul or the entity of Realm II is the philosopher, but conscience reduces Wisdom's philosophy to human practice. *Con*-science is the phenomenon of Realm II logic; the human phenomenon of soul's presence in the form of wisdom. Thus wisdom may be called the noumenon of which conscience is the phenomenon or the right presentation showing itself to the human consciousness as a hint of wisdom's prescience.

Conscience is one's own moral property; one's own peculiar property. It is one's own philosophy or individual theology; one's individuality or one's morally sophisticated and spiritually wise self dictating its science or its spiritual philosophy to one, consciously.

Conscience is true theism. It is warm with zeal, fervor, and an ardent devotion to right and to moral honor. It lavishes its sciences and sentiments upon humanhood, even as the sun lavishes its warmth and enlightenment or light upon the figurative Earth, Ear-th or ear of understanding.

Conscience is a great word. It puts one's own convictions into words and dictates them. It (or he) is a great speaker, lecturer, orator and friend; a great moral-spiritual scientist, speaking with wisdom's authority.

Con-science is that science born of Omni-science or The omniscient Good, which is the Anglo Saxon synonym for God. It is the innate or natural capacity to know Good; the spiritual-moral ingenuity and intuition inherited at the birth of good, which good and which intuition is mothered by the logic of The Logos, or the science of Omniscience.

Con-science is the genius of Good; the natural, moral talent which wisdom maintains. It is the morally natural aptitude which teaches, directs, dictates and urges the practice of wisdom's moral principles. It is that exalted moral lecturer who is constantly drawing the line of demarcation or differentiating between good and bad; between that which is beneficent (well-doing) and that which is malevolent (illdoing or the ill-will).

Conscience is the moral science that abides with one (consciously); the spiritual intelligence that hovers over one in spite of one's semi-disobedience or one's semi-unconscious disregard. Conscience represents the ever-present wisdom or the omnipresence of the more rational faculties or the abiding faculties. It presents and represents (again and again) the ever-present consciousness which is itself—as representation of the good that wisdom discerns. Thus conscience is that consciousness of one's innermost self or soul which constantly protests against wrong, false science, sense-knowledge or human knowledge; knowledge of that which is bad or vile.

Hell is only the loss of this abiding consciousness of right; the fall into an abiding belief or a tormenting sense of the absence of right and good; a consciousness or belief of right having drowned in the inflow (influence) of wrong.

Conscience is the entity within oneself, at work, making decisions or conquering indecision; stabilizing, securing and maintaining one in moral honor. It makes one conscious of himself as being that entity who is honest or honesty himself; as being veracity herself in action; as being moral stamina, firmness, steadfastness, courage and validity, or the whole moral integer representing these and all of the other moral excellences.

Conscience is one's own integrity expressing itself, while wisdom is master of the thinking integer and of the logic of The Logos; master of the sciences which conscience embraces. Thus there is a mutual collaboration between wisdom and conscience as they work to counteract the follies of human knowledge. They constitute a great moral force. Wisdom leads. Conscience appeals to human reason.

Conscience acts as go-between driving the human esse into the audience of wisdom; dictating the way into a sense of appreciation for wisdom (soul) and his logic.

Conscience is one's own human reason or rational faculty reasoning with oneself silently, so that one may put his own sentiments or convictions into words and voice them audibly. Conscience is always with one, never against one.

Human knowledge, called science, is foreign to con-science. Humanly established sciences may not be with one, but they may be unfamiliar to one, while conscience and the moral thinker are a unit —Latin, unus-animus. That is, of one mind or one soul. They are consentient and in agreement on all things pertaining to the logic of Realm II, the prescience of soul, and the substance of the moral law.

Conscience is the feminine form of prescience or moral science (not ethic; not humanly established philosophy of morals; not human ethics). It is the outcome of spiritual logic. Prescience and conscience are moral mates. Prescience is masculine. He is the agent of wisdom presenting wisdom's perceptions to humanity via conscience. Prescience presents spiritual-moral foresight to human consciousness to instruct. He is far-seeing; a seer, seeing far into the science of reality. He and conscience think in unison.

Prescience—the seer—must act first. He must present his rudimental or elemental perception to the fertile consciousness or conscience. Conscience must accept, conceive, quicken or act upon his virile perception for it is potential until the fertile consciousness acts upon it, honors it, and makes it actual or existent in human affairs. Thus conscience, acting upon her convictions or her moral instincts and intuitions, becomes the moral law (in action or in operation), and this shows how important conscience is in her office. She and the prescience upon which she acts constitute the virile and fertile powers of reason, or the highest mental-moral ratio of power. They preserve all that is right or good in civilization. They lead all thinkers who are with them (all conscientious thinkers) on to and on through moralization. They teach the human race to think in terms of soul, in terms of wisdom, in chaste terms of soul science and under the didactic rod of both prescience and conscience. They teach what to love, how to love, and what to worship and how to worship Good.

Conscience is that consciousness (soul consciousness) in which the individual holds judicial sessions. Conscience, looking to soul (one's own soul) for rule of right, is the judge. The thinker is his own defense attorney. The science of con-science is the moral-spiritual law, rule or principle which prescribes its own recipes for executing this law.

Conscience identifies the individual. He and conscience are one and the same ego, having the same judicial power in common, or having the same good judgment. This thinker is a single individual, entity or identity who is in constant and immediate contact with soul, the science of soul, or the science within himself. Thus self, soul, ego, entity, and conscience are a combine, or they combine to form the thinker, the conscientious thinker, or this highly principled individual thinker. This self may be identified by its moral-spiritual disposition or its conscientious functions.

Conscience is not the moral law maker. Its science, born of the logic of The Logos, is the moral law. Wisdom is the logician who, as soul consciousness, supervises, oversees and inspects or looks in upon the moral sessions, to represent, express or to ideate or to point out the object, the spiritual motive and the moral intention. Wisdom and his logic represent The Logos. Conscience and its science represent and present Wisdom's logic.

Conscience, being a representative and an expression of higher law, has a constructive and preservative power. It protects and defends the human race against all of the unsavory, injurious, destructive, foolish, and unmoral agencies.

The immoral, unmoral or popular amoral or impious agencies—these unmoral agencies—are skilful, adroit, magnetic or well schooled in their arts. They dexterously confuse, worry, harry, fret or harass. They dispute, argue, deny and make nothing of the piety or pious nature of conscience. They work or function by means of magnetic personality, hypnotic tendencies, hypocritical means, exciting influences or the human imagination to get control—mental control—of the rational faculties belonging to the human being.

Con-science—the science of soul within oneself—may not be controlled, disputed or confused. It is an element of wisdom, with the power of spiritual discernment, speech, understanding or true conception, and with dominion—with a domain, manor, house, dwelling or realm quite removed from these impious and opposing agencies.

The human being, the human race or humanized kind is in the middle; is in between these opposing forces and the patient, gentle, wise and loving forces of spiritual discipline—as presented by conscience. Thus mankind, humanity or the human mentality is kept in subjection; is kept in a struggle; is kept away from his mental temple of quiet and conscientious contemplation; is kept out of the auditorium of wisdom's address, or out of the consciousness of well-being, and is kept in the consciousness (dwelling) of ill-being. One human being's mentality is used as an instrument with which to reach another. Thus two mentalities are under the control of this evil human king of the realm, which realm is regarded by humanity as being the only realm, and thus the only escape is through conscience, by means of the armor and rod of conscience.

Conscience is a very important word. It speaks the language of the human race. Its science (its truth, its literacy, its legitimacy or its logic) reaches the human ear or the ear of humanhood when no other science can lead or instruct. It is the only intelligent and rational way leading out and away from Realms IV and V; away from the finite consciousness; out of humanized concepts and precepts; the only right and safe way leading the individual thinker to his infinite consciousness in Realm II.

Conscience leads in the way of logical and literate and legitimate supremacy or in the way of the science of soul (the logic of Soul) only as the thinker is able to follow and only so fast as his self-discipline promotes him. Conscience is the science which leads in the way of intelligence up to Intelligence, and away from human intellect, which human intellect—compared to Intelligence—is only the recorded findings of the human brains, or the humanized and finitized sense of things; the corporealized consciousness.

Conscience is the gateway, the gatekeeper and the gate-tender on the way, pathway or course which leads to Realm I.

Conscience is one's intuition—*judex* or judge; one's judicative presence and moral faculty and sentiments dictating, saying and wording the law (*jus*); one's most wise and discerning self; one's executive talent and one's most rational moral faculty always at work. It is the thinker presiding over and directing his own affairs in the dignity of his logically and literately appointed office; in his legitimately justified and spiritually begotten house (*domus*) or conscious home.

THE WORD, Consider

The word *consider* is made up of root *sider,* and prefix *con-*. The root is from the Latin *sidus* (*sideris*), star. The prefix *con-* means with or together.

> Literal and original meaning: to contemplate the stars.
> Common meaning: to reflect upon; to meditate, cogitate, or ponder; to observe wholly.
> Common antonyms: disregard, heedlessness, inattention; to forget, ignore, overlook, slight.

The verb consider indicates exaltation, loftiness of thought, or the intent toward heavenly observation. It means that the thinker is with the stars, figuratively, seeking enlightenment or a brilliance such as they possess. It typifies that the thinker aspires to being spiritually illuminated as with wisdom; is interested in figurative ascension far above the mundane; is interested in celestial transition so that he may see or discern as wisdom or as spiritual seer. It means that the thinker would regard, observe or ponder things from wisdom's heavenly or high point of view; that he would be with the stars wholly; that he would cogitate, reflect, meditate, muse or contemplate jointly or observe closely, and with his back turned upon limited, earthly or temporal considerations.

Honesty is star and is a star in the moral heavens. He is a most honorable character. He typifies moral vision, discrimination, honor, splendor and clarity of thought. He thinks in a morally ethereal manner and with consideration for truth or for that which is true, equitable, just and right.

Honesty is not the only star in the moral heavens. All of the splendid qualities or virtues are stars reflecting their morally vivid light or their considerate enlightenment. These stars are higher and brighter than ordinary human considerations, human kindnesses or human standards of excellence. These virtues have a moral splendor and a glory of their own. They are morally candid. They beam or gleam and emit their candid enlightenment by iterating and by reiterating and by illustrating or by illuminating such virtues as chastity, constancy, affection, patience, compassion, moral stamina, vigor and virility. A bright star is hope and its considerations. It is moral prosperity, ever flourishing and ever fortunate. Faith or fidelity or spiritual confidence is one of the greatest and brightest. It is vividly sparkling. It is quick or morally and spiritually alive, for faith is animated by soul and is substantiated by understanding.

The stars are silent and meek, friendly, playful, considerate. They are like wisdom in substance and in nature, because they inspire thoughtfulness, provoke highest discernment and attract the loftiest attentions away from that which is unlovely, unwise, unkind, invalid and immoral or humanly morbid, impure and unwholesome; away from the arrogant, inconsiderate nature.

To temple with the stars or to contemplate in their light is to love, to believe, to be lofted or lifted. Lovers love the stars, love to contemplate them, love the sentimental environment that they seem to produce or to occasion. They seem to stimulate the lovers' ideals and to cause them to forget, for a time, the physical environment that disappoints their ideals and sentiments.

The Latin root of the word consider is *sider*. It is the root of the word desire—*de-sider, de-sidus* or *de-sidero*. It means down, from away or completely away from the star. While the word consider would indicate that one is inclined to temple *with* the stars or to contemplate the stars (where they are, in the heavens), the word desire indicates that one would bring the star down to Earth; that one would wish to have and to hold that which the star represents to one.

Desire means to wish for, to ask, pray, yearn or long for; to long to possess; to hope to coax the star to descend from its heights where it is out of reach, and to come down.

Stars indicate things beyond human comprehension or above human grasp. They symbolize things dazzlingly wonderful; things that stimulate one's highest sentiments, or things intelligent enough to look into one's heart or core.

The stars of the moral realm are the virtues. They have their own moral luster. Each star has seven points. All virtues or stars together form a moral constellation, the crux or the pivotal point upon which all human welfare, human progress or moralization depends. It is that constellation which is at cross purposes with unmoral, wrongwilled, headlong human considerations and human knowledge.

The seven points symbolize the completeness, wholeness, integrity or the moral perfection of the star. Their candid light typifies the virginity, moral chastity or immaculacy and clarity of the valid conception of right, by way of conscience and by virtue of conscience, as individual moral law. Their *candidity* is like the accurate perception of individually verified right and its virtues.

In the star-lighted realm of human imagination the lover finds refuge from the humanized patterns and the physicalized Earth. With

the stars he may lose this physical and mammal and mechanical hum-
drum sense of things; may lose the limited or physically confined sense
of himself, so that the unlovely, adverse mortal existence seems non-
existent, and so that the ugly and irksome circumstances of the earth
(ground, *humus,* or *mundus*) do not seem to have reality. There with
the stars he loves his loftiest ideals as realities, and there he weds
that which he loves. Hence the lover is, for one brief moment, enjoying his ethereal devotion or his sentimentally abstracted meditation.
Then he is brought down to earth to be rebuked for his idealism; to
be reproved for wasting that one moment in abstracted adoration; to
be admonished for being a dreamer, for being impractically romantic,
visionary and inconsiderate of the facts of anthropology and the other
ologies. Nevertheless the lover will go on catching these resplendent
glimpses of himself and of that which he considers to be. He will continue to enjoy moments of heavenly irradiations, made luminous by
his own exalted perceptions; made real by his own unconfined aspirations and inclinations toward such reality. This reality is in his own
lofted heart.

The thinker who is spiritually considerate, thoughtful, attentive,
intuitive or contemplative of such lovely ideas, realities or heavenly
things, will find himself somewhat at cross purposes with human knowledge and the humanly prescribed enlightenment, but he will forever
consider the heavens with its promise of harmony, and with its fixed
stars that symbolize universal logic, literacy and law.

Desire is a virile element of the mentality. Consideration is feminine in its function, in so far as it means to think with (him); to ponder
or to weigh in the (matrix) mentality; to collaborate with, to meditate
with or together with the virile thinker, or to deliberate together. It
means to cogitate (agitate with) or to muse together; to reflect or think
together constructively, harmoniously and lovingly; to contemplate
or to temple together; to estimate or to esteem thoughtfully.

The feminine agency gives the desire her fondest and sincerest
consideration, which means conception and gestation. If this were not
so a desire, a prayer, or a worthy design could never come true or be
carried out. If the female element of the compound mentality of man
did not consider, ponder, act upon, carry out, quicken, bring forth and
nurture a worthy desire or a moral-spiritual design; if the female thinker
did not sustain and nourish the potential issue desired and prayed for,
then man's most solemn prayers, desires and expectations would never
come to issue; his hope would be in vain, and the multiplication and
the realization of these potential issues would be deliberately ignored;
not considered, but neglected; not lovingly regarded but disregarded,
slighted, and forgotten.

This does not mean that the feminine element of the compound man (mentality) is a god to whom he must pray, but that it is the feminine power of conception and fruition whom he must consider as his collaborator, since he has only the powers of perception and presentation or address, or petition.

THE WORD, CONSTANCY

The word *constancy* comes from its Latin root *sto* (*stare, status*), I stand; *statum,* to stand; *stans, stantis,* standing; *sistere* (*sisto, statum*), to cause to stand; *statuere* (*statuo, statutum*), to station, or fix or to place.

The prefix *con-* means together or with.

The suffix *-y* or *-cy* gives the adjective constant its abstract noun form as state or quality.

Literal meaning: the quality or entity that stands with its troth, its positive verity or its invariable principle; the state of being fixed, placed, stationed or stanced with, together or together with a standard of excellence or of virtue.

Common synonyms: stability, firmness, steadiness, fidelity, faithfulness, perseverance, industry, invariability and others.

Common meaning: consistency and fidelity in thought, purpose and action; freedom from change; steadfastness in affection or in attention.

A stance is a position, a foundation, site, or a station. To stand is to abide, endure, continue, remain or stay. Hence *con-stans, sto,* or stance would be stance with, station with; to abide together; to endure together; to continue with or together with one's principle, one's standard of excellence, one's troth, promise or ethical obligation; to stand by or with one's conscientious precepts, or one's highest concept of moral law; to stand with the other highly refined characters, entities and qualities as a member of understanding, standing permanently, under Infinity, Divinity or The Logos-God who is not only permanent (staying to the end; to stay or remain to the end, as the human intellect defines) but who is interminable constancy itself, standing as Father-Root of all logic and Mother-Word of all literacy, and as Principle-Life executing the vital principles of parental love which *is* Love.

Human parlance or mode of speech has no word for the divine classification of constancy and such other qualities that are timeless. For instance, the word perpetual is defined as continuing or lasting throughout. It gives no definite noun, subject, thing or classified or

[76]

specified kind of thing, excepting a finite thing such as time, year, season, action or some other humanly outlined thing.

The words firmness, stability, fidelity and invariability are synonyms of constancy, yet they become antonyms when they take their position in the human realm of parlance, and thus they stand opposite or in *op*-position, as opposed to that which has no end, no element of time and no element of human nature, human intellect or its finity.

There is human conception of constancy, physically limited concept of it, and moral concept, but the spiritual concept is an infinite realization of the divine Ego who stands fixed in place, as Premise of all that may be logically concluded and as Precept of all that may be directly conceived to be divinely judicial, beneficial or perfectly and completely doctrinal, even wholly profitable. This concept involves no inference to finis, the end, the finish, or the finity of time.

The following table will classify and further define the word constancy:

REALM I
DIVINITY: The infinite Logos-God; The Root and Word of all understanding; The Ego or I principle.

REALM II
SPIRITUALITY: the logician understanding The Logos; the literate, logical, legitimate thinker who stands under, and understands Realm I; the wisdom and substance which The Logos causes to stand, fixed and firm forever.

REALM III
MORALITY: the ego, conscience; the thinker who stands with moral law, stands by moral science, or stands faithfully set and steadfast with the science of soul within himself, which is conscience. This is moral firmness, stability and moral equity standing and functioning.

REALM IV
PHYSICALITY: the realm in which there is a series of change, inconstancy, and discontinuity; the realm of variability, infidelity and misfortune; the realm of no infinite abiding, remaining, enduring or sustaining of its substance — physicality, the human physique, person or mammal.

REALM V
IMMORALITY: the realm of moral inanity, spiritual ignorance, or unmorality; emptiness of conscience or moral sense; moral deadness.

In this realm there is no moral precept to stand by
or with, and no concept of right to stand with it.

Constancy is a virtue that exists only in Realm II, but it may
exist in Realm III as a human ideal possible of attainment, or as a
moral precept governing that ideal or concept. It is a quality or virtue
of infinite scope or universal application. Faithfulness, loyalty, stamina and moral stability are the synonyms best suited to humanity.

The thinker of Realm II does not think or estimate in rounds,
cycles, circuits, or intellectual orbits. His thinking is not governed by
the human sense of events, places, or the completion of cycles outlined by the human intellect.

The constant thinker perseveres in obedience to his never ending,
fixed, firm, and immutable premise or Principle which has no end, but
which is like a circle—without either beginning or ending. This kind
of premise, Root, or Logos-Mynde is unbelievable and inconceivable
to human nature.

Human reckoning considers an ending for every beginning, a variable possibility for every humanly set up premise, a possible (probable)
deviation or mutation for every obligation, a lack of obedience, industry, and fidelity in every human undertaking. Hence humanity's undertakings fall apart because of the lack of such qualities as steadfastness, steadiness or stability that is stanced in the logic of foreverness.

The thinker of Realm II knows that his word, troth, duty, promise,
and his reason for existing is to The Word, with The Word, and sustained by The forever Word. Thus he takes his stance in Realm II as
a compound of the forever spiritual excellences, as fidelity itself, as
virtue itself, as troth herself, as wisdom himself understanced or substantiated by The forever Logos.

THE WORD, COURAGE

The word *courage* comes from the French and Latin root *cor* (*cordis*), or the radical *cord-,* meaning heart or the heart. The suffix *-age* means act or condition, quality or process. It may mean aggregate or sum of, or it may indicate the function of the metaphysical or figurative heart.

The common meaning of courage is that mental quality which meets danger with calmness; the dauntless, firm, or valiant temper; stout-hearted disposition.

The common synonyms are fearlessness, pluck, boldness, bravery, daring, mettle, intrepidity, fortitude and others.

The word courage may present an aggregation of the bold or stout-hearted characteristics; a collection of these resolute and gallant inspirations; the sum of all of the brave and hearty qualities.

Courage may mean act or process or capacity for hearty or strong impulses or emotions; vital and central emotions.

The heart is often used as synonym for soul.

The word encourage is a verb. It means to put courage in (another); to hearten; cause to take heart; to inspire or to promote hope; to reassure; to animate with confidence or faith. To be or to feel encouraged, would mean to be full of courage; to be *in* courage, not out of it; to be in action and in demonstration of that courage; to be in or into a condition, whole-heartedly; to be acting with all one's heart, and with all of the courageous qualities in action. This is whole-heartedness.

There is a physical heart and a metaphysical heart; a literal heart and a figurative one. When one thinks of heart as the core and the soul or the self, one may find many different states and stages and concepts of courage.

The following table classifies the word courage:

REALM I
DIVINITY: The divine creative Logos-Soul.

REALM II
SPIRITUALITY: the soul or heart that is fully inspired or heartened; the soul or thinker who has all of the qualities essential to spiritual courage or courageous action.

Realm III

MORALITY: the moral courage and stamina that belongs
   to the conscientious and bold thinker; the courageous
   factors of moralization; the moral zeal, intents and purposes of the mentality, the core or the heart.

Realm IV

PHYSICALITY: the physical heart (muscular organ) of
   the human mammal; the metaphysical animal or mammal
   courage, motivated by resentment, pride or revenge.

Realm V

IMMORALITY: the unmoral and criminal; the heartlessness or hard-heartedness of the inhuman mammal nature.

Realms IV and V present the negatives or antonyms of the word
courage: fright, cowardice, timidity, awe, dread, alarm, anxiety, fear
and such.

Realm II is one of accord, concord and spiritual courage.

Realms IV and V present discord, discouragement and an inner
emptiness; a lack of core, soul or heart.

There is a fear which is reverence. There is an awe and a fright
which purely spiritual and unfamiliar symbols or phenomena present
to humanity. There is a courage which embraces such a degree of intelligence that it amounts to hope, faith or spiritual expectancy.

There is a low morale or state of discouragement which amounts
to spiritual ignorance or moral exhaustion, human hopelessness or
desperation, and the natural human lack of understanding (understance or sub-stance) and its confidence in conscience—the director
of courage.

There is a dread, an anxiety or a feeling of alarm which divorces
one from his inner self or soul. There is a lack or absence of one's
natural spiritual resources which bring in courage, logic or con-science
with its science of soul. This is a feeling of being at sea, divorced
from the dry land or one's established sense of home with its sense of
protection and provision. Courage is akin to at-home-ness. One may
be king in his own home. Discouragement, fear or reverence for other
heads (rulers or strange kings than the one dear to one's heart and
home), creates a sense of alienation or of moral-human desperation,
even utter desolation. Here the word desperation may mean dis-spirited
or without and away from one's spiritual home. The word disconsolate
or desolation may mean asunder or apart from soul, sol or one's spiritual identity or sole entity or soul self, and one's mental home.

Adverse human opinions swamp and discourage one. To lose one's treasures or fear of losing that upon which one's heart is set, discourages one.

Moral courage is not afraid of being too moral or too radically set in and on moral premises; never afraid of being too kind, too affectionate or too compassionate in the face of opposition; never afraid of being too tolerant or too patient in the face of moral-spiritual ignorance.

Moral courage is radical, but spiritually wise or conscientious in defending right; always meek before The God of his spiritual principles, but bold before the opposition; always having his heart set on the right side, but his defense (his heel) set against the wrong side.

Moral courage feeds upon prayerful desire, expectation, strong faith, high hope, inspiration, aspiration and anticipation or the vital elements of moral prosperity.

It is said that right is might. It may be said that courage is moral might leading on the great processes of moralization. Courage is a great leader whose heartfelt serenity leads on and encourages those of weaker zeal.

Courage is a thoroughly heartened or hearty virtue; a completely healthy, sound or hearty state of being; a very warm, lively or alive quality of being; a deeply felt earnestness, or a stouthearted sincerity; a normal condition or a condition of having the utmost and innermost feeling of sincerity or a sincere heart; a quality that functions as conscientious depth and in profound frankness.

There is no place in Realm III for discouragement, depression, lack of morale or a dispirited and disheartened moral invalid. Realm III is the forefront. Moral courage commands the *foreward* march. Dismay cannot follow.

Courage is the natural moral stimulus. It is stamina of the highest moral character. It partakes of spiritual consolation and it is held up or upheld by wisdom and his benevolence. This holds the morally courageous one superior to fear of the despots, below. It strengthens, gives assurance and enhances certainty of one's moral ingenuity. It holds one up in harmony with his own heart. It keeps one's reason in authority.

There is always a reason for one's discouragement, but this kind of reason is not fully rational. It does not reflect full ratio of one's reasoning power. Hence discouragement is a form of moral weakness; a state of semi-invalidity; a condition of semi-irrationality that gives up or gives in or gives over some of its heart, or some part of its soul sense, to an unreasonable influence, or to a relatively immoral and humanly lordly pressure.

There is a fear, fright, or intense alarm that victimizes the morally weak heart. The strong heart (the spiritual core or soul) functions undisturbed, in spite of that discouragement which may be felt in Realms III, IV, and V. The strong heart is maintained and sustained by The Great beneficent Soul. He is constantly full of spirit (spiritual energy), whole-hearted or whole-souled. He stands resolute in his understanding. No human authority depresses or dismays his soul for he stands soluble and resoluble only in Soul's Principle. He stands in Soul's solution, which solution dissolves the problems, mysteries, and difficulties that promote discouragement. He stands in soul's calmness and at-home-ness—even spiritual tranquillity.

THE WORD, CREATION

The word *creation* comes from the Latin and Old French *creo* (*creare, creatus*), I create; or *creatum,* to create, make, or to make.

The suffix *-ion* forms the verb create into a noun of action or condition.

Literal meaning: the act of creating; state of being created.

Common meaning: the act of producing out of nothing; the act of producing or creating without use of preexistent material; the act or fact of causing to exist.

This treatise, THE WORD, begins with The Logos as The Creator; as The Beginning, Principle and Origin; as the only preexistent, self-existent and true Source of the ever-existent logician, his logic, his literacy and his legitimacy. This Origin, Source or Logos can hardly be designated as not existing in The Beginning, as The vital Principle and first principle from which the whole compound idea of creation springs into being. This Word or Omni-existent Creator can hardly be said to have created the divine or spiritual universe out of nothing, but out of all; out of The Re, The Noumenon or The Thing Itself, which is omnipresent Intelligence, or The omniscient Logos.

This Re is Creator of reality, all that is real, and all that may be divinely realized; The Noumenon of all purely logical phenomena (creation). Both Creator and creation are far removed from that which the world calls creation, and calls substance or material.

The Logos-Creator made or created that which is entirely dependent upon The Logos for expression, for being, for classification, for entity and for identity.

The word creation, therefore, is wholly dependent upon The Creator (The Word) for its existence, for its literacy, and for its rational power or judgment. However, there may be two schools of thought, two opposing theories, and two opposite beliefs based upon two bases or premises of thought and of conclusion.

The following table classifies the several creations conceivable and inconceivable to humanity:

REALM I

DIVINITY: The divine creative Intelligence; The independent Soul, unapparent to the human intellect and unregarded by human knowledge. The I Am Spirit, farthest removed from human nature.

Realm II
SPIRITUALITY: the creation which the Logos maintains, sustains and substantiates; the realities, ideas, verities, understanding, images, forms or spiritual products; the divinely designed or the spiritually divined and the ideate forms defined as the concrete result of having been created by The Logos; the concrete result of The divine creative Logos's (The Word's) deliberate intention to design, to divine, to define and to create the holy spiritual thinker, logician, conceiver, understander, or understanding intelligence.

Realm III
MORALITY: the creation seen within human horizons; humanity's concept of Creator, creature and creation.

Realm IV
PHYSICALITY: the finite physical aspect of creation.

Realm V
IMMORALITY: the morally depraved aspect and concept of creation; the finite point of view that embraces hostility and all deadly destructive impulses; unmorality or total spiritual ignorance.

This Realm V is the creation of envy, jealousy, dishonesty, infidelity, disloyalty, inhumanity, self-exaltation and mad personal ambition.

Realm IV is the human nature point of view, embodying the mineral, vegetable and animal natures, and embracing the knowledge of these physical properties and the legends and humanly established traditions and premises—physical.

Realm III is the moralist's point of view; creation that is made of moral or conscientious properties; that is peculiar to moral sentiment and sense; morally substantial concepts and precepts, and their honest convictions.

Realm II is that creation which The divine creative Logos or Word has fathered and mothered into being; that highest, most literate, most logical, real, true and legitimate point of view (realization, revelation and demonstration); that vital or living or vivid concept of Realm I; that divinely unique Soul-like, Love-like and Spirit-like creation which expresses, manifests and represents Realm I; that compound ideation (absolute but humanly abstract); that substance or understanding or power of realization which stands under and understands The Creator; those spiritually clarified concepts and properties belonging to *mon*—the thinker—which have originated in Realm I or in The Mynde of The Logos-Creator—Creator of the spiritual and divine universe.

The word creation is often regarded as the work of the gods whom the world regards as creators of everything and everybody—good and bad, spiritual and anti-spiritual.

The verb create is often regarded as a power that causes something to exist which did not exist prior to the time of its being made apparent to the individual's power of perception. For instance, two units plus two units makes or creates four units. There has never been a time when this was not (or will not be) true. It has no creator or maker in the sense that humanity ascribes to God.

When an idea becomes apparent to the individual thinker, when it begins to make sense, or when he first perceives it to be true, he knows that it is an element of everexistent logic, literacy or law-principle. He knows that it is an attribute of the divinely legitimate premise and precept which is Source and Origin of all divinely (really, truly, wholly and holy) existent ideas.

The thinker knows that as two plus two units constitute four units so does two and two make or create four whether that fact appears to the human mentality or not.

Creation is the compound ideation of The Logos; the divine property or compound understanding of The Logos; the elements of reality set forth by The Logos-Re of all *re*-ality.

THE WORD, DEATH

The word *death* is an Anglo Saxon form. It adds the suffix *-th* to the word die. The word die is a verb meaning to decease, to perish, depart, expire or to cease to live.

The suffix *-th* forms the word die into an abstract noun, meaning the result or process of having died.

Common meaning: cessation or expiration of physical animation or breath; the act or condition of dying or of passing beyond the termination or end of natural energy or of physical vitality; extinction, as of things extinguishable.

The word death comes from the word (adjective) dead. This word *dead* is pronounced with a dull, dead thud. It is made up of dead, lifeless, uninspired or breathless letters. It includes no aspirates for inspiration or for respiration. It presents the sense of expiration. It has no *o* vowel to express continuity. The final literate character *d* in the word dead suggests finality or the past tense. It has no sustained vowel; no long vowel to continue its voice or sounding. Its vowel sound is the short *e* as though the word were *ded*. Its vowels are muted, abruptly stopped or deadened by the final letter *d*.

The word death has a negative meaning, being the antonym of the word life. It indicates the opposite or the complete departure from life; total lifelessness; deadness. Its Anglo Saxon dead is as spelled. It is from die (ME. *dien, deyen,* and Ice. *deyja*). The Anglo Saxon word death is as spelled—death.

The word decease is a synonym for the word die. It means to cease from, down or out; to part from or to depart; to cede, yield, abandon or go from, out or down from; to give up or to surrender completely; to pass away, out or from; to leave off; to end, finish or terminate as extinct, extinguished, lapsed from, down or out (lifeless).

The Latin radical *mort,* and the forms *mortis* and *mors,* mean death, as in the words mortal, mortify, immortal, immortality, mortalize, and immortalize. Its antonym is *vita.*

The Greek *nekros* means dead or dead body. It is found in the words necromancy and necropolis (literally, city of the dead). Its antonym is *bios.*

Death is the end, finis or finish of that which may be rendered void, invalid or of non (not or nul) or no force; that which is exhaustible because of being corporeally, personally, humanly, locally mortal or finitely existent; that which is destructible or mutable because of being naturally material or physically and materially natural; that which is perishable because of being of the literal or figurative humus, or because of being subject to or dependent upon the organic matter and matters (or the organisms) of the humus.

Death is the humanly established god of all finity; the god most feared, and the enemy most revered or reverenced by humanity; the end of all humanly measured things; the finis of all humanly created and humanly instituted things.

Death is that which human intellect and human knowledge has named it; that which physical science calls it.

Death is that curse pronounced by the god of human knowledge, of humanity or of mortality (which humanity and mortality are synonymous), as the prescribed end of that which has been called alive. It is according to the consensus of human belief or opinion set up, settled upon, ordained or installed in office by the human sentiments, beliefs and instincts or impulses, wholly peculiar to human nature.

Death may be the humanly outlined end of a humanly perceived and conceived being, which being human knowledge had granted organic life, as a human being, and which human being is perceived to be of the humus or a humus-man being.

Death is the end of this human assemblage of stuff (humus, organic matter, humic stuff, soil, ground or this organized material) which the human race has called the human being, which human being has been induced and produced by and from physicality as basis and as ground.

The following table shows physicality and its relation to the several other bases or premises:

REALM I
DIVINITY: Life, The vital Premise, Beginning and Principle of life; The self-existent Logos.

REALM II
SPIRITUALITY: life or health continuity in the sphere of the compound, vital or ever-living idea; the spiritual thinker or logician who stands under and completely understands The Logos.

REALM III
MORALITY or the moral metaphysicality: that which is morally alive or animated by conscience, by moral instinct or the science within oneself; the orthodox human conception and apprehension of all things virtuous.

Realm IV
PHYSICALITY: that which is physically animate as human nature and as the Adamic concept.

Realm V
UNMORALITY: moral ignorance and immorality which is moral indifference, insensibility or death; misconception, misunderstanding and misrepresentation of all things—noncarnal or noncorruptible things.

This is the end where human knowledge ceases, deceases, expires, is spent or exhausted. This is the realm in which all of the antonyms of life (of Life or of The divine creative Logos) may be found.

Death belongs to the realm of disintegration or that which human knowledge has made or integrated. It belongs in the realm of decomposition or that which human intellect has composed or human assumption has assumed or has accepted or has conceived to be. Death of the human animal or mammal is as human knowledge has assigned, has appointed, has confined or limited. It is the humanly conceivable, tangible or believable (not probable but inevitable, necessary and unavoidable) evidence of an event, even as birth of the *humus-man* is an event. Death is a cursed event, while birth is called a blessed event, and each event comes according to humanity's settled rules and established theories concerning both, according to mortality's knowledge of both.

The Anglo Saxon *bana* means death. A bane or *bana* means murderer; a scourge; deadly poison; disease; anything pernicious or noxious; death; destruction; anything bad, injurious or deadly. Thus death may be called the bane of human (humus-man) existence or experience. It is simply mortality's bane; humanity's bane or the status lacking logical validity or soul vitality—which status itself is the bane or murderer; which status is materiality, humanity or mortality, which is the antonym of immortality or soul life—belonging to the thinker of Realm II.

Death is the deep (mental) sea of finity in which the human intellect loses itself or reaches the end (finis) of its ability to sustain itself. It is the sea in which humanity (mortality, animality, sensuality) or the humus-man mentality is at sea; is in a state of bewilderment trying to promote and prolong animation while it promotes and fosters death.

The mortal or humus-man mentality exists in Realm IV. Its basis or premise for life is physicality, as is also its basis, cause, precept and premise for birth and for death. Thus the humus-man concept of death partakes of his physical sense and outline *for* life and *of* human life, and thus life is limited to the conditions prescribed by this humus-man concept, and this bewildered intellect.

Human knowledge would, if it could, subordinate all conception and perception to this very finite or humanly limited—mortally bound and corporeally restricted or confined—sense of things; this very puny, desperately feeble, and metaphysically humanized sense of things. Thus human knowledge allows and disallows, causes and effects, animates and mortalizes. It materializes or humanizes and dematerializes or deprives of human form. It organizes and disorganizes or destroys the organic structure of that which it has constructed or created, or that *in* which it—human knowledge—has invested its intellect or itself. It is the human intellect that fails and falls or gives up. Death itself is nothing of itself, excepting the final process (the dying process) in which the human intellect (as power to sustain) finds itself powerless, either as passive victim or as active pride in advantage or in disadvantage (at the end of its resources).

Death is as wide-spread, as active and as authoritative as it has consensus, sentiment, and conceivers to sustain it, to carry it, to bear it, give it its event or to bear it out in its Eve theory.

Death is that cursed event belonging to the realm of humanity, which humanity is equivalent to and synonymous with mortality; that which is most conceivable to humanity and therefore, most inevitable in its realm; most customarily and ordinarily regarded. Thus birth is beginning, while death—physical or mortal or human death—is the usual end of the usual beginning; the human custom or manner of conceiving or of believing; the traditional and conventional way of thinking or perceiving; the orthodoxical way.

In the realm of mortality, humanity, materiality or literal physicality which is corporeality, death is the usual, the habitual practice; the common usage. It is very general, very customary and as humanly natural as birth, since human nature is the mother or the conceiver of both; since human nature is the mater who matures both events, or who nurtures and mater-ializes both events.

Death, without its humanly established instrumentalities, humanly instituted agencies or the agents which subordinate the human animal (mammal) to it, could not have its common or usual event in the realm where humanity or mortality reigns—that is, in the realm where human impulse begets and human nature quickens and brings forth.

In the last analysis death is the mortal or human nature concept of all things; the mortal conceiver carrying out her conclusion, end, fulfilment or mortal design.

Death is an ominous thing; a fateful destiny prescribed by mythological gods. It is as its perceivers and believers have made it. It is as authoritative as it has human conceivers, human sentiment and consensus to sustain it, or mortal Eves to carry it, to bear it, to bear it out or to give it its predetermined or predestined event.

Death is that cursed event overtaking the innocent—innocent and ignorant of its nature—and the bewildered and the betrayed human race. It is human nature's triumph over humanity, which humanity is synonymous with mortality and with *mater*-iality, which *mater*-iality is synonymous with Eve who is believed to be the mother or mater of all living persons, and that means that she is first the mother of fratricide or death, its victim (Abel), its guilt, its fate, its necessity, its agency, and the physical and metaphysical instruments of destruction or doom.

Human nature is that which gives birth to the mortal physicality, person, personality, and corporeality. It is human nature, or mortal nature that takes or destroys that which it has made after its own nature.

Human nature quickens and brings forth her own. Human perception, mortal pater and pattern begets his own kind of impulses and fathers fratricidal tendencies and agencies. These agencies may be mental, physical, or mortally metaphysical. They are without either virtue (moral excellence) or manhood, since the word *vir-tue* means man or man's state of being morally and spiritually excellent, good, right, pure, true and altogether just. Virtue is not born of human nature (*mater*-iality) nor begotten of the mortal pater or the Adamic condition of being.

Death is a mental thing; the ripening of humanity's fear *of* it and particular belief *in* it. It is the work of theory; the result of fear and reverence for the god (*theos*) which is Adamical knowledge, materialism, atheism, or the theism of finity. It blasts its theory of Adamic life or mortal birth.

Life is a thing of soul; of mon—the spiritual creature—created by The Logos-Soul or Infinity.

Death is of the dust to dust, or flesh and bones (soulless) doctrine; the work of human knowledge. It is Satanic in its character. It is malevolent or bad in its state. It is unhealthy, impure, maculate, distressing, calamitous, hurtful, morbid and wholly antispiritual in its condition. Thus human knowledge is the soulless god.

Human knowledge, corporeal knowledge and its sense may delight the human nature, but this same knowledge is the death of the victim of this knowledge, this prevailing influence or this nonspiritual orthodoxy. Its *theos* or theories mortalize.

Human knowledge calls death inevitable, and calls birth only the beginning of this slowly maturing, but inevitable death. This is mortal knowledge or the knowledge of mortals adhered to, honored, believed, beloved, given lief, leave or permission. Thus birth—the beginning of physical breathing—is condemned to die in due time, or is consigned to death at the end of this breathing time; is doomed to physical expiration, exhaustion, or cessation.

The newborn of human nature—under human intellect—is never exempted or absolved from the death penalty or the expected end (of this finite condition).

Human knowledge constitutes the human environment. Death, being a thing of which the human mentality has knowledge, is existent in that environment.

The spiritual mon, soul or mentality or thinker lives in and by virtue of the divine environment.

Virtue claims man, because *vir,* viril, virtue and all moral and spiritual excellences belong to man and they constitute his environment. Virtue embraces truth, justice, purity, integrity, worthiness and uprightness. These virtues conform to the law (precepts and principles) of an eternal and imperishable nature. They do *not* conform to the rulings of human nature and its knowledge—cursed Adamic adverseness.

Human nature (human intellect or knowledge) claims man, believing that there is virtue in human nature and its kind of existence. But there is *no* virtue in Realm IV nor in the person (human, humusman or mammal creature) that human nature says inhabits it. Thus human nature keeps this theory alive. It promotes, prospers, popularizes and elects and reelects it to keep itself in favor in the human mentality or mental environment. Its decisions, decrees, mandates and ruling (orthodox) verdicts constitute the tyrannical gods of the human nature. Human nature is the bane of the human environment. It is holding the threat of death over humanity, and with hypnotic influence forbids the human race to look higher for being (deathless being or soul-being).

Human nature and its knowledge is carnal in every respect. Its function is to circumscribe the human race within this carnal aspect of existence. Thus it can reign as the king, the god and the knowledge of the elect—under which one may elect or choose but to die.

While death and its kings or gods are reigning in their realm, Soul —The divine creative Logos—is reigning in Realm I, and is sustaining the life and spiritual wholeness, soundness, vitality, virility, fertility, prosperity and health enjoyed in Realm II.

While human nature and human knowledge combine to execute the law of death, Soul and spiritual logic combine to execute the Principle which *is* Soul, *is* Life and is in the form of infinite continuity of intelligence or intelligent action.

While human nature and its mentality constitute finity—which denies the existence of Infinity or Intelligence or The Logos and His divine logic—The divine nature or Soul continues to be Life or The living God; The true Infinity.

Humanity claims it creates itself. The human nature mothers itself. It maintains that it maintains or *keeps* (preserves) itself. Yet it keeps no longer than flesh and bones (organized as organic matter) can keep or can be preserved or can be maintained by human knowledge. It believes that it exists with the benedictions of The true God, and *under* and *by* the rulings of The true God, but it is a destructive force warring against the constructive forces of The Logos-Soul and refusing the ministrations of wisdom and soul. It is not spiritually quick or quickened as is the wisdom, the soul, the understander and thinker of Realm II. It is not alive to the quickenings of Soul or The Deity. It is the negative of every positive truth in Realm II; the imaginative but prevailing belief in the Adamic mythology, preying upon humanity as its mortal foe and fate.

The human being, mammal or animal lives under the mental pressure of human knowledge or intellect—the instruction amassed or stored up as argument against the logic and reality of Realm II. The human race lives under the influence of this instruction, which instruction is the agency or instrumentality that would control its mentality.

The word instrument is from instruct-ment. It may mean to build in or into the human mentality; to set its agents as tools within the human consciousness or to make it a subordinate agency. Thus the word animal is so constructed and construed to mean human animal or mammal, rather than to mean the *animus* soul or mind, the *anima* life, breath, or inexhaustible breath of Spirit.

The human being is instructed as humus-man (animal); is taught all of human nature and animal nature having some of the nature of the lion, some of the characteristics of the wolf (avarice), some of the swine (spiritual ignorance), some of the beast (lust), some of the animality or the animosities peculiar to the human animal.

Human nature (or human knowledge) stands mentally adverse to all but its own agencies which serve to mentally assassinate all higher than human nature; serve to murder all teachings and teachers of higher than human knowledge. Thus death is the instrument of the most popular (ancient and modern) wonder-worker, magician, mental manipulator, liar (about the *animus,* soul), and general misdescriber and misplacer of soul, yet quoting its own misconceptions of soul incessantly, thus presenting them for conception.

THE WORD, DEVIL

The word *devil* is a name for that character who characterizes evil or that which is vile. The function of this character is to devil, to devile or to defile, and to revile; to vilify. This word devil embodies the word evil, and it stands for all that is base—not high; all that is bad—not good; all that is worthless—of no virtue or moral worth.

The function of this character is to defeat every good purpose as the negation (negative element) of that good purpose; to misrepresent everything good or right that is presented in good intent, by reversal to bad intent.

The devil is that god of mythology to whom Adam prayed for a wife and who answered by creating Eve. Thus the devil is the god and lord of all misfortune, the creator of all evil or *Eve-ill* or Eve's ill-fortune. Eve typifies human nature, the mammal nature or mamma (mater) of all evil matters. Eve's ill or evil conception (of the serpent) brought forth adversity, curse, calamity, and finally fratricide. She is, therefore, the wife of the devil and matter (mater) of his most devilish issues.

REALM   I   DIVINITY: The Logos, who is God.

REALM   II   SPIRITUALITY: the logician, who is man.

REALM III   MORALITY OR HUMANITY: the human being and the human intellect governed by moral instinct or conscience.

REALM IV   PHYSICALITY: human nature governed by physical knowledge, instinct or sense.

REALM   V   IMMORALITY: unmorality; inhumanity; self-condemnation or damnation; moral depravity; complete spiritual ignorance; carnal, finite, odious, foul or vile mindedness.

Evil is that which exudes a vileness offensive to good metaphysical taste. It is bad taste, or a lack of moral sense and good sense. It is ignorance of good taste; a lack of moral instinct. Evil is the state, quality or condition of being vile or vileness itself; the state of being the opposite of goodness. Thus evil or devil imposes itself upon the company of those of better and best human taste. It would associate with its betters or with the better human sensibilities, in order to practice its traditions which traduce and induce the unwary, the morally weak or ignorant.

Evil or devil is the state of being dishonest, deceitful, dishonorable, disloyal, irreverent and farthest removed from honesty, integrity, charity, chastity, veracity, constancy, fidelity, loyalty, moral stability and such good and right characteristics. The devil however wears the mask and the garments characteristic of morality in order to operate in human society; in order to maneuver more unobtrusively in human affairs (as one of good intent or as one of moral purpose), and in the currently popular manner.

Evil or the devil operates in human consciousness as envy or deceit; as an inordinate desire to acquire a good name which belongs to an honest man. It may operate as covetousness or jealousy, conscious of its own depravity. As a male element of evil consciousness, he functions to impregnate the feminine mental matrix with the germs of his conspiracies. He exudes, utters, emits or sets forth his dictations to counter-roll or to control the dictations of con-science; to mute the voice of conscience and to amplify his own in her ear; to keep her under his spell, magic, charm or magnetic influence.

Eve herself may serve as symbol of feminine evil. She has a natural susceptibility, pregnability, impressionability or impressibility for his deviltry or devilry; for his villainy, sinuity or his covert suggestions. His potent germs of hypnotic nature, creep, wind, flow or flux into her mental matrix, by way of hint, allusion, or human nature's dreamy delusion. Thus they would, if they could, supplant or sterilize every honest intent, and every conscientious purpose by simply impregnating the human mental matrix, and by keeping that matrix impregnated.

The devil is master of many evil arts; a linguist speaking in every native tongue; an agile fellow capable of wearing the official costume of every humanly honored office, and every humanly adored and adorned personage. Here let it be said that *con*-science also speaks every native tongue; that *con*-science is master of the science of correct and accurate thinking and speaking, and master of the good and true arts sponsored by Realm II. Thus *con*-science, under the superintendency of wisdom, works most effectively to guard the conscientious thinker, and to unclothe the devil before the eyes of the thinker. The devil, without his glittering or glistening costume, is naked indeed.

The devil, as king, has his subjects over which he reigns tyrannically, but so courteously (with such courtship or in such a courtly manner) that his subjects enjoy it. Their great desire is to be as devilish, as clever, as fascinating, entrancing or enchanting as their king.

The devil, as lord, is devilishly sophisticated, smart, popular, agreeable, famous, occult, and the idol of his worshippers.

The devil reigns most popularly in that realm where conscience is absent and human vanity of personal reputation is the thing most cherished. He is the model of the mundane people whose first desire is to be as devilishly clever as he; to be as charming a fellow; to have such a magnetic personality or to wield such an hypnotic influence as he. Thus he is that characteristic human vanity which would outmaneuver the other fellow, so as to appear more devilish than the devil, or than the world's most flattering concept of the devil.

The devil is that evil fellow (in evidence) who is morally illogical, contrary to the moral law, opposed to the will of conscience or the law of right. His vileness, however, is not evident or externalized to those who are in sympathy with him—those who are on his mental level of human vanity.

He is a pretentious fellow, affecting what he wants to affect, and blandly telling lies (as champion liar) when he wills. This devilishly charming fellow is only a human nature characteristic. It or he is characteristic of the human nature and its vanity, its pretense, and its morally idiotic affectations. He is human nature itself; the corporeal personality honoring, respecting, reverencing, adoring and worshipping itself as king and as god in his own world.

The devil's function (his act on every human stage) is to devil mentally; to slander or to deceive by throwing his deceptive, mythological fancies across the path or in the way of the human thinker. The word calumniate (to accuse falsely) and the word diabolic tell of his nature and his function of throwing into every scene his cross purpose or his dia-bol-ical (*dia-ball-ein*) part, meaning to throw across, and *dia-,* dividing into two parts or factions.

The word devil could mean doubly vile, twofold or twice bad and base or degraded. The first part of the word may be *dia-* (Greek, dividing into two parts) and the last part of the word may be vile. This would mean that the devil's adverseness is (and functions in) in two parts or functions as two vile characters or as a character functioning through duplicity, deceit, simulation and dissimulation.

In order to function the devil must have an accomplice to help him or to mind him. This accomplice must be a fictitious character even as he. If he is male his accomplice must be female, for he is a twofold point of view, viewing with malice, deviltry or fiendishness whatever he views, and thus the devil is simply an adverse point of view, seeing through his own eyes, that which is adverse to good or that which is the reverse of good or that which slanders good.

The devil without a worshipper or an accomplice would be impotent. His slander would be audible and his deviltry would be obvious and his identity would be more tangible to the human sensibility. But with feminine cooperation he can function through his worshippers who hold within themselves his ability to carry out an intent, or his only ability to function, for he could not make a statement (a slanderous one) excepting in his own audience because the male element of honesty has the power to decapitate or to deprive him of reproductive power. His worshippers (hearers) conceiving or accepting his germs of deviltry (are excited and incited) begin at once to enfold, envelope, enwomb and embrace his false report or vile design, to sustain it.

The devil is a character of ill repute. Hence he must ride, occultly, upon a person's social reputation and must keep his victim (the person who acts and speaks for him) well covered or protected from ill repute and well cloaked in favorable reputation. This person is, of course, devilishly charming and charmingly devilish and he is most popular in human society. He is proud, vain, egotistical and altogether selfish. But since humanity is vanity itself, short-lived and mortal, he makes the most of his timely opportunities, as he plays upon his audience.

The function of the devil is to defile; to render foul or dirty like himself; to vitiate everything and every person excepting himself and his kind; to impregnate the *feme*-ones whom he delights, with the germs of his own kind so that he may become even more popular and increase his own kin and kind, which kind is enmity for and enemy of goodness.

The devil characterizes the most morally vitiated concept of a male person. His foul perception of a female person characterizes his mate —she who is most enslaved by his possessive and ruling ego. This female of the devil species is she whom he enraptures, ravishes, captivates, fascinates and enchants and holds under his spell or under his control.

The devil is physically and metaphysically magnetic and hypnotic. He is a personalized conception of magical, mental and physical elements. He is a personality having only those elements which the human imagination gives him or assigns to him, yet he is the first and last enemy of manhood, womanhood and humanhood. He typifies inhumanity or inhuman enmity.

The devil is the king of vice, adverse to virtue. He is the metaphysical symbol of the hypocrit; the metaphoric character presenting hypocrisy in all human affairs.

The devil's accomplice is the Eve character. She is the metaphysical symbol of susceptibility to her master, and to his impressions. She is of his temperament, feelings, nature, sense and emotions. She is the character presenting sympathy with and sentiment for the devil. She is the mamma, the mammal, or the mammary element who nurtures her master's desires and purposes; the producer of the egg or ovum that matches the devil's potential germs, and the sustainer of them. These germs produce war, fratricide, murder, bane, ill fortune, desperation and all that is morally odious or objectionable. Eve has no will but to act upon them.

The devil, like human knowledge, has no good side. The de*vile* is the antonym of that which is noble, wholesome, clean or spiritually pure. Human knowledge gives credence or belief to the Eve hypothesis which, like the devil, is the bad side and has no good side. Eve, being the mater of all human nature and human knowledge, will produce the devil's designs so long as there is an Eve to conceive them and to carry them to their devilish fruition.

THE WORD, DIVORCE

The word *divorce* is from the Old French and Latin form *verto* (*vertere, versus*), I turn, and from *versum,* to turn.

> The prefix is *di-*. It means away, apart, asunder, aside or aside from, apart or apart from; opposite of.
> The root is *vorce, vers* or *verto* (versum), to turn.
> Literal meaning: a separation; a disunion; turned apart.
> Common meaning: a dissolution of the marriage relation, by legal means.

That which is turned apart never was turned together, in reality, in literacy or in logic. That which is the opposite of or is opposed to, never was in agreement or in harmony *with* that which it opposes. That which may be turned apart, aside or away from the other element of a compound idea, never *was* a part of that idea.

No part of that which is (holy) inseparable can separate. That which is divinely, spiritually, really or morally united may not be disunited, separated, disjoined, disassociated, severed, sundered or divorced or diverted into different forms or substances, but must exist as complementary and component parts of each other or of the divine, spiritual, real or moral whole.

There can be no breaking up of units; no disintegration of united, married or closely wedded elements—logically related.

Marriage is any close union. Divorce is the disunion of that which humanity has caused to be married or closely united. Marriage is the union of two individual and essential elements. Divorce is the breaking up of those uncomplementary elements which cannot or may not be conciliated, consoled, consolidated, confirmed or validly established, or truly compounded.

In reality divorce is a mental and moral struggle to free oneself from those human forces which claim to be legitimately wedded to one.

Fidelity divorces itself from infidelity. Loyalty divorces itself from disloyalty. Wisdom, integrity or honesty is divorced from foolishness, folly, vanity, animosity, dishonesty or deceit. Hatred is opposed to affection. Impatience and passion divorce themselves naturally from patience and compassion. Pride separates itself from meekness, humility and beneficence. Envy and jealousy separate themselves from moral prosperity, abundance and amplitude.

A legal divorce separates a male person from a female person, but a metaphysical divorce separates dissimilar and inconsistent elements from the impersonal thinker.

A wife may be divorcing herself from the lordly male personality or ego, while a husband may be divorcing himself from that female characteristic or female character which he cannot conscientiously support or embrace.

If human marriage and divorce are both controlled, more or less, by human nature, which nature is insubordinate to moral and spiritual law, then marriage is not good.

Inconstancy and unchastity are not marriageable. They cannot stand with or stand by a troth or an element of law, neither can they stand alone. They fall, unsupported, while every virtue stands as the versus of vice. Human pride is always false. It is false pride trying to cover its faults and its littleness by inflating itself.

In the metaphysical realm marriage is the union of masculine or virile elements and virtues to feminine or fertile elements of the human mentality. Divorce is the disunion of those elements which are not sentimentally, mentally, really or truly related and morally essential to each other, as morally supporting each other.

The process of divorce may be the constant and continual search for the matching elements and the elimination of the superfluous ones, since every masculine virtue has its feminine mate:

> Constancy is the mate of steadfastness, moral stamina and firmness.
> Purity is the immaculate wife of spiritual accuracy, integrity.
> Feminine intuition and comprehension is the wife of masculine discernment and apprehension.
> Feminine powers of veracious, valid conception wife the masculine powers of honest, zealous or pious perception. They honor honesty, and actualize his potentialities.
> Feminine sentiment is the affinity of masculine vision, provision, prophetic opinion or foresight.

The feminine powers of metaphysical fruition are silent, obscure, quick, but retired and hidden from human sense or human knowledge, while masculine powers of presentation—such as speech and advocation—are overt.

The feminine powers of conception, gestative action and fruition are magnificent, because they magnify, amplify and appreciate that which has been advocated. They are not the properties or powers of the human intellect, but they are spiritually and morally intuitive.

They are not related to human nature but they are married to him who has a natural moral aptitude, instinct or affinity for their degree of intelligence.

In human civil affairs marriage and divorce take place supervised by the civil law. But marriage is governed more by the moral law, moral principles and ideals. These ideals may be stable or fanciful, conscientious or superficial.

The human nature is author of its own law, mandator of the mating instinct in its physical or natural realm.

Marriage was instituted to function under moral law or the conscientious sentiments, to prevent human nature from completely adulterating the moral nature, and to keep human nature from robbing matrimony of its essential ingredient—mother-*mony* or the peculiar virtues of motherhood.

She who loves, honors, and obeys the moral law must wed him who expresses and represents it. She who dislikes, dishonors, and disobeys the moral law is not under its protection; not husbanded by its wisdom; not manned by its strength.

Faith and fidelity may not divorce herself from confidence, but she is already divorced from infidelity or faithlessness. She keeps her troth to her high concept of manhood, not to a human person. She loves and honors honesty's moral precision.

Honesty may not divorce himself from her who honors him with her veracity and chastity, but he is already divorced from those unmoral and unwomanly (human nature) characteristics which have little or no appreciation for honesty. Thus these virtues separate themselves from the human nature vices by means of the law of conscience and its science of right reasoning. This right reasoning begins where and when human nature is found to be unreasonable and morally unnatural.

Intelligence is the thinker's whole mental faculty. Ignorance is not a faculty of thought, but of thoughtlessness. It is that state of the mentality which ignores what it does not apprehend because intelligence is beyond, over, and above its metaphysical reach. Ignorance is a lack of intelligence.

Every individual thinker is more or less divorced from intelligence, yet every individual thinker (if progressing) is divorcing his or her thinking faculties from ignorance.

Intelligence embraces logic, literacy, and judgment or judicial power. Thus it is divorced from the elements of ignorance, but ignorance claims to be a part of intelligence; claims to be identical as human intellect.

Neither human intellect nor ignorance are any part of intelligence; no part of an element of wisdom; no part of an element of moral stamina, firmness, courage, validity, constancy or soundness, but they are divorced by means of their wholly separate existence. They are divorced from moral and spiritual soundness, wholeness, holiness or holy completeness; divorced by means of their humanly limited state.

In reality, where the rational or thinking properties are spiritually real, the very spiritual purity of each element makes it belong to the whole intelligence. These properties are wedded, held together, quickened, sustained and maintained by their creative Logos-Intelligence.

The thinker is constantly going through the processes of elimination. That is he is divorcing himself (soul-self) from that which is no longer a part of his intelligence, his soul, or his true self. Divorcing a person may not improve one's essential processes of elimination.

Wedlock, in its spiritual and highly moral purpose, is designed to lift the human race out of its human nature—even sub-animal nature —by means of the holiness of matrimony, home, mother love, purity, wisdom and constancy. These conditions are intelligently stable. There is no breaking up of these spiritual states or qualities—these elements of intelligence. They are leagued together in the compound *mon,* or male and female intelligence. They are bound, banded, or united by the moral intent to moralize and to spiritualize the concept of marriage.

Each individual must have the bitter experience of divorcing himself from his own human ideals, idolatries, glistening objects, personalities, magnetic, hypnotic but vacuous nature. Without this struggle there could be no moral or real spiritual birth, for the struggle is like that of the bird or the baby moth breaking out of a shell or eliminating the shell. It brings both strength and color to the wings.

THE WORD, Duty

The word *duty* is a noun formed by adding the suffix *-ty* to the Latin *debere (debeo, debitum),* to owe, or due. The French form is *deu,* or devoir, to owe; service or duty; owe.

The suffix *-ty* gives the word *due-ty* its state, quality or condition of being. Thus its literal meaning: state of being due; that which is now due; condition of being owed; that which is now owing; indebtedness; obligation.

Common meaning: that which binds or obligates or is due morally, financially, socially, civilly, spiritually or in some other legitimate way, as one's individual duty.

The word duty ramifies into many different states, conditions and relationships of individual being. Each individual assumes his own obligations according to his state, qualities and recognition of being. For instance, one's moral obligations are moral. One's moral duty is in proportion to one's moral ability to perform it; in proportion to one's conscientious rational faculties, talents, or capabilities to perform it fully.

One's duty may be civil, social, or literal or literally financial— neither moral nor figurative. Duty is according to one's state of being in relation to others, and according to one's own recognition of himself, his state, his quality or condition of being. One's duty to humanhood ramifies into many, and ramifies from his or her first three duties.

1. Manhood owes virtue. He owes the kind of moral manhood which IS virtue itself manning the man. This is moral virility, stamina and courage.

2. Husbandhood owes protection, providence, honesty or his honest convictions; owes firmness, trustworthiness, sobriety, solemnity, profundity, deep earnestness or solemness, foresight, steadfastness, moral uprightness, with hope or moral prosperity. This he owes as marital relative.

3. Fatherhood owes highest paternal pattern of integrity, forth-rightness and the wholly mature virtues, which virtues are those of manhood, tripled—not divided into thirds, but triply intensified—through wisdom and experience gained from manhood, husbandhood, and

thirdly fatherhood. Thus his obligations are tripled as are his abilities.

1. Womanhood owes her highest sentiments, affections, charity, modesty, chastity and genuine moral womanliness; owes her highest concept of love; her love for the morally good, sincere and beautiful; her love for virtue and her love of and regard for the dictates of conscience; owes her moral fertility.

2. Wifehood owes her troth, her veracity, her vow and her word; owes her patience as wife (*wif, wefan,* weft) or material of which the moral fabric is woven; owes her faith and expectancy and fulfillment of her vows as conceiver and weaver of moral issues.

3. Motherhood owes only that which is most (spiritually and morally) natural to her; her highest instincts and mature intuitions; her ability to be constant, compassionate, gentle and faithful to the holy bond of matrimony or mother-*mony*.

These duties are not performed in reverence to persons, relatives, or to the civil law. They are performed as one's duty to one's conscience—the soul within oneself—and to one's highest concept of Soul —The Logos-Soul.

THE WORD, EARTH

The word *Earth* has many literal and figurative meanings. The literal, physical Earth (planet) is defined and well treated by the popular geologies, the physical sciences, or the geophysics or geographies and geometries and whatever pertains to this solar system.

It is the purpose of this treatise to define and treat the word Earth from its literate character and from its symbolic nature.

The word Earth is from the Anglo Saxon *eorthe,* meaning land. The Anglo Saxon *erian* means to plough; to ear the land or the earth. Thus to plow involves the ultimate purpose of fruition; involves the ear of wheat, corn, or the like. It involves seed, sowing, germination, and vegetation, by means of cultivation or land husbandry. This sense of the Earth gives her sex. She is that which brings forth; that which germinates; that which is fertile; that which vegetates, quickens, develops, or promotes growth and maturity, and that which sustains and nurtures upon her vast bosom the whole of the animal and the vegetable kingdoms.

In the higher metaphysical sense she symbolizes continuity, eternality, and mother constancy. Her spherical shape and her constant spinning action has no beginning and no ending. The peoples of the Earth may depend upon her mathematical measurements as she coordinates with the sun in seasonal, timely, orderly fashion.

She is didactic in her nature. She illustrates and demonstrates what she teaches. She typifies a nice sense of science and of art, of symmetry and of natural beauty. She teaches profound lessons in all of the virtues. There is a sense of meekness and humility in her tremendous capacity to follow pattern and recipe of her universal principles. Her troth, truth and trustworthiness and her obedience to the sun, is beyond human comprehension. Her punctuality in keeping her appointments, at each station in her heavenly orbit, typifies her dependability and her legitimacy as an heaven borne and heaven supported idea. She teaches and fosters hope, expectancy of good fruition, faith, confidence in orderly precepts, fidelity to orderly principles and honor of literate and logical powers. She teaches moral and spiritual prosperity, growth and constant or perpetual development.

The Earth has great metaphysical meanings. Her frankness and her candid honesty (showing everything on the surface); her mothering of tiny seeds within her matrix typifies reality, lifts human thought out of its smallness and selfishness into higher and more heavenly contemplations; into moral and spiritual spheres of thought.

As the thinker revolves in his moral and humanly ethical orbit, in obedience to the principles and precepts of his sol, soul or individual light of conscience, and as he turns things over and over in his mynde, he is learning to be obedient to the eternal premises which conscience teaches.

As the Earth revolves on her axis, so does the thinker revolve on the moral axis, axiom, and polar axis or maxim which he honors; so does honesty, veracity, loyalty and conscientious integrity keep and hold the thinker, always in line with his axis principle; so does conscience (the science of soul, sol, or the sole self, and the individual thinker) act as moral-spiritual magnet, holding the thinker within the scientific radius of his polar line.

The Earth, in her literate or letter sense, is the word ear, which adds the suffix -th to form the word Earth. This suffix (-th) means result or process. The literal meaning is result or process of earing or of hearing. Thus it is ear-th or hear-th, and to hear means to understand or to conceive thoroughly.

The function of the ear is to hear, to listen, to receive, to regard or to harken (hearken). Figuratively, Ear-th is the audient element of heaven or of the heavens. Her function is to lend an ear, to give attention, to list, listen, luf, luff, love, leif, or to belove and to believe, favor, regard, to observe, to list or take note or notice, and to record or to give concrete form. Thus she complies with and cooperates with the other elements of the solar system or this soul system, and thus she must symbolize the illimitable, universal powers of conception and fruition; the infinite element of love herself, receiving, conceiving and understanding wisdom, and bringing forth his rudimental or potential issues. This she does as spiritual womanhood and wifehood, making his issues actual or set, and in harmony with wisdom (spiritual integrity).

Earth, in her more universal and infinite meanings, is a member of soul's enlightened or wise spiritual system, even as she is a member of this solar system. She reflects the enlightenment (light) of soul or spiritual integrity, even as she reflects—by means of her water surface—the light of the sun, so brilliantly. She represents that sound, valid, solid spiritual substance of understanding; that compound of realities (divine), even as she is that solid mineral substance that makes a lovely home for the human race, and even as she is that mineral sphere which mothers the animal and vegetable kingdoms.

Earth, in her symbolic sense, is the home-land of the human race, where it may bathe in the sunshine (of sol or soul), where it may

breathe in or be inspired by the breath of heaven (spiritual atmosphere) and where it may drink in the heavenly rain (spiritual influence). Indeed, this it *may* do. But the human race, humanity or humanhood rarely lifts its mental eyes above the land of physics or the
sphere of physicality, or the human nature (the human physique) to
inquire or to seek wisdom.

Earth is modest. Her function is silent. Her ear takes in. The
abstract noun *Ear-th* adds the suffix *-th;* adds the breath (voiceless
consonant) to the ear or to that which breathes in; to the ear that is
inspired or inspirited by what she hears and conceives. Then she
quickens, gestates, vegetates, inspirits, inspires, integrates, makes hale,
makes whole, nurtures or sustains that which she has conceived or
received in her silent and modest way.

The Earth, being that which ears or hears, is also the state, quality,
agency and condition of being that which ears, hears, listens, hearkens
and heeds. Her orbit symbolizes the progressive earing of truth as the
process of being on the scent of heavenly truth. Earth is heaven bound
or bonded, but heaven is not Earth-bound. She is held in her orbit
and office by the sun (sol and sole light and soul enlightener) around
which she rotates and revolves in her own systematic way.

The Earth must be a brilliant spectacle from the Mars (planet)
point of view, and Mars could be the marital relative of Earth. Mars
could be marry, *maritus* husband.

Much has been said about Earth communicating with Mars, but
from the literate nature of the two words, Mars will communicate with
Earth when Earth's ear is attuned to the more universal and spiritual
form of speech, expression, utterance or communication. When Earth's
ear has become fertile to his sidereal desires and heavenly speculations,
deliberations and considerations, then she will hear from him, for they
are married by universal law and this law will function via their natural affinity.

Earth and Mars are lofted in the same heavens, and lighted or
enlightened by the same sun. This heavenly sense is not sensible to
the mundane and physically minded, however. Mars is believed to be
the god of war. Thus the marriage (communication) may be attended
with war between the factors of ignorance and the elements or faculties and factors of intelligence or soul, but the angels of soul or spiritual sentiments and intuitions that soar above, will win the war.

The Earth is the dry land. It is also that land under the sea. Earth
symbolizes that very substantial sphere or heavenly body, separated
from the other heavenly bodies of this same solar system by the realm
of heavenly understanding; by the firmament of contemplation.

Mars is not the home of man, as Earthlings regard man, but Mars has its own kind of thinker who is specifically adapted to it and divinely assigned to it. Thus the method of communication between Mars and Earth must be solar in its nature, and must carry a symbol of solace. It must be mental and yet spiritually audible to *Ear-th*. It must be something like music as music is understood on Earth. It must symbolize the art and science of good legitimate thinking to those who have an ear for good.

The thinking creature of Mars may differ greatly from the man-creature and the other creatures on Earth, but they are metaphysically related and they live under the rays of the same sol which gives solace to both. They must have the same or similar sense of harmony, as music or some other kind of harmony is appreciated on Earth.

As the Ear-th has opened her ear to neighboring races, and as the once isolated countries have become one human race, in constant communication, in one Earth, so must Earth prepare to deal, amicably, intelligently, and spiritually, with the Martians. The spiritually refined and morally delicate or sensitive natures must represent Earth's sentiments or else Mars will not come into the scene as husband of Earth, but as a modern Goliath—thick, coarse, gross god of war, indeed.

The following table shows Earth (*Ear-th*) in its several realms of conception:

REALM I

DIVINITY: The audient Intelligence; The divine Ear or conceptual capacity of The Logos.

REALM II

SPIRITUALITY: the ear of understanding and of complete realization; the intelligence of the logician or the wholly (holy) spiritual and spiritually literate or legitimate thinker who understands the speech of The Logos, perfectly.

REALM III

MORALITY: the ear that hears (obeys) the speech of conscience, or the thinker who has an ear for moral precepts, ideals or conscientious scruples.

REALM IV

PHYSICALITY: the Earth planet as defined by the physical sciences, and which symbolizes the metaphysical ear or the state, quality and condition of hearing, earing, comprehending, acting upon and bringing forth.

Realm V

IMMORALITY: the realm without moral principle, or
sense of conscience which wars against the animus of
soul, because it is active animosity defending its egotism;
because it is soulless. It has no ear or audience with
soul, or with Realm III.

The Earth, as a great sphere, has infinite meaning. Its equatorial
line has no point of beginning. Its polar line is a great axis, hub,
pivot, principal theme or infinitely strong law of balance, equity or
right, presenting the idea of The Logos axle of correct and accurate
thinking; of logical reasoning or the science of (soul) reasoning.

Ear-th typifies that which has been understood of The Logos; that
which has been spiritually substantiated; that which will continue to
be understanding, and continue to be contemplating, considering, conceiving, perceiving, demonstrating and realizing further, and farther
as the spiritual ear listens to The Logos-Word—The speech of Soul—
expressing infinitely literate, logical, and legitimate ideations.

Ear-th typifies the landing of the thinker, in that he hears, understands, settles and lands.

To land means to come to rest.

To land morally, spiritually or understandingly would mean to
come to the realization of a pertinent element of logic, fact, truth, law,
science, literacy or wisdom; to discern an evident element of intelligence, or an idea enlightened or lightened by sol-soul; to find a landing
place in one's search for a universally true idea; to find a place to stand,
understand, sit or reside on the land; to be satisfied in a settled (conscious) abode—neither adrift, nor on wing; to be on a solid metaphysical or moral platform.

Earth typifies that spiritual platform where wisdom stands as the
divinely instituted and divinely substantiated thinker; stands in soul
contentment, in soul consolation, and with his solid, universal ob-
jectives. Here stands love—in her spiritual glory—ready to conceive,
nurture, love, and cherish wisdom's perceptions and to bring them into
intelligent evidence before the eyes of solid thinkers. Here Earth is
a spiritual point of view and a spiritual ear presenting the powers of
perception and conception.

Earth is that spiritual symbol which has no sun-set and knows no
darkness, no inactivity, and no figurative darkness. She presents the
idea of complete enlightenment as an ideate thing; as phenomenon
of The noumenal ear of The Logos.

Her relation to the sun symbolizes and presents understanding of
The Logos-Soul and her relation to Soul; symbolizes and brings forth

metaphorical morning or brings to light (to the human sense and vision) by means of her fruit — vegetable kingdom; brings forth, quickens or makes grow, animates or vegetates and gives her motherly nutriment. Her dependence upon the sun or sol symbolizes her dependence upon Soul (as Source of wisdom and enlightenment).

When the equitable wisdom of the Earth has reached the point of universal realization or the reality of complete understanding of Soul, then the thinkers of Earth will think of Mars as neighbor and will be ready to hear his kind of speech, his kind of expression, or the Mars kind of ideation.

When Earth has learned her lessons from the manifestations of the animus (sol, sun, soul or soul-life) as soul is made manifest or as soul (sol) makes manifest on Earth, then Earth will be ready to hear from Mars and will be capable of learning how sol is made manifest there; how *anima* (breath), living creature, spiritual essence, substance are reflected and presented and represented there.

When Earth has verified, likened, compared and brought forth the images of wisdom here, she will probably find that Mars has a polar axis very similar to ours; an equatorial line and a governing principle, precept, and premise similar to ours but expressed differently.

When Earth's concepts are deduced from the one (same) creative Principle or premise, then the logic and literate conclusions in action on Mars will be found to be familiar to us because Mars functions under the government of a polar axis and our familiar sun, and because precepts and concepts must be of one spiritual family if their premises and precepts or principles are related.

Both Mars and Marslings must be very different from Earth and Earthlings, but when a more logical and literate point of view is reached they will be found to be in the same sol (solar) and soul light or *soul-ar* light, whatever their physical aspect may be.

When Earth becomes the audient ear (audience) of The great governing Logos-Soul that emits enlightenment and that speaks the language of The Logos, then that which we know as truth, as wisdom, as spiritual logic and as intelligence will be found in evidence on Mars, because seen in the right light.

Mars may present a more strenuous aspect; a different and virile or masculine style; a kind of energy indicative of potent wind—latent and potential—but fundamental; a kind of might as the wind manifests it; a kind of potence and a kind of atmosphere (metaphysical) that differs from ours; a mental motivation and a spiritual encompassment more boisterous than ours, yet affording breath for the creature and inspiration for the Marsling.

The Earth (sphere) is round, having neither beginning nor ending, but having continuity as a type or symbol of eternal hearing, quickening or spiriting. Her mineral body symbolizes her solid or solidified spiritual properties. Her vegetable kingdom symbolizes and teaches the miracle of soul or spiritual life standing on spiritual substance or understanced by Soul's logic. Her animal kingdom vegetates, germinates (from seed), generates, gestates and multiplies according to its nature.

This Earth Sphere begins its description with the principle or polar axis at North or at the North Star, which directs as first point of direction or as directing principle. It continues to the point of East—the origin or the rise of mon in spiritual (soul) enlightenment; continues to the point of South where the crux marks the place of crossed purposes and crosses that place outlined by the human race, in order to demonstrate divine logic or spiritual consideration; continues to the point of West—having risen up against the soulless purposes at the South— where this highly principled idea meets Truth's equatorial line—Her golden brilliance—where Her equity, troth and promise is fulfilled by carrying the thinker (idea) up to the point of beginning or of complete realization; point of perfect fruition and demonstration.

Thus all of Soul's ideas are presented to the ear of Earth for conception. Thus Earth typifies the solid ground and the oceans of water (solution dissolving spiritual ignorance) typify the constant clarification of concepts going on in her very capacious and concipient auditorium.

THE WORD, EDUCATION

The word *educate* comes from the word educe, which is a Latin word built upon the form *duco* (*ducere, dustus*), I lead, draw or call. Education functions to lead out.

The prefix is *e-* (*ex-*), meaning out or from.

The root is *duco,* meaning lead.

Literal meaning of the word educe: I lead or call out.

The word educate adds the suffix *-ate,* which gives it its office or function.

The word education adds the suffix *-ion* or *-tion,* which makes it a verbal noun.

Literal meaning: the state, condition or result of leading out.

Common meaning: the systematic training and instruction that develops the natural powers.

The Latin forms *docere* (radical, *doc-* and *doct-*), *doceo, doctum,* mean I teach, or to teach. *Doctrina* pertains to that which is taught—doctrine.

The I or ego who leads out, teaches or educates is the doctor. The student is the docile one who is teachable or who may be taught. The doctrine pertains to a principle taught, which principle disciplines by means of recipes and rules, and which principle nurtures or educates. This I who teaches may be in highest classification, or the doctrinal principles may be reduced to lesser and simpler classification.

REALM   I   DIVINITY: Omniscience; Intelligence; The Logos-Principle; Soul.

REALM   II   SPIRITUALITY: the logician—wisdom or the spiritual thinker whose powers of perception and conception are innate or in soul; intelligence—the natural disciple of The Logos-Principle.

REALM III   MORALITY: the morally docile thinker whom conscience instructs in the science of soul or the ways of wisdom.

Education is that which reaches the subject's reasoning ear or the hearer's understanding. To educate would be to cause to understand; to rouse or to stir the thinker to listen so that he may be taught.

There is a leading in and a leading out. The speaker speaks out and the hearer leads (or takes) in or is led to hear or to take in by way of conception. Thus they are led to think and to speak or to teach together. The speech is conducive to conception. The speech or speaker educes or evokes, calls forth or leads out. His hearer draws out his potential ideas by her gracious hearing, attention or her attentive listening. At the same time she draws in or is induced to lead in his rudimental outlines.

To educate means to lead forth or bring out. An educator is a leader leading (or driving) or conducting or inducing students to deduce from or to lead down from premise to conclusion, directly and positively, so as not to be seduced (led aside or astray) or induced to conclude wrongly.

To educate may mean to lead out, bring out or lead forth from ignorance or from misinformation; to adduce or to offer doctrine which leads to correct conclusions (to lead to or to cite correct and accurate reasoning, led or leading) from highest rational premise to reasonable conclusion. Thus the educator educates or produces (leads before) an awareness of principles for practice, for discipline and for concipient thinking. He calls forth the desire to learn to form concepts after the likeness of a true precept, so that one may not be traduced (led over) to infirm or unstable propositions or didactics.

This doctor who teaches is as impersonal and as universal as the doctrine taught; as infinitely true and trustworthy as the principles and premises (of The Logos) which are followed to conclusion, demonstrated in practice, or ideate (manifest) in the understanding. He is as trustworthy as his doctrinal principles are true or in accord with The Logos-Principle.

The I who teaches or leads is the doctrine, not the person humanly authorized.

Doctrine is a principle, precept or universal premise taught. The logical, literate and legitimate thinker is the understander of it. He is standing under the discipline of that doctrine, as recipient of it and as percipient and concipient conceiving accurately and correctly of it.

This doctor and this doctrine constitute The Logos and the logic taught. Both The Logos-Doctor and the logic are unconfined, illimitable and interminable. Both The I who teaches and the I (thinker) who is led (educated) pertain to The Logos-Ego or Soul. This is education in its highest degree. This is The Word teaching the doctrine and use of all literacy, speech or word properties. This is The Logos

Principle disciplining, as doctor of all law. This is The Logos Love teaching the doctrine, the logic and the science of love; teaching the substance of understanding, the love of reality, and the bliss of its realization.

THE WORD, ENVY

The word *envy* comes from the Latin *video* (*videre, visus*), I see, and *visum,* to see. It also means look, a look, to look, or a seeing.

The prefix *en-* is *in-,* meaning against. It is *an-, ant-,* or *anti-,* meaning opposite, against, or instead in its Greek sense.
The suffix is *-y.* It forms the verb to see into an abstract noun (as French *-ie,* as Latin *-ia,* or as Greek *-ia*).
Literal meaning: a seeing against; to see against; a looking upon; a seeing instead; see upon.
Common synonyms: jealousy; ill will; a begrudging; covetousness; hatred.

Envy is a difficult word to define (as a noun) because it is a feeling. It is difficult to explain a longing, an individual desire, an unsatisfied craving for something not one's own but possessed by another. This feeling is so strong that it will acquire or possess at any cost. It is an inordinate desire to possess, leading to betrayal and even murder. It prompts and leads to stealth or stealing of things or of character or of reputation, by means of every or any criminal action.

Envy is occult, yet bold. It is an inhuman trait. It is without character and therefore, the envier would rob another of his character or his good name. It is a feeling deep within, murmuring and grumbling at its own ill fate or lack, while looking upon the fair reward of others. It is a willful determination to obtain that of which one is not worthy, does not merit, but feels an obsession for and to obtain or to possess. It is an unrestrained covetous and rapacious feeling peculiar to human self-esteem and personal pride; a self-justified feeling of prestige striking out against another whose character, qualities, or state of being makes the envier look small, unworthy or insignificant.

The only good thing concerning envy is the fact that it strikes out against itself in making itself prominent. It leads to its own predestination and damnation as it elbows its way toward that cursed end or damnation.

Envy is mental larceny; the thief robbing himself, in an attempt to rob or steal from another. It is a mental laziness; a lack of industry in building up individual character; a loathing to give credit to another or to see credit given to another. It is the bastardlike mentality, having neither right nor reason for its existence.

The envier robs himself of his own peace of mind. He undertakes or sets his eye upon that which is impossible of attainment or acquirement. He feels only his grudge. He is insensible to his potentialities. He robs himself by admitting that he does not have that which another enjoys or has in evidence.

Envy is one of the most depraved characteristics that lives in the human mentality or the inhuman mentality. It wears all of the marks of grossness or gross dishonesty, disloyalty, revenge and all that is self-justified against equity, conscience or metaphysical feelings of compassion, morality, temperance and affection for the better and higher sentiments.

There is no good side to envy. It is all bad and on the bad side. It entertains only itself—its bad self. It has knowledge only of itself. It is a lack of the good and the virtuous disposition.

The highly moral and semi-spiritual virtues, qualities, characters or thinkers counteract envy and its conspiracies. They detect its invidious nature. They see through its pretense, or see beyond its mask. Wisdom, being spiritual vision, seeing, discernment or sight, is the antonym of envy. Envy or the envier may not enter wisdom's domain but it strikes out against him as envy sees him by way of its ignorance. Thus the moral-spiritual excellences and graces abide as in a walled city, while envy's feud contends against the wall in vain.

The word invidious means looking against. Evident means clearly seen. Provide means to look out for. Visage means the countenance or the face.

Envy has no factual, actual, logical or legitimate existence, since it is only the negative or antonym of wisdom; the lack of wisdom; the total absence of good sense, and the sum total of bad sense or of no sense—nonsense.

Envy, having nothing good to sustain it, spends itself or exhausts itself in an effort to get what it sees lacking. This may be the fact that the envier is beginning to recognize his own misfortune or lack, and is beginning to quarrel with himself for not having those qualities which he so sadly lacks. It may be the first step toward a more constructive existence.

Envy is a state of feeling excited or inflamed concerning what one sees and continues to see in one's environment. Thus what one sees or feels chronically may become a chronic mental disease, making one irritated, uneasy, incensed, and morbidly affected. It may become a form of mental iritis.

Envy is a state or condition of the human view, and view point of a situation. It may be called a chronic and stubborn view; a chronic concept always before one, burning one mentally. Thus that which would pacify or soothe (if applied, mentally) only chemicalizes the envious condition, and thus envy goes on inflaming and chemicalizing; goes on fretting, gnawing, and wearing itself away. It may be called a state of mental erosion, or mental agitation or discomposure. It may be called mental harassment. It may be one of the hells or places of torment; one of the Satanic promptings of the human nature; one of the major impulses that harasses (harangues) human multitudes. It has the features and elements of fire, of burning, of inflaming, or firing as mentally inflammable—even combustible. The high tempered mentally chemical properties combust—burn up.

Envy is like a disease. One may have it and yet one may not know that one has it. The more chronic it becomes the more the passion or habit of envying becomes natural to one. Envy is like a disease also, in its natural destructiveness. Its chagrin destroys content and composure. Its discontent and burning and longing destroys one's ability to give out mental substance to others, and it crowds out even a faint trace of a desire to give. It is an obsession to get, without either equity or ethic.

Human pride is back of envy. Self-justification is with envy, and self-deception incites it. Selfishness is the essence of it. Littleness, ingratitude, fear, and all of the spiritual depravities, poverties or states of destitution stand with it in its metaphysical penuriousness. Thus, by being deprived of good mental food for thought, the envier starves himself to death by his very meagerness of intake, or by his very need for the mental vitamins that he has denied himself. Envy, therefore, may be a state of mental-moral starvation; a lack of mental nutrition; a state of spiritual emaciation, or a state of being spiritually stunted, starved or undeveloped. In the last analysis it may be starvation of the sentiments or the affections; an hunger for the beauties and graces of soul; a form of mental assassination by starvation, or by the famished condition of the human being. When, therefore, the human being begins to feel his hunger for the qualities which antidote his envy he may cure himself of the disease called envy, which is spite, resentment, a belief in personal ill fortune, a disposition to begrudge, a covetous feeling that inflames and angers, or a continual longing for something that is manifestly not one's own, yet may be plainly manifest in another or in others. All this calls for self-discipline, moral improvement, via conscience and self-knowledge, or for a command of self in every way, via the mandates of one's better self.

Envy may be a very quiet and unobtrusive character unless and until it is excited, aroused, or inflamed by some specific contrast or unfavorable comparison. It is a very occult mental method of stealing or desire to steal in order to obtain that for which one has no mental capacity (to receive); to steal honor for which one has no faculty (to grace).

The envier has a belief of having been discriminated against. He hopes to obtain his portion by cheating or by lying or by betraying any and every trust.

Envy is a condition of shame, shaming and pointing out one's lack of honor. It is a condition of moral poverty and a state of inhuman desperation when coming face to face with that which one lacks so desperately.

Envy acts on the ever irritated and ever agitated stage and in every scene of human action whereupon it is provoked by comparison with the reality of which it is only the proud and revengeful character— the wanton character, wanting in all real character. Envy's act or motive or will is always the same. It is to destroy that which stands in the way of having, possessing or acquiring that upon which it looks with an inordinate desire to obtain.

Envy operates in the physical and personal world. It belongs to the realm of the physically minded, in which realm the person or human personality is the character, the actor, and the envier. Being thus physical it is obvious to the impersonal, universal or highly moral thinker; obvious to wisdom who makes envy feel very foolish.

Envy is prompted and motivated by mad ambition, blinded by selfishness. It is the fool seeing against wisdom.

THE WORD, ESSENCE

The word *essence* adds the suffix *-ence* to the Latin *esse,* which means to be, or be. The form *en, entis,* means being.

> The suffix *-ence* is *antia* or *entia,* giving *esse* its noun form. It signifies degree, state, quality or action.
> Esse means actual being; existence.
> Common meaning of essence: that which makes a thing what it is; the intrinsic nature, primal character and immutable substance of anything, especially a spiritual thing or being.

The word essence is identified as spiritual. It is an entirely dependent word, existing only as the phenomenon of its Esse-noumenon —The Thing in Itself—which *must* be Spirit, since essence is classified as spiritual, as supported attribute, as inherent quality or as the essential property inherent in The Esse. If it were possible to separate the essence (entity) from its Esse, it would not and could not exist or be, or have existence or being—so absolutely dependent is it upon its Esse for being.

The word essence embodies three aspirates. The two literate characters *s* and *c* (the double *s* and the *c*) give it breath or spirit or spiritual action, and its state of being. This breath is sustained by The Esse. Thus the word essence is filled with spirit, breath, essential power, desire or lift; filled with radical worth of its Root-Esse, as the divinely rooted quality of being. This essence or this entity is spiritually substantial or divinely substantiated, realized and maintained.

There is a moral phenomena of the spiritual esse, entity or essence.

This moral phenomena exists in the realm of conscientious humanhood, where the thinker or entity believes himself to be essentially of the humus, earthy or unspiritual by nature.

His honesty, his conscientious reasoning power is the attribute or essence of what he understands of The Esse. His moral qualities or his ethical virtues are somewhat humanized or removed from The Esse. He follows the humanly orthodox, the popular, and the traditional ways of thinking and believing. He observes the human intellect which is the quintessence of being human, or of being the human being. This intellect is essential only to itself and it depends upon the physique for entity.

The human physique, the human animal, mammal or person calls The Esse that which is unknowable; that noumenal, essential thing which transcends human intellect, human knowledge or human apprehension; that Logos-Spirit which is least understood and most misunderstood by the human being's sense of things; that Esse or noumenal thing of which humanity is most ignorant and is farthest removed because of humanity's human nature. This human nature is physical, since natural and physical are regarded as nature and physique, each essential to the other. Human nature is the essence of the human physique and the human physique is the essence of human nature, its impulses, its beliefs, and its actions or activities. Since, therefore, essence is the spiritual phenomenon of The Esse-Spirit, what is this quintessence of being human or being the human physique? Is it not the most unessential substance and essence instead of being the most essential noumenal thing? It has no continuity.

THE CHARACTER, Eve

Eve is that allegorical character employed by Moses, to characterize false conception and the false concept of the female of man; to characterize human and inhuman false activity (giving activity to that which is false or faulty) in a lively manner or with human animation; to characterize ignoble and infamous womanhood.

She characterizes the first daughter of the "worm of the dust" theory; the eve or beginning of night and of the carnal family or physical mindedness, carnal knowledge, moral depravity, spiritual ignorance, or mental night.

She characterizes the first wife (chosen and designed by human impulse—Adam) as bone of his bones and as flesh of his flesh; as meet, fit, adapted, mete, measured or in appropriate measure, and suitable for Adam.

She characterizes the first mater, the first *humus*-man woman to give prenatal culture to the unborn human mammal. Here she symbolizes human nature, *mater*-iality with their activities and agencies, and all carnal culture; symbolizes that which is native to mortality, humanity or materiality; stands for that which is mater or matter of the Adam kind, and producer of organic (Adamic) animation and action; stands as producer and amplifier of Adamic matter and matters; stands as nurturer of Cain (acquisition, possession, by spear or lance); mater of fratricide, mater of Abel (vanity, transitoriness, or breath in the nostrils); mater of war and its fratricidal tendencies; mater of all bane and Eve-ill.

The word evil may have originated with Eve and the tree of evil or vile knowledge, which brought the ill, the ill fortune, or the vile fortune and misfortune to Eve. Eve brought forth and brought out evil, or the aspect of evil. The word evil may be evile or ex-vile, or ex-vil, meaning the vile aspect out, or is out; the bad is out, set out, or brought forth. Eve did conceive, quicken or act upon, and did bring out or bring forth (into view) the bad aspect of the situation. Eve did give leave or leif to evil. She gave attention to it.

Eve, as a character, is human activity, acting upon, or quickening, or giving activity to evil. Eve, therefore, is a symbol of ignorance of good. She is the denial of spiritual benevolence or beneficence. She is the wife of the character Devil (de-vile). She is the fault of every virtue; the beguiled of the fraud or the guile; the traitorous woman character, depicting total ignorance of goodness and the womanly graces.

Both the character and the name Eve suggest the eve or evening; suggest the beginning of darkness and night, which is a figure of moral-spiritual ignorance, or a sense of conscience stricken fear of this darkness. Eve suggests the very denial of morning—the beginning of day. This day symbolizes the appearance of all things in their true light, and the disappearance of things pertaining to the night and to human knowledge of night time that limits good, and multiplies Eve's ill or evil matters. Eve is mater of all cursed events, and multiplier of them. She is the opposite of the symbol of motherhood—mother of blessed events. She typifies a beginning for shame, dishonor, fratricide and all human misfortune or human misconception, which is human mistake.

Eve is that character introduced by Moses to show, by way of direct and immediate contrast or comparison, the antonymous nature of Eve compared to the female created on the sixth day in Genesis 1:27; to show the negative nature of evening and night as compared with the positive nature of morning, the Logos enlightenment, light or Day by means of which true understanding of The Logos is illumined and is sustained in that wholly (holy) illuminated state.

Eve illustrates the difference between hearing, conceiving, acting upon and bringing forth the issues of the serpent—his suggestions, claims and conspiracies—and the believing, letting or permitting and bringing forth of the issues of The First Principle or Beginning of Good—The Logos.

Eve as woman is false womanhood, having no sense or intuition of good, right or conscience; no constant sentiment.

Eve as wife is a metaphysical adulteress. She betrayed her husband and his best interests by having metaphysical knowledge, conversation or communication with the charming but malicious conspirator—the serpent. Here it may be said that there is no record of Adam's addressing his wife, or of his having verbal intercourse with her. Thus her active mental matrix had to imagine the talker to impregnate and to stimulate her gestative processes.

Eve as mother (mater or matter) was so named by her husband Adam, who called her *vita* because she was the mother of all living persons; mater of all *mater-iality;* mother of all that is profane; mother of moral vacuity, moral inactivity, invalidity, nullity, fear, mortality, envy, jealousy, pride, death, fury, quarrel, murder, decay, crime and revenge.

Eve was made for Adam, and by Adam's god, and this god or lord put them in the garden Eden—in the environment of physically natural pleasure and delight—where they dwell together. This delight is typical of the mating season and instinct which is very brief but which holds out great promise of delight, and it is this promise of delight which animates or impells them, for Adam typifies *humus*-man impulse (physical or sensual impulse) and Eve typifies flesh and bones activity, quickness or liveliness acting upon her own concepts or conceptions.

Eve is bearer of wrath, war and fratricide; mother or mater of corporeality, sensuality, inequity and inhumanity as they pertain to mater or matter; mater of the *humus*-man, as Cain (slayer) and Abel (victim of lordly, aggressive wrath).

Eve is wife of personal pleasure, personal pride, or the sense of person; pride of human physique as physical premise or father; wife of the Adamic supposition, the Adamic dream, the dust to dust theory or dust of the ground premise; wife of the corporeal or *humus*-man impulse.

Eve was made by Adam's maker and designer; made after the design, the pattern, the imagery or imagination of Adam and at Adam's unvoiced request, but to meet Adam's need to be productive as a complete mortal or *humus*-man, so that Adam's god, lord or designer would be glorified. Thus she is daughter of Adam's god which is the god of disintegrating, decomposing and degenerating premises and matters. She is the image of his unholy imagination; the character of his fleshly minded specification or his incited and excited imagination or physically minded agitation or incessant endeavor to excite or to stir. She is nurturer of human nature and nourisher of its every infant issue—its every Cain and Abel.

Eve is that character—present in the human imagination—who brings forth moral ignorance and acts upon that ignorance and its idiocy. She is that character in every human drama who accepts, believes, proudly takes and acts upon every unwise and idiotic suggestion, for she is idiocy (unmorality) itself.

Eve typifies vanity in its highest or most inflated form. She marks the changes in every human scene, from bad to worse, because she signifies mutability itself. She stands for false pride and falsity itself. Her affinity to badness or with that which is bad leaves her with no kinship for that which is good, a good woman, or true womanhood, or real manhood.

Eve is the feminine human mammal physique in every humanly imagined drama; the very magnetic, hypnotic and pleasing female person—lively, sportive, vigorous, physically animated and frolicsome. She has no metaphysical, moral or true mental significance excepting as her who countenances, aids, abets, helps, conceives and acts upon the rudiments of mythology, falsity, sensuality, finity, adversity, idolatry, dreamy delusions, curses, lies, vileness, and all that is morally base. Hence she is that form of feminine idiocy, or that metaphysical character who brings forth and nurtures and gives vitality to all that is morally base and sensually dreamy. She is the matter, the mater and the character mater-*ial* out of which all malediction, malevolence, and moral offense, and malformation are made; that matter and mater from which all that is morally abnormal is born, and is called human nature since it has no conscience or moral nature.

Eve represents, symbolizes and epitomizes *mater*-iality—mater or mother of all human misfortune. She typifies the secret action and mental quickening of those mater-ial concepts which she conceives (becomes pregnant with), gestates, or allows to take form in her matrix of human imagination.

All of these Eve-ill ill fortunes are quickened, born, and brought forth into human experience before humanity is aware of their existence, because all of the conceptual processes are hidden, silent, obscure or seen to be inoffensive because they are not going on, obviously— to the human observer. On the other hand the male element of the human mentality advocates, outlines, specifies what he desires or advocates, and his actions are obvious. His gestures are apparent. His person is eminent or prominent in the affairs of humankind.

Eve's kind can do more harm to the human race because it cannot trace her Eve-ill action and its fruition. The human race is much more ignorant of the powers of false (or true) conception than it is of the powers vested in the male and his powers of perception, advocation and war on other males. All male efficacy is of a very potential nature. He depends upon the female human nature to conceive, quicken, and sustain his propositions. Even the subtle serpent that impregnated Eve with his Eve-ill theories and delusive lies, was a potential power or proposition but for Eve's very thorough action.

Eve's action and agency of quickening was the power. The serpent's part was a suggestive germ outline which acted upon Eve's imagination by way of charm and impression or charming manipulation of her mental matrix.

It was Eve (the woman), not Adam (the man), whom the insinuating and treacherous reptile accosted. Was it because Adam is more subject to the hypnotic control and influence of the gods of mythology than to the reptilious, sinuous, and charming male personalities represented by the snake?

Adam was putty or clay in the hands of his suppositional, mythological or dreamy gods who quenched his desire for a mate, by making Eve according to his specification.

Eve (the woman) was the first woman to find herself in a man's world. Perhaps she did the best she could in dealing with Adam and his own peculiar, personal (idolatrous) imagination and admiration, while (at the same time) having to deal with the charmer, opposer of all truth, all good, all honesty or veracity; having to deal with the most magnetic male personality, the most learned talker, the most glistening, fascinating, glamorous, and amorous pair of beady eyes.

Adam was Eve's inventor, the demand for her existence, and the first witness accusing her of a crime, concerning which she had had no instruction, either from her husband—the agriculturist—or from his god. This tree of false knowledge had been designated to Adam, but the female nature had not been considered. Thus Eve, being unconscious of the existence of injustice, wrong, injury, immorality, seduction, deception, and betrayal, conceived of falsity and brought forth the desires of Adam's false gods—personified by the serpent.

It was not until the lie was out, evident or made obvious by Eve's fruition, that Adam's evil god was exposed, or that his evil doctrine was demonstrated to be false knowledge, trickery, strategy, or the artifice of the beguiling gods.

THE WORD, EXPRESSION

The word *expression* comes from its Latin root *premere, premo,* (*pressus*), I press, or *pressum*, to press.

The prefix *ex-* means out, out of, forth, off, from, away from.
Thus I press or breathe forth; I speak out.
The suffix *-ion* forms the word into a noun of action or condition. It changes the verb express into a noun.

An expression may be an utterance, a gesture, or some other mode of representing an idea or an embodied thought. An expression conveys, presses out or presents some statement, saying or sentiment. It must, therefore, have a precept or premise from which to press forth; some motivating, animating soul-sentiment or principle from which to press forth; some intelligence to convey.

An expression is the entity, idea, or spiritual agent or instrument by means of which Soul may be made known to humanhood; by means of which wisdom, verity, reality and their Principle may be ideated. An expression is that which is pressed out or born or borne into evidence. It is a purely metaphysical, moral or spiritual thing (a phenomenon of The Soul or creative Premise), which thing is spirited, motivated, animated or pressed out by its primal, noumenal Logos-Premise; which thing is effected or made real by this noumenal Logos-Cause.

In the realm of human experience a true, honest, moral or right expression may be suppressed, pressed back or repressed by oppression or by oppressive and opposing beliefs, doctrines and opinions.

In this realm of human experience (with human nature), an expression must be morally virile, valid or valiant in order to stand, unimpressed, nor yet *de-pressed* by immoral oppression. To be depressed means to be pressed down or abased. To be oppressed means to be pressed against. To impress means to press in, imprint, influence or to produce a marked effect upon. An expression having a strong moral intent or purpose may not be repressed. A spiritually empowered or motivated expression is irrepressible, because its power or force is irrepressible Intelligence.

Immoral forces, impelled by human nature's impulses and desires, strike hard against the expressions of honesty, troth, veracity, chastity, integrity, fidelity and such, to oppress them, to dispirit, to press the breath (voice) out of them; to tyrannize over the kingdom, realm, or moral domain, which indeed these immoral forces cannot occupy.

An expression or idea is the highest degree of literate, logical and legitimate being, being pressed out from The Mynde or Soul of The Logos. It is reason in highest ratio, being divinely energized, sent or dispatched or pressed out, breathed out or explicitly pressed forth, in the form of speech or spiritual gesture or manifestation. It is a representation of reason or of Wisdom; an ideation reflecting reason, troth, verity or truth.

A complete, perfect or intelligent expression is pressed forth by means of divine pressure or the Spirit which is omnipotent; by means of spiritual, universal, logical pressure or compression. It is an emission, issue or offspring emitted or sent or pressed forth from The Logos-Spirit or Premise.

THE WORD, FAITH

The word *faith* comes from the Anglo Saxon *fides*. This root is found in many words such as fidelity, infidelity, perfidy, confide and confidence.

Faith can have no true synonym because she is a progressive quality, constantly developing into her higher forms; constantly leaving firm beliefs for firmer and more trustworthy trusts or more solid understanding.

Faith is radically moral or morally absolute. She depends upon *con-science*—the science of soul, within—rather than upon human consensus and human parlance.

The common meaning of faith is the state of being faithful, the state or quality of being allegiant; loyal or sincerest expectation expecting certain result from having utilized a recipe of a certain principle, or from having deduced from a spiritual premise. It is a firm and unwavering trust in reality; a solid conviction based upon one's own con-science or understanding of truth. It is an individual mental condition born of one's own intuition or based upon one's moral instinct and experience. It is a feeling of certainty arising from one's best sentiments and inspired by wisdom, or by wise intuitions.

Faith is that substantial quality which is the very substance of truth and the very essence of troth or trust. It is spiritual stamina presenting itself, through conscience, to the human sentiments. It is the fore-runner or herald giving warning, admonition or good news of that which is to come, or prophesying with hope—her associate.

Hope and faith collaborate. He depends upon faith to conceive and to bring forth (into evidence) that for which he faithfully hopes. That for which they hope is spiritually substantiated or established. It is above or higher than the human realm of self sufficiency, and it is beyond that for which humanity strives. It is entirely apart from human ambitions and mundane interests.

Faith is like a courier running from highest understanding, to bring evidence, to bring word and to sustain one's hope and trust. Faith follows moral courage to his heights. Neither courage nor hope nor faith would trust human perception or knowledge; would trust their high hopes, higher destiny, or highest welfare to human intellect. Faith looks upward—never backward or downward. She looks forward, trusting her heart-felt sentiments, her highest intuitions and her highest moral principles. They lead her to that which she hopes and prays to understand more completely.

Faith is the animus of hope; the trustworthy agent and quickener who acts upon every worthy and potential hope. Without faith to honor, to conceive, and to sustain this germ of hope, it could not appear, it could not prosper as the worthy issue hoped for, and it could never be born, because faith must test the moral virility of hope; must test and verify hope's worthiness.

Faith is that fundamental quality that gives credence to heavenly expectations. She loves and lives upward or heavenward, and through her heavenly constancy and her valid fidelity, she sustains and realizes her heavenly anticipations and expectations, for she is morally strong and tenacious.

Faith is a form of moral courage rising upward; a form of moral fertility, substantiality and fecundity. Because of her highly rational power of conception, she is able to comprehend, adhere to, sustain and bring forth the simpler realities, or the more elementary verities that abide in higher temples of contemplation.

The following table shows these higher temples:

REALM I DIVINITY: The Logos-Principle.

REALM II SPIRITUALITY: wisdom — the logician; the most highly principled compound thinker, and adherent of The Logos-Principle, or the substance and essence understanding and realizing and standing under Divinity.

REALM III MORALITY: faith, standing *with* hope under spirituality; standing *with* honesty, moral stamina, steadfastness, or firmness; standing *as* feminine veracity, troth, loyalty and the meek, chaste sentiments.

REALM IV PHYSICALITY: human nature.

REALM V INFIDELITY: unmorality, immorality; amorality; moral ignorance ignoring conscience; disloyalty; unfaithfulness; distrust and dishonesty; that nature which rebels against all radically moral restraint in social, civil, or domestic affairs; perfidy, slander, perjury, treachery, falsity and all that is devoid of moral substance and precept.

Faith never enters the lower realms, because they have no appreciation of her morally refined, subtle, or finely acute sensibilities. She does not argue or contradict or dictate. She does not contend with the ignorant and faithless, but her correlative—conscience—does. Conscience, as agent of faith, can dictate and can argue with the Adamic consciousness.

Faith is *candidity* or sincerity itself. Her only secrets are those abiding in Realm II.

Faith is one of those more exquisite or ethereal qualities whose state, condition, and character makes it impossible for her to be tangible to the mundane, sentient or physically minded, but conscience can make itself heard in the human consciousness, as sure as there *is* a conscious ear. Faithlessness may vitiate and corrupt human character, but it cannot close the human ear.

Faith reasons from cause or premise to conclusion. She is one of the highest of the human faculties, and an element of highest human virtue. She typifies the spirit or motive of trust, constancy, chastity and fidelity, and the hope of human enthusiasm or devotion. She and her colleagues — honesty, piety, prudence and trustworthiness — replenish their vital substance from the intelligence of Realm II. They aspire to having the wisdom of Realm II, and they are inspirited or inspired by its vivid light. They are the human phenomena of noumenal wisdom, substance or intelligence. Indeed, without faith and her colleagues, there is no inspired hope, and no fruition for the moral seer who hopes. Without faith to purify or to moralize human impulses and desires, the human race would never realize a worthy hope or substantiate a faithful belief, or bring forth an honest conviction. Her silent influence (inflow of moral-spiritual energy) is a power in the human realm, where human nature would *Adam-ize,* personalize or *human-ize* all purpose, all desires and all things desirable, and where human knowledge would summarize and epitomize all things as being of or pertaining to the Adamic experience.

Faith differs from belief. Faith takes up that to which the moral sentiments give *lief* or leave, or *luf,* or love. She takes this potential hope by way of conception, gestation, or adhesion. She sustains this hope. She nurtures and nourishes it, as mother of it. Belief is only the first mental action of realization. Faith begins where belief leaves off, and then faithful affection and the substance of conscience carry on.

Religious faiths or beliefs are dictated by conscience. The dictates of conscience and the higher ideals and sentiments must have expression in human society. The various religions give opportunity for the higher sentiments, beliefs and ideals to have that expression. Each individual may identify himself with the religious belief or faith most akin to his own.

Faith has her own individual standard of excellence. She is as a fixed star, firm in the moral firmament. Faith does not need religion as much as religion needs her and her firm substance. Faith is the substance which substantiates all genuinely substantial religions, because faith takes her stance immediately and directly *under* Realm II, or spiritual substance. In this office both faith and the most conscientious human beliefs or sentiments are understanced by conscience.

The Latin form *fido* (*fidere*), *I trust,* is a higher form of faith. It partakes of spiritual truth, troth, confidence, or complete trust. It pertains to the verities or truths of Realm II. It pertains to holy or purely spiritual fidelity. This does not mean that faith is unimportant. Without faith there could be no hope of spiritual realization or enlightenment. Without faith to lead on the aspiring and hopeful individual thinker, human aspirations would be without breath or spiritual animation. Without faith human hope would cease to express moral prosperity and would express utter despondency.

Faith functions as the wife of hope who hopes for vision and for wisdom. Faith conceives of masculine hope (for wisdom) and tests his moral potency. She verifies his moral-spiritual virility. Her blessed event is the demonstration and the realization of his hope; the evident manifestation of that for which he hoped. It is the blessed event for which he hoped—the event that proves the potency of his wisdom. It is the potential hope that she conceived and sustained by her faith and intuition. It is a bit of heavenly substance made evident on the human Earth.

Both conscience and faith are individual properties belonging to the individual thinker. This faith is more spiritually natural and more genuinely individual than his religious faith or belief. Faith goes into, and lives deeper within the thinker's being, his self, or his soul, than his sincerest religious convictions, beliefs or faith, because faith is that substantial quality and that moral property upon which all religious faiths depend for their moral support and spiritual substance. Faith is that most essential stimulus or stimulating property that establishes a religious faith. The religion only names its kind of faith or belief, but faith can never be fully embodied in any form familiar to humanity. It is more infinite than human concepts, sentiments or their sincerest prayers for something, since faith is that which one *has.* It is like conscience, one need not pray for one (conscience) and one need not hope for spiritual substance, since faith *is* that substance. And in exercising one's faith confidently one has the blessed event or the evidence.

The word faith pertains, specifically and literately, to Realm III.

The word confidence or the word fidelity can be used most correctly
in Realm II, because the letter *i* in the root *fides,* and in fidelity or confidence, is more literate than the letter *a* (with the letter *i*) in the word
faith. Hence faith must function in Realm III, as go-between for the
absolute confidence (or spiritual fidelity) of Realm II and the human
nature of Realm IV.

Faith's silent, serene influence tends to promote every human virtue
to its moral zenith or highest degree. She is queenly, gracious, gentle,
excellent, chaste and delicate in her moral elegance. She is affectionate, tolerant, always right and very compassionate, but she is never
humanly sympathetic, for this would mean that she must be *with* the
hopeless and the faithless, feeling what they feel; that she must change
her state, quality and condition of being; that she must share the mental and physical states of the faithless in Realms IV and V. But she
has no affinity for and with her antonyms. Her compassion does not
commiserate with the physically minded or sympathize in the human
sense of feeling; but she holds her position in Realm III and administers faith, with power and with spiritual benevolence, and it is through
her compassion and faithful ministrations (as go-between) that she
functions as faith, to eventually lift humanly stolid, impassive or spiritually insensible natures. She stands in Realm III as a constant invi-
tation to the hopeless and the faithless, but she could not enter or live
in their physically orthodox realm. Her moral courts are filled with
the veracious, the just, the upright and such as have a good and right
reason for their existence, and for their radical faith.

Faith is an element of science because she is a factor and faculty
of conscience, and science (as coherent and adherent of *con*-science)
is the art of reasoning logically.

Faith is not a wandering or a wondering element of human consciousness, but it is a stably assigned virtue. She does not play at
random on the human sentiments, nor does she deviate from the true
course which leads and directs human reason upward to highest premises.

Faith, being an element of moral science (*con*-science), and being
thus related to soul, does not divide her confidence or trust between
the premises of Realm IV and the principles of Realm II. She keeps
her face turned expectantly toward Realm II, never looking back or
down to Realm IV, and never becoming involved in the itinerant or
the transcient pride, conceit or vanity of that realm.

Faith, in her gentle meekness or semi-spiritual humility, is submissive only to the premises and precepts of Realm II. She is whole-
souled and whole-hearted. She is whole or undivided in her scientific
stance. She may be called a scientific thinker, coherent with *con*-

science and adherent *of con*-science. Thus her scientific stance is protected by conscience, and thus the forces of Realm IV may not restrain, control, subdue, subject or subordinate her. She holds her stance, substance or under*stancing* with conscience as her metaphysical ruler and dictator, while the world (or realms) below her continue to believe that which is faithless, false, untrue and perfidious. Conscience is the mouthpiece, and faith is the silent grace ever at work demonstrating the phenomena of reality.

Faith is a foretaste of spiritual substance; a forecast of spiritual action; an anticipation of spiritual benefits, understanding or reality; a fore-sense of that which is to be understood. It is moral in sense and in sentiment, but it looks to Spirit (in Realm I) for spiritual enlightenment, for moral confidence and evidence to substantiate faith.

Spirit is the *theos* (The God) of faith's enthusiasm; the creator of faith's inspiration. Moral enthusiasm (*en-* or in *theos*) spirits, drives or motivates faith's aspirations and transports thought to higher interests. Hope of spiritual advancement, progress and promotion is moral prosperity or *pro-spirit-y* thriving or growing into spiritual stature.

Hope and faith are in hale condition, breathing or inhaling the rarefied and pure atmosphere of *spirit*-uality. They are in moral health, order and right being or in an hale condition. They are not *in* Realm II but they receive inspiration and health or haleness from there.

Faith is that moral genius which is fed by spiritual ingenuity.

Hope hopes to see and to enjoy that which faith brings forth or brings down from Realm II. Faith is a vital light. Hope is a glimpse of that light understood and *per*ceived, but not acted upon. Hope perceives and whispers his hope, but faith *con*ceives, gestates, quickens or acts upon that hope. Thus faith is the wife of hope, and thus they trust their destiny to higher than human abilities. They bring forth their peculiar spiritual-moral phenomena. They bring down the stars.

The morally ignorant call faith's rewards good luck. The spiritually ignorant call them personal ingenuity, human intellect, a strange happening or an amazing event.

Hope desires (*de-sidero, desidus, desider*) to bring the *sider* or star down. He hopes, he prays, wishes and requests. Faith con-*siders* with him. They consider and contemplate and temple with the stars. This temple is morally and spiritually removed from human nature and its perception of things.

Faith typifies the spirit of constancy and the zeal of moral chastity. She contemplates in confidence, in loyal trust, in heavenly con*sider*-ation, in honest expectation and without human collaboration. She thinks in terms of moral-spiritual reason. Her mental faculties are morally substantial and spiritually attuned.

Faith inspires or lends confidence to her fellow workers of the moral realm. She conspires, concurs and lends moral energy, stability and the phenomena of intelligence to her moral associates such as hope, honesty, veracity, patience, compassion, humility, modesty, humanity, tenderness, virtue, affection, equity, sobriety, obscurity, profundity and all of the morally worthy. She lends aspiration and exaltation. She lends dignity, true quality, moral excellence and honor to her realm and to its workers.

The moral realm is beset, harassed, or besieged from underneath (from Realms IV and V). The immoral forces, the physics (physical knowledge), the physical, natural or human nature forces and moral-spiritual ignorance or human conceit and pride are like armed forces. They are armed with physical evidence or that which is right evident to human sight. Thus we see that faith does not sit on a cloud and play a gold harp, but she *does* rejoice with hope and her other morally sensible entities, in the fact that their talents, gifts or spiritual endowments are superexcellent, subverting physical knowledge.

THE WORD, FATHER

The word *father* comes from the Anglo Saxon *faeder,* as feeder, or as one who provides food, or as one who feeds. Anglo Saxon fodder (*foddor, foda*) means food. Feed is *fedan* (*foda*) or food; to fodder is to supply with *foda* (food).

The word father comes also through the Anglo Saxon feather (*fether*), in the sense of providing covering, clothing or protection, and also as the feather clearly shows the kind and classification. The feather, or the feathered coat of a fowl, marks its species or its breed. The color of the feather, its texture and sort, tells of the father bird, male fowl, cock or full-grown male bird.

The word father is related also to the word founder, in that the father founds or institutes his house and his home, and then he supplies it and supports it. He forms, founds or sets up a home in his name. He supplies it with food and lodgings or he equips it. Thus he establishes his house and home, and it is founded upon his good name.

The Latin form of the word father is *pater* (*patris*).

The Greek *patria* means lineage or race. A patriot is one who loves the country established by his forefathers. The Anglo Saxon papa, the Latin *papa,* and the Greek *papas* mean father or pope.

In the metaphysical and moral realm honesty is advocate, counselor and father of all that is most honorable, and all that stands in honor. Honesty, moral virility, potency, stamina, courage, piety, sobriety and such male excellences father all of the higher human virtues. Here virtue pertains to man, the state of being a man or manly excellence. It is the complement of virgin.

The moral excellences must be multiplied. They must be fathered and mothered, propagated, and prospered. The issues of honesty and virtue are begotten, generated and maintained by their father, who is pater and pattern or model of excellence. The pater is the potter in whose figurative hands the issues are shaped. He is the model or pattern of the vessels or issues.

The moral thinker perceives and sets forth the kernel, the gist, the rudimental elements, the pit or pith, the germ or the seed of his most excellent mental treasures to be conceived and brought forth by the moral sentiments. He is profound. He fathoms or sounds and penetrates into that which is deep and morally and ethically sound.

The moral thinker is founder of the moral law, or he is father of it.

He is pater and peter (*petros*); rock like or stone like; he is adamant, and morally substantial—unwavering in his stand.

The father element is fundamental as rock foundation; as solid or true or right foundation or as fundamental principle in the building of character and in the moral support of his house—mental and metaphysical, literal or morally figurative. He has the spiritual dignity, humility and moral worthiness (intrinsic worth, blended with modesty), and courage to expose the vain, the proud and untrustworthy characters who stand, occultly, in honored positions. He it is who must uncover their conceit.

Every state, quality or character has a function. Every word must have its verbal action or function, or it must have place, position, relation and reason for its existence in that place. Thus father or human fatherhood has its metaphysical position in the world of human affairs.

The function of father is to father those metaphysical issues which lead on moralization and which advance a more moral, right, ethical, worthy, chaste, upright and virtuous civilization. Thus to produce and multiply his kind.

The function of moral fatherhood is to uphold honesty and its peculiar honor, which spontaneously nullifies or makes *un*-virile those pretentious and self-exalted misrepresentatives of honor, so that the morally conceptive world of thinkers will abort these dishonest issues.

The dignity and duty of fatherhood is like that of motherhood—to increase or multiply that which is morally sound and good, and to forewarn conceivers of the fraud.

The self-exalted is subtlety itself seeking favor, honor and trust, of the gentle, unsuspecting conceiver who will carry out his will or his dishonest purpose; who will conceive, give form, give action, quicken or act upon his desired purpose. The truly elevated or morally exalted thinker has a duty to guard the unsuspecting conceiver and truster, so as to cause her to contraceive of subtlety, and to conceive the more heartily of the moral virtues or the morally virile.

Virtue fathers that which is virtuous. He mans that which is honest, morally potent and wise. He husbands that chastity and moral fertility which wifes him.

Father may be a symbol of wisdom who is not confounded, confused, perplexed, defeated or overthrown by any human instrumentality, but who leads all morally, faithfully or conscientiously inclined thinkers or peoples into highest understanding, and away from or out of confusion.

Father may be a symbol of masculine intelligence, power of perception or spiritual-moral potency and mental virility. He may be founder of human precepts and practices which develop or demonstrate human honor, honesty, veracity, fidelity, integrity, chastity and moral stability. These virtues do not fall into the habits of dishonor, disability or the ills and complexities of human nature, but they distinguish themselves by honoring their father or founder—honesty.

Wisdom is not the father of mixed theories or confounded premises, but of spiritual principles.

Honesty is not the father of human ethic mingled with human nature, but of moral precepts—chaste moral ethic and equity. He presents and represents moral stamina, courage, valiance worth and worthiness and he is never overwhelmed or overthrown by the weapons of moral ignorance or the illegitimate human practices. This father—honesty—is the father of all legitimate moral operations, while wisdom is the father of conscience and con-science is the mother of honesty and veracity functioning, profoundly or conscientiously or honestly and somewhat wisely in human affairs.

THE WORD, Fear

The word *fear* is of Anglo Saxon form *faer,* meaning danger, or sudden danger. This kind of fear is not chronic, or of long duration.

The Greek form *phobos* means fear. A phobia may be a sudden or lingering dread or fear; a persistent and unreasonable emotion; a deep seated and obscure aversion.

The Latin *timeo* (*timere*) means I fear; *timidus* means to fear. Timid means fainthearted, fearful or afraid.

The common synonyms of fear are dismay, fright, alarm, horror, panic and terror. It may be a mental feeling of painful dread, apprehension or doubt of one's ability to escape from the painful situation so frightening.

The antonyms of fear are metaphysical poise and tranquillity or quietude; a feeling of safety, certainty, assurance, confidence, security and well-being. These metaphysical states support physical boldness, bravery and validity, or strong-heartedness, or physical normalcy.

Fear is an abnormal, negative, unstable, fearful or faintful condition; a drifting of human thought or attention upon the physically local and current waters, or a state of being caught in a mental whirlpool that intensifies the dread and makes the fearful one more dizzy, more involved, more out of control or more thoroughly intoxicated by his immediate environment, as he views it. Fear therefore is a humanly individual thing, although it is as contagious as any other uneasiness or diseased state of diseasiness. It may become more intense or severe according to its further aggravations. It may be the agitation of a fixed superstition. Here superstition is that which stands over or above one in authority to control or to tyrannize over one. This authority may be real or imaginary.

There is a form of fear, called reverential fear, such as one feels for his God and before whom one stands in awe or in an attitude of worship. This differs from human superstition. It places one's best concept of God (as Good) above one, while superstition believes that there are evil, harmful or hurtful gods above, around or encompassing one. Superstition enthrowns its own malevolent gods; its own fear-created images or cursed things and forms which threaten to overtake and to overpower.

[137]

Fear carries with it its own peculiar maledictions always oppress-
ing and opposing or intimidating; always dictating urgently and loudly
to drown or counteract the benedictions and dictations of conscience
(the science within one).

Both fear and superstition constitute that which is over one's
head or beyond one's capacity to understand—indeed, beyond one's
power to reason out—because fear is unreasonable and is an irrational
state.

If superstition or fear stands above one, then where does the
fearful one stand? He must stand beneath and subjected to this
unreasonable state, or on a less than irrational basis. One may not
understand superstition, but one may suspicion or suspect (look up to
it; esteem it highly) if one can drop low enough to stand beneath
or under such unsound, impious and unrighteous theories. Thus one's
low position or point of supposition is very low.

The following table classifies and defines fear, and compares it
with its antonyms:

Realm I
DIVINITY: The Word; The Logos; Soul; Good.

Realm II
SPIRITUALITY: the literate, logical and legitimate
thinker and soul born of Realm I.

> Here fear is an holy reverence and a complete under-
standing of Realm I.

Realm III
MORALITY: the conscientious thinker who fears or worships his morally good concept of soul, and his morally
radical soul precepts and principles within him.

> Here fear is reverence deduced from Realm II, but
mixed with fear induced by Realm IV.

Realm IV
PHYSICALITY: the physical impulses or sense perception; the physical sensibilities and instincts that fear and
that act and react according to human consensus.

Realm V
IMPROPRIETY: the lowest metaphysical depravity; superstition; supposition; suspicion; *fear;* dread. These
mental states depress, disable, alarm, deject and appall
or make pale with fear and horror. They are states of
desperation (without moral hope). They are metaphysical cholera (or the gall and bile of melancholia).

Realm V typifies moral and metaphysical night, blackness, darkness, self-ignorance, self-deception and a mortal fear which shows itself in either self-condemnation (con-damn-ation) or proud self-justification or self-reverence.

Mortal fear convulses, diseases and throws the human physique into a state of abnormalcy which may be either chronic or acute; either fatal or detrimental.

THE WORD, FEMALE

The word *female,* like all terms that refer to the gender other than the male of the human species, is made up of a common root. Here the feminine gender is indicated by the addition of the prefix *fe-* to the word male, which is primary. This makes the word female secondary and very dependent upon the male.

The word female comes from the Old French *femelle,* and Latin *femella* (young woman), or *femina,* woman.

It is interesting to note that the dictionaries give woman, female or young woman a place in the realm of the human animal or mammal or physical or physique, and that female is given a place in the botanical realm, but she is given no place or note in the metaphysical, mental or moral world or realm, excepting that female is inferior to the male.

Male is defined as indicating superiority or strength and quality of anything. He is distinguished from female by means of his characteristic qualities which denote an intensity or superiority of his peculiar characteristics.

The female of the moral, spiritual and wholly metaphysical realm is probably the one creature that the world knows or perceives *not at all.* The mundane realm has no definition for her and no words with which to define her; no spiritually literate words that pertain to her. Hence she is confined to the animal, botanical and mechanical things and is given no place in the realm of thought. A thinker has always been pictured as a male.

Woman or the female has always been pictured as Eve. Motherhood is the only role in which woman or female has been revered or held to be of superior quality.

The female conceives and loves above herself, never below her realm. The female has a high, higher and highest realm in which she functions as thinker and conceiver.

Intellect has granted her a place only as mother of a great man, but never as equal of him (in the role of womanhood—the female of the male or man), because the world has not been able to trace or to perceive the divine, the spiritual or the morally metaphysical functions of the female as they may be traced from conception to fruition. The human intellect can take no cognizance of the feminine functions that go on in Realm I, Realm II and Realm III, because human knowledge is several realms removed from the female (conceptual) intelligence.

The following table will show the female intelligence functioning under her infinite Principle:

REALM I

DIVINITY: The Logos Principle; Intelligence.

REALM II

SPIRITUALITY: the logician, man; the female of man who conceives, ideates, concludes or brings forth purely spiritual concepts fathered by Intelligence or infinite Wisdom.

REALM III

MORALITY: conscience—the female element of science who conceives and acts upon the potential moral issues fathered by the principles of spiritual wisdom and realized by woman's intuitional concipiency.

REALM IV

PHYSICALITY: the realm of the human physique.

REALM V

IMMORALITY: the realm in which the female accomplice (Eve) carries out the outlined plans of criminal conspiracies fathered by the serpent.

The foregoing table shows that there are five very different realms in which the female element of that realm carries on and carries out her functions.

In Realm I She functions as Intelligence Herself. In Realm II she functions as truth, verity or the conceptual intelligence herself. In Realm III she functions as veracity, affection, patience, compassion, confidence and expectancy; functions as the wife of honesty, hope or moral prosperity; functions as the female element of virtue.

There could be no morality without the female element (of the moral virtues) to love, to honor and to obey the moral laws and principles under which honesty functions.

There could be no spirituality without the female element (of spiritual reality and understanding) to love, to conceive and to gestate or to obey and carry out wisdom's potential perceptions; to bring forth his blessed events.

There could be no Divinity without The audient One (The Hearer; The Listener) to whom The divine creative Logos addresses or directs His Speech or His divine petition. But this audient One is so silent, so invisible and so divinely obscured from human intellect that humanity does not find Her to be tangible or real.

It is true, however, that the male element in every realm is first or primary actor, but not in a superior sense.

Without the female element or the feminine mentality or mental matrix, without the *womb*-man to function in coordination with the male element, he would be altogether ineffective—mentally or metaphysically sterile—and morally incapable of producing his own potential issues. He may be wisdom and the power of perception itself, but he would be powerless to effect progeny or blessed event; he would be impotent within himself, as isolated from the power of conception. Without the female element of man, the male element of man is incomplete, and man (as a compound issue of intelligence) is or would be only half of the elements of man; only half of the rational functioning agent.

The female element presents the sentiments and the intuitions; presents the powers of verification, demonstration, illustration and fruition. However, these powers and these illustrations are invisible to the human being or the human intellect. They may be traced by the spiritual thinker, and their moral significance may be traced by the highly moral thinker. This is true because her sentiments and intuitions are factors of conscience and its soul-science, which science is unrecognized in the realm of human intellect (and its natural cognition, which cognition is humanly instituted knowledge).

The female agency, being second actor, depends entirely upon the strong, soul-sure intelligence (not intellect) of the male agent or representative. Thus the thinking sphere can widen its horizons only as far and as fast as the male thinker furnishes the germs or seeds of wisdom.

Let us say that the Earth is female; that she is that ear of understanding which ears, hears, receives, conceives, and brings forth; that she is that mental, metaphysical matrix upon which impressions of moral, spiritual and even divine impressions are made; that she symbolizes the concipient intelligence which conceives, gestates, quickens, develops, nurtures and brings forth or effects universal cause.

Let us say that Earth is a universal element; that she belongs to this solar system or world, and to the universe, as well; that she is not mundane or worldly—not temporal, earthly, or profane and not pertaining to mortal, human existence—but that she is essentially constructive and productive of spiritually universal ideations.

Let us say that she typifies the female powers of conception, realization or effect; that she effects, carries out or carries through, as effecter (or power of conception and fruition) that which the male agency—wisdom—causes; that she has the power to effect, to do, to make, fulfill, to make effective, to understand, to substantiate, to verify and to bring to issue or full success that which wisdom has perceived and has advocated or set forth for conception.

Wisdom is universal. Conception is universal. The male and female of true literacy, logic and principle are universal as a compound ideation of spiritual substance (understanding and powers of realization), or as a unit of universal power. Thus the ear of Earth must be universal and spiritually effectual, intelligent, excellent and of infinite continuity.

The world of human intellect and human parlance gives no place to concipiency which is the female term matching percipiency. To perceive is a male or masculine function. To conceive is a female or feminine function. The mentality is a compound of many different but complementary functions.

The world of human parlance uses the word perceive (perception, percipient or percipiency) and it is familiar with the word conceive (and concept and conception) but it allows the male to usurp rather than share in the mental functions. In this way there would be many unconceived, unquickened, and motherless nonentities or undeveloped potentialities.

All mental issues have their (first) percipient forms. Then they must have their concipient (conceptual or concept) forms. Then they must mature until they are independent of either their perceiver or their conceiver. Infant issues must be mothered, nurtured and sustained in this world of moral inadequacy and spiritual incompetency or they perish.

The power of conception (concipiency) as it pertains to the female mentality, must be a discovery. The thinker must discover that spiritual and moral potency (wisdom and honesty) are masculine in their functions, while concipiency is that female power which makes wisdom actual and makes honesty powerful. The thinker must learn that the female mentality is as different from the male mentality as the female disposition, character and temperament, and that her thinking functions do not duplicate those of the male.

THE WORD, God

The Word *God* is the most literately concise word in existence. It is The self-existent Word, Logos or God; probably a contraction of The Word Good. It is perfectly symmetrical in form, logically precise, literately concise, and judicially or juridically regular. It typifies elegance, superlative dignity and divine grace or gracious intelligence.

The Word *God* is made up of three infinitely literate characters: *G, O* and *D*. They spell God. They define, describe or portray God, and they classify The Word God by setting forth the three most highly literate letters or characters, and the three most divinely significant characters. This *G, O,* and *D* designates, marks and presents the genius, the temper, the sort or The Spirit which *is* God.

Each literate character is taken in order of its individual function.

1. The letter G forms the first semicircle or hemisphere.
2. The letter O forms the sphere; completes the sphere.
3. The letter D forms the complementary hemisphere, or semicircle.

The entire word God or Good (GOD or GOOD) may be written by tracing and by retracing the same spherical line, to form this letter-perfect word. These three literate agents, characters or divine entities, function in sequential order:

1. The *G* characterizes The First Person, The Speaker-Logos, or the first divine creative action.
2. The Second Person is characterized by the *O* as The Hearer-Logos, or The Person spoken to; The divinely audient One; the infinitely capacious matrix or conceptual Intelligence.
3. The *D* characterizes the third person; the person spoken

of; the compound creature (m*o*n) and that creation encompassed by The divine matrix Mynde or Intelligence. This letter *D* finishes both The Word God and the divine creative action, outlined by The Speaker.

The letter *D* has an axis line which marks the center of the sphere. It is like the axis line of the Earth that runs from pole to pole.

The axis line in the letter *D* both divides (differentiates) and unites the two individual characters—the *G* and the *D*—while the *O* has already encircled, encompassed, embodied, or embraced all three. This *O* presents the full orbed idea of creation. Thus each letter is individual in character, and each character speaks for itself as to its individual function, while it fulfills its part in giving form to the whole all-inclusive God-Principle or Good-Principle and the included conclusion (or conclusive idea) which is *dis*-ciple of this *Prin*-ciple, and is The Creator's conclusion following out The Good Premise.

The axis line divides or divines evenly between the one or the two *O* characters giving each one its half ratio and divine proportion; marking two entities of one God.

The letter *G* presents the outline of an open mouth; presents The Speaker-Logos.

The letter *O* does not close the mouth in the open letter *G*, but it does encompass and retrace its outline.

The letter *D* does close the mouth outline with its axis line, but not until The Speaker-Logos has completed His divine creative oration.

The Greek *logos* is lo-god or lo-good. The word *lo* means observe or behold. Thus we have the exclamation Lo! your God, or Lo! our God; Behold our God! Observe The Gos or The God.

The Word God or Good is so great, so fraught with infinite meaning, so *literally* concise and so far above and beyond human thinking and human parlance, that it is necessary to analyze and define it by means of its several synonymic names or titles—all of which are treated in this book.

The Word God is of such high ratio of Soul light as to be utterly dazzling to human discernment. The two *O* vowels in GOOD (Good) intensify, double, or make more vivid that noumenal God (Good) of which all holy (wholly) good is phenomenon. This abstract and absolute good may not be brought down to relative degree or conceived to be finite in slightest degree, but it remains with mon— the wholly spiritual thinker—as his divine inheritance, his properties or endowment. Thus *mon* (the holy spiritual man) teaches the wisdom and substance of absolute good to the moral thinker in terms of *con*-science. But the spiritually ignorant find Good unknowable and unknown.

The spiritually re*cip*ient, per*cip*ient and con*cip*ient mon is under the dis*cip*line of Good as dis*cip*le, following The God endowed re*cip*es; learning to divide, divine, differentiate, distinguish, discern and discriminate by means of The Good or God Prin*cip*le.

The following table classifies The Word God:

REALM I

DIVINITY: God; Good; The Deity; The Word; The Logos, The vital Principle of all divinely good recipes; The Logos-Spirit and Father of all good; The Logos-Intelligence or Mynde; The divine creative Word, Love —Mother of all love, of mon, of truth and of true wisdom.

Divinity is The Logos-Soul—The whole integer of Good or divine beneficence—giving solace and solution through the logic, literacy and law of Good; giving life or the continuity of Soul; giving intelligence or truth and minding, tutoring or giving thought to mon.

REALM II

SPIRITUALITY: good or spiritual goods, substance or the essence of Good; the compound thinker or logician understanding Good; the legitimate spiritual entities realizing the beneficence and the literacy of The Word.

REALM III

MORALITY: moral goodness expressed in honesty, veracity, chastity, validity, stamina, charity, moral prosperity, fidelity, integrity, and a good conscience; a moral concept of equity and right; humanity; human reason; the human concept of God, Good, or The Deity.

REALM IV

PHYSICALITY: the human physique; the human nature; the human mammal, mortal, or animal; the physical person who neither thinks good nor prays for good, nor knows how to worship any god excepting those physically tangible ones peculiar to this realm.

REALM V

UNMORALITY: moral and spiritual ignorance; the lack of or absence of goodness; consciousness of badness, deceitfulness and all unrestrained human nature and its will.

Realm II is the product of Good. Realm III is the product of the good, conceived to be good or the elements of Good or God. It is a moral product; the human manner, custom or tradition of believing and conceiving of God; the human concept of God, humanized or mixed with humanity's most conscientious and most reverent grasp, apprehension or perception of God as Good; the human concept of good, with its two *o* vowels denoting (sounding, voicing, speaking, avowing, or acknowledging) the eternal continuity of Good, in its infinite, divine and inexhaustible capacity; the human concept of The Deity or Divinity (The divine Good) with its two *i* vowels denoting the vision of Spirit and the wisdom of Soul.

The Word GOD (capitalized) may not be used in a plural sense or form. It is so concise and so fraught with infinite meaning, that it is necessary to analyze or define it by analyzing and defining the seven major names or the several titles which, where capitalized, mean God. Each and every one of these synonymic words, titles or names is treated in this word treatise. Each one of these names is of such high ratio of Soul light as to be dazzling to the human (metaphysical) eye. Each one is so logically and literately bright as to give off divine enlightenment or logic or infinite brilliance beyond human ability to behold, to observe, to discern or to see.

Conscience, as it exists in the human realm, brings to humanity its best concept and precept, science or logic pertaining to God or to Soul, since con-science is the science of soul or the science deduced from soul, from wisdom or from the logic upon which wisdom stands. Thus as human honesty honors conscience, as veracity brings forth the fruition of its moral standard, and as all of the moral virtues abide by conscience, they are observing (in human degree) the science or logic of The Logos or God.

The two *O* vowels in GOOD (Good) intensify, double, or make more vivid or sensible (to the human comprehension) that God or Logos which is Good; that noumenal Good of which all holy good is phenomenon as being wholly or purely good. The Logos may be Lo-Good or Lo-God; may be The infinite, absolute and supreme God (Good). This absolute God may *not* be brought down to the relative degree. This infinite God may *not* be taken to be finite in slightest degree.

The Word, The Logos or The word God is divine; is Divinity. This means that God is of highest degree of literacy, logic, authority and speech; of infinite or supreme classification in all things most excellent or good; is of divine condition; is sublimely perfect or complete; is entirely intelligent, fully or wholly coherent and cognizant of that creation which is of highest degree of The Logos logic and which belongs to the supreme and infinite classification of literacy, and is under the discipline or government of The Good or God principle, or divine beneficence.

God, as Divinity, is of divine disposition, of most loving constitution and of most lovely character and state of being.

God, as The Logos, is fundamental principle of all logic which logic is positively true or is The Good Truth. This God is The vital principle of all living attributes, ideas, words or concepts having literate and logical and legitimate life or continuity; is The Father and The Mother of them.

God is essentially constructive, substantially instructive, and lovingly and gently self-interpretative to those who belong to Realm II, but to those who belong to the physical and relatively physical realms the logic of this fundamental principle (this Logos or God) is not understandable, and the literacy of this Word (God) is not readable; the log or the record of The Logos is not legible and not interesting.

This true God (as The Word) has the power of record—the power to record itself, the power to speak for itself, and the power to make its reader altogether wise as the power of spiritual realization.

The word divinity, as The Deity, or God is never plural and, as The divine One, it should be capitalized to indicate The one Divinity, The one *Deus* or Deity. If this is not so considered, then divinity could mean that which is believed, named or so designated by the spiritually ignorant, and then the word divine would pertain to gods known to the spiritually ignorant, gods familiar by way of humanly popular legend.

Divinity is the state or quality or condition of being God, of being The One Supreme Being, The one God who is altogether good and who is Love in its wholeness. Only the spiritually or divinely enlightened thinker may divine or know such a God as this. The spiritually ignorant find this Divinity unknowable and of the unknown.

The God who is Good may be divined, defined or taught only by divine logic, and by means of divine literacy, and by means of the recipes of The Logos-Principle which disciplines the spiritual disciples, the logicians who are spiritually concipient, recipient or percipient, and the spiritually wise, substantial, and sentimental.

Divine may mean the same as *divideo*. It may mean to divide, differentiate, discern or discriminate, wisely. It may divide (*dividio*) as devise or device, or as a thing mentally designed and constructed; as a thing seen, a thing mentally witnessed or perceived to be, or found to be spiritually visible by the spiritual seer or logician. This thinker distinguishes, divides, separates or sees as put asunder, and as opposite and apart, those things which are not divinely logical, literate, and spiritually legitimate. Thus he makes evident or causes his ideas to be clearly seen.

THE WORD, GOSPEL

The word *gospel* is related to the Greek Logos. It is the last syllable, *gos,* of The Word Logos, meaning God or Good in the infinite and divine degree.

Literally the word gospel means good spell, good time or period of rest from bad; good interval.

Commonly it means good tidings; all is well.

The Anglo Saxon is godspel, gospel or goodspel or spell. The Anglo Saxon spell is a message, discourse or gospel.

The Greek *evangel (euvangelion)* means glad tidings, angel messages or news. The prefix *eu- (ev-)* means well, hence to bear a message of well-being or well-doing.

The French *legende* and the Latin *lego (legere, lectum)* mean read or to read; to gather, pick or choose. Literally and originally it meant stories of the saints to be read—*legen'da*—in church; good or well chosen legends; narratives (good narratives); selected, elegant Bible legends, lectures and lessons; sacred readings that hold the reader and the hearer under the good spell; under the spell of heavenly or spell-binding news; a spell of heavenliness, as from God; a spell of godliness, spiritual spell, sentiment and heavenly reality, which is heavenly verity.

The word gospel means real, verily, really, veritably, truthfully or infallibly true (in its adjective sense), as "this is the honest or gospel truth."

The word gospel is a verb meaning to teach; to fill with piety; to preach the good doctrine; tell the good story; to read or to write the good speech.

A gospeler is one who sings or reads the good tidings.

In its human, moral sense the gospel brings its message of piety, honesty, charity, sobriety and inspiration. It brings its good spell and its aspirations of hope and moral prosperity, courage and stamina; its moral lessons told by prophets and saints; its axioms and precepts or sayings, or proverbs, or teachings prescribed by psalmists in sacred songs. It brings good news to the faithful. It brings angelic truths to the meek and the hopeful, the expectant and the good or humble. It brings courage to honesty and it honors him. It moves or influences affection, charity and compassion and sustains patience. Thus humanity loves and cherishes the gospel and the gospel loves moral humanity as cherisher; environs it as charity.

In the purely spiritual sense, the gospel is that true word which comes directly from The Word, The Logos or The true God. It is the embodiment of spirituality and reality; all that is divinely and universally good; all that is infinitely good, infallible, invariable, immutable and completely spiritual in substance. This substance embodies wisdom, integrity, wholeness or holiness or the whole integer—man. This spiritual man is the gospeler, singing, preaching, reading and teaching the God spell (Gos or Logos-spell), or The story of Good. He brings the moral significance of the good story down to human conscience or to its moral utility, according to the human ability to hear or to read (the glad tidings) what it reveals. He ministers to human consciousness or to the humanly conscientious, veracious and morally capacious.

When speaking of God, *Gos,* Good, Logos, or The Word, human conception and human usage is of no importance and of no significance. Human understanding or human usage has many names for God. It should be stated here that Eli, *Deus, meus* (my God), and Elohim is the one upon which the four gospels or New Testament is based, and the one upon which the first chapter of Genesis is based. It is the one abstract (or most highly conceived) name for the absolute *Deus* or The Deity. The people of the times choose their own timely names for that Deity to whom they pray, but the people's conception of The infinite Logos and their choice of a name or a word with which to express their conception, has nothing to do with The Word or Logos-God.

The Anglo Saxon name for God is Good. In this age this name Good seems to be most conceivable. It is decidedly the most literate name according to the alphabet.

The human intellect is not capable of thinking in the absolute, but in the relative or even in the finite, since humanity bases its knowledge upon that which is obvious or is known, or is knowable at the human point of view—which point of view is finite. Thus the human intellect cognizes where it stands and understands. This stand is relative because it relates to humanity, because it depends upon human instruments of perception, because it does not stand immediately under The Logos standard, because it is not related to the positive (infinite and perfect or completely absolute) *Gos,* but is *unrelated* to The Infinite—Logos. It stands under its own humanly peculiar standards, premises and precepts; stands *by* its own established concepts.

THE WORD, Hate

The word *hate* is an Anglo Saxon word, hate or *hete,* or *hatian.* It is both a noun and a verb. The radical form *hat* is heat or hot. The Scot form *hete* or hot (pp. of heat) may be *het* or *hat,* the root of heat and hot. This form pertains to heat of mind, temper or anger; pertains to mental irritation (inflammation), passion, violent vindictiveness, wrath, ire, and rage. A choleric nature or condition is called so because it is a hot or firey (fiery) nature; because it is a bilious nature or a boiling condition. (Cholera prevails in hot weather or in midsummer.) Hate may be called mental heat or an over heated mental condition.

The Scot form *haet* or hate means a whit, an atom or bit. By adding certain prefixes we may have: not a bit of love, not a whit of affection, or not an iota of friendship.

The word hate defines itself and classifies itself by means of its own letter construction. Its *a* vowel tells of its negative and ignorant nature, since the *a* vowel is the most illiterate vowel. Its initial letter *h* tells of its adverseness, because it is supporting or standing with the prominent *a* vowel.

Hate and hatred have many synonyms in which the initial *a* and the *a* vowel are in prominence. Abomination, aversion, antipathy, animosity, abhorrence, anger, acrimony, abuse, annoyance, rancor and malice are some of them.

Abominate means omen off; aversion means turn from.
Abhor means shrink from; antipathy means pathos or feeling against.
Animosity means will against or the will of revenge.
Animosity may mean to contend against.
Acrimony is an acrid (sharp, bitter, burning, irritant, caustic) or morose taste or sense of another; an acidified feeling, concept or intent; harsh, critical or cutting remarks; a virulent or malignant temper.
Rancor and rancorous mean: full of or evincing rancidness; vehement ill will; deep seated or chronic enmity; intense sourness; spite or an active resentment. This rancidness (rancor, rancid condition) indicates that that which is well advanced in sourness or in rancidity may have been previously well advanced in sweetness.

Hatred is a morbid, malignant mental corrosion; a lack of human affection; absence of moral and spiritual integration. It is the madness of the fool emitting foul mental odor; a pungent effluvium (out flow) of mentally foul or offensive fumes coming from morally decayed matters or hated issues destroyed by human vengeance. Hatred is a state of moral pollution or of spiritual depravity sending out its taint, poison, infection or its putrid influence to vitiate or to contaminate.

The human mentality, heated by hate or by the heat of hatred, is like the humus in a stagnant, filthy puddle. It is like the humid condition of the humus (under dead water) in high degree of *temperature,* causing it to deteriorate (rot) from bad condition to worse. Acrimony is the humic acid of the human (*humus-man*) or the human mammal's mentality at work in the human mentality. The intenseness (or intensity) of the resentment is measured by the mental temperature. The boiling point begins to destroy the germs; begins to sterilize or to vaporize. This is the way hate destroys itself or its hatred. In its processes of self-destruction, it functions as the most inflammable element of the human and inhuman mentality. Hate keeps seething, keeps boiling, keeps aflame or keeps inflamed those human jealousies and ill wills. It keeps steaming with envy and revengeful tendencies. It keeps the envy in human nature aflame.

Odium is one of the synonyms for hatred. It comes from the Latin *odi,* meaning I hate. Odious means provoking repugnance or belligerence, or having a flare or flame for exciting hatred (odium). One may hate, and may be thus under the influence of hatred, or one may be the victim of another's odium and malevolence. This hate is a malevolent attitude, wishing and doing ill occultly. It is an inhuman agency of the human nature. It indicates harmful action; evil or vile doing. Hatred or malignancy corrodes, frets, cankers or eats itself away.

The word hate (coming from Greek) is *misos* (hatred); *miso, mis, misein* (to hate), means also intolerance.

Misology means hatred of discourse or enlightenment, while
   philology means love of or loving speech, discourse or
   enlightenment.
Misanthropy means hatred of mankind.
Misogamy means hatred of marriage.
Misogyny means hatred of women. A misogynist is one
   who is intolerant of women.

The Latin form *odi* means I hate. It is the root of the words

odious and odium. One of the synonyms of odium is detestation.
To detest means to bear witness or testify against; to hate intensely;
to loathe; to witness down or off; to testify down, off, from, away
or completely away from; to abhor completely; to curse. Odious
means exciting or provoking fight, hatred, dishonor, disapproval, and
repugnance; being of hateful nature.

Hate is that element of the human nature, or that natural personal, human impulse, or that element of human will which wars
against the higher and highest natures. It fights every manifestation
of love and its spiritual sentiments. It wars against every manifestation of moral affection, human compassion, charity and the moral
sentiments. It is at war against the faculties of conscience and its
high sentiments. It is ignorance at war against wisdom's love.

Hate is a condition or state of feeling malevolent. It is a silent
wishing of ill, evil, vileness or badness to fall upon another. It is
a wish for harm or for that which is harmful to curse another. It is
the act of malicious wishing or maligning, slandering, defaming, tra-
ducing, aspersing and harming for the purpose of vilifying or making
a vile report, or a villainous testimony. It is a deliberate intention to
revile and to punish another for believing unlike oneself. It is malicious intolerance or intolerant malevolence being the cruel lord and
master; being egocentric. It resents and would punish that which is
benign or benevolent. It antagonizes, opposes, abuses, denies, quarrels and contends with that which is its antonym—love and verity.
Thus hate would, if it could, gainsay all but its own ignorance.

Hatred may be detected by its disposition to flatter. It may maneuver to use personal influence. Its peculiar artifice is to get without
giving; to mingle with honest folk as one of them — not as enemy
and not as enmity. It is disaffection pretending affectionate relationship and friendship, trying to enter the sanctuary of love and verity.

Hatred takes pride in being a forceful hater. It is animated by
selfish pride or self-pride or being self-proud. Human nature is proud
of itself, of its me, its I or myself, and of its selfish nature, and human
pride animates and fathers hatred. It always justifies and sanctions
its action.

Hate creates and maintains its own hellish environment, its own
proud but subtle character, and its own hateful mental atmosphere.
Thus hate wars with its own mentally created images. It loses itself
in its own world and dies in its own unbreathable, noxious atmosphere.

Hate is the venomous reptile of the mental-moral realm. It would
bring enmity into the human mentality as the noxious and deadly
enemy of human affection. It would poison human charity and stop
its compassion. Its mental virus would spread itself like a physical

disease and its paths would be as wide as a field of deadly battle with
a physical enemy as in war, but moral affection and courage and
sentiment are not victimized by this serpent. Moral honor, compassion, humanity and equity hold the moral realm intact, and moral
excellence holds Realm III (Morality) unimpaired, completely faithful, hopeful or full of hope (moral prosperity).

Hate is a form of indulgence, intemperance, insobriety or mental
violence, but the moral virtues live, as it were, within a walled city.
Every virtue is stationed in its place, as watchmen are stationed
upon the wall. There is a noble virtue to handle every vice. There
is moral equipage in Realm III which has withstood the vices of
hatred and the forces of hate thus far. Indeed there is a strong and
tender affection—a mental feeling or sentiment—that may be called
equipage.

THE WORD, HEALTH

The word *health* embodies the word heal, to which the suffix -*th* is added to form the noun health.

The verb heal is made into an abstract noun by the addition of this suffix, which means result or process, as in the words grow-th, weal-th and steal-th.

The word heal or health is from the Anglo Saxon form *hael,* meaning sound or whole. It also means holy, wholesome, hale, hail, and holiness.

Literal meaning: state, result or process of being sound, being in health, being whole, wholesome or healthy.

Common meaning: state of being sound, hale or whole in body, mind, or soul.

The Icelandic *heill* or hale means sound also.

The word sound means free from flaw, defect or decay; healthy, perfect, reliable, safe, stable, firm, strong and figuratively secure, sturdy and trustworthy.

The word health or heal turns in all directions. It is a universal word having four parts of speech, four voices or four very useful forms: the verb heal; the noun health; the adjective healthy; and the adverb healthily, or healingly. It speaks from the figurative North, East, South and West. It speaks *from* the East—the rising up of the radical idea—and it speaks *of* The Root (The Word, Life) or The Beginning vital Principle which is The Origin of life, soul and soul health, which health is spiritual soundness, perfection, and infinite continuity.

The following table will classify health in its relation to Life, and in its relation to the human concept of health:

REALM I
DIVINITY: The Word Life; The vital Principle of life, soul-continuity or health.

REALM II
SPIRITUALITY: the word health as that state or condition derived from Life; health as that status of wholeness, soundness, completeness or spiritual perfection; that quality of being perpetually valid, good or strong, substantial or substantiated by The Logos, as logical; spiritual continuity; state of spiritual prosperity or di-

vine thriftiness; well-being; state of having and enjoying
all that is essential to life or to health in its fullest representation, liveliest manifestation and holiest ramification.

REALM III

MORALITY: health in this realm is a human concept.
It is variable, intermittent, inconstant, mutable, exhaustible, physically local and metaphysically inconstant
or uncertain, depending upon physical sentience. This
realm has its periods of ill-being or its states of being ill.
It has its periods of consolation (con-*soul*-ation) and its
periods of disconsolation or deep dejection; periods of
comfort and of discomfort; periods of normalcy and of
abnormalcy, disease or disorder and uneasiness, because
this realm partakes of physical temporality, and partakes also of intellectually calculated salubrity. Hence
health is a fluctuant human concept of a physical condition.

REALM IV

PHYSICALITY: sickness, disease, invalidity, lack of
health; absence of health; state of what is incorrectly
called bad health.

Bad health does not exist either literately or logically, because
health is good; is a quality and condition of soul, and is not to be
found in its negative or antonym.

Health, soul, love and such spiritual factors, elements, entities
or states may not be humanized; may not become unspiritual. Nevertheless human intellect would humanize soul; would physicalize
health (or call it a state of the human corporeality); would carnalize
life; would animalize love and would mammalize man.

Health is a scientifically fixed spiritual state of being. It is an
inheritance from Divinity. It is a divine endowment; a heavenly
grant; a natural gift bestowed upon Realm II as its naturally peculiar
property; as its inheritable or descendible property falling to one by
reason of his divine birth, lineage or descent, by reason of The
divine nature. Thus health is a quality to be received as an inheritance
or as a present, proper for *mon.*

Illness is of the human nature—an inheritance from it. Human
salubrity is exhaustible, finite and confined to Realm IV, while
health is inexhaustible, infinitely spiritual or universal. It is completely unconfined, yet completely manifested in Realm II.

The human concept of health is *not* derived from The Logos-
Principle of life, or The Life-Principle. It is derived or inherited

from human nature, the human physique or that which it presents, gives, confers, offers, introduces, proffers or donates as essential to the human race, or as natural and normal to its physique. This concept includes dis-ease in physique as well as ease. It regards life as that normal animation which begins at birth of the human animal or mammal; that with which the animal is endowed temporarily.

Health is the state, quality or condition of being spiritually well, quick, sensible, prompt or lively (in obedience) under the discipline of The vital Principle-Soul. It is a manifestation of complete humility allowing the individual to be wholly vivified or quickened or alive to divine discipline; continually mindful of Principle's recipes.

Health is an element of quick understanding, hearing and obeying. It stands under Life or understands Life. It stands in a position of humility (lower than and submissive to) under the quickening ministrations of The Word or The living Logos; stands in humbleness or meekness ready to be led or instructed. Hence health is a form of lowliness with receptivity, receiving that which is called health, but which is a form of life, which life is the direct opposite or antonym of human pride, conceit, arrogance, lordliness or vanity, all of which mortalize themselves.

Health is a form of mental or metaphysical quickness or spiritual sensibility; an acuteness, promptness, alertness or spiritual drive, or aliveness continually inspired or constantly whole, sound, strong, valid and vivid or quick; constantly maintained and sustained in the condition of health or life; interminably enfolded, employed and retained in that healthy, well, wholesome or sound condition.

Health is like wisdom. It does not fluctuate; does not have periods of foolishness or sickness. It is like complete understanding which does not have periods of misunderstanding and confusion. It is like power, having no periods of impotency. It is like spiritual integrity. It has no condition of disintegration or unwholeness or unsoundness or unwholesomeness or unloveliness.

Health, being born of The Word Life or The living Word and Logos of Realm I, exists as attribute of its Source. It stands under Realm I as a divine substance, as spiritual under-*stanc-ing* or as wholly substantiated as an holy entity.

Health, being the ideate manifestation of The Logos-Life, exists as life exists—as a living idea, a vital entity or as an expressed identity emanating from The Logos—which Logos embodies no element of unsoundness, but embodies all of those eonian states and qualities belonging to The living Beginning or Principle which has no ending.

Health, being the substantial essence of The Logos-Life, is essentially *like* Life—divinely excellent, supremely beneficent, gloriously good, actually existent, positively and perpetually articulate or speaking for itself. Health, being thus, is sublimely perfect. It exists as true or as truth. It exists as a living and eonian element of intelligence; as the wife of wisdom—conceiving always of him. Health, being thus, is altogether wise, altogether lovely and completely coherent—adhering always to his logic, literacy and spiritual premises. Health, coordinating thus, lives by and with the living precepts which are essentially constructive.

Health abides in Realm II where there is no blunder, no mistake, oversight, fallacy, delusion or mental wandering; where she is the recipient of life, as constant liveliness or as being constantly enlivened by Life.

Health knows no misconception of Life and knows no deviation from complete realization of life, and being thus divinely motivated and actuated, she is—in reality—life or spiritual healthiness, or the aliveness that heals as healer.

Health is an element or an agent of infinite logic. It is a member of the established qualities or properties belonging to man. It may be likened to the numeral character five or six in that it is fixed in science as a scientific member of a complete whole. Health is that literate and legitimate character which, like love, reality, substance or spiritual integrity, does not fluctuate to greater or to lesser proportions in status. The numeral character six does not rise and fall in value, neither does it change its degree of value from lesser to greater degree or ratio of power. So it is with health. It is a fixed, firm and infinitely substantiated divine property. Man—the spiritual logician—may enjoy health in proportion to his understanding of Life, which vital Principle sustains and substantiates life or health.

In like manner the thinker of Realm III may enjoy his understanding of mathematics and he may use the characters that express or manifest mathematical ideations with complete confidence, knowing that they will never grow more valuable or less valuable; never have more power and will never characterize less ratio or power. He is not afraid of running out of fives or sixes. He is not afraid of forgetting his understanding of the principles and rules that govern his mathematical processes of thought.

Contrariwise, many believe health to be a random thing that comes and goes by chance. The human nature, and its knowledge, thinks of health as it does of love—that is, as a purely physical or as a semi-physical and semi-spiritual condition—as being in love or as being in health. Human knowledge is aggregate spiritual ignorance.

Human nature is spiritual depravity. Human intellect is that mental agency which competes with spiritual intelligence; that human impulse which contends against con*science* and its science; that conventional and traditional sense of things which is disputing, reversing, denying and opposing spirituality or the whole of spiritual substance. It is that human self-justification within one which would destroy all but itself, in order to justify or preserve itself. It is the human ego or self-esteem within one which would (if it could) make itself an all-knowing sort of god; an embodiment of knowledge (physical, material, corporeal, mundane, sub-animal, unmoral and spiritually false knowledge) belonging to the human being or personality.

Health may not be personalized. It is universal. Health is an idea or an ideate manifestation belonging to the holy and wholly spiritual being whose structure and substance is also spiritual. Health, wisdom, soul and love are spiritually consistent. Human knowledge is inconsistent, Adamic, short lived, fantastic, chaotic and altogether finite. Human intellect and knowledge are lordly. They are minus the wholeness, integrity or holiness of the spiritual integer, health. They are two realms removed and many mental or metaphysical leagues removed from and lower than infinite health which is spiritual living, divine thinking or intelligent reasoning.

Health is originally and ultimately itself. It makes no concessions to human theory or consensus. It is spiritual healthfulness enjoying itself; omnipresent healthiness being itself; an element of divine logic being maintained by The Logos.

Health of the moral sort may be enjoyed in Realm III in so far as conscience is allowed to live, or to be active and lively. It is a vivacious consciousness intent upon its conscientious activities. It is the condition of being morally healthy. It is a highness of morale, moral joy and moral zeal; a spontaneous moral action impelled by or moved by the thinker's individual principles or conscience or moral energy. It begins with moral character and rises.

Health may be a state of the moral thinker; a state of being above, not under or below par or the natural, normal state of morale; an *aboveness,* not a lowness of morale. This high morale is spiritually caused, and it leads on up to Realm II by way of inspiration, higher and higher above human concepts of health, as the thinker develops.

Health may be a state of being morally clean, wholesome, honest, trustworthy, loyal, sincere and sound, not sickly, and not vulnerable to moral weakness or to deterioration.

An healthy moral status is alive with moral prosperity, thriftiness, and growth. It is promoted by conscience and its metaphysi-

cally moral-spiritual science. It is sustained or mothered by con-
science and its science of soul which feeds Realm III and keeps it
in moral order; keeps it enjoying moral normalcy (moral supremacy)
or honor and glory over the immoral conditions of Realm V. Thus
Realm III has a right to hold its healthy, thrifty jurisdiction over the
unwholesome, unholy, and unhealthy or the morally infectious diseases that would infect or contaminate the higher human affections
or would affect or taint moral honor.

THE WORD, HEART

The word *heart* comes from Anglo Saxon *heorte*, meaning *heart* or *the heart*. Many compound words embody this form, such as heartbreak, heart-string and heart-whole. Many adjectives and adverbs and verbs are made up of it, such as heartfelt, heartily (heartly) and hearten. It lends itself to many parts of speech because it pertains to many figures of speech; many metaphysical and figurative aspects of heart.

The Latin *cord-, cor, cordis,* means the heart; the core (the inner part); cordial (hearty, sincere); concord (with the heart, or unity of sentiment); discord (apart from the heart or want of harmony); record (to remember or to get by heart or to register); courage (heartiness, or the heart as the seat of bravery); accord (heart to—not apart from—or heart to heart; agreement).

The heart or core of anything is its innermost part; its vital, central or most important part. The core of an apple, for instance, contains the seed or the most important part and the most treasured part.

The word heart is important in the animal kingdom, in the vegetable kingdom and in the mechanical or mineral kingdom. It pertains to the core or pith, the central theme or the heart of a subject; the pit, the kernel or gist of a matter spoken of; the pithy substance written of; the essence or quintessence, sextessence and septessence, or the several angles of an essential and important subject; the core from which every sense of a concept, a thought or an idea may unfold.

In its physical or animal sense the heart is the organ that propels the blood.

In its moral and first figurative sense or metaphysical sense the heart pertains to the emotional nature of the human sense of things; pertains to the affections or the sentiments (human feelings); pertains to the mental feelings of the person or the human personality, as the seat and center from which the hearty and sincere and tender impulses take rise. It is that which is said to suffer in sorrow and to rejoice (or to register), beat or throb in joy. As a moral figure it is related to conscience.

The heart has no intelligence any more than the brain is an organ or element of intelligence. But the heart may represent the humanly sensitive center of the mentality which is highly susceptible to the harshness of disagreement, the pain of discord, and the vitiating

[162]

influence of discouragement. That which is cordial acts favorably on the mental heart, or it stimulates and cheers one.

The heart is that which registers and records as a great mental matrix or tablet of memory. It is impressed by things of a moral nature; by such things as moral axioms and wise prophecies or such verse as promotes moral progress or prosperity, and thus lends hope rather than depression. Moral courage and moral stamina, sincerity, veracity and honesty—these are qualities of the moral core which must be sustained by hearty spiritual substance and these axioms provide this substance. Thus the heart is called the seat of bravery, intrepidity, courage, prowess or that kind of dauntlessness which is peculiar to a high moral sense of radical right.

The heart is the drive or driver that propels and impels the leading human agencies of conscience. It stands for the sincerest intents and purposes and it stands undaunted in the face of human perplexities, because it stands for valiance as a character of moral instinct. It is that something (that drive) within one, speaking intelligently or wisely, within one, for it is conscience itself, with its science within one, ever impelling one.

The heart, therefore, in this moral sense is a rational power or reason herself, within one, acting within one, as one's innermost feelings in agreement with one's own sentiments, or acting and speaking as one's innermost self. Confidence, faith, hope, compassion, patience and all good qualities, stimulate and prosper the heart. Confidence disallows despair and desperation, thus it strengthens the heart by feeling certain or confident.

A trustful or trustworthy heart is whole-hearted or a whole-heart. The human heart cannot love, for love is a spiritual state, condition or experience. The human heart is affected by ideals or human sentiments, by charity or by the human affections themselves, or by the sense of being right or being good, or by a sense of equity and well being. Thus the human heart may be sorrowing at one time and rejoicing at another. It may hold a sense of great benevolence at one time or feel the lack of benevolence and the presence of malevolence at another time, and these experiences may come from without or from within the finite human concept of heart.

There is a loyal heart, a faithful heart or an aching heart, and a happy heart localized in the human concept or in the human sense of self and soul. The human heart is not the soul, but humanhood speaks of heart and soul in one breath. A person is called a good soul, called goodhearted, or called a lost soul. One may be said to have put his whole heart and soul into a purpose. This promiscuous use of the term soul must either promote heart into a higher sphere in which it cannot literately or logically or genuinely exist, or it must demote the term soul into a lower realm where soul cannot exist. The heart can have but three realms—the physical heart and the morally metaphysical one or the bad, hard, cruel and inhuman and unmoral heart. The soul can have but two realms; can occupy but two spheres—the spiritually metaphysical one or the divine one. Soul must be spelled with a small initial *s* or capitalized to present The Deity (Soul). The word soul may present man (mon).

A good, honest, affectionate heart is a conscientious and morally enlightened consciousness, a contented heart or moral contentment. The spiritual *mon* or soul presents spiritual contentment. In this condition of contentment there is no heart labor; no pressure from emotional strain; no harassments of fear; no excitement from animosities, hostile feelings or inhuman revenge; no anguishing perplexities; no terrifying emergencies; no dreadful and enervating situations to weary even the physical heart organ, but all action is inspired by contentedness.

The foregoing analysis has defined the word heart or has treated it from several points of view. The following table will classify heart and soul:

REALM I
DIVINITY: The Logos-Soul; The Word Soul; The Deity.

REALM II
SPIRITUALITY: the logician or literate soul; the whole expression or the legitimate attribute of The Logos; the intelligent thinker whose infinite and eternal drive comes from Soul.

REALM III
MORALITY: the human heart which is humanity's perception of soul; the human heart that yearns for higher measures of soul and wisdom.

Here humanhood has established its own perceptions and moral principles which are very orthodox; has instituted its own conventional sentiments and traditional opinions; has mixed or diluted the strength of them by accepting consensus of human opinion and the strong influence of the literal, physical status.

REALM IV
PHYSICALITY: the heart of the human physique; the heart of the human mammal; the human brain as the seat of feeling and impulse.

Here the human person has established himself.

REALM V

UNMORALITY: moral ignorance; metaphysical soul-
lessness and heartlessness.

In reality there can be no more heart identity in the physical gray
matter than in the muscular matter (of the heart) or the region of
the elbow, the liver or the pit of the stomach; no more than in the
tip of the finger, the palm of the hand or the sole of the foot.

In reality there can be no soul excepting in Realm II, and no
Soul but in Realm I.

THE WORD, HEARTH

The word *hearth* is one of the primitive and homey words that has lost much of its meaning because modern means have taken the place of the hearth. It is like the word threshold which used to be a part of a granary; a bin or a storehouse for grain having a very high threshold, over which one must climb. It was thus so as to hold the threshed grain (thrashed ripe grain) from pouring out when and if the door were to be opened. This structure was used as the threshing room or floor itself, or as a bin having a high window-like entrance. The threshold could be lowered as the grain was used or taken out. Many happy neighborhood gatherings were based upon the harvesting and threshing of the wheat and other crops, whereas the modern meaning of threshold is simply a term used in regard to building, as the sill (of whatever material that lies under a door); figuratively, entrance.

The word hearth was once fraught with figuratively moral and spiritual meanings. It was heart having the letter *h* added. It was home. It was hear having the suffix *th* added. It was at the hearth that readings were heard and lessons were studied, and sacred legends were heard. It was the heart of the home where writing, reading, listening, harkening or worshipping was the activity. It was the *hear-th,* the vital core, the heart or the most essential part or center of the home; the place where precepts and premises were cited and recited and learned by heart. There were no books as books are known today.

The word hearth comes from the Anglo Saxon *heorth*. The word heart comes from the Anglo Saxon *heorte*. Hence the fireside is called the heart of the home or the home itself.

There is the human house and home or hearth and there are several figurative, moral, metaphysical, and even spiritual classifications of hearth and home. It can symbolize warmth, cheeriness, and family and community affection.

In the earlier days food was cooked at the hearth. It was hung over the blaze, set on the coals, or placed in metal or stone ovens. It meant nourishment, comfort, rest and human contentment, yet it meant vital activity.

The following table will give four classifications of the word hearth:

REALM I
DIVINITY: the heaven, the divine home or the divinely

harmonious house (Mynde) in which Good or God or
Soul — The beneficent One — abides; the divine hearth
from which the warmth of Love and the nutriment of
Soul issue forth.

REALM II

SPIRITUALITY: the realm in which the logic of The
Logos and the literacy of The Word is heard; the realm
in which wisdom, spiritual integrity, power (as the
power of infinite realization is understood), and the
love, vivacity, and immaculacy of Spirit are substantiated.

REALM III

MORALITY: the realm where the ethics of conscience
(*con*-science) is heard; where moral axioms and precepts are learned by heart; where moral hope, faith
(and its expectancy) and courage and stamina are
nourished and warmed; where honesty is honored as
being in power or in moral force.

REALM IV

PHYSICALITY: the realm in which hearth has only its
material significance.

THE WORD, HEAVEN

The word *heaven* is of Anglo Saxon formation—*heofan*. The letter *f* is interchangeable with the literate character *v*, as in the words life and live, half and halves, left and leave, and many others. Heft is from heave. Heave means lift or *habban*, to lift or to raise or to rise or to throw upward. This Anglo Saxon form (*heban, hefan*) meaning to lift or to heave, is the root of the words heap, heaven, heavy, upheave, upheaval and others.

The suffix *-en* forms the verb heave or lift into its noun formation heav-en or *heof-an*, or it may belong to the Old English *-en* which would be liften up or made of heaved up things or the plural form as in children. It may be that which relates to or is relating to heaven as that which is heaven up. The heavens are the heaved up things. Heaven is that which is spiritually lifted up, heaved up, helt, held, or hove up high. In the Old English times the suffixes *-en* and *-es* and *-ens* were used somewhat differently than in modern time. Oxen sounds much better than oxes, yet we may say either brothers or brethren, but not brothern.

Heaven or the heavens hover over. It may be a hover, a spiritual shelter, a divine *hoven, hofen, heofan, hof* or conscious house that is hove up high; the divine haven (*haefen*) or harbor; the place of continual security. It may mean that divine atmosphere which hovers over, broods over, exalts, lifts, cherishes and sustains all heaved-up things, all heavenly or lofty qualities, states, and conditions of being.

The word celestial means on, over, or above the heavens; upon or beyond the heavens, as being beyond humanity's metaphysical vision. It is a Latin form (*caelum*) meaning ceil, heaven, ceiling or sky.

The Latin form meaning firm, strong or stable is *firmus*. The word firmament is another name for the heavens. It is that which is confirmed, made firm, is fixed, is divinely solid, constant, and secure.

Originally firmament meant firm foundation; that which is divinely affirmed or is spiritually firm and confirmed or verified. This word firmament is rudimentally *firmamentum* from *firmare*, to make firm, steadfast, immovable, decided or immutable.

It may be divided into two parts, *firma-mentum,* or *firma-mens, firmus-mentis* (mind), being mentally immovable, spiritually or mentally firm and steadfast. *Firmamentum* means support, hence heavenly support, or supported in and by heaven, or lifted up and held up in the upper firmament. It would be a condition of understanding. It would be a mental and spiritual condition of uplifted consciousness; a state of being lifted over, above and beyond human metaphysics, human ideals and highest earthly sentiments. It would be a state above humanity's most exalted hopes and desires. It is that mental environment in which only the loftiest thinker may find heaven or hover. It is home of the wholly (holy) spiritual sort. It is spirituality or that condition of continual harmony which only the wholly spiritual entity can enjoy, and in which only this kind of entity can or may feel at home.

Heaven has been pictured a place of rest; as the home of angels who play harps and wear filmy robes, but this is not true because even the angels work. They have their God given assignments.

One may not become bored with life in heaven, since it is experienced in proportion to one's individual capacity to appreciate its harmony, and since heaven is enjoyed by degree or by spiritual promotion and development. Heaven comes to one as one's individual requirement. It comes by process of spiritual education; by degree of love-power; by ratio of wisdom's merit; by experience with human mediocrity—spiritual ignorance and hypocrisy or mere formal simulation of reality.

Heaven is the state and condition of spiritual reality or full realization of that which is divinely glorious or superlatively harmonious.

Heaven may be experienced in degrees by higher humanhood as it advances heavenward, Spiritward or Soulward into higher grades, stages, or states of progressive realization, even as a child is promoted into high, higher, and highest grades or classes for the study of mathematics. The Speaker, Heaver and Teacher, being The Infinite Logos, heaven teaches logic of The Logos, literacy of The Word, and the legitimate principles of The Logos-Principle. This is highest Heaven. The next one is higher heaven which is spirituality, spiritual concord or understanding in harmony with The Logos. The next lower one is high heaven or the metaphysical human heights, morality or mental harmony with conscience. Thus heaven has infinite potentialities for one, and one may not be demoted from his own point of view—heaven—or his own mental status, but rather promoted into higher realms for higher development. Demotion would involve going back to one's undeveloped status or state of metaphysical inadequacy and forgetting one's spiritual attainment or soul degree.

One may not be demoted from heaven for the same reason that a child may not unlearn his multiplication tables; for the same reason that virtue never becomes vice, or wisdom becomes foolish.

Heaven is constituted of wisdom, virtue, spiritual immaculacy (purity), accuracy, precision and all that is soluble to Soul's science. Whatever is not in line with Soul's logic—the logic of The Logos—is not in line for promotion into heaven.

Heaven is constituted of spiritual completeness, soul freedom, peace, reality, soul consciousness, perfect enlightenment, an harmonious state of being wedded or of being closely related to all that harmonizes with one (that one being soul, and that related one being spirituality or one's complete understanding of Soul).

Heaven is attained gradually. The first lessons are taught by *con*-science. This teacher is within one's own consciousness giving constant reviews, recitals, tests, experience or tryouts in moral-spiritual science, for *con*-science is the science of soul or the representative of wisdom and soul within oneself. The lectures of conscience are mentally audible—going on day and night—preparing one for the place called heaven.

One of the best ways to define heaven is to show it as that which is most unlike hell. Since hell is the fire of remorse, the suffering and pain of moral and human deterioration, the pangs of inhumanity, and the mental agonies of desperation trying to exterminate consciousness, then we may assume that heaven is the bliss of innocence, the contentment of understanding The divine creative One (Spirit), the peace, the inspiration and the state of feeling the housing, hovering, mothering, fathering environment of The Logos (Soul).

If hell is an accumulation of sorrow and sadness, then we may assume that heaven is the opposite of that distress. Heaven must be the state of being qualified to enjoy real spirituality or spiritual reality; the condition of being able to fully appreciate the divine encompassment and to live in this divinely protected and divinely provided and divinely pure mental sphere.

If hell is like a bad dream, or is like an awful, dreadful, deceptive, defective, and noxious experience, then heaven is the experience of being ever awake and alert to the harmonious liberties and glories of divine excellence and its perfection. It is the experience of being in harmony, in accord, or in the same heavenly (heaved up) heights, or in joint relationship to and with The Logos-Love. It must be living in, trusting in, moving in, minding in, and loving in the divine heights of Soul. It must mean being in heaven (harmony) *with* The God who *is* GOOD, by being in unison with God's good assignments to the individual.

Heaven may not be understood without understanding Love; without feeling the spiritual sentiment which is love, or without a highly moral sense of loveliness or love-likeness, or without a love for that which is spiritually lovely. One must feel an affection or a spiritual motivation toward and for love.

That which is heavenly is that which is lovely. Thus love, being a purely spiritual quality, heaven must be a realization of that loveliness in every sense. It must be the opposite of the erroneous nature of hell and hate. It must be the forever home of the divinely tutored and spiritually disciplined logician who loves his literate and legitimate home.

That which is morally qualified as heaven is freedom from the spurious, immoral, illegitimate or bastardly condition that constitutes the mentality of hellish birth.

That which is called heaven (in a physical sense) is that physical ecstasy, that dreamy rapture, that human impulse or excitement and incitement of the physically manipulated imagination. It is a high enthusiasm (in-*theos*) for the god of physicality; a trance or hypnotic and very extravagant sense; a physically animated kind of worship of and for this god of the human physique.

Heaven may not be coaxed down to human level. Highest heaven is three realms or spheres removed from human or physical heaven. Heavenly nature is far from human nature. The great Principle of heaven governs or disciplines by means of infinite recipe; disciplines all lesser principles and creates all that is infinitely harmonious, wise, ethical, equitable or truly proper. Thus spiritual actuality is heaven in harmony with this Principle.

THE WORD, HOME

The word *home* comes from the Anglo Saxon *ham,* as used in the word hamlet. A hamel or hamlet is a village. *Ham* or home pertains to the individual hearth, residence or dwelling; one's fixed place of abode; one's family fireside, hearthstone or habitation; one's place of peace, shelter or security; one's natural resting place or abiding-place where one cherishes and is cherished; where one understands and is understood.

The word home in its wider sense may be country or nation to which he belongs as native or as native to one. It may—in the coming centuries—mean Earth, Mars or some other planet of this solar system or of the universe.

The word home has many figurative meanings, from the most finite and literal or physical, to the most infinite or spiritual (spiritually or divinely universal). It means protection, love, provision, hover, cover, place of birth or brooding. It is the figurative atmosphere (or sphere or realm) in which one feels most at home; that moral or spiritual environment most native or natural to one, and in which one feels housed, homed or hovered and feels that he belongs.

Home symbolizes constancy, steadfastness, a settled condition and a homing nature or indwelling instinct or an ever-dwelling intuition. Thus home must be the place, realm, figurative sphere or spiritual basis or base where one feels supported or sustained by well grounded premises and precepts; where one feels nurtured by fundamental principles.

The word home has one vowel or sounding, speaking letter which is *o.* This vowel is spiritually and morally capacious, literately all-encompassing and continual or continuous in its image or form. The word house is also highly literate, having two good vowels. The final *e* is not important.

The literate *o* shows the nativity of the word home or shows its higher nature. For instance, love abides in spiritual dome (domicil) along with wisdom (wise-dome). It belongs to and lives in the spiritual domicil or settled abode which is universally and completely permanent. This word permanent is per-*maneo* (per-*manere,* or *mansus*) meaning to stay or to remain through; to dwell throughout or to remain steadfast. It pertains to a constant, immutable or perpetual home. Thus it is thoroughly settled as a dwelling place, spiritually substantiated as an abiding place, and fully occupied by the holy or wholly intelligent thinker who understands or stands under The Logos-Intelligence.

The following table will further define and classify the word home:

REALM   I   DIVINITY: the home of The Logos-Soul.

REALM   II   SPIRITUALITY: the divine phenomenon of Soul; the home of wisdom, soul, spiritual sentiment or love; the home of *mon* —the spiritually correct, accurate and immaculate thinker; the home of the literate and logical thinker or the legitimate consciousness who has the natural talent for thinking from The Logos-Principle, through practice, and back to Principle again; the thinker with the homing instinct for Realm I.

REALM III   MORALITY: human orthodoxy, the popular intellect; human knowledge or metaphysics where the human being feels at home, metaphysically; human sentiments and settled affections.

Let the word home be classified and defined again to show its several meanings:

REALM I

DIVINITY: the home of Good or divine goodness; the home where intelligence is born; where the literacy of The Word abides; where the logic of The Logos is revealed and taught; where the soul of the thinker is nurtured.

REALM II

SPIRITUALITY: the home of the good, the holy or wholly legitimate perceiver and the hallowed or immaculate conceiver of Good or of the virtue, substantiality and continuity of Good; the home of the wholly good and the fully appreciative ones who enjoy the universal utilities provided by The Logos, Good, or God.

REALM III

MORALITY: the home of the morally minded; the realm in which the higher human virtues, hopes, aspirations, and ideals are at home or feel at home; the realm in

which *con*-science and its rules or science dominate
over the unrestrained human nature.

Realm IV

PHYSICALITY: the home or residence of the mundane
or physically minded; the realm in which the human
physique constitutes the home or place of abode, and
in which it constitutes also that person or personality
living or dying in it.

This realm presents the physical or natural sciences
as they exist in the many departments of human knowledge, but in this table it characterizes both the physical
and the metaphysical home of the human mammal.

Realm V

IMMORALITY: the realm of the unconscientious, the
unscrupulous wanderer; the moral vagrant, the morally
ignorant and illegitimate ones who have withdrawn
from Realm III and have demoted themselves to Realm
V because they feel more at home here.

This is the home of the unmoral and the wholly unspiritual characters, qualities, and states of human being,
or of being a human mammal in moral-spiritual oblivion,
misconception, or false impression, or sad delusion.

THE WORD, Honesty

The word *honesty* comes from the Latin *honestus* and the word honor. Literally it is *honor-est-ty:* the character standing in the superlative degree of honor; quality of being most honorable, trustworthy, candid, sincere, upright or most genuine. The form *honestus* means full of honor, and honor means literally a nice sense of what is right; that virtuous quality to which respectful regard, esteem or reverence is due.

Honesty, being thus reverenced, possesses a dignity of character; a certain moral worthiness; a station of excellence; an office of power; a genuine moral stableness, or a nice sense of moral and virtuous justice to be honored.

Honesty is supreme in his realm—supreme in power and in dignity and in authority. He is masculine in character, and he may be addressed as the honorable, or as His Honor. He is that honest character whom faithful sentiment honors, and that character who imparts dignity and stability to his environment. Veracity is the wife of honesty.

Honesty is not a humanly acquired, or a humanly dignified position. It is an honor bestowed by conscience and by the authority and power of wisdom. Honesty is a radical form of most honorable, creditable and equitable character, as adjudged by wisdom—not as paid by human respect, or by human sense of credibility and worthiness.

Honesty stands in highest position or rank, under wisdom's power and direction, which power he honors, reveres and even worships.

The following table classifies honesty:

REALM   I   DIVINITY: The Supreme Being; The Logos.

REALM   II   SPIRITUALITY: wisdom — the spiritual logician and thinker—standing and understanding in highest degree of realization of power, or power of spiritual realization.

REALM III   MORALITY: honesty, veracity, chastity, fidelity, humility, moral sentiments, compassion, hope or prosperity; all of the most

[175]

honorable qualities that lead on moralization.

Here honesty functions with conscience
—the science of right thinking—as that
morally natural instinct which prompts
one to be radically honest.

In the realm of human affairs there are degrees of virtue and
honesty: a, b, and c, or high, higher and highest. The highest degree, as exhibited by Realm III, is somewhat unpopular with humanity. It is too radically honest. The higher degree is humanly
practical and considered to be honorable enough, and more honorable
than most human codes require. The *a* degree is high enough to
satisfy the social, civil and humanly customary demands, but it is
relatively dishonorable because it compromises with human nature
or the lower nature which has no appreciation of honesty's virtue or
value or worth.

Honesty is a quality or attribute deduced from The Root and
Source of honor; deduced as an element of logic, from The Logos;
deduced and reduced to human appreciation or comprehension and
utility. Neither honesty nor wisdom demand esteem, but they are
entitled to it from below, even as they inherit it from above. Honesty
and conscience are moral energy and prosperity counteracting dishonesty. He is moral virility, itself; a prince in power. Human orthodoxy and tradition hold no jurisdicton over him.

Honesty, based upon the word honor, has full and double moral
capacity and capability. The two *o* vowels typify this capacity or
capability. Thus there may be states, stages, or degrees of honesty
in its fullest and most literate sense.

Realm III may be divided into three degrees. These are honorable, more honorable, and most honorable; high, higher, and highest
degree of honor and honesty, thus:

(a) is high enough to be distinct from dishonesty, and
to stand out as honorable, in the eyes of the world.

(b) is higher in degree, quality and proportion of conscientious honor, and embodies little of the skill of deceit;
little of the art of self-defense or personal self-justification
for embodying a fraction of deceit with which to defend a
humanly honorable reputation.

(c) is highest degree of honesty (honor); state of
being most in honor, in the eyes of wisdom; state of being
characterized by moral integrity, straightforwardness; direct-

ness and steadiness in thought; state of being guileless, ingen-
uous or frank in speech; quality of being invariable in conduct, steady and firmly established in honorable and honest
purpose—that is, unadulterated with any least degree of
fraudulent sentiment, of falsity or of trickery. Thus acting
as moral ego, not as self-conceit.

Honesty, because of its positive properties, embodies no degree of
its negatives; no degree of its antonyms. It is therefore with full
power and in fullness of its power and moral energy. He is an entity,
agent or moral ego in force, at work or functioning under wisdom.

Honesty, like wisdom, is a male faculty; a potential producer and
multiplier of moral, right and honorable issues. He requires verity,
with her veracious nature, to wife him, so that his issues become actual
and evident in human affairs. She preconceives his thoughts before
he expresses them. Her moral and semi-spiritual intuitions and instincts are in sentimental harmony with his sentiments and precepts.
Her faith and confidence, and her enthusiasm, are allied to his hope,
or his hope and her enthusiasm blend into expectancy.

It is through Honesty's perceptions and veracity's conception that
conscience is duly esteemed in the Earth; that moral science or ethic
is honored; that integrity is unadulterated, or that truth and virtue
are evaluated.

The male power of perception, his honorable nature, or his stability and morality, his courage or his strength, require the female
power of conception to honor that nature, to promote the prosperity
of that hope, to sustain that courage and to make evident (to honest
folk) the virtue of honesty and the reason for his existence.

Honesty, in his masculine form, requires verity, veracity or the
feminine form of honor to nurture his infant issues; to make them
thrive in the realm of morality.

Honesty, like wisdom, standing in honor, requires the tact, the
quick and silent understanding, and the spiritual ingenuity of the
feminine thinker to embrace, to mother and to protect his infant
issues lest they fall prey to the dishonest folk who envy him of his
honor. Neither he nor his conceiver (veracity) compromise with
human nature—unrestrained self-indulgence—for he is head of the
moral house and she (veracity or moral verity) is heart of it, and
their soul, sole entity or identity, is beyond personal human impulses
which indulge human nature; their individual characters or identity
is to be found only in *con*-science and its soul-kind of science, not
in random human wills, impulses or personal ambitions, and not in
personalities or egocentric forms.

Honesty, under the discipline of wisdom, houses and husbands verity, chastity, veracity and the feminine virtues or true womanhood. Integrity cherishes her. Fidelity permits no unwholesome or profane element to enter either his house or his moral domain. Thus the moral virtues may bring forth and sustain their moral issues or infant verities (infant or new to human vision and even invisible to human nature), and thus they may protect their good works from the disloyal, deceitful and licentious human nature. Indeed, if chastity and constancy were unhusbanded, unhoused or unprotected, then civilization itself would fall, and moralization would fail and fall, because human nature embraces deceit. It acts without consulting conscience—acts upon impulse—and thus human nature, with its ravishing and rapacious forces, would terminate human progress.

Honesty and veracity are morally inviolable and altogether honorable in the face or fore of conscience. He trusts her even as one trusts the rules that govern mathematics or the harmony of music. She is his power of test, proof, conception and verification, and together they demonstrate honor and counteract dishonor or ignorance of moral rule. This they do spontaneously and instinctively or intuitively, and to human sense of time, instantaneously or immediately.

THE WORD, HOPE

The word *hope,* like faith, has great moral and spiritual import, significance or weight. It is trust, confidence or expectancy in the triumph of an honest and worthy hope, over the human disputations and mutations that would counteract this inspired hope. It is the masculine complement of faith.

Hope is an Anglo Saxon form (*hopa*) which may be akin to hop or hopping; to leaping upward or spirtward.

The Latin *spero* (*sperare, speratus*) means I hope. Its antonyms are despair, de*sper*ate or de*spera*tion. Its synonym is pro*sper*ity or pro*sper*ous (according to one's hope). Thus it is that hope is moral triumph or prosperity leading to (hopping toward) one's spiritual goal.

The Latin form *spiro* is spirit. Hope may be aspiration and inclination toward spirituality; may be inspiration motivating one according to one's hope. Thus to be full of hope or to be hopeful would be to have that transcendent quality which knows by way of having been inspired to rise above the influences and gravities of human nature and the consensus of human opinion. It would be a state of moral prosperity leading to spiritual realization, and leading away from human desperation, hopelessness, hope-sickness, morbidity or heart-sickness.

Hope is a vital, urgent quality. It is a quick or working energy, always at work within one, anticipating freedom from some humanly inflicted, humanly induced and humanly magnified, and humanly promoted mental spectacle, which display or spectacle is also sustained humanly.

Hope is one of the most spiritually advanced qualities of the human virtues; one of the essential elements of conscience that looks upward and away from human desires to let thought soar into the heavens of wisdom's realities.

Hope, like wisdom, is potential. Hope may be ever so virile, but without faith to sustain masculine hope, and to quicken or act upon it, hope would always be a mere hope. It would never develop into a reality.

Hope has the power of perception within him. Hope is a desire within the masculine consciousness. It is like the blue-print, plans and specifications of a house that one hopes and aims to build, while faith is like the material out of which it is made. Hope is like the pattern. Faith is the material, or the essential substance. Hope sym-

[179]

bolizes the pater (pattern) element, while faith is like the mater (matron, meter) element. Neither element may prosper without the coordination and collaboration of the other. Thus hope is only one of the essential elements of the inner self; only one of the natural moral instincts that prompt aspiration. It is an innate quality of the higher intuition; an intuitive factor of conscientious thinking.

Hope cannot exist alone. Faith, sentiment, affection, patience, honesty and all of the profound and good qualities move with him; all that is valid, vital, sober, meek (but valiant), pious (but morally courageous) and teeming with stamina, work with him as spiritual determination and resolution. All of these moral forces follow hope's pattern, his anticipation, or his leading aspiration.

Hope may be likened to the good grain in the old-fashioned corn bin. It represents the farmer's hope of a good crop—all of which is potential. The realization of this good crop depends upon many elements. Faith is one of these elements. Faith, like the earth, is the fertile ground that brings forth. Honesty, veracity, moral, virile precision, troth, allegiance or devotion to conscience, zeal or moral enthusiasm—all of these constitute the weather conditions which promote or demote the good crop. Thus hope (in a figure of speech) terminates in realization of the condition, circumstance, state or presence of the particular thing hoped for. Hope, himself, is like seed; like a great store house of good seed or grain. He must be given the opportunity, the right, the support and the occasion to replenish himself.

Hope is ever in operation. One individual hope goes through its cycle to realization, while new experiences give birth to higher hopes and wider undertakings. Hope is one of the students in the great school of human experience, working out the patterns of virtue.

Human nature is hope's most natural enemy; most subtle deterrent; most formidable organization set up against him. Thus hope is a thing of solid inspiration or substantial aspiration which leads the moral forces higher and higher until they are led out of reach, touch, sight or hearing of human nature's habits, customs or manner of doing things, or manner of claiming, usurping and imitating all good things to be hoped for. Hope is not a member of humanity's traditional organization. It is a member of the moral faculty. He has the gift of reason, and has a good reason for his existence.

Hope, being masculine in his qualifications and characteristics, cannot conceive of himself, cannot act upon, gestate, sustain, quicken, bring forth and nurture his own rudimental desires, wishes, hopes or expected issues.

Hope, without the feminine elements of thought (to develop, unfold or amplify a specific hope; without the mother constancy and the mother instinct to expect; without the mother affection to prepare for his issue), would be without issue or prosperity, or thriving, flourishing, good fortune or happy ending; would be without his hoped for blessed event.

Hope, without the faith and confidence of his conceiver, could not prosper or succeed in realizing his hope, and neither could his infant issues thrive, nor could they truly exist in their sturdiness, without the feminine moral nature that mothers and nurtures them.

Hope may provide the potential issue; may advocate it, protect it and promote it. He cannot mother it. He cannot conceive, but perceive. He cannot gestate, but advocate; he cannot sustain, but maintain (that the issue is a beneficial or desirable one). When his issue has come forth or been made evident, he can protect it. The higher and more spiritual the hope, the more inspiration accompanies it. The higher and more radically moral the hope, the more human nature influences assail it, and the more the issue needs protection. Hope provides that protection. He has the masculine quality of foresight or provision—see forward or before; foresee. He has the intelligence to protect his issue, and he has the intuition to see that its moral rightness preserves it.

Hope, being that moral condition which is moral prosperity, becomes immoral desperation when it is not spiritually nurtured. Thus when hope does not cooperate with faith, and does not continue to look up or upward to wisdom, it begins to be morally negligent—not morally intelligent. When hope yields to discouragement — loses moral stamina and courage — the individual weakens, becomes invalid and falls into a state of human desperation. One such state leads to a more desperate one. Still the individual refuses to look up to wisdom and his advice or counsel, because he is so far from moral prosperity and so buried in panic or desperation.

The state of desperation is a form of moral ignorance, ignoring all moral hope, confidence, virtue, virile stamina and fertile understanding.

This very unfortunate condition of desperation is the cause of many civil, social, and general crimes. It is a case of the development of the vice rather than the virtue, or the moral qualities. It is a mental running in the wrong direction; an attempt to out-run the vice on its own track.

Hope is a spiritual emanation; a moral relative of higher understanding; an impulse born of wisdom; a state in which one identifies himself with highest moral virtues as a member or student of the university of magnanimous virtue.

Hopelessness or desperation therefore is a deadly enemy of the compound moral thinker. This thinker should be warned by the least suggestion of despair, and should right-about face or reverse and turn his face toward the morally and spiritually substantial virtues which, in reality, belong to him as his own self or as *con*-science—the science within oneself.

Hope is always standing ready to protect himself and his companion — faith or sincere expectancy — against discouragement and against the disheartening suggestions which would check progress in the direction of that for which they hope.

There is neither hope nor faith nor the substance of moral-spiritual expectancy in human nature or in its realm. Physical substance is expected to produce physically evident results, because of the nature of that physical substance, and because of the exercise of the natural functions inherent in and natural to that realm of physicality.

Hope is the simplified form of spiritual anticipation. It cannot stand alone. It must be morally substantiated, faithfully attended, and spiritually inspired with a high and higher degree or form of expectancy. It must not become intimidated by physical knowledge and it must not lose its element of constancy. It must follow out and follow through in observing the recipes of the moral principles upon which hope is based.

Expectancy leads hope to his tryst with faith where all premise or principle, that may be trusted, rewards expectancy; where moral demonstration (or conclusion of moral precept) reaches the culmination of hope or moral prosperity.

Hope (with faith) is that living, animating virtue or that driving and leading force which conveys thought from human environment up to the realm of moral science or con-science which is the environment of the science of soul. Hope leads the thinker into his native mental, metaphysical, or moral environment where he finds the answer to his hope to be within himself; within conscience—the science of the true self.

THE WORD, HUMAN

The word *human* has no root or parentage. It is something that humanity has named itself, which humanity means also mortality or of the nature of the humus, the ground, earthy, dust, soil, humous (relating to or derived from the ground or vegetable mold or humus); the organic matter of the soil (leaf-mold and such decomposed materials).

The human body or physique is said to be seventy-five per cent water. The form *humeo* (humor) means be moist, humid, damp, or humic.

The word man should not be suffixed to the word humus, composing *humus-man*. There could be humus-kind, or the humus kind of a man, which kind exists only in the human mentality as the lowest and most abased conception of man, which conception is a product of ignorant speculation, supposition, conjecture, assumption and imagination, and which kind of man is mythological, allegorical, carnal, sub-animal, illogical, and is established in the mundane realm as a legendary character or creature, made of the humus. This legend is a human tradition, an orthodox belief, or a conventional figure or pattern, which pattern is based on Adam, as pater or pattern, or patron; based on Eve as matter, matron, mater or maker of the carnal Cain who made a bloody slaughter of Abel.

This Adam-kind has never risen any higher than his own pattern or conception of himself, which conception is negative, passive to all misfortune and contraceptive of all good, good fortune or moral prosperity.

The word human is an adjective. The word humanity is a noun; a synonym for mankind, civilization, the human nature or the humane kind; the state or quality of being human. This state and character of being (human) is the quality of being humane, benevolent, charitable, compassionate, forgiving, gentle, kind, merciful and so forth— all of which are adjectives.

Being a human being requires having certain humane, moral or excellent standards; certain positive and humane premises or principles to demonstrate and to practice—all of which are moral precepts.

The human race is inclined to make its own rules and to fit them into its own humanly conventional, ethical and formal way of living or being.

Humanity does not afflict nor does it inflict distress upon a neighbor. Humanity is humane—neither cruel nor unduly severe in dealing with others.

Humanity is a moral grace and a graciousness; a moral excellence; a morally elegant and refined taste; a gracious attitude; a sincere and honest dignity; a state of being metaphysically or mentally graceful, affectionate, morally alive or prosperous. It is a state, quality or condition of being faithful to human obligation and moral duty; a state of being sober, equitable, steadfast, and courageous; being meek or humble before the throne of con-science—the science of soul within oneself; within one's truer and most conscientious self.

The human being must learn to be humane before he may learn to be the soul of which con-science speaks; must learn to be spiritually refined, benevolent or gracious.

THE WORD, HUMILITY

The word *humility* comes from the word humble; Latin *humilis,* meaning on the ground; lowly. This Latin *humilis* is from its radical root humus, the earth, ground or soil. To be humble means to be (literally and figuratively) on the ground, or that may be bowed (low) to the humus.

The suffix *-ity* forms the adjective humble into a noun of state or quality of being. Hence the state of being humble; the quality of being lowly; capable of lowliness.

The common synonyms are: lowliness, meekness, modesty, lowness, kindness, submissiveness, humbleness and such states of being which express freedom from pride, arrogance, self-deceit, self-conceit, self-love, vanity, pretence or self-exaltation.

Humility is that quality which shows itself in being humble where there is need for submissiveness to higher authority. Humility is an element of wisdom understanding its relation to supreme wisdom and standing or bowing under that supreme authority.

Humility, lowliness, or meekness in the face of equal station or equal authority, is not wise but foolish; is not right but wrong. One need not contend with self-exaltation in oneself or in another, but one's lowliness is in reverence, in reference, and in recognition to and of that which constitutes a legitimate principle, a logical mandate, or a literate demand; that which constitutes something high above the earthy and earthly, the humus and humanity; that which constitutes infinite or universal wisdom, not human authenticity.

Wisdom is that intelligence which has dominion over foolishness. He has and he holds the position of judge as having jurisdiction over the human thinker, over human reasoning, perceiving and conceiving.

Humility, meekness, modesty, lowliness and such place confidence in wisdom or in that impersonal intelligence which is universal, instead of placing the confidence in human intellect, in personality or human ability, which ability is limited to self. Personal ability is isolated from impersonal wisdom. Wisdom is not confined within oneself, but it is unconfined intelligence flowing forth from its Source, which Source is The Logos-Intelligence.

Humility is most essential to the thinker's progress and prosperity. It takes the course that fulfills the thinker's hopes, and makes obvious the ideas for which he entertained faith and hopes.

Humility is as essential as integrity. It is the acknowledgment of one's ability to cognize or understand wisdom, and one's disposition to obey its scientific rulings, decrees or mandates. It is that kind of meekness that may be told and may be directed or led, instead of trying to tell wisdom where to lead. It is a silent power and way of reasoning; a sign of due reverence to wise dominion. It is a gentle modesty that is in contact with humanly invisible power and position. It is lowliness kneeling in recognition to highness or the highness of supreme Wisdom. It is that kind of submissiveness which never submits to lowering his identity but at the throne of Wisdom.

THE WORD, HUSBAND

The word *husband* is of Anglo Saxon origin; a contraction for house-band, the house-bond, band or bound.

The house to which a man is bound consists of those who bear his name or belong to his own individual house; those whom he must house, houze, shelter and cherish—literally and figuratively.

The Latin *maritus* means husband. The form *maritalis* means of or pertaining to an husband or to marriage. The word marry is rooted in this form, *maritus.* Thus a married man is the marital relative of his wife. He is her spouse, sponsor and partner in marriage.

The Greek *oikos* means house. The husband is economical manager of his house (his *oikos*). He mans it prudently, frugally, providently, thriftily or wisely and in a practical manner. He is supervisor of his house and he is bound by law to maintain it.

Husbandhood is one of the states, conditions or characters of being in the realm of human relationship:

Manhood
Husbandhood ———Humanhood——— Wifehood
Fatherhood

Womanhood
Wifehood
Motherhood

Marriage is based upon the marital relative—the husband—mainly and directly. The quality of husbandhood depends upon the manhood to the fore of it. Humanhood is the consequence of marriage and of the quality of its six hoods. Thus humanhood itself depends upon the union of these six strong and morally sound characters which husbandhood houses, protects and provides for, literally and morally.

Marriage pertains to husbandhood, while matrimony pertains to motherhood specifically. The whole world praises motherhood and sets her on a high pedestal as a thing of miracle or of worship. Womanhood and wifehood are left for husbandhood to cherish, prize, appreciate or praise.

The husband is the family seer and *fore-seer; pro-seer,* pro-*video* or provider. He has vision and the moral courage to guard his figurative domicile with great care and with perspicacity. This house is a metaphysical thing existing in his consciousness. It is an ideal or sentimental thing which calls out his moral virility, virtues or true character.

This house or this marriage must stand through every kind of social, civil, economic, legal, moral and natural challenge. It must

[187]

stand as a unit, an individual house (a figurative house, solidly set), and it must rest upon his own sagacious shoulders. He must be shrewd in dealing with the world that environs his house. He must be farseeing, tender, steadfast, trustworthy and honest or morally honorable if his marital house and contract is to endure. Thus he becomes defender of the standard which he has set up. His human ideals may fall, but his moral standard never.

Husbandhood is the outgrowth of manhood. If the man has learned to man himself, then he may undertake to man his house. If he has learned to restrain human impulses and to overcome, manage or subdue human nature in the man, then the husband may be master of his own house and his marriage will have a home, a sanctuary or a true domicile.

This does not mean that husbandhood is the fulcrum, prop, lever and support of the other hoods, but of marriage.

When Moses instituted the moral law for marriage, husbandhood and wifehood were of a simpler nature. The distaff side, the wife (Anglo Saxon *wif,* woman, *wifan, wefan,* or one who weaves or holds the distaff, or the woof, weft and warp *mater*ials) had her peculiar feminine functions to perform, while the husband had his well defined and simple masculine functions to perform. But modern modes of living, modern ways of thinking, economics and industrial and political affairs—all human affairs—have made changes and complications; have tended to mix, confuse or fuse together these two distinctly different functional entities.

The male is that one who begets, generates, propagates or multiplies his kind, as generator. The female is that one who germinates, causes to begin to grow into higher form or causes to sprout or to vegetate as germinator and as quickener. She is that genius having the peculiar female ingenuity, aptitude, or essential talent to weave, to furnish the *mater*-ial and to *mater*-ialize that which she is to bring forth.

Modern civilization has complicated marriage. Only complete moralization and spiritualization can correct what human nature and human knowledge have caused to overlap, fuse, duplicate or to compete rather than to complement.

In the physical realm one may find many changes in many things, but in the metaphysical, morally mental and highly ethical realms, the principles governing the *sixual* functions have not changed. The wife has only that peculiar female dexterity, skill, natural intuition and ingenious sentiment which is opposite but complementary to the husband. She weaves into higher form, she constructs, and she furnishes the *mater*-ials (be they physical or metaphysical).

Husbandhood is a further development of manhood. Manhood is *vir-hood* or virtue (as presented, expressed, reflected or manifested by true manhood) in its male form, only. Wifehood is a further development or expression of womanhood. It is virgin-*hood*. The Greek *gin, gyn, gyne* or *gune* means woman, or the female kind of man. (Latin *vir-* is man.)

The male virtues do not duplicate the female virtues in any least degree. She is womanly. He is manly. She is verity or veracity while he is honor and honesty. These virtues are complementary but not duplicative. She performs the functions that pertain to conceiving, developing, and bringing forth. He performs the functions of perceiving, advocating (setting forth), and maintaining or fathering that which he has advocated. He embraces all of the male or masculine excellences while her heart is set upon being mother of those excellences. Her powers are conceptive. His powers are perceptive. He takes or grasps thoroughly or by way of or through discernment, seeing or witnessing as wisdom. But wisdom is potential until conceived of and brought forth in form (after wisdom's pattern, plan or specifications).

The husband qualities must be those upon which woman or wife depends to supply those elements which match (but do not duplicate) her own wifely qualities or mental properties. He must have the virile substances or essential qualities while she must have the opposite fertile ones receptive to and consentient with and appreciative of them.

True husbandhood means that he shall be as dependent upon the distaff (that holds the *materi*als out of which his ideate forms are woven) as she is dependent upon him for the *pater* or pattern elements.

Husbandhood embraces all of the virtues of the individual manhood, all of the masculine abilities to perceive, to advocate or to provide the rudiments and pattern, the plans and specifications for that which is to be acted upon by the feminine capabilities or capacities. Thus husbandhood embraces all of the virtues, excellences or honorable qualities of manhood, of himself—husband—and of potential fatherhood.

Husband is the demonstration of manhood—its virtues or *vir-hood* or virility — while fatherhood simply maintains and cherishes that which husbandhood has proved to exist or has proved to be true, excellent, virtuous and honorable.

Husbandhood should not be robbed of its dignity by manhood or by fatherhood. It should not be robbed of its full importance as the individual presenting mature manhood or metaphysical virility (virtue).

Husbandhood should never mix or blend with the other two male *hoods* or states, qualities or characters of being. But it should stand as central axis and action, utilizing the dignity, power (potency), virtue, faculties of reason or rational states belonging to his office, and it should fill and fulfill all of the requirements of that office, and it should have the glory, the honor and the dignity of that office. It need not be shared.

THE WORD, IDEA

The word *idea* is immediately derived from its Logos-Root, I. It is one of the most literate of words, having the initial *i* vowel and two other vowels and only one consonant, all of which speak or are sounded in speaking. Literally it means I see. This I who sees is The Ego or creative Word-Entity.

The word idea is the more literate form of the Greek and Latin *idein* (to see), and *eidenai, eidolon,* image. It is pertinent to note that the form *iden* is the central theme in this *eidenai* (*e-iden-ai*) and is root of the word identity.

The word idea is made of the four literate characters: *i, d, e,* and *a,* which are found in the midst of *eidenai.* The other three letters are silenced, leaving the word idea unencumbered with silent letters *e, n,* and *i* in *EideNaI;* leaving the initial letter *i* which is the most literate of all vowels. It eliminates the more bulky, unwieldy, and unspiritual human baggage, and carries only its own identity or ideate self which is the idea that Soul (I) perceives or sees. So it is that neither The I nor the idea may be humanized or may be brought down to a less literate degree.

An intellectual human concept is not an idea. It is only an image, picture or metaphysical form or figure (figurative sense) of some physical figure, person or thing perceived in the human mentality. An ideal of the human sort is a sentimental fancy; a product of the human imagination; an illusory thing or phenomenon of human intellect; an unrestrained, dreamy, dramatic fantasy excited, designed and created by human nature and human knowledge, and given form in the human mental matrix as something identical with human nature.

An idea and an ideal are elements and entities of Intelligence. They are immaculate, accurate, holy or wholly complete or perfect integers representing Intelligence as intelligent realities, qualities or spiritual verities emitted and uttered by Soul. An ideal pertains to this idea which idea Soul sees. Thus an ideal is one of Soul's ideas, and so each letter (literate character) is an entity with the power of spiritual speech; the power of Soul expression; the power of spiritual realization, ideation and identification. Each letter in the word idea breathes forth and sets forth that which Soul sees, sends, emits or expresses.

The following table will classify the word idea and show, by comparison, that it is unrelated to human patterns and paters; unrelated

to human matters and maters who give birth to mental objects or who
objectify and project and sustain such matters:

REALM   I   DIVINITY: The I, Logos-Ego or Soul.
REALM   II   SPIRITUALITY: the idea and the ideal;
                     the ego-logician; the seer, wisdom who has
                     infinite and universal vision or soul vision;
                     realization.
REALM III   MORALITY: the human concept of soul as
                     humanly idealized, idolized and identified.
REALM IV   PHYSICALITY: the physical forms or the
                     images from which humanity forms its
                     metaphysical conceptions; the human na-
                     ture from which these forms are born, and
                     by which they are sustained.

The I, Soul who sees, needs only the one literate (divinely literate) character with which to be divinely identified, for, as words
take on their more literate (logical and legitimate) meanings, they
lay off their humanly applicable and humanly popular meanings (together with the letters and the forms or the literate bulkiness necessary to interpret, transmit, define and explain the higher meanings).

All words that belong in Realm I must be defined in divinely
literate and logical terms. All words that belong in Realm II, such
as idea, must be defined in spiritually pure language or diction—
because of their spiritual *con*-diction or condition.

The concepts of Realm III rest partly upon physical condition
and partly upon the intellectual, moral, and metaphysical condition
dictated by Realm IV, and partaking of the language peculiar to
Realm IV. Only the elements of con-science are unburdened by
illiterate and illogical and illegitimate luggage (corporeal, personal
luggage), for conscience is the science of soul, dictating the spiritual
condition or *con*-diction of Soul, and thus conscience, adhered to,
carries the thinker over, up, above and beyond; carries, bears, trans-
fers or translates and conveys the thinker into the realm of soul and
translates or interprets the ideas that wisdom entertains. Solid conviction begins here where the humanly considerable objects leave off.

Soul is the giver of divine enlightenment, science or logic and
thus the logician or the idea sees in this light as wisdom which word
is *witan,* see; wit or witness, to see as spectator, observer or one who
beholds, and which Latin *specio* means see, observe or behold.

The human intellect is not capable of discerning an idea or an ideal, but human progress or moral prosperity depends upon conscience for vision and ideal expectation; for foresight.

An idea or ideal has the power of universal, infinite conception and realization. A human concept is localized within the mental horizons of Realm III and it is finite-*ized* by the influence of Realm IV. An idea is a compound embodying wisdom. It is the substance of wisdom's understanding. It is the essence of The I, Ego-Spirit or Soul, as the spiritual continuity, life, love and ever-thriving health of soul (or Soul's ideal) vividly expressing itself.

An idea must be diminished in ratio of universal power in order to be brought down to human utility. Thus moral honor, honesty, veracity, charity, affection, patience, compassion, faith, fidelity, hope and its prosperity (expectation, quickened and carried out), and all of the virtues dictated by conscience, are the qualified elements of ideas reduced to human appreciation. Thus human integrity is spiritual holiness in its lesser or diminished degree. Faith is a glimpse of wisdom's understanding. It is faithful, loyal and constant in its moral essence or degree, or substance. These virtues kept inspired or alive by their spiritual intent and purpose, are motivated toward Realm II. They pertain to the moral degree or ratio of enlightenment. They pertain to the moral integer and entity.

The enlightenment of Realm II would dazzle the moral thinker by its infinite brilliance and wisdom. Its verities and ideas would carry too great spiritual intelligence and import to engage or to interest humanity. But human concepts must not remain too orthodox, too conventional and traditional in standard, or humanity will never emerge from its relative darkness.

Human egotism or self-sufficiency, and the popular human intellect, have used the I pronoun (which should indicate the Deity as the Supreme Being or I AM) to indicate itself—the human being. Thus it falsely assumes preeminence.

The capital I should indicate The living Word, The Speaker or The speaking Logos as speaker, as The first person, as The greatest, highest and most literate I or Soul, supreme over all other egos, nouns and pronouns. The word idea is the direct and immediate offspring of The I or Soul; the entity or ego, manifestation or identity so set forth, so described, so spoken, defined or divined.

Idea is the third person or the ego spoken of. He is the wise, immaculate, potent, valid, sound, purely or wholly good idea set forth and brought forth or made so; made as designed, as specified and as intended; made as the compound ramification of The I or as the product of The Word and Root; made like Soul—The Logos-Soul.

The following table will classify The I and idea:

Realm   I   DIVINITY: The I, Soul or The Deity; the all-seeing Logos; The all-ideating Word.

Realm   II   SPIRITUALITY: the idea or soul of Soul; the spiritual seer; wisdom, who sees and witnesses and who presents and represents what he sees, discerns or ideates, or finds demonstrably evident.

Realm III   MORALITY: the *eidenai* who identifies himself as conscientious thinker or as a morally minded entity, identity or integer.

Realm IV   PHYSICALITY: human nature and its observations.

Realm   V   IMMORALITY: the state of idiocy; total absence of con-science, of moral stability, stamina or understanding; total spiritual ignorance or imbecility; state of being *under* the occult, hypnotic or magnetic forces ruling as human nature (its impulses and knowledge).

An idea indicates Soul and identifies itself *with* Soul—even as the sunlight identifies itself with the sun. An idea is an infinite expression of its producer which producer is The Logos, and an idea is as dependent upon The Logos as the sunlight is dependent upon the sun.

It may be seen that humanity glorifies itself, violates the law and logic of divine reverence, or commits a kind of sacrilege in using the I pronoun. But the languages do not provide ways and means for expressing The Word and its literacy. They only provide for the human person and the human physique and the human point of view. The I, The Word, and The Logos point of view is the beginning and premise of all logic and of all literacy—all science and art of reasoning or correct and accurate thinking. Thus correct and accurate writing should take the Realm II point of view. In this realm idea is us, me, our and expressed identity or spiritual phenomenon of The Word. Idea is entity (soul) identifying itself with Soul.

In Realm III human usage has humanized all ideas, all words and identities; has personalized concepts and things; has given each thought or concept a thing, an object or a human being to represent it. Thus it has established or instituted its languages.

In Realm IV physics has physicalized all concepts and knowledge has identified its own mortal, mundane phenomena. Thus Realm III becomes the metaphysical, figure or figurative element of Realm IV, plus its human, moral conception of Realm II. Its language has been deprived of the true soul qualities.

The world has made no reservations in its languages for The Deity or for that idea or ideate being derived from this divine creative Word. The world's self-sufficiency has precluded the necessity for having words of the Realm I sort. It has moved itself into Realm I and has usurped it and all other realms. It has presumed itself to be the all and the *omni* in all physical and highly metaphysical logic.

The world of mundane thinkers would use Realm III as that metaphysical field in which to cross breed its mundane with the moral, the inspirational, intuitional and conscientious; in which its crossed purposes may contend for place and for metaphysical power or control.

The world has made Realm III a mental battle ground and has succeeded in leaving some of its hybrid beliefs, peculiar to human nature, in that realm. It has brought in its barren arguments and its illegitimate or sterile concepts and precepts, but it has not disorganized Realm III—the moral realm. Morality does not mix with physicality, nor does its conceivers become fertilized by amoral or foreign points of view.

Realm III is made up of honest and veracious characters whose moral ideals are as useless to Realm IV as its physical and finite and heavy knowledge or beliefs are to Realm III.

Ideas are infinitely enlightened. They carry great spiritual import, but no human or physical weight. They have no form visible or tangible to the lower realms. They signify infinite vision. Idea means to see, but only to see as wisdom sees and as he witnesses or discerns, and as he judges.

Logical, literate or legitimate ideas are compounded or made of purely spiritual and divine substance, and they are sustained and substantiated by The Logos-Spirit as ideate things or thoughts. These thoughts are made of worded forms, word forms, worded concepts, or spiritually mental images understood. Without words, a thought has no substance.

All thoughts, ideas or concepts must be perfectly, completely and spiritually worded, else they have no instruments (no literate instrumentality) with which to perceive, outline, or be instructed and constructed; no mental implement with which to form and to set forth these perceived images; no divinely created vehicle with which to carry out or to deliver vocal or written speech. Thus an idea must be thought out before it may be spoken or written out or taught.

Ideas are representative of The Word, manifestations of The

Word's import; the similitude of Soul's literate Principle; forms or images existent in worded form, and formed by The Word or Logos —The Root, Cause, and Source of them.

Ideas are not only literate in highest degree, but they are wholly logical as reflecting the logic of The Logos. An absolute or wholly compounded idea is the soul-logician, the most vital thinker, perceiver, and conceiver.

Ideas are literate, logical, and legitimate. A legitimate idea originates or springs from The Logos-Principle, as conclusive, and as universal conclusion in the form of wisdom, infinite sentiment or love, spiritually pure and potent virtues; in the form of valid, vivid images or immaculate conclusions from this Logos-Premise. These ideas reflect their Logos, and express nothing less. They understand their Logos-Origin by being man (*mon*) the compound understander.

An idea responds to its creative Logos as the spiritual creature; as mon—the logical thinker—saying I see, I understand, I perceive, I conceive so, I realize that this or it is so, I discern or I see the logic in this.

This idea or mon—being the power of ideation—is *literateness* itself who reads, chooses, gathers, picks up and finds The written Word to be divinely elegant or select, and to be spiritually legible, intelligent or intelligible; finds to be as spoken, as said, as presented or as intended to be.

An idea is issue, attribute, offspring and representation of The Word—The living, loving Truth. Ideas are spiritually solvent in this Soul-Truth. They see well, see good, see as divinely described, outlined, specified, defined or set forth.

THE WORD, IGNORANCE

The word *ignorance* is based upon the Latin *ignoro* or *in-,* not, and *gnarus,* knowing. Literally, not knowing.

The suffix *-ance* gives it action, state or quality of being. Literally, the state of not knowing or the state of being ignorant.

The word ignorance has only a negative existence. It is the antonym of the word intelligence or conscience. It does not ignore the science of *con*-science or the wisdom of intelligence, but it is the state of being unfamiliar with them; the state of being unassociated, unacquainted, or not in the family with them. Wisdom lives or abides in Realm II, which is reality or spirituality, and conscience is the science of soul (the intuitive soul) within one, which soul also dwells in Realm II.

The following table classifies intelligence, wisdom, conscience, soul and the negative ignorance.

REALM   I   DIVINITY: The Logos-Intelligence; The all-perceiving Soul.

REALM   II   SPIRITUALITY: the logician whose powers of perception and conception are inherited from Realm I; that holy intelligence peculiar to soul.

REALM   III   MORALITY: the intelligence or science peculiar to conscience; the power of honesty and right.

REALM   IV   PHYSICALITY: the knowledge peculiar to physics; the sense perception of the human physique or human mammal.

REALM   V   UNMORALITY: moral ignorance, depravity or insensibility peculiar to this realm; state of being amoral.

Ignorance excludes itself from intelligence because it includes that which is bad, deceitful, false, worthless, unprincipled, unstable, abnormal, vile, valueless or incorrect.

Ignorance is made up of that knowledge which includes the knowledge of badness—the state or quality of being bad—and bad includes that which is incorrect, abnormal and unsound.

Ignorance is the human consciousness knowing what it knows. It knows by means of its natural capacity to gather and to hold, and to develop its own literal physical concepts. These concepts make up human knowledge and they exercise the human intellect which intellect looks to physical premises for all of its conclusions—good and bad. Thus human intellect is fraught with calamitous conclusions and concepts, and with all sorts of physical and metaphysical adversities.

Intelligence excludes itself from human intellect and all human knowledge, by simply being that which human knowledge cannot humanize, corrupt or make incorrect; by being that which humanity cannot physicalize or finitize or utilize.

It is the infinite positive of humanity's finite negative, which negative is ignorance, which ignorance is the state of being devoid of divine logic, but counterfeiting it with human knowledge. A finite knowledge fills the human mentality as humanly acquired intellect, which intellect misrepresents intelligence through its ignorance of it.

Ignorance picks up that which is humanly, physically, literally—not figuratively—obvious or evident. It has no moral (conscientious) instincts, but only its physical or natural (human) instincts. It has no intuitions; no moral-spiritual tutor (con-science) to teach it to counteract its misunderstanding.

Ignorance thrives on finite concepts. It cannot touch or invade the integrity of intelligence, but intelligence can (through the processes of legitimate thinking) annihilate ignorance, even as sunlight annihilates darkness. This darkness is nothing more than absence of light in its literal physical sense. In the moral sense, it is absence of or lack of moral enlightenment, conscience, instinct or intuitive moral sense. It is the absence of the moral qualities such as veracity, honesty, loyalty, fidelity and chastity, and it is the presence of human nature with its instincts, and its overwhelmingly magnetic physique.

There is an ignorance which falls even lower than the natural mammal instincts. It is the sub-animal or sub-mammal instincts; the sub-normal, unnatural and inhuman sense of things; the unmoral intellect, trained in its immorality. It is that form of sentiment and sense which has no higher sense than the physical sense; no morally metaphysical sense, but is non-moral, not moral or is unmoral because of being morally ignorant; spiritually insensible.

This kind of ignorance is not hostile toward intelligence or toward the moral law, because it is unmorality, unconscious of higher law (such as conscience). Immorality is the deliberate intellectual artifice that breaks the law, consciously, and protects human reputation by immoral art, or by the machinations peculiar to the immoral character.

Ignorance is not a force. Immorality and its art *is* a force to be nullified or abolished, individually and metaphysically and conscientiously. Thus conscience is that intelligent force which is annihilating unmorality, moral ignorance and spiritual ignorance.

Human ignorance is human folly, falsity, vanity and pride. It is envious of wisdom, verity, validity and natural worth. Ignorance can only covet intelligence, wisdom and such, or it can imitate it. Thus the spiritually ignorant prefer their own environment where immoral craftiness, artifice or sophistication is popular and where the cleverness of the worldly-wise excites human pride.

Ignorance is moral neglect, neglecting to pick up or to adopt or to embrace the premises of wisdom, but collecting, gathering, or picking up the elements of folly; neglecting to pick up the firm, the sound, valid and secure logic of highest understanding, but procuring personal prosperity to insure personal standing, which standing is misunderstanding or a mistaken reversal of intelligence or understanding.

Ignorance does not stand under intelligence as a student of wisdom. It stands under physicality or human personality or human nature, as student of it.

The following table will show the stand of ignorance:

REALM   I   DIVINITY: The Logos.

REALM   II   SPIRITUALITY: the logician of The Logos, governed by the recipes of The Logos-Principle; intelligence; wisdom and understanding standing under The Logos.

REALM III   MORALITY: the student of wisdom and conscience.

REALM IV   PHYSICALITY: the natural sciences, physics or human knowledge; human nature; the human physique, person and personality; the humanly natural (orthodox) concepts; human intellect; the knowledge adverse to *con*-science and its wisdom or science; the intellect premised and established on physical perception, sensibilities, evidences or conceptual conclusions.

REALM   V   IMMORALITY: this is the stand of ignorance. This is where ignorance stands— isolated from con-science, but studied

or learned in the art that ignores it; an
artist at doing whatever is physically or
humanly possible, without reference to
moral science, law and equity.

Ignorance—being without moral stability—is without or outside
of moral understanding. It is morally infirm, unstable, insubstantial,
inaccurate, invalid, worthless and useless; is without reason for its
existence; without virtue or use to man; without a place or stance in
the realms of moral values, dignity or worth.

Ignorance is not lack of knowledge (of the human sort) but it
is that knowledge, intellect, information, or instruction (humanized)
limited to humanity's realm. It is not lack of learning but it *is* learning, humanly directed, humanly circumscribed, and humanly confined to that which humanity knows by way of physical (sense perception) observation, physics, and humanly established rule or law;
that which humanity has gathered or picked up (with great diligence
and industry); that which humanity appreciates and chooses to know,
and it is that with which the human race is most familiar. Intelligence is the direct opposite of this, for its premise is The Logos.

Humanity (with its ignorance of intelligence) has translated and
interpreted the infinite and absolute (positive) into the finite, relative and negative.

THE WORD, IMAGE

The word *image* is one of the most dependent of words because it depends wholly upon the subject, the thing understood, or the topic introduced. It has no form of its own. Its form is the image or similitude or formation *of* the thing under consideration, or *of* the topic placed before one. It carries with it no subject, no premise, no thing (nothing) to denote its classification.

The word image must hang (depend), hang down, hang to or exist as contingent upon some thing. This thing must be established by context, because image must have something with which it may join, may attach itself, or may become related as pertaining to something (textual).

The word image (in old French and Latin) is *imago,* meaning likeness. In Greek it means be like.

Its common synonyms are: conception, emblem, picture, idea (Greek *icon, eikon, eioka*), representation, figure, similitude and others.

The verb image shows its function. It means to portray, describe, exhibit or represent vividly; to mirror; to typify, reflect or to form a mental picture of; to think to be or to imagine. The verb imagine is simply the exercise of the human and literal imagination. It may go far afield from logic, literacy or ruling principles of every kind. It may guess, suppose, contrive, scheme or conjecture and misrepresent or misconceive.

The noun image must be a representation or true concept of something; a picture closely resembling something; a precise reflection of that something. It must be true to its kind, and it must function as the phenomenon of its noumenal element, and in the rank or the office for which it is equipped.

The following table will classify the word image:

REALM I

DIVINITY: The Root and The Source of which mon (man) the thinker of Realm II is attribute and image.

REALM II

SPIRITUALITY: the logician, mon; the thinker who is completely equipped with understanding and with all of the powers of realization or spiritual demonstration;

the image, the essential expression, or the compound entity of wholly spiritual condition.

REALM III
MORALITY: the moral consciousness or *con-science;* the honest, patient and faithful or very conscientious student who is studying the science within himself (*con-science*) or the simpler forms of the logic of Realm II.

Here the moral virtues or qualities constitute a collection of entities, or the aggregate of these moral entities, functioning as the sum and total of honor, moral stamina, steadfastness, courage, confidence and spiritual tractability.

REALM IV
PHYSICALITY: the physical figure, model, form, potter (pater), pattern or kind of which the physical image is similitude; the physical phenomena of physical mindedness; the aggregate or sum of forms, figures, objects or images attributable to human nature or to natural causes or to artificial or manual craft; all images pertinently related to human nature premises and their conditions, actions and conclusions.

REALM V
IMMORALITY: the metaphysical phenomena of the physical noumenon, thing, precept or concept; the mental images adverse or opposed to or hostile toward the thinker of Realm II.

In the realm of physicality or humanity the first person or speaker —the me and the I; the us and the our—pertains to the human being, the human physique, corporeal being, body (somebody), or to the humus-man. All images—physical and metaphysical, literal and figurative—are dependent upon the physical object after which they are designed. Such images are the physical phenomenon of their physical or human, natural noumenon or premise.

The phenomenal images of Realm IV are sustained, nurtured, actuated, animated or moved, verified and glorified by their physical premises. They are the conclusions representing some form of physicality.

The images of Realm III are wholly metaphysical. They take their elemental or elementary forms from physically illustrated things, as the morally figurative sense of those things. The spiritually figurative sense of things is taken or deduced from Realm II. If this were not so the physically minded would be forever confined to Realm IV with no hope of moral, figurative, or mental, or metaphysical prosperity; with no way or highway out toward Realm II, and the physically minded breed—with their physically outlined imaginations —would never enjoy the tutelage of either morality or spirituality.

This physically minded breed or brood is the image of its own physical kind or kin. It cannot metaphysicalize itself. It cannot moralize itself or its status while it stands upon its own physical premises, practices or human fundamentals. It cannot save itself from its very finite, self-imposed and self-righteous or justified condition. It cannot change its own human imaginations to spiritual forms and images, because it has no spiritual premise and no morally scientific basis, but only its physical and humanly natural basis.

The Realm III thinker leaves off human imaginations to take on moral realities.

The Realm II thinker is a divine reality; a real or true image instituted by and constituted of The Logos. He is designed or divined by The Logos as logical thinker, as literate image, and as legitimate dependent.

THE WORD, INFLUENCE

The word *influence* is in three parts or syllables: *in-, fluo,* and *-ence.*

Prefix *in-* means in or into.

Root *fluo* (*fluere, fluxus*), I flow, or flow; *fluxum* means to flow.

Suffix *-ence* simply forms the word inflow or influx into a noun of action, quality or state.

Literal meaning: a flowing in of mental elements; an inflow or influx of persuasion that actuates or impels; that drives, elevates, promotes or demotes.

Common meaning (verb): to act upon mentally so as to command, induce or cause to believe; to exert mental power upon so as to affect rightly or wrongly.

Common meaning (noun): that inflow of mental energy or action which masters and may maintain authority.

Common synonyms (verb): actuate, compel, excite, draw, incline, induce, instigate, move, prompt, urge, mold, stir, sway, dispose and others.

Common synonyms (noun): power, prestige, ascendency, control, authority, impulsion, affection and others.

The word influence is an indefinite noun and verb. It does not classify or define itself, but only its action. It is a noun of action, or a verbal noun which may be used in several senses, qualities, states and conditions:

The following table classifies the word influence:

REALM I DIVINITY: the influence that flows out from The Logos into the mentality of the logician or thinker of Realm II.

REALM II SPIRITUALITY: those mental properties and spiritual promptings and powers that flow in from Realm I, such as wisdom.

REALM III MORALITY: those mental, moral powers of conscience which persuade and prompt honesty, veracity, verity and such qualities to act, and which maintain and sustain that action.

REALM IV   PHYSICALITY: the magnetic, electric, hypnotic, ethereal or physical fluids that actuate the human animal, or that exert organic force through the nerve fiber, brain and sense.

REALM V   IMMORALITY: the mystic, occult and persuasive impulses excited by human imagination.

The influence flowing in from Realm I comes from The Mynde of The Logos. Its influence flows in with such thoughtful affluence or magnanimous mental resource as to make one know that it is from The Logos-Mynde. Its logical influence is power. It speaks with highest and greatest ratio of word literacy and reason. It speaks with the authority of The Word and with the fluency of thought, and *to* the thinker's spiritualized mentality.

The thinkers or ideas of Realm II think in harmony (confluently) but individually. They think together or in unanimity because influenced by the same governing Logos-Principle. They partake of the same mental substance (understanding) and logical essence. There is nothing to obstruct the flow (or course) of tranquil contemplation.

The thinkers or concepts of Realm III are not in conflict with Realm II but are somewhat ignorant of its high premise or mental principles; but are greatly influenced by the crystal clear thinker of Realm II, and find solution in his great flow of wisdom, for the Realm II thinker does impart, let flow and let overflow the divine solution or solvent waters in which the radically moral thinker may solve all that seems problematic.

This flow of wisdom and its potency flows in with such mental (metaphysical) energy, moral impulse, moral influx, control and influence as to keep the moral thinker in balance and on his feet, in spite of the contrary influence brought to bear from underneath (Realm IV).

Human nature is the greatest or most influential factor with which humanity contends. Its instruments are the natural or physical manipulative forces such as pride, self, charm and such as carry the thinker along with them. It coaxes the person to flow along with its trend, or it commands, demands and forces concurrence by means of sweeping the person off his moral feet.

The finite human nature (influence) is constantly confronting one with its natural or physical evidence, with its natural human impulses or currents of thought. This influence may be verbal, silent, or known by gesture, but it is insistent, subtle, artful and occult or naturally persuasive to the human mammal, person or personality.

The moral one whom the human nature confronts with its flood of influence, is not easily confounded or made to flounder. He does not acquiesce, but resists and restrains human nature (humanly finite conceptions). He is not easily washed out to sea, or made to be at sea and at the mercy of human mindedness. He holds his own. He stands firmly upon the rock of morality or on the mountain of conscience, or in the heights of the solid convictions of conscience. He is not moved or driven by the human instincts.

The thinker of Realm II is wisdom, the logician. He is a spiritual scientist who understands and demonstrates the science of conscience and of his own soul. His logic flows in from The Logos. His literacy is the inflow or influx of the substance and essence of The Word (The divine creative Word). His law is The Logos-Principle which loves and disciplines, tutors and protects.

THE WORD, INNOCENCE

The word *innocence* comes from the Latin *noceo* (*nocere*), I injure, hurt; *nocere, noceo, nocitum,* meaning to hurt; noxious (*noxius*), meaning hurtful; *nuire* (French) and Latin *nocere, nocentia,* meaning hurt as in the word nuisance.

The prefix is *in-*. It means not.

The literal meaning is not hurt, not hurtful or injurious.

The suffix is *-ence*. It gives the word innocence its entity as that which or one who. Thus it is one who or that which does not hurt, harm or injure. This suffix gives the word its *antia* or its *entia* (its state or quality of being); gives it *idem* or identity; gives it its actor and its agent, its agency or its activity; makes it a noun of action or quality and makes it the condition of being innocent or pure and untainted, or free from those qualities that can hurt, and free from the liability of hurting or of harming or of doing injury.

The word innocence is a positive word as to quality, but it is a negative word as to its formation. It derives its positive strength from the fact that it counter-acts and counter-rolls or controls that which is hurtful. It is set, fixed, established and maintained as the antithetical state, quality and condition of being which hurts or is liable to injure; as the agency of benefit, help, consolation, solace, profit and comfort. It is the counter-actor of its antonyms: corruption, fault, hurt, harm, impurity, wrong, abuse, insult, offense, affliction, plague, curse, crime, vexation, or desecration.

Innocence is that character, agent or entity who performs the functions of remedying, blessing, purifying, making free from hurt, from violation or profanation or foulness of any kind.

Innocence is the state of being compassion itself, the state of being angelic or in a state of spiritual purity which counteracts that which would plague, and inspires that which perfects and makes sound or complete.

Innocence is a virtue. It may exist in the civil world as innocence or as innocent of offending the civil law. It may exist in the moral realm as freedom from moral offense. Thus honesty is innocent of deceit. Human affection or charity is innocent of hate, of malice or of disaffection. Faith or fidelity is innocent of infidelity. Constancy and moral stamina are virtues that stand in innocence, as free from vices or from that which is morally vicious and pernicious and insidious. Human honor may not be injured by the elements of dishonor, neither can human honor and honesty injure or hurt the human race. Humanity, chastity and such virtues may not be abused, damaged, offended or insulted by the mockery (effrontery) and indignity of their opposites or their affronters, and neither can these virtues inflict harm upon those people who mentally (figuratively) leap upon or insult them. Thus the word innocence holds its moral position or its positive meaning. Thus it maintains its moral nature, and thus conscience serves spiritual innocence, purity, love and soul innocency by leading, dictating or directing the innocent.

THE WORD, INTEGRITY

The word *integrity* comes from the Latin *integritas*. It means, literally, an unbroken, untouched, and unimpaired state of the integer. The suffix *-ity,* added to the word integer, makes it an abstract noun of state or quality of being (an whole integer), a complete or completely qualified integer; the state or quality of being sound, whole or wholly completed or perfectly made; the quality of being holy or an holy individual unit, in tact or intact, or in the condition of intactness, as being wholly intelligent.

The radical (root) of the word integrity is *tango* (*teg* or *tig* or *ting*), as in the words tangible, contingency, contiguous and integer. This root *tango* (*tangere, tactus*) means I touch; *tactum,* to touch. The prefix *in-* means not. Thus it means not touched or untouched, undivided or left entire and entirely whole; maintained and sustained as an integer or as a complete entity in its entirety, and in its peculiar and individual completeness, as the following table classifies that peculiar completeness:

REALM I DIVINITY: The wholly good or holy God; The Holy One; The Logos-Soul; The divine creative Logos-Unit.

REALM II SPIRITUALITY: the wholly spiritual integer; the state of being holy (holiness, itself); the condition of being spiritually sound or untouched by that which is unspiritual, or divinely unessential; spiritual integrity itself, which self or soul is immediately derived from The Logos-Soul or Integer.

REALM III MORALITY: the realm of moral integrity, uprightness, honesty and the other moral virtues; the realm of moral soundness, courage, stamina, steadfastness, loyalty, compassion, faith, or spiritual confidence, hope or moral progress and prosperity; the realm of all of the instincts or intuitions peculiar to conscience.

Integrity is that quality of thought which speaks of the thinker's rational wholeness; speaks of his full or complete ratio of understanding and of wisdom. It defines itself as being untouched by any lesser degree of reason. It sets forth the holy or wholly rational status of man—the thinker—whose state or status of being is purely spiritual, and is commonly and religiously called holiness.

The moral integrity of Realm III shares in the absoluteness of holiness; shares in the blessedness of Realm II; shares in the hallowed or holy condition of the entity, the identity or the holy integer, but he does not possess the whole spiritual capacity for conception and for understanding as the thinker of Realm II possesses that capacity. He does possess the capacity and the moral capability to conceive and to bring forth his sound moral issues; his sturdy, vigorous, and morally zealous issues for human utility in human affairs. These issues are outlined, lectured, elected and dictated by his moral conscience, as his own affluent understanding of that which is right with his own conscience.

Moral integrity is moral amplitude bringing forth its own potentialities in the form of moral substance or under-stanc-ing (understanding) which is honest faith and confident expectancy (hope) *understancing* the moral entity.

Integrity, in its whole sense, is spiritual health which is manifest throughout all human ramifications and physical manifestations. Integrity, in its most pure and wholesome sense, is the state of being whole, complete, perfect or sound in soul—therefore in body—temple of contemplation.

Integrity is the condition of being an whole integer, untouched and unmarred by the soulless, the unsound, the unwhole or the false sciences and physical curses.

Integrity is that quality and character which guards the body as the sole owner and as the soul-logician who allows no element of human knowledge to enter in or to claim ownership or control of the body (as well as the soul) properties.

Integrity is that form of intelligence which allows nothing of the human nature or kind of thinking to touch either the soul (the mind) or the body, but holds intelligence to be out of reach of human intellect and knowledge.

Integrity is not in sympathy with humanity, with human physics, or with human metaphysics. It is that kind of wholeness which needs neither remedy nor recipe that human sciences may or can prescribe. It has neither physical nor mental plagues.

Integrity would not be itself (integrity or holiness) if it needed help from human hand or from any kind of material thing. It is like soul. It stands wholly supported and spiritually sound, under the direct discipline of The Logos-Principle. It stands and understands, independent and free from that realm which believes that soul (and its man) can be both whole and unwhole; both wholly spiritual and holy, or truly a divine integer (entity, idea or identity) and still be unwhole, living in an unholy or unsound temple where he must suffer the effects of the laws of physics, or allow the knowledge of humanity's law to govern him or to pilot him into its realm of invalidism or unwholeness.

Integrity is spiritual health. It reaches to the realms of reason, conscience and intuition. It reaches to the realm of contemplation or spiritual consideration and it carries its thinker with it up to The Logos-Premise, where all conclusions are in harmony with Soul; where the thinker is whole and is controlled by the wholeness and perfection of Soul; where the thinker is two realms removed from mental unwholesomeness or from physical unwholeness; where he may not be touched by human sagacity, erudition; where knowledge or its sense of things cannot invent disorder, cannot divide thought between the absolute and the relative, cannot disturb the tranquillity of soul.

Integrity is the condition of soul living under the care of divinely tranquil Soul, and enjoying all of the great benefits of soul health; enjoying perfect health or complete soundness, as an individual thinker, as an wholly spiritual integer, as holiness itself, untouched by those mental germs which infest the lower realms, and which first cause and then care for the physical victims.

Knowledge of the human physique or physical knowledge creates its own victims. Integrity, on the other hand, is not associated with, but is divinely divided from, human knowledge. Hence its wholeness or holiness, or its wholly spiritual status of soul and body, entirely hidden from human science or knowledge, which treats of inaccurate and incorrect, unwhole or abnormal states and conditions.

Integrity does not pertain to realms four and five, because the physical realm (four) and the immorally, unholy, and unsound realm (five) embrace the antonymic nature of integrity.

The following table shows these antonymic states, qualities, and characters or conditions peculiar to these lower realms:

REALM I

DIVINITY: The Logos-Creator of the spiritual creation and all that is essential to completeness, wholeness, or the integral whole—reality.

Realm II

REALITY: the logician—real creature who contemplates untouched and uninfluenced by that which deviates from infinite completeness.

Realm III

MORALITY: the conscientious thinker who tries to practice human virtues prescribed by conscience, while the world which environs him is not virtuous, but thinks in an unholy, unhale, unwhole, and unwell vein. This thinker is untouched by that which deviates from moral standard.

Realm IV

PHYSICALITY: here the human physique or person may be called a perfect specimen, intact as a mammal integer.

Realm V

DEPRAVITY: that which is farthest removed from the didactic truth, conscience, and integrity; that which presents all of the antonyms of integrity; the state, quality, condition and character of moral depravity.

The Realm III thinker stands between the low and the high or highest forms of integrity. He grows morally strong, vivacious, sound, cognizant of being go-between, and scrupulous as he practices his high moral precepts. He is a moral integer. He holds himself to be above that which is unprincipled, unsound, dishonest, vain, self-proud, hateful or disloyal to the moral principles.

THE WORD, INTELLIGENCE

The word *intelligence* comes from the Latin radical *lego, legere; lectus,* I gather, pick, choose or read; *lectum,* to gather, or to read. It points to literacy and away from illiteracy. It leaves off the *e* vowel in the radical root and takes on the *i* vowel as *ligo* or *lig,* which vowel is of highest literacy.

The prefix *intel-* is *inter,* meaning between or among.

The suffix *-ence* gives it entity; gives it state of being or quality of being. It forms it into a noun of state, quality or of action.

Literal meaning: the perceiver, the entity or the idea who chooses between the absolutely literate and the relatively literate.

Common meaning: the power or act of understanding; readiness of comprehension.

Common synonyms: instinct, intellect, mind, news, information, tidings, knowledge and understanding.

In the realm of human parlance the word intellect is given as a synonym for intelligence. Literately it is not a synonym. It may not be identical with intelligence, because it is of lesser and lower degree of comprehension; of a lesser form of wisdom, cognizance, understanding or power of verification; of a lower sphere of action, industry or mental diligence and not so highly endowed with or identified with the powers of realization.

Intellect may be said to be intelligence humanized, humanly esteemed, humanly interpreted, humanly collected, humanly selected or gathered; that which is of human import or of human perception; that which is reasonable, conceivable and familiar to the human race. Thus intellect elects to collect and to recollect that human sense of things with which it is most familiar and in which it is most interested, and thus intellect is acquired by human diligence.

In the realm of common meanings the word knowledge is used as identical with highest intelligence or highest spiritual instinct and understanding, but knowledge is only that which humanity has perceived or apprehended and which it holds to be scientific, reasonable or reasonably acknowledged by its own rational faculties. It is that with which humanity is self-indoctrinated and it is the antonym of logic derived from The Logos. It is that for which humanity has a liking—a predilection. It is not intelligence.

[213]

Intelligence is an endowment of soul; the result of conscientious (spiritual) diligence; a property of the science of soul. It is as morally, mentally and spiritually industrious or active as conscience or as wisdom. It holds the infinite significance of an idea or concept, while human intellect holds to the relatively finite significance, reason or meaning of all things.

The word neglect means not picking up; not gathering, selecting or choosing. Intellect, because of its lesser capacity, neglects to pick up, to understand or to gather that which intelligence gathers or finds to be eligible, intelligible or intelligent. Intellect reads its own human concept and elegant legends into whatever it reads and then ledgers this concept into a written system of knowledge.

The following table will classify Intelligence, intelligence, intellect and knowledge:

REALM I
DIVINITY: Intelligence as that which The Logos-Mind embraces or that which is embraced by and in The Mind of The Logos; infinite logic of the divine sort which originates in and with The Logos; Truth of the universal sort giving birth and true substance to all intelligence or intelligent ideas of the spiritual or divine sort.

REALM II
SPIRITUALITY: intelligence of wholly or holy origin; divine tidings, news or information; intelligence peculiar to the logician—the fully representative or wholly logical thinker; wisdom and understanding of the completely spiritual sort; the substance of Truth or the substancing and understanding of Truth; wisdom—the dominant and true-*ly* empowered thinker who dominates in the realm of true or intelligent realization; spiritual diligence.

Intelligence is the logic of soul within one; the intuitive, informative, instructive tutor within oneself, which self is soul being logical, literate or wise. This soul-principle disciplines, teaches, guards and directs. This soul, logician or thinker is under the tutelage of The Logos-Principle.

REALM III
MORALITY: intellect, human reason, the moral instincts, the conscientious sentiments and verities that take rise in Realm II or are deduced from its logic, literacy or principles.

Conscience is the expression of intelligence, or the representative of Realm II logic bringing the substance (understanding) of soul down to the moral ear or ear-th. Con-*science* is that science, verity or spiritually veritable and morally understandable soul-ego that dictates its instinctive science or its scientific instinct to tutor, lead or discipline one.

Morality is a spiritually prompted, spontaneous sense of right. Human intellect is not moral but conscience is. Thus conscience, not intellect, comes from Realm II intelligence.

Realm IV

PHYSICALITY: the human nature with its natural animations, impulses, instincts and instituted knowledge.

THE WORD, INTUITION

The word *intuition* is made up of prefix *in-*, root *tuere, tueor,* and the suffix *-tion,* which suffix forms the word *intuit* into a noun of action or condition.

The prefix *in-* means in, on or within.

The root *tuere, tueor, tutus,* to watch, guard, or to tutor; *tueri, tuitus,* I watch, I look after, I guard or protect.

The suffix *-tion* or *-ion* means the act of, denotes verbal action or condition.

Literal meaning: the act of keeping watch on, or watching within; the act of protecting or looking after, or of guarding as tutor.

Common meaning: apprehending or cognizing by instinct (of a moral sort) or by the powers within; insight.

The following table will define and classify the word intuition:

REALM I DIVINITY: The Logos-Principle; Giver of all recipes; Origin of all discipline; Word of all defense, wisdom and logic.

REALM II SPIRITUALITY: the logician, soul, man or mon divinely tutored; the spiritual genius; spiritual instinct or talent supervised by The Logos-Soul; literate perfection; spiritual purity of conception and wholeness (holiness) of perception.

REALM III MORALITY: con-science (the moral science within one) or one's tutor watching within one; the moral genius or one's highest and most conscientious sense of right deduced from Realm II and providing insight, foresight or discernment; a true sense of the moral law that defends, tutors, guards, urges, commands, instructs, informs and disciplines.

Intuition may not be reduced further. It is a spiritual genius; a highly instructive moral and spiritual intelligence with, in, on or within one; a divine inheritance utilized; a peculiar property of soul; an endowment of Soul from Soul.

Human knowledge, human sensibility, human sentiment or the established human intellect cannot know the science of intuition. Only the highly developed *con*-science and its sense of things, can sense intuition. Conscience is the agent of intuition, because it is the science within one, the science that knows within, the science of soul dictating from within or tutoring within oneself.

Intuition is not a random thing or a weak thing which only the weaker sex may feel or sense. It is an wholly, truly, and real sensibility or the faculty of reason.

Reason, when loosed or freed from human intellect, may become spiritually rational or may enjoy the wholly (holy) spiritual ratio of intelligence (under which intelligence, both conscience and reason function).

Intuition depends upon conscience and reason to carry on and to carry out its messages or its instructive and constructive recipes to their ideate conclusions. The female of man is the one who carries, bears, sustains, quickens, acts upon, develops and bears out or carries out the issues—physical and metaphysical—which are entrusted to her. This may be the reason why intuition has been assigned to woman.

Intuition is a form of faith or faith is an element of intuition— the capacity to believe what the world neither feels nor sees. It is the capacity to receive messages from wisdom—words of advice—or from higher reality and its spiritual realizations. Intuition, like faith, leads to this reality, which reality is wisdom's understanding of The Re or The Logos—the divine Re-ality.

In Realm II the logician is teacher or tutor. He is wise, wholly enlightened, literately perfect and divinely substantiated. This tutor functions as savior to save the thinker from maculate and inaccurate concepts. He functions as defender to defend (strike away) that which would attack or strike out against his pupil. He functions as preserver to preserve, to maintain, and to guard as guardian. He functions as confidant to make secure, safe, firm in stance and confident under The firmly fixed Logos-Principle. He functions as demonstrator exhibiting or showing the spiritual phenomena of this noumenal Logos-Premise or Principle.

In Realm III conscience and its science is the tutor, furthering faith, prompting hope and prospering the morally teachable or tractable. Its function is to refine humanity, to teach patience or compassion and to discipline passion or to restrain the human impulses that are passive to the untutored human nature. Its function is to keep watch—untiring watch or constant watch—over and in the mental vestibule where believing and thinking goes on or go on spontaneously or of one's own free will.

In Realm I it is The I, The Word or Logos who is Tutor, The Teacher, The Instructor and The I Am Divinity, or I Am Protector, protecting from that which is illogical, illiterate, and not of divine origin or not under the tutelage and discipline of The Logos Principle.

In Realm II it is mon—the thinker—who teaches the wisdom, infinite vision, universal discernment and the accurate and immaculate art of highest realization; it is wisdom himself who is tutor supervising Realm III.

THE WORD, Justice

The word *justice* comes from the Old French and the Latin word *just,* which is an adjective. The radical root is *jus.* (*Juris,* right law; *justus,* lawful; *judex, judicious,* a judge.) The suffix *-ice* forms the adjective just into a noun. Justice is that which is just; the act, quality or condition of being just. Justice acts upon a right law or a law that is wholly equitable. Justice stands at dead center, in an upright position, indicating erect and correct standard of legal excellence. It marks the center of the sphere of law. It stands erect, and thus it marks the moral plumb line of the principle of equity. It admits no ambiguities. It represents the bull's-eye or center of the legal target. It rests upon the vertical line, the zenith, principal or summit of up-rightness or universal rightness. Thus it verifies its correctness or its position, stand, and standard of excellence.

Justice deals with human nature, the human animal nature, and the inhuman, unmoral nature. It deals with every form of inequity, injustice, prejudice, mental jaundice, envy, personal opinions, be-liefs, bias, or ambiguous points of view—having other than the right point of view, or having the sentiments colored by prejudice or envy.

Justice judges from universal precepts—which applied to local and intellectual problems of the human sort—adjusts, settles, rights, rectifies, or practices in conformity with universal precepts; adjusts the ambiguous, penurious and pernicious human prejudices that hold the human race in a state of self-justified and self-imposed injustice, or false concept of justice. This concept may be symbolized by a crooked equatorial line, or by an off-center polar axis line, neither of which exists in fact. Justice may be symbolized by these true-*ly* cor-rect lines which need no adjustment. Thus does justice practice to relieve the victims of a false concept of justice, or an ignorance of it. Thus does justice teach humankind to abort its false and ille-gitimate conceptions, and to nurture conscience as the phenomenal attribute of justice.

Con-science is the spirit of justice. The statute books are the letter of it. Con-science is the science of law, which speaks or dictates its mandatory statements or sentences in the ear of human reason. Thus conscience is the moral and spiritual agent of justice; the substance of law; the essence of innate intuitions or moral instincts; the informa-tive and leading rational faculty that collaborates with justice.

The human intellect and personality plead as self-justification and self-conceit. Conscience pleads for individual honor, honesty, integrity, veracity, uprightness or the law of right, against artifice and ignorance, or negligence.

The following table classifies justice:

REALM   I   DIVINITY: The Logos-Principle.

REALM   II   SPIRITUALITY: the logician-disciple under the discipline of The Logos-Prin-*cip*-le, and following the recipes (re-*cip*-es) of this Principle, as re-cipient of its fundamental substance, as governing law, and as Source of doctrine and justice.

REALM   III   MORALITY: here *con*-science is the silent counselor; the essential spirit of the law, or the moral energy motivating, presenting, dictating, and ruling. Conscience is moral instinct or the higher nature, defending, tutoring, guarding, protecting, supervising and pointing out the rulings of right or the familiar moral axioms that sustain it.

Here honesty defends human honor, and equity maintains ethical law and order.

REALM   IV   PHYSICALITY: human nature with its selfish sense of justice; physics with its natural sense of justice, its self-justification (proud and willful).

REALM   V   IMMORALITY: inhuman nature with its revenge, its injustice, inequities and iniquities; with its anger, animosities, and destructive mental weapons.

Justice and truth use their metaphysical weapon which is Truth —the constructive principle of The Logos. Justice and truth are elements of logic and they work through conscience, to reach mankind. They cannot and do not work through dishonesty, injustice, envy, immorality, will-power, flimsy beliefs or such logic as humanity may reverence. They work through or by means of the verities which Truth or the logic of The Logos substantiates.

This logic is its own sword or weapon. It strikes and slays that which is not infinitely, divinely, and spiritually logical, or morally conscientious—not of con-science.

The Logos-Principle or The Logos-Truth is judge. Truth's logical ideas ideate, perceive and conceive under the immediate supervision, authority or judgment of The Logos-Truth. They function as they are directed. They operate as the most highly principled ideas or as justice itself. It is corrective and counteractive, remedial and right or just in its rulings or its ruling ideas, because it is justice, truly just or justly true.

Justice is not without its quality of benevolence or its element of loving-kindness or lovingness. It is not without its state and character of wisdom with its valid, vital continuity.

THE WORD, KNOWLEDGE

The word *knowledge* comes from Anglo Saxon know.

The root is *cnawan* (know); to know; knowledge.

The suffix may constitute another word, ledge, and thus make it a compound word.

> Ledge is from *lecgan,* to lay, or to let lie, as leger or as ledgered law; as laid down in ledger.

Literal meaning: that which is known or is certainly apprehended.

The common function of the verb to know, is to experience, to learn, to acquire information or knowledge.

This Anglo Saxon word knowledge covers a wide sphere of human learning and it represents education itself to humanhood. It may mean that which is shelved or laid upon the ledge or shelf (as books are laid upon shelves) and as ledgers (records, history and sciences) are bound into book or ledger form.

Knowledge is that which is alleged to be true and is so ledgered; that which is commonly known to be lawful, authentic or so, as delegated sent and bequeathed (as knowledge or science) to succeeding generations or to human posterity. Thus human judgment sets forth and it causes to be recorded (or ledgered) all learning that is the rule, the findings or the result of humanity's search for knowledge. Thus human acumen may be judge and ruler.

Knowledge is that which humanity has found and has ordained, instituted, organized or set in order. It is that which humanity has acknowledged and reported to be true, or has perceived to be supreme in precept, and to be remedial or beneficial to humanity, judging from physical precepts.

Knowledge is that which humanhood or the human race has searched out. It constitutes the precept for every human conception; the premise for every human conclusion; the theory (established) for every human practice and human action. It is the *know-leg* or *lego* handed down as that which speaks as tradition, that which is selected to be read, and that which is legal and lawful to cite, quote, allege, to state or to affirm as being a material fact.

Knowledge is that which is conclusive and conclusively orthodox in the conventional human realm or the educational world. It is that which the Greek *gignosko* (know) indicates, and that which the Latin *scio* has designated as being knowledge or science.

The following table places knowledge in Realm IV:

REALM   I   DIVINITY: The Principle and Premise of all logic; The Logos; Intelligence.

REALM   II   SPIRITUALITY: the realm of the logician, wisdom, or the doctor of divine logic; the thinker who fully understands The Intelligence, as intelligence; spiritual substance (*under-stancing*) or understanding itself, perceiving.

REALM III   MORALITY: the realm of human reason, human intuition, moral sagacity or *con-science* where mathematics is humanity's most rigid and inflexible school master and where conscience is its most radical and rudimental and fundamental dictator of right. Its other sciences are induced from Realm IV.

Here the human intellect is in opposition to intelligence.

REALM IV   PHYSICALITY: human knowledge; that which humanity has instituted as peculiar to its needs; that which human nature wants to know as peculiar to its apprehension of existence; corporeal, carnal, physical or the human animal kind of knowledge gathered from physical bases or premises, and so established.

Knowledge is by no means a synonym for science, although it is ordinarily so used. It is created by human nature and the human intellect in proof of itself or of its consensus. Knowledge belongs to the human mentality—its sense or senses, opinions, theories, beliefs or elements of humanly established doctrine. Thus knowledge may function in Realm IV only, where humanity believes it to be science (scientific) or logic, and logical as the only kind of logic, and where physicality is believed to be the basis of existence as well as the avenue through which one may sense and gather all knowledge.

Science comes from logic (Realm II) and logic comes from The Logos (Realm I). Knowledge is not deduced from science for absolute, universal science belongs to con-science and is comprehended, perceived and embraced by the thinker of Realm III, while knowledge is peculiar to Realm IV and is localized in physicality in its theory and in its practice, in its precepts and in its concepts, in its premises, and in its conclusions. It profanes the name of science (which science con-science teaches under wisdom and his logic) and which science takes no cognizance of human intellect, learning or knowledge, or the finite human point of view.

Human knowledge is based upon that which is mortally doomed; upon theories which are to be spiritually exploded when the science of soul within (con-science and wisdom) begins to undermine or to supplant that which has been called science.

Science dictated by con-science is immutably trustworthy, right, just, and uncompromising (with the human and mundane).

Science is the highest form of logic conceivable to the human race. Science teaches its doctrine via con-science.

Let the following table contrast knowledge with The infinite origin of logic:

Realm I

DIVINITY: The Logos, Root, Origin, Soul and Source of logic, of the rudiments of science, of the spiritual logician, and of his powers of expression.

Realm II

SPIRITUALITY: the spiritual attributes and logical ideas that represent The Logos; the realities of Soul and the verities that originate in Soul as Source; the literacy born of The Root-Word.

Realm III

MORALITY: the moral status and the state of being morally sound, firm, steadfast and conscientious; the quality of being right (with con-science) and being right because superintended by right reasoning or by the science of con-science constantly.

Here the human faculties are devoted to moral usage and development.

Here the science of con-science (which leads to soul, wisdom, Realm II logic and ideas) is paramount, and when morality is in question this moral science has preponderance, but when physical knowledge and its established natural sciences are in question they may be the stronger influence; may rule or sit in judgment.

Here abides conscience (faith, moral prosperity or hope) with its confidence in soul-science, and here fidelity may cause the thinker to doubt the finite physical knowledge, or to deem it secondary.

Realm IV

PHYSICALITY: the physical status of the human physique; the physical mindedness of the human nature; the human mammal and its physical and metaphysical states or conditions of being.

Realm V

IMMORALITY: the human person and human intellect that is morally abnormal, ignorant of conscience and its science, and is unmoral because of this abnormalcy and ignorance. Thus Realm V presents dishonesty, envy, malice and all that is mentally noxious or morally obnoxious.

Realm V is false assumption based upon finite physics; error in premise and in conclusion based upon humanly satisfied theories and humanly instituted systems and premises; humanly accepted culture, established learning and discourse based upon precepts within Realm IV. It is misconception of higher than physical science; mistake or the taking amiss or for granted of the substance of realms above. It is anti-science as con-science presents it. It is anti-logic as Realm II or wisdom presents it. It is anti-Truth or anti-Soul and anti-spiritual as Realm I presents the logic of The Logos.

Realm IV presents physical finity. It is not deduced or reduced from moral-spiritual substance or understance.

Realm III presents that science of con-science which is the science within oneself, science of soul, wisdom, understance or spiritual understancing. It is logic of The Logos reduced to human appreciation (in the form of conscience), altogether independent of Realm IV, but having the sense of spiritual intuition, vision and discourse, having a moral sense or high morale within; having inspiration and higher aspiration—not weighed down by physical ponderance or preponderance of physical knowledge.

No relation exists between physical mindedness (with its phenomena) and moral mindedness (con-science) and its right or moral law (equity) phenomena. But this right mindedness may show its right phenomena in Realm IV.

In Realm I there is The Logos-Truth. In Realm II there is The logic of The Logos. In Realm III there is the science of con-science.

In Realm IV there is human knowledge and its institutional, conventional, traditional and learned awareness.

Knowledge is a noun. To know is a verbal action. The last syllable of the word knowledge is ledge. This ledge is an inactive thing. It means to lay or let lie as laid down. It is stored as dead record, not as living, growing unfolding, or not as that which is being further revealed. It confines itself to the physical or mundane aspect of things, and to humanity which means mortality. It pertains to the physique, the human animal or mammal, the earthy, temporal human person, and is devoted to his terrestrial delights as well as his sorrows, or undelightful impressions made upon the human physique.

To know within oneself is to observe con-science—one's living, prospering ethical sense or moral intuition. It is honesty, veracity, sincerity, verity or one's most conscientious sentiments in action under the urgency of soul or by the motivations of spiritual wisdom and its potency. It means an ever active adventure into the domain of wisdom and his logic; into the realm of literate wholeness.

The following table separates knowledge from science:

REALM   I   DIVINITY: The Logos or Word, Creator of all logic, literacy and law; Source of all that is essential to man (mon, mind, or the soul), the spiritual thinker and understander.

REALM   II   SPIRITUALITY: the logician; wisdom; the realm of divinely substantiated logic, and of divinely verified literacy, and of those principles, premises and precepts which govern realization.

REALM   III   MORALITY: the science which is identified by conscience.

REALM   IV   PHYSICALITY: the knowledge fathered by physics; that which is physically patent or naturally patterned or pater-ed (fathered) by human nature or that which it makes evident; knowledge familiar to the human family, the human race or human kind.

In the eyes of wisdom—the spiritual seer—knowledge is a false assumption of science and of wisdom; a conglomerate mass of all things claimed to belong to itself, as well as all things that do belong to itself.

In the ears of con-science—the moral tutor—human knowledge is that which claims to be science, but which is the disputer of con-science, as adverse to its kind of science (which kind of science is morally metaphysical, tending definitely toward the spiritual).

The kind of science which con-science teaches does not mix with those of the humanly natural kind, because it is not in accord with human nature and its kind of knowing. Conscience does not hear to such and is unrelated to such.

Knowledge includes all human *isms* and *ologies*—even anthropology. It claims to embody all logic and to express all science, and it does for the knower who is content to think in Realm IV, or to stand under the premises and theories of Realm IV, or to abide by its proud, despotic systems.

Knowledge is a mixture of human ideals and idols; of humanity's firm convictions and its infirm and invalid beliefs; of its collected and recollected matters of intellect elected and selected to stand as knowledge, and humanly acknowledged (believed) to be right, true or good; humanly admitted to stand as humanly understood to be.

This peculiar mixture is gathered from the mundane side of things. It fathers and mothers all human fears, mortal envies and hates, warlike theories, and inhuman premises. Its source and resources are mutable, infirm, and not morally radical, or not spiritually confirmed.

Knowledge (as that which must be known, must be had, observed and followed) has been honored by the peoples of the Earth throughout all human generations. It has exacted and demanded honor, yet knowledge or human intellect is made up of human assumptions, humanly confirmed. It is composed of the consensus of beliefs, wills, evidences, conclusions, judgments and opinions which the human race has accepted upon its own evidence or information presented.

Knowledge belongs to the human race because it is a product of the human race and is essential to it. It was and is originated by it or begotten of it. Here the word origin refers to Eve, the human character, woman-parent or female ancestor from which all human concepts proceed. Here Eve is the woman (*gin,* as in *gyn-ics,* or *gyn, gyne,* from Greek meaning woman or female) who originated knowledge, who conceived and made evident that knowledge which was presented to her—and who gave it rise and origin. It rose from her as its beginning. Here the word be-*gin* and beget are native to Eve, innate in Eve and natural or initial in Eve.

Knowledge is true to the commencement of its existence, its origin, its cause, its first conceiver, its generator and its originator—

the woman Eve who gave it rise, who gave it birth, action and institution. Knowledge is therefore modeled after her. It is her concept—
the flesh and bones concept; the corporeally evident consequence and
conclusion. It is her conception upon which all finite, material
(mater-Eve) or *mater-ial* doctrine is based. It is her natural assumption made evident to the natural, the physical, the mundane or matter-
ial ear and ear-th.

THE WORD, LAW

The word *law* has its root in Greek, in Latin and in Anglo Saxon. The Greek *nomos* means law. It is often used in compound words, as the suffix *-nomy*. The Latin *lex* (*legis*) means law. The Anglo Saxon *lagu* (*licgan, lecgan*) means law, lie, or to lay.

There is a sense of law, rule, ruling word, word of law, rule laid down, ledgered and caused to lie and let lie. There is a sense of science or logic being the law; a sense of The Logos-logic in the Greek *nomos*. There is a sense of the law being a thing of action or the actor who is "to lay down the law," or being the statute book in which the word of law is laid down; in which the law is laid down and let lie as a ledger or book of law for the purpose of edict, principle, decree, code or mandate (to preserve order). This is the Anglo Saxon sense. The Latin sense brings out rule, a rule, to regulate, to govern, to keep in order as by being a ruling system. This law may come from the throne of a ruler, while the Anglo Saxon pertains to a ledger, a book, or statute of basic rules. Thus the book is the ruler and the authority and is an impersonal sovereign (Word) of justice. This book or ledger of law is a three-in-one written and worded impersonal ruler. It legislates or makes the law. It judges or acts as justice in being that which is laid down (written, given word form, or recorded to let lie). It executes the law or serves as the administrative or executive agency and department of the law. All this is above and beyond human personality, human office and human conception of law and order.

Law is a thing that lies, sits, is settled, and stands. In the Anglo Saxon sense it lies. In the statute sense it stands. In the sense of rule it is a system settled upon or established. It rules by settling disputes.

The word law is spelled with the illiterate *a* vowel. It therefore applies to civil, social or human kind of law, or to humanity's concept of law.

Moral law begins with that which is *right,* honest, fair or humanly ethical and equitable. It is a sense of justice as dictated by conscience, veracity, charity, affection, compassion, patience, mercy or the moral instincts, whereas human nature deals with self-justification, self-will, personal opinion or the consensus of belief. It obeys civil tradition, polite formality, social propriety and courtesy or human orthodoxy which dictates that which shall be observed as *right.* Thus human nature becomes law as dictator of human action, in opposition to moral law.

The following table will classify the several different bases or sorts of law:

REALM   I   DIVINITY: The Spirit and The Letter of The Word, The Logos—logic or law.

REALM   II   SPIRITUALITY: the spiritual principles of wisdom; the stand or stance of understanding or spiritual substance of law and logic; the thinker who observes the letter of the law and lets or permits it to operate as letter; the logician or the correct and accurate thinker who reasons from Realm I premise to legitimate, literate conclusion. Here, The Word is law.

REALM III   MORALITY: the moral law in force, via the human faculties of reasoning.

REALM IV   PHYSICALITY: the law of human nature.

In Realm II logic is law. It is that which the thinker deduces from The Realm I Premise, Precept or governing Principle. It is a divine logic or law. It is a divinely worded law or Principle from which the logical thinker gets his directions, recipes, order, rules, doctrine, judicial command, divine mandate or prescribed and *pre-written* precepts and divinely worded instructions. In this realm (spirituality) all things are interpreted spiritually as the essence, substance, spirit and letter of The Word. Wisdom is dominant soul-judgment or sound judgment, or the logical thinker in action; the wise agent and logical agency of the universal law. He is the seer of infinite foresight, soul-enlightenment or spiritual integrity.

In Realm III the highest human sense of right is law. Honesty, moral stamina, loyalty, moral courage, piety, modesty, meekness, veracity, profundity, sobriety or temperance, hope or moral prosperity, faith, or fidelity, and humanity or the human kind of benevolence—all these are agents of the moral law. They are humanity's best concepts of right, justice, virtue, honor, equity, truth, human excellence, uprightness and devoutness. They stand as substantiated by the human heart or sentiments. They lie as laid down by the morally conscious or conscientious thinkers of the ages. They sit in judgment in the human consciousness, and from there they perform their judicial, legislative, and executive functions, because they are not words, but they are moral characters, qualities, instincts, intuitions or states of being (moral); states or conditions of being just; states of being in action as moral agitators; morally impelled beings who are leaders of the people, in all civil, social and ethical affairs.

These leaders belong to Realm III, while the people whom they lead belong to Realm IV, as morally retarded or as slow of law conviction or slow to respond to the higher (than human nature) law, administered by conscience.

The people may represent public opinion and a strong sentiment for human nature as being the normal and natural order. Thus the civil law (or the law that civilizes but does not moralize) is the law of the people who are being educated to live in a state that is one realm above savagery and is concerned with domesticating the human creature so that the human animal or mammal may live in a house instead of *silva,* wood, or the woods; so that the human creature may be mentally or psychologically ferocious, savage, cruel and rapacious, rather than being kind and gentle like many so-called lower animals. The processes of civilization are essential only as they lead to a sense of individual moral honor, and only as they support a universal system of education based upon virtue; only as they lead up to or lead on to complete and radical moralization, as the following table classifies:

REALM I

DIVINITY: where the logic of The Logos, the literacy and letter of The Word, and the legitimacy of The universal and infinite Principle of law *is* law, holding jurisdiction over all rule, order and orderly dominions that coordinate with and are in harmony with the logic and the letter of The Logos-law.

REALM II

SPIRITUALITY: where man—the logical and literate and legitimate thinker—is *mon* governed and controlled and dominated, ruled and commanded by The mandate of The Word and its radical Root or Principle.

In this realm of complete understanding there is a law peculiar to spiritual intuition, or divine instinct or intelligence. This law functions as wisdom itself, as spiritual holiness or divine integrity and as constancy, immaculacy, validity, verity and the other powers of perception, conception and realization. It functions (not through force) gently as the dove or the angel, through love or the wholly and holy spiritual sentiments.

Realm III

MORALITY: where the human race or humanity or
human kind or mankind lives and trusts, hopes, prays,
cherishes, worships, honors, obeys and holds moral restraint over human nature and its disposition to control
or to counter-roll the impulses of moral nature prompted
by conscience.

In this realm of moral standard, the moral thinker
looks to Realm II for higher interpretation of right, of
right rule, right principles, and right laws; for greater
wisdom in its application of law.

Realm IV

PHYSICALITY: wherefrom natural science or the physical sciences ramify and thus become a law to humanity,
which humanity represents Adam or the Adam-kind, the
Adam kin or kind of a man.

Here human impulses or the Adam impulses govern,
and the Eve nature and the Eve sentiments control the
physically minded.

Here the intent of the civil law is to carry out the will
or the better judgment of the people; to institute as high
a system of government as the people can appreciate
and find practicable—thus maintaining civil order.

Realm V

IMMORALITY: unmorality; moral depravity or insensibility; all that is unlawful, illicit, improper; all that is unrestrained and unregulated by moral influence or law;
all that is unruly and not in conformity with the civil
law; all that is licentious or lewd and offensive to civil
and moral taste; all that is alien, hostile or adverse to
conscience and its science.

In the realm of humanhood morality is recognized as a governing
factor. But the consensus of human opinion, human convention and
orthodoxy is also recognized as a governing factor and as an influence.
Human nature (of Realm IV) is an influence which does not easily
let go of humanhood. Thus morality must be radical, fundamental,
innate or natural if it is to survive the unrestrained and unmoral influence of human nature in social usage and formalism. Moral integrity must be developed and must serve as the law within one; as the
law of conscience (within one) governing one, and thus law and one's
obedience to it must become as natural to one as human nature is

natural to humanhood. (Humanhood is the state, quality or character of being human.) Morality is the state, quality or condition of being moral—customarily right, proper or of conscientious habits.

Morality is based on right, equity, justice or the law dictated by conscience—not by human nature. Thus the moral law is the right manner or way of conducting oneself; the right convictions which stand as law within oneself; the best and highest human sentiments and virtues which take the lead as law, consciously and individually.

Law, in any sense, must be developed and matured and well established in the individual. Law, in its highest sense, may mature into a principle, precept or high moral premise from which the individual concludes, judges and practices and deduces his proper conduct. This kind of law is obeyed, habitually, customarily or as a thing of right manner or of ethical usage. Thus the individual carries his own principles, manners, morals, precepts and practices with him.

The law of human nature fights, wars and persists. It has come down through the centuries as king of the natural (physical) impulses which impulses impel as law. Thus, the mammal human being has no defense, no help, no remedy and no weapon excepting a persistent and constant moral alertness.

The individual must educate himself to cope with this natural instinct which rebels against moral restraint, moral discipline or education. Practice in counter-rolling the cleverness of human nature (and its immoral nature) is the only way of becoming expert in this contest. Experience teaches that human nature is hypnotic, magnetic and occult. It is crafty in its approach. It is subtle, artful or humanly clever in its suggestions, always leading the victim toward its amoral (but natural), unmoral den.

This law of human nature in which the mammal nature holds jurisdiction and dictates its natural action, has been honored and served for centuries. It will take absolute thinking, wisdom, the nature of the dove, the lamb and spiritual love to lead the thinker to the secret place or covert where wisdom makes one wiser than subtlety or the immoral intent.

THE WORD, LETTER

The word *letter* may be defined as a literate character. A letter may be a writing made up of words which are made up of literate characters or alphabetic characters.

The literate characters have several degrees of literacy. The most literate ones are v or f, c, l, u, o, t, r, p, s, d, n, i, and m. The final *e* is used in all degrees, but it has no literate standing. The most illiterate ones depend upon the *a* vowel and assemble themselves or associate themselves, primarily, without the use of the most literate characters.

Again, the word letter may pertain to that which lets, allows, permits, believes, gives leave, lief or permission. In this sense it takes the form of power, truth, law, a principle or thing in authority. There are several of these degrees of authority.

The following table shows the letter as truth:

REALM I

DIVINITY: The divine creative letter—Truth—who conceives, quickens and gives divine form to the ideas specified by The divine creative Intelligence, First Person or Speaker.

Truth—the letter—is The audient One or The Intelligence (person) spoken to.

REALM II

SPIRITUALITY: the person spoken of; the percipient and concipient (compound) intelligence or intelligent entities let, given form as true, or given true form as truth or truths, realities, or Truth's legitimate attributes and qualities.

Here truth or true understanding of Truth is the letter.

REALM III

MORALITY: honesty, veracity, the science of or pertaining to or belonging to con-science; the verities which substantiate moral science.

Here conscience is the letter who lets, honors, and lets honesty's issues come forth.

She lets or allows him dignity and moral authority as wife—correlative thinker.

REALM IV

PHYSICALITY: the feminine element of material knowledge who conceives and lets its issues thrive.

REALM V

SUBANIMALITY: the feminine element of mythology or the accomplice (letter) who permits and carries out (gestates), acts upon, and brings forth the offspring of myths or such legends as oppose The Truth or truth.

In the moral realm the letter takes form in moral axioms; in worthy statements of truths; in worded dictations or written dictums involving or embodying a moral precept; in recipes deduced from spiritual principles; in proverbs, words or verbs of action and condition.

These axioms lead, direct, encourage, offer solution, counsel and consolation to the thinker in transit from humanized letting to moralized understanding.

A printed page sets forth the letter of a concept, but the reader must have the zeal, ardor, active interest, or enthusiasm (spirit); must furnish or have the kindred sentiment; must have an innate sense of moral values in order to glean the substance from the axiom, rule, recipe or remedy. The reader must supply the intelligent energy, the heart and the vital properties which animate the letters.

In the great beginning of all creation Moses presents The Logos-Speaker as saying "let" fourteen times in the twenty-four verses.

The Letter to whom The Logos speaks is The divinely concipient Intelligence or Truth Herself; The Holy Ghost of Biblical language; The invisible and humanly intangible Mother-Spirit of logic, science or truth who conceives, quickens, develops and brings forth all things perceived and set forth by The Holy Spirit.

If there were no Letter—no audient One—to hear and to let why should The Speaker entreat, pray, ask, petition or address His audient One so earnestly and repeatedly?

Human intellect has never discovered The true Creator. Human speculation calls him Father as a Christian gesture, but human hypotheses would never embrace such a God only as the unknown *theos* or deity. Spiritual intelligence appreciates and embraces Elohim as The compound God — Speaker and Hearer or Letter. This is the whole God; the holy, wholly infinite.

In the realm of human intellect and knowledge the human physique usurps the spotlight as speaker, hearer, and actor. In this realm there is no end to prayer and petition, and no end to trouble, because the function of the letter—the element that lets or allows—is not clearly defined, and is not at all understood. Hence humanity keeps on praying.

The divine Letter conceives only that which is divine; only that which originates in The Logos-Mynde.

In the realm of human desires, wills, passions, impulses and propensities, humanity finds itself pursuing its own kind of methods and using its own kind of powers—will-power. It works through intrigue and deceit to satisfy envy, jealousy, rivalry, insatiable ambition and greed to answer its own prayers; to let itself.

In this realm the letter (conceiver accomplice) is the passive element. She is without the science of con-science to teach her how to contraceive that which the instigator presents as the active element. His impulses are without patience, compassion, charity, humanity or moral affection.

In Realm III the letter is the recorder. She gives form (permanent letter form) to the moral law. She is verity conceiving veritably and verifying all recipes, formula, remedy and instruction by means of truth (verity) of Realm II. She multiplies the letter to let it speak again and again as moral law prescribing, instructing, directing and reiterating.

In Realm II the letter is truth recording the infinite spiritual substance and essence of wisdom and the law of his high domain, the principles of his practice, the precepts of his perceptions (and her own conceptions), and the premises (drawn from Realm I) from which the compound thinker of Realm II draws real and substantial conclusions.

The letter who conceives and gives import to a potential thing, also carries it, ponders it, or she harbors it in her mentality during its development. This is (mental) prenatal culture. Thus the *sub*-animal nature is a thriving concept nurtured and cultivated in the human mentality.

The letter who conceives and develops the potential perceptions of wisdom or divine logic, gives spiritual import to them and gives them the benefit of the divine (highest) prenatal culture. Thus there are no physical or animal impulses — no human nature — to be restrained; no potential misfortunes to be contraceived or counteracted by this highly intelligent letter—conceiver.

In the realm of human reasoning, the conceiver or letter takes an important part. Her part is one half. Here she represents an intuitive sense for truth or she recognizes a truth, intuitively. Queen Isabella illustrated this fact when (about the year 1492) she believed, beloved, mothered and sustained a fact or truth which Christopher Columbus had proclaimed and maintained.

She is the letter, cooperator, collaborator, coordinator, verifier, demonstrator, and the concipient, or intuitive intelligence which brought forth this fact or brought it into human view and has now caused it to be recorded as an element of fact. But when Columbus said "The Earth is round and I can prove it" he may not have known that he was dependent upon the natural function of the letter who must honor, conceive, gestate, quicken (act upon, mentally), give form, substance and development to his potential and unlettered, or his unconfirmed and uncorroborated (yet factual) perception.

She is the letter who validated and recorded the whole plan. It was, in that day, a miracle because of the hazard of an uncharted, expansive ocean. But since it was intelligently perceived, and heartily conceived, it was mothered into its factual birth and, like an infant child, it was a tangible, perceivable thing. It stands as a mature fact and as a valid thing.

THE WORD, LIFE

The word life is the Anglo Saxon *lif,* life, or *libban; lifian,* to live; to have life; to continue in life; to be alive. This means to abide, dwell, reside, or to remain alive or in life or in living condition, state and character. The Anglo Saxon *leofian, lybban,* mean live, or to live. They constitute the verb form of the root *lif.* The adjective form is lively, and the adverb form is livelily.

> The Latin *vita* means life as in the word vitamine. The Latin *vivo* (*vivere, victus*), I live or survive.
>
> The Latin *anima* means life as in the words animal and animate.
>
> The Greek *bios* means life as in the words biography, biology and bioplasm (germinal matter from which all living things spring).

There are many conceptions of life. The most common human concept of life is that one which pertains to the living organism or animal life as it appears in the human mammal; as it appears to be animated or breathing organic human matter.

In divine literology the word life cannot exist in the same realm (of literacy, logic, or substance) with death because the letter *i* (its only vowel) is of divine literacy and of interminable, inexhaustible or continual duration. Since death and human animation exist in the realm of human parlance and human knowledge, life is assigned to the realm of spiritual literacy or divine literology.

The following table classifies Life and life:

REALM I
DIVINITY: The Logos-Life; The divine creative Word Life or The living Word and Root of all living ideas; Soul-Origin of all soul-life; The creative, vital Principle or beginning of that which may be correctly attributed to The Logos-Deity; The Root-Principle, Soul and Source of all divinely sustained entities or spiritual identities; Life as a name for The Deity.

REALM II
SPIRITUALITY: the spiritual logician, man or *mon* who lives an uninterrupted and immutable life which is sustained by The Logos-Soul; the soul, mind, thinker or

mon who is unrelated to the popular human conception
of man and living, but directly related to Life; the highest spiritual significance of life as life is manifested by
mon who is in a state of soul-health or divine quickness.

REALM III

MORALITY: the human concept of life or the living virtues; the kind of life or quickness that con-science acknowledges; the kind of aliveness that the moral qualities have within themselves; the vital virtues, such as
honesty with its moral honors; meekness with its susceptibility to Soul's science or logic; humanity with its
sense of equity and justice; temperance with its moral
and conscientious sense of restraint; faith with its up-
turned face, its troth, constancy, confidence and intuitional expectancy of the continuity of good and right;
human sentiment with its better and higher ideals; moral
instinct with its inspiration and thriftiness or liveliness;
patience with its industry and moral zeal or diligence
that chooses to pick up or to gather up and to perform
all moral duty. (Negligence chooses not to pick up or
gather.)

REALM IV

PHYSICALITY: the human physique and its physical
and terminable animation; the human mammal with its
human nature and human knowledge of all things finite
or limited to physical forces; the human animal with its
natural instincts and intellect.

In the realm of humanity (Realm III) the human being assumes
that he is an amalgamation of physical and metaphysical properties;
a compound of spiritual, moral, immoral, unmoral, mental and animal elements. He divides his premises between two or more realms
and thus he has divided or disunited conclusions. He confines himself within the humanly tangible and identifies himself with human
nature and its concepts and he looks to the human intellect for
knowledge of himself, of life and of all things. He finds finity and
discontinuity.

Conscience presents the first glimpse of man's living soul. Conscience teaches the science of soul (one's living soul) within oneself; one's living consciousness (*mon*) as wisdom, spiritual logic,
substance, or that which is vital, valid or founded on truth—the logic
of The Logos; that which is strong and healthy, is in health, in power,
in force, indispensable or divinely essential, forever.

Human intellect, the physical sciences or knowledge, however, have classified life as *anim, anima* and as animal, meaning something having life; a sentient living organism other than a plant; pertaining to the sentient or bodily life of man. The word vital (from *vita*, life) is associated with organic life. The word biology (*bios, bio*) pertains to living organisms or to the science of life which life is in plant or animal organisms. Thus it is that the natural sciences have defined and have classified life, and thus it is that human intellect has accepted it. But this concept of Life is finite and physically localized in a corporeal realm several metaphysical leagues below Life.

Realm III is established as the metaphysical element of Realm IV. Here the human intellect decrees, assigns and allots or measures the human life-time and death-time. Humanity has a very certain sense —limited sense—of life-time and a very certain sense of death-time. Human knowledge is a mandatory will that organizes and disorganizes. It is a well established consolidation of beliefs which govern humanity according to these humanly instituted beliefs. It times life-time. It controls all things under its control. Human knowledge or intellect is made up of the consensus of human will, belief and opinion. It rules by its popularity or by means of its intellectual sovereignty, by means of its well known rules and by means of its familiar human concepts that govern human nature so naturally.

Human knowledge or intellect has its human concept or its apprehension of all things. This apprehension is spontaneous in that the human intellect responds, individually and collectively, to whatever it apprehends. It shapes all concepts and decrees the time of animation and the time-point of inanimation. Thus humanity lives in obedience to these humanly originated rules and these humanly sanctioned traditions, doctrines or sciences, while life, spiritual health or soul-normalcy go on infinitely in Realm II realization.

Life in Realm II is the complete manifestation of Life; the perfect condition of the entity—soul, or individual thinker—who is the spiritual logician born of The Logos-Soul. This wholly logical thinker, this divinely literate representation of The Word, this holy and truly legitimate offspring of The Logos-Spirit, is the spiritual mon or mind or man—a composite of living ideas.

This whole, sound, compound *mon* who lives and who continues forever, forever embodies the properties and elements of infinite continuity. He embodies nothing imperfect to be perfected. He embraces no degree of incompleteness to be made complete; no mutable sense to be changed; no exhaustible substance or limited essence to deteriorate, and no inaccurate, unsound, insincere or unhealthy condition to be cured (ac-cur-ed or made accurate). He is wholly and holy made and wholly actuated. He is divinely (not humanly) actual as mon.

He is wholly literate, fully logical, and completely or worthily legitimate as mon—the holy thinker—whose thoughts originate in The Logos.

He thinks. He does not guess, suppose, assume or conjecture. He understands, as wisdom, standing under The Logos-Life, and as the recipient of life. He is divinely substantial and spiritually substantiated. Thus he stands upon nothing that is *not* divinely solid or spiritually solidified, confirmed or firm. He stands under Divinity. He stands in highest position, place, or positive degree as thinker, forever, because he embodies nothing that may be discontinued. He stands or lives in Realm II.

He realizes his own living condition in relation to Life. He stands sustained by Life, as living thinker with the power to think (conceive and perceive) in this most vividly lighted or enlightened place, realm, degree or sphere, forever, because this realm includes nothing finite, feeble, foolish, corporeal, impotent, mundane, material, unspiritual, physical, mythical or conjectural, even in slightest degree.

Life, in its highest and most logical sense, is one of the names of The divine creative Word, Logos-Life or Deity; The living Root of intelligence and of all literate and legitimate existence.

Life, being a state, quality, condition and character of The Logos-Creator, is divine. This means that both Life and Life's complete and compound manifestation—the logician or thinker of Realm II—are altogether wise, supremely good, lovely, loving, beneficent and sublimely excellent; that this logician (mon) is divine—not human; that he is wisdom and the powers of realization, living in a state of inexhaustible continuity; that he is perpetually articulate as a perfectly compounded or composed idea; that he is entirely coherent and adherent to his Root or living Origin—not as a *humus*-man being, and not as adherent to human knowledge.

The thinker of Realm II lives in a state of wholeness, living soundness or thriving health; in a state of health or spiritual existence which may not be impoverished by humanly instituted systems of knowledge. He lives in that condition which is without either beginning or ending, and which is beyond human capacity to calculate—beyond what is called eonian. He lives in that state of continual health or whole life which can only be defined by the use of symbols and cannot be described or explained to humanity (or Adam-*ity*) at all.

Realm II is beyond Realm III. The Realm II concept or idea of living health (or infinite life or spiritual existence) is far beyond and above those who live in the *humus*-man concept of things, in the lower realms. He thinks, loves, lives, conceives, perceives, acts upon, sets forth, quickens and brings forth. He possesses infinite energy and an interminable power of motivation and an ability to appreciate his Origin—The Logos-Spirit that motivates him.

This thinker of Realm II is positively true and real, but not real or not so to human appreciation. Humanity would bring Life, life, infinite or complete health, love, and all of the Realm II substance down to Realm IV where the human intellect could appreciate them, feel them and enjoy them. But humanity and its knowledge or intellect *is* mortality. Its origin is allegorical and Adamic; theoretical, not vitally logical. Humanity generates, germinates, gestates and creates its own kind of life and by means of its own kind of exhaustible, calculable or divinely impoverished materials. Humanity presents and represents itself as the human race which embraces the human physique, the physical brain, intellect, knowledge and humanly instituted learning, but which learning does not embrace an iota of soul life, health continuity, or Soul-Life, and is embraced only within human perception of what humanity calls life or living.

The thinker is freeing himself from humanity and from its limited and small world of what it calls the living; from that which has been humanized, physicalized, and mortalized; from that which human intellect has acquired, created and recreated or caused to stand in physical evidence of its physicalized conception or perception. This creation is three worlds, three realms or metaphysical spheres removed from Life and from The Logos, from logic, from literacy (The Word), and from The vital Principle of life.

Life—as Life—is a primal, radical condition of the living Logos; a vital, radical Root-Principle of life—which life is the legitimate attribute of The Logos-Root Source, and which life is the state of being of the *mon,* mind, or thinker of Realm II.

The state of being The Supreme Being, and the state of being the supreme *mon* (man) embraces the only two possible states of life or of living—according to the logic of The Logos, and the literacy of The Word.

Humanity has named Eve *Vita* or life. But the literate *i* vowel in *vita,* and the one in life cannot be classified with either Eve or Adam. The initial *E* in Eve is the very opposite of the final *e* in life (Anglo Saxon *lif*), even as the teeming Eve is the opposite of the purely spiritual conceiver of Realm II who propagates wisdom's vital kind.

Eve is human activity, physical aliveness, or the conceiver of all characters (Cain or Cains) who would possess all, who would acquire all, who would get all with spear or lance (skill) to amplify self.

This kind of activity is without a vital principle or a living premise; is without either moral vivacity or spiritual vitality; is without a vivid precept. It is the activity of moral ignorance, and is without the energies of a living conscience to maintain it. Eve acts upon, quickens, and propagates her Eve-ill kind.

This Eve activity is human nature in action, quickening or animating its own kind, which kind is subject to total devitalization or the totally inanimate condition of the human mammal. It has no maintained existence above Realm IV.

Life, in its highest, infinite or universal sense, is not easily defined to humanhood, because human parlance has already so thoroughly established life as it pertains to humanity and as it is taught by human knowledge.

The word life, as a noun, includes the verb live or living. This kind of living is unknown to humanhood because human parlance teaches such verbal action as pertaining to human persons, animals, human mammals, physical formations or vegetables.

The Word Life, and its living realities which express Life, can best be defined to the human ear as a verb—a functioning quickening force—with a specific function to perform. Thus by outlining the function of Life or by showing its action as the Cause, Source, Beginning or initial Principle of life or spiritual living; by showing its action—its phenomenal action—upon humanity, we may better understand Life as the vital law noumenon.

The following table shows that phenomenal action:

REALM   I   DIVINITY: Life.

REALM   II   SPIRITUALITY: life; spiritual health or living continuity of immortal substance (the stance under Life); understanding.

REALM III   MORALITY: the living con-science or the science with a living moral principle whose practical or essential phenomena is seen in honesty, veracity, sobriety, profundity, compassion, charity, human affection, chastity, fidelity, modesty, humility, trustworthiness, hope or moral prosperity, moral courage or heartiness, moral stamina or understanding and all of the morally vital qualities; all that is vitally essential to mankind's moral and spiritual progress, promotion or furtherance.

> That which is morally metaphysical or beyond physics or above physicality or its figure and form, and out of reach of its death or disintegrating processes.

REALM IV   PHYSICALITY: death and all of the antonyms of life and of the moral-spiritual phenomena of Life.

Physicality or the human physique is animated by breath and is physically tangible and physically formed as the human animal or mammal according to human nature.

Life is The Great (I AM) Quickener or quickening intelligence that functions or works through intelligence—not through human impulse, human nature, human knowledge or human intellect. Life is *of* The I AM (I am Spirit); The Logos-Spirit.

Life is The Holy Ghost, The conceptual intelligence conceiving, quickening and sustaining that which is intangible, invisible and insensible to human sensibilities. Hence ghostly because Life is an element of Spirit which is bodiless to human sense—even non-existent because of natural estrangement or lack of communication. Thus human animation begins and ends within its own physical bounds, two realms removed from life and three realms removed from Life, The I am The Logos-Infinity.

The human being, the human race or mankind may reach life only by way of Realm III, wherein it finds moral power, force, energy, stamina, vigor, strength, validity or vitality to promote or to move or to carry it up into Realm II where life lives as the function of Life in action, quickening that which is born of Life—The divine creative Principle—in Realm I.

The human race cuts itself off from soul-life or spiritual life by confining, restricting or limiting itself to Realm IV; by imprisoning and encoffining itself in physicality.

Life, in its divine, infinite, universal and ever abiding sense, must be something that cannot deteriorate; something exhaustless, wholly metaphysical or incorporeal, and immediate and immaculate; something in the form of intelligence, logic (The Logos), or that Mynde of The Logos which ever thinks, ever keeps (is preserved) and ever keeps thinking. It must be something like consciousness, since *mon*— the living and ever spirited thinker—is in the form of soul consciousness or intelligence, which intelligence is originated by The Logos. Thus life, as it pertains to man or *mon* and his consciousness (his conscious life), is like that of his Origin, his living Root-Life.

Humanity, humanhood, or the human race is inclined to accept a transitory concept of physical animation or of the animated physique, or the human animal vitality as the sole concept of life; but life may not be materialized, mortalized or confined to that which humanity humanizes or reduces to human impulse, pulsation or that animal which throbs, pulsates, breathes (air) and exists as *earth-man*—a mundane creature subject to fratricide, homicide, suicide, infanticide and so on. The animosities peculiar to humanity, are not conducive to soul existence. Transitoriness of conscience is unthinkable. A transitory consciousness is illogical. Conscience lives in soul, not with the physically minded. Conscience is that vital, ever-living element that pervades intelligence. Neither conscience nor intelligence may be mortalized or humanized by humanity. They are the vital properties of the soul, and like wisdom keep (alive) forever, sustained and maintained by The Logos-Mynde.

THE WORD, LIGHT

The word *light* comes from Anglo Saxon *leoht*. It gives little or no idea for analysis, excepting that the literate form of the word light is of greater literate value and virtue than the rudimental *leoht*.

The word light is a universal word turning in all directions, or in four parts of speech:

As a verb, it means to illuminate.
As an adjective, it means bright; full of light.
As an adverb, it means lightly; brightly.
As a noun, it means many literal and figurative, physical and metaphysical things.

The highest and most literate concept of light is that one which the sun or sol presents to Earthlings, or from the Earth's point of view. The sun at noonday is brightness itself, and the absence of that light is darkness, according to the literate sense of things, the literal sense and the physical perception or sense of things. The sun therefore is the highest humanly comprehensible figure from which to draw a highly figurative sense of light. It is the most familiar material figure from which to deduce and introduce the metaphorical or metaphysical sense of light and the source of soul-light.

This treatise deals with words as words. The sun, sol or solar light is treated exhaustively by the natural or physical sciences. This may be called natural light. This treatise does not undertake to inform its readers on any point concerning artificial light or other classifications of the various causes, sources, effects or phenomena attributable to these.

This treatise begins with The Word or The Logos as Source and Cause of highest metaphysical sense of light or enlightenment; as Creator and creative Beginning; as Origin of logical and literate light, discernment, wisdom or the spiritual seer.

In the universe of Soul, light is derived from Soul. The Logos-Soul emits light to the ear of understanding, even as the sun (sol) emits light to the Earth (the ear-th). As the sun is the only giver of light to Earth, so Soul is the sole and only Giver of light or divine enlightenment (ideas, essential realities or substantial verities) to the ear and eye of the discerning thinker who witnesses to what he sees. Thus the thinker may be fully enlightened and wholly mindful of the logic of The Logos and the literacy of The Word.

The following table will classify the degrees of light:

REALM I

DIVINITY: The Word emitting words of wisdom; The Logos from which all true, real, pure and genuine logic emanates or issues forth.

REALM II

SPIRITUALITY: the realm of spiritual enlightenment; the sphere of universal vision; the thinker discerning all things in highest degree of direct light.

REALM III

MORALITY: the realm of moral enlightenment, or light reflected from Realm II (not direct light from Realm I). Here the thinker observes the science of con-science which is reflected or re-emitted from Realm II logic and wisdom.

This realm enjoys the logical and literate light which is redirected, reiterated, replenished and reideated by the thinker of Realm II. It enjoys the honor and glory of honesty which is a lesser form of spiritual potency— the moral version of power. It has loyalty, fidelity, faith, courage and confidence which are the lesser forms of Realm II discernment.

This moral realm exists as the morally enlightened; as the morally correct and accurate thinker; as the science and art of right reasoning which he deduces from the reflected logic of Realm II.

This moral realm is of lower degree of light intensity than Realm II.

The brilliant light of Realm I is of no use to this realm. It would only dazzle and bewilder (daze or confuse) rather than instruct. It has infinite power of illumination, whereas this realm has capacity to utilize the light which conscience brings from soul, or which moral intuition brings from wisdom.

REALM IV

PHYSICALITY: the realm of human learning, knowledge, or intellect which teaches what light is.

REALM V

IMMORALITY: the realm of human darkness where the light rays of soul (conscience) cannot obtrude or intrude; the realm of contradiction or denial of light, in its moral-spiritual meanings.

Light, originating in The Logos-Soul, reaches Earth (ear-th or the human ear) only in the degree that the human eye enjoys inward, soul-vision to see it, and only in as much as the human eye is opened to discern or to differentiate between what soul presents and what human intellect presents.

The human discernment of Realm III is torn between the evident realities which Realm IV presents—as enlightenment—and the spiritually scientific enlightenment which conscience presents as coming from wisdom or soul in Realm II. But there is a gradual lofting or lifting of hope which tends to look upward (heavenward) for light of the continual sort—the soul sort—and as Realm III looks upward to wisdom for vision, to the spiritual entity (soul) for light, it sees all things in a better, wiser and more essential light.

It is evident that a clear conscience is a most essential factor in clear thinking. Justice, equity, compassion, meekness, kindness, sincerity and such virtues are like a flame (a living, burning flame) of moral light and energy. They are candid lights lighting the way. They are splendid things or qualities reflecting their moral splendor. These human virtues or worthy qualities are alight and alive with the vital science of conscience. They are moral integers who are sagacious, pious and morally peculiar. They see through or by means of the moral lens, the moral instinct, intuition, sense or sentiment. This lens is conscience. This lens magnifies the elements of soul and clarifies the atmosphere of soul for the conscientious one who aspires to rise beyond and above the human horizon, to peer into the realm or atmosphere of wisdom.

Wisdom comes forth from Soul in a direct line, even as a sunbeam comes forth from the sun in a direct line. The light of Soul or the direct light of wisdom (soul) is of such divine brilliance as to be dazzling to the eye of humanhood, even as the direct light of the sun is dazzling to the eye of humanhood, and must therefore be reduced to lower degrees of intensity or brilliance, in order to be morally practicable to humanhood.

The infinite power of enlightenment belongs to The Logos-Soul who, as God, is creator of light, and who, as The Word is illuminator and giver of light, which light takes form in understanding, in spiritual substance or under-stanc-ing; takes form in wisdom, in the powers of ideation (perception and conception), reflection, fruition, and expression.

The thinker of Realm II presents all of the essential elements of reality and all of the powers of essential and substantial realization; all of the faculties for the full utilization of infinite Soul light. This thinker thinks or discerns in highest degree of light, for he is a soul entity reflector, reflecting the Realm II light to Realm III. This thinker perceives in highest degree of spiritual light, direct light or radiant energy. He thinks, reflects and conceives by the divine noonday sun, irradiated through the logic and literacy and law principles of The Logos; through the brilliance of The Word.

Wisdom represents this spiritual seer, this fully enlightened and brilliant thinker, wholly mindful of himself as soul—thinking in the radiant light of Soul. Wisdom's power of re-illumination serves to teach Realm III.

The moral thinker of Realm III enjoys morally radiant energy in the form of faith, confidence, fidelity, hope or moral prosperity and expectancy. He radiates affection, patience, humanity, modesty, compassion, trustworthiness and all such virtues that make him the moral seer and sage.

The moral thinker's conscience is his radiant light within, teaching him as master of moral science and law.

The immoral realm is impervious to moral light. It is environed with a moral opaqueness which best suits its beclouded, unconscientious or soulless mentality; best suits its contradictory and wholly darkened, sensual, material personality.

Light or spiritual enlightenment typifies the day of The Logos and the spiritual logician; the day of divine brilliance or universal light and literacy wherein is no spiritual ignorance or moral night doubting and contradicting soul.

THE WORD, LOGIC

The word *logic* is born of The Word; born of its Root (root word), or Logos. It comes directly from this divine or divinely rudimental Source. Hence The divine creative Logos or The Word is capitalized because it is a name belonging to The Deity, and thus the word logic is that kind of science which pertains to The Logos, is like The Logos or is made of like rational substance or scientific essence.

The word logic is derived from the Greek *logos* which means many things: speech, ratio, description, science, reason, word, saying, oracle or thing.

The suffix is *-ic* (*-ikos*). It signifies or means that *log-ic* or *log-ikos* pertains to The Logos, is of The Logos, or belongs to The Logos, or that it is the science and the oracle of The Logos; the literate science of The Word. It is the speech or the message or is the monologue (oration) presented *by* The Logos, which is The divine creative Word. This suffix means also that logic is characteristic of The Logos; that it is patterned after The Logos; that it resembles and is peculiar to The Logos; that it is comparable to The unique and singular speech of The Logos.

The Logos is reason itself. Therefore logic is of or it pertains to that rational power (that full ratio of reasoning power) which reason or truth herself presents.

The logos is science. Therefore logic is the science and art of reasoning; the science and art of correct and accurate thinking; the science of its Principle-Logos.

The Logos from which logic is immediately and thoroughly derived is infinite; is universal; is divine. Therefore logic is unconfined as to its literacy, its science and its principles, which principles belong to The Logos-Premise. This makes logic divinely practical or practicable. It makes logic conclusively like its Premise.

Logos, as The Word or Speech, teaches and embraces all of literacy. Logos, as thing (The Thing, itself) is the re, the *res,* the real or *realis;* is the genuine, the absolute, the real, and the spiritually veritable thing, cause or divine entity, from which all logical realities and real verities issue forth. It embraces and embodies all law, all precept, and all recipes or instructions, rules and directions for confirming this real logic individually.

Logic is *not* made up of humanly established sayings, axioms, adages, maxims, or excellent moral utterances. Logic leaves off where

human reasoning begins, where human intellect or the humanly instituted sciences begin. Logic is science of highest degree. It is the
essence of The Logos-Esse; the substance of The Logos-Speech or
Word. It is driven, spirited, inspired, motivated or actuated by The
Logos-Spirit, and it constitutes the substance or the understanding of
the logician. This logician is of highest ratio of power (of realization or of infinite demonstration) and of highest degree of excellence
or logical virtue. This logician is the full or complete representation
or expression of The Logos-Verity. He is skilled and versed in the
logic of Verity, or in the verities of The Logos-Truth.

The Logos is The Word, wording all truly literate speech or sayings. The Logos is Speech or Speaker or description, describing, outlining, specifying or setting forth exactly what He would form or
would create. The Logos is that Speech and Speaker who describes
ideas or puts them into specifically worded form, to be conceived, sustained, quickened or acted upon logically, literately, and divinely by
The concipient or audient Logos.

The Logos has the quality, state or condition of literate continuity.
The logician has the same quality and is of the same continual, im-
mutable or perpetual condition. He is as continual as his Root, his
Premise or Logos-Principle.

The Logos, as a word, embraces two *o* vowels. They are of highest
and fullest or greatest literate and logical capacity. They denote
continuity and infinite capacity or capability. They signify highest
ratio of intelligence. The Logos may be written speech, scribed, script,
or scriptural; may be inscribed, described or engraved. It may be
committed to memory or impressed upon the heart or the soul of the
logician. It may be a record or the log of the logos (the log of *gos*)
which logos and which *gos* mean God and mean Good. This log and
this logic, being infinite and universal, never closes its record and never
ends or comes to a finis or conclusion.

The Logos lessons, assignments, lectures, speeches, revealments
or constant instructions never cease pouring out the logic, the science, the literacy and the infinite judgment or the universal wisdom
which the logician utilizes. Thus it is that The Logos and the logician are of infinite vitality or quickness. The Logos is infinitely vivid.

The following table shows, by comparison, that which logic and
the logician are, and that which they are not; shows the absolute
logic in the relationship between the logician and The Logos:

REALM I
DIVINITY: The Logos; The Word; Good or God; The
divine creative Word or Soul; The sole Creator; The infi-

nite Premise and Principle from which all logic, literacy and law issue forth.

Realm II

SPIRITUALITY: the logician and his infinitely logical conclusions, conceptions and ideations; the radically good or divine logic which the logician embraces; the intelligence and understanding deduced from The Logos.

Realm III

MORALITY: the human intellect which is a collection of knowledge. Here the only element of logic deduced from Realm II is that which con-science presents to human reason. It is the science and art of reasoning, or the science of correct and accurate soul thinking and of infinitely logical, literate and legitimate thinking.

The human sciences and the orthodox learning offset or counterbalance the influence of conscience somewhat since the premise of conscience is in Realm II and the premise of the human -*ologies* is in Realm IV.

Realm IV

PHYSICALITY: the corporeally evident world, called natural or physical; the premise of the natural or physical sciences; the home of human nature, human knowledge, the human physique, the human animal, or the human mammal.

This Realm IV presents to the logician, only the humanly tangible symbol of Realm II, by its expression of the three natural kingdoms—animal, vegetable and mineral. These physically or humanly natural kingdoms are the humanly visible teachers of beauty, form, precision, grace, color and delicacy, on the one hand, and teachers of the logic which involves great power, great wisdom, magnanimity or great soul, on the other hand. The delicacy of a flower contrasts, obviously, with the greatness of a mountain, and the mobility of an animal contrasts with the immobility or fixity of a mountain.

Realm IV is like an open book, elaborately illustrated in infinite color. The color is true. It is not touched by human hand; not misrepresented, but it is presented to humanity, even as The Word, The Logos, is presented, in its true color, and in such a form of logic, literacy, and principle that it is suspected of being a miracle. A flower is the miracle of the vegetable kingdom, yet humanity calls it natural —humanly or physically natural.

Realm IV teaches infinite logic by means of finite or physical—animal, vegetable, and mineral—illustrations.

Realm III teaches infinite logic—the logic of The Logos — by means of con-science and its moral instincts; by means of the science and art of reasoning conscientiously, or by means of morally confident correct thinking. Here in this realm, conscience is school master, constantly endeavoring to teach and to establish the science that pertains to Realm II, rather than give way to the learning or the knowledge of Realm IV with its exhaustible and radically physical aspects.

That which human intellect has found to be satisfactory as science, is only that which physicality or nature exhibits of spiritual order, coordination, operation, cooperation, natural relation, and correlation of ideas, divinely outlined and divinely created by The Logos. Therefore, physical perfection, such as a flower might symbolize, is only the thing sent forth or set forth to human view, to familiarize humanhood with the metaphysical perfection of Realm II and its kind of logic.

The physical completeness of the three earthly kingdoms (animal, vegetable and mineral) only symbolizes or gives veritable sign of the spiritual completeness of Realm II, where logic, or verity, and sentiment or love collaborate; where power and reason or wisdom consolidate in understanding to form an infinitely substantial realm, which may be typified by the solidly fundamental, mineral Earth.

The animal kingdom symbolizes all that pertains to the spiritual animus, *anima, anim,* or *animos,* before the human intellect sensualized, humanized, physicalized or gave it its physically sentient or sensual nature.

Human intellect, human knowledge, and human nature have established a carnal animus, soul, or mind. They have honored even the sub-animal nature, to give it breath, or life or animation or passion to war against the loving and lovely principles of Realm II.

The vegetable kingdom typifies The quickening Spirit or Mother Spirit—highest conception of nature. It sets forth the beauties and graces of soul. It signifies the health, the growth, or the thrifty, lively activity peculiar to Realm II. It portrays the ever vegetating and ever living vigor of the thinker—his power to multiply, reproduce and replenish the Ear or the Earth with wisdom and loveliness.

Logic, literacy and law or spiritual principles constitute the power of realization, compound and complete understanding, the understander, and the logician or idea. This compound logician perceives as male and conceives, ears, hears, understands or comprehends as female; speaks or sets forth as male and brings forth as female.

The Logos is The Principle of logic or of these spiritual principles

which constitute the logician's power of realization. The Logos is a
compound of Speaker and Hearer; of Him who sets forth and Her
who brings forth; of Him who perceives and puts ideas into words
and of Her who conceives and makes potential ideas evident, manifest, or spiritually real and able to speak for themselves.

The Logos or Word is a compound of The percipient or petitionary
One and The concipient or audient One. This concipient One is The
Mother element of The compound Logos. She is least understood,
because most obscure, altogether silent in Her gestative function, and
in Her divinely metaphysical realizations or revelations or creations
or demonstrations. Thus the spiritual logician of Realm II is a compound of percipient and concipient elements—male and female elements; the male breathing forth that perception which must be given
form (literate form), must be recorded, written and made readable;
and the female bringing forth that which constitutes all of the essential
properties of the perception spoken of; bringing forth that which she
has made intelligible to all readers and comprehensible to all thinkers
who are of her degree and ratio of intelligence.

THE WORD, Love

The word *love* comes from Anglo Saxon *luf,* and from *lufian,* to love. This root forms also the word lief, which means willing, ready, agreeable, gladly, pleasing, dear or free. Thus to belove is to believe, or to *beluf.* To be beloved is to be believed, and to believe is to give leave or to grant permission. To be dearly loved is to be gladly believed. The form which means leave, belief or believe is *lyfan.* It means to permit.

The word love is one of the most shockingly misunderstood words of all of the universally divine words. It is not only stolen from its spiritual environment, but it is demoted to humanity's unspiritual, material or wholly physical environment. Thus conceived human nature becomes its nature, whereas human nature is opposite in nature.

Many generations of human progress, moral achievement, and of spiritual advancement may bring the human race nearer to love's logical, literate and legitimate realm or environment. Love's era is approaching. Human nature will *not* change, but the moral standards *will* change and climb. Moral nature will transcend and will leave human nature farther and farther behind. Moralization is going on. It is lifting human hope to consider the loftier conceptions of love. Moral faith, troth, constancy and affection are believing and beloving more genuinely; are learning to look higher and higher for that which is worthy of trust, troth and love.

Love is a divinely animated sentiment; an expression of The Logos-*mentis* (*psuche*) soul or mind, or (*animus*) soul or mind. It feels. Its function is to be conscious of Love and of loving or of cherishing; to be conscious of or to have the sense of loving and of being loved by Love, and of being loved because love is lovable and spiritually and completely lovely; because love is the most adorable virtue.

Love is that consciousness which feels or considers by way of being in touch with Love, or by way of its spiritual sensitiveness and intactness. Love is the feeling of Love expressing Her divine Self; the feeling of Intelligence being tender and considerate, being thoughtful, being wholly aware and cognizant of its own intelligent images. It is the feeling and the choosing of Intelligence. It is the highly esteemed and highly intelligible quality which functions under the direction, and in the presence of The Logos-Intelligence. Love partakes also of the power of this intelligence, because love is a factor or an element of logic or of science in its highest form. It is *not* a humanly sensible feeling. It is not personal adoration.

Love is an intelligent conclusion drawn from The Logos-Premise or The Love-Principle. It is a spiritual concept derived from and fathered by The Logos-Precept or beginning of logic, literacy and law (or legitimate being). Thus love is a vital or living reflection or it is the logical thinker reflecting or thinking or considering or pondering or esteeming in the most intelligent or wisest way; in the most elect, elegant, select, holy and highly diligent way; in the most highly principled way.

Love in its highest classification, is a name for The Deity, and love, in its higher (spiritual) classification, is a name for mon—the thinker and worshipper of Love. This kind of loving, beloving and believing lifts and belofts all worshippers to the loft of heaven or into spirituality; lifts, transposes and translates all thinkers.

It is simpler to explain to humanity what love is, by mentioning that which love is *not*. Love takes no cognizance of the human patterns, but the human inclination is to worship, love, and idolize the human person or physique, and other physical things. Indeed it is a very popular form of idolatry, since humanity gives lief, belief and its best understanding of love to physicality and since humanity finds it to be dear, pleasing and agreeable.

The amativeness of the physical realm is a popular burlesque that portrays the complete absence and ignorance of love. It is the human concept of love, physicalized and lost in human nature, which is the sub-animal, mammal nature. This sub-animal nature constitutes the pit or snare into which all physically minded human beings have fallen, and have thereby lost their metaphysical treasures.

Love is in no way associated with the magnetic, electric, romantic, esthetic or humanly ethical practices for love and for loving. Love is not an image or an ideate form on the human, mental level. Human affection and human charity serve that level or that realm. Human compassion and human kindness are more practical and applicable for human utility. Love may not be affectionately impressed by romantic, human manipulations.

The *o* vowel in the word love indicates its capacity to enfold. It indicates feminine capability to enwomb by means of the mental, spiritual matrix of the logically adept, fertile womanhood, completely pregnable to wisdom's precepts and principles.

The Anglo Saxon *luf* and *lufian* use the letter *f* instead of *v*. These letters are interchangeable, as in the words life and live.

The verbal action of the word love is to *luff*, elate, inspire, exalt, or to elevate; to lead or guide into the *lyft*, loft, or higher degree or higher atmosphere of harmony, unanimity and logical continuity or literate reality.

Love is the companion and the affinity of wisdom. She is an element of verity and of logic; a member of understanding or of purely spiritual, universal substance. She is in no way related to the realm of human thinking. She is a spiritual quality that may not be reduced to human consistency. Love does not simplify itself in order to accommodate human kind. It does not become illogical in order to be more kind to the human race, even as a numeral character does not become less logical in order to accommodate a school boy's mistake in mathematics. Love is spiritually didactic or scientific. Mathematics never has changed in order to be kind to humanity. If it were to do so the whole world would be in chaos. There is no miracle in mathematical perfection, even as there is no miracle in spiritually natural love, or in the true understanding of Love. There is no miracle in wisdom. It is an element of reality and intelligence. Numeral science may not be physicalized, humanized or finitized, because of its infinitely logical nature and its perfectly literate nature.

Love enjoys a complete and perfect immunity from the false human concepts and misunderstanding of love. Human imagination perceives her to be a pleasingly sentient dreamy sense sentiment or a personified or personalized thing which may be captured by the human dreamer, and may be held captive or embodied in somebody.

Love is an element of science because she may be classified and defined, as the following table shows:

REALM   I   DIVINITY: The Logos-Love; The Love Principle of love.

REALM   II   SPIRITUALITY: the logician-love who loves, worships and adores Love; love is the daughter of Love, the sister of truth or intelligence; the wife of wisdom (bringing forth his holy or wholly and highly exalted vital sentiments).

Wisdom's sentiments are projected as wise issues, in Realm III.

(This is love's loft.)

REALM III   MORALITY: the human sentiments; human affection; ethical regard; moral reverence; sincerity; honest charity; true compassion or the patience of verity and conscience.

REALM IV   PHYSICALITY: the human nature and its
                natural passions.

REALM V   UNMORALITY: the inhuman hates; igno-
                rance of the higher sentiments and of ver-
                ity or the science of con-science.

If love were not a member of the faculty of scientific realities
(intelligence), or if there were no love element in Spirituality it would
seem stern, very precise, scholastic, exacting, formally wise. But
love is there to inspire, vivify, exalt or glorify.

Love is a science because it can be defined and classified. It is a
science because it is an element of reason; a rational faculty or entity;
a spiritually rational power to think, to ponder, to consider, to discern and to conceive. Love is a science because she is an element of
logic. She is the power or the highest ratio of appreciation of those
things (qualities, states, conditions and characters) which are wholly
and purely lovely, loving and lovable or appreciable to Love—The
Logos.

Neither love nor Love are humanly appreciable. They are praiseworthy but the human race is not worthy of love, but of human affection. The human race does not merit and cannot appreciate love
for she is not reasonable or sensible or estimable to the human race
or to human nature. Indeed love is two realms removed from human
nature and is not natural or native to humanity but is foreign to it.

Love is the most lovely and loving rational faculty; the most lovely
metaphysical quality; the most lovable and holy (completely) adorable character; the most wholly (perfectly) spiritual condition of
being; a divinely assigned state of being; the dearest and most beloved
attribute of Being.

Love, being the offspring of The divine creative Love, is altogether
intelligent, is divinely excellent, is supremely lovely, loving, beneficent
and good; is positively true, is troth and is trustworthy or constant;
is actually existent, is perpetually articulate or expressed, and is of
infinitely literate and logical continuity as inexhaustible love.

Thus love is queen of that kingdom (spiritual domain) in which
wisdom dominates as virile perception or discernment.

Love stands in authority, as a divinely stable or substantiated
science; as a power in power or in force in the realm of infinite substance. Love is a science because her Source and Root is The Logos
—Father of all logic, man or *mon*. She is that spiritually powerful
senti-mentality that senses the most intelligent qualities of wisdom's
mentality.

Love, as love exists in mon—the logician, is the very phenomenal image of The Logos-Love which is The Noumenon of both mon and love; The Source of both mon and love. They exist as attributes or as images attributable only to The Logos Source. They may *not* be humanized or mammalized.

Love is an element of science or of logic; a firmly fixed element of infinite literacy. She is constancy herself, while human misconception of love is unstable or inconstant. Human affection vacillates. The human heart breaks, but love is aloof from human avidities and from personal affinities. Love feels the dignity and magnanimity of soul, the bliss of reality, and the joy of infinitely immaculate ideation, fruition and realization. Love understands the universal or divine language which is foreign to humanhood. Her spiritual philology is gloriously interesting and thoroughly inspiring.

Love is a thinker of full ratio and of infinite spiritual proportion. The human heart cannot encompass her, but there is not one who has not felt the holy, heavenly touch of love; not one who has not been lifted to her spiritual loft for one brief moment: not one who has not been in her angelic or pure presence to be inspired by her beyond words to express or to explain.

Professor Drummond says that love is the greatest thing in the world. But is it *in* the world (the mundane realm)? No, neither love nor Love can be of the mundane, worldly or earthly. Love is purely spiritual, and Love is divine. Both are heavenly. Therefore, Mr. Drummond must have been very much out of this (mundane) world when he found this out. He must have been in love's loft.

Love (capitalized) is Good or goodness of superlative or divine degree. Love (not capitalized) is spiritually pure and good—the attribute, substance, essence or entity of divine birth—and is good (not capitalized).

Love has all of the distinguishing characteristics of The Logos-Spirit. It is a verbal noun. It is moved, inspired or spirited by The Logos-Spirit.

Humanity, materiality, corporeity or human nature cannot grasp the significance of so infinite a thing as love.

The Anglo Saxon *thing* means also cause. Authorities name *thing* as one of the synonyms for The Logos. Thus The Logos-Love is cause, maker, producer and origin of love, while love is the thing effected, realized or produced.

The function of love is to love, to belove, to bring belief (and relief from that which is not spiritually lovely), to relieve, to help, to comfort, to free or to give lief, gladly, fully and completely. Love is divine sentiment flowing out. In this sense, love is an orator—a flowing out of loving speech, prayer or pleading. Here the Greek *rhetor* means, a flowing out as oration of master, teacher and tutor. Thus Love or love is teacher of logic, science, truth and speech or the science and art of divinely expressive speech or discourse.

The human race is inclined to worship, to idealize or to idolize persons, humanly prized things and objects. These humanly patterned, humanly outlined and humanly maintained concepts are the objects of human affection; prized, praised, idolized or idealized persons which are the phenomena of the worshipful concept so conceived to be.

The human concepts are mutable. The human ideals are subject to change. The human idol is subject to change. Clay feet and human imperfections may begin to show as characteristic of human nature. So are all human ideals and idols worshipped only so long as the worshipful illusion or concept lives or is uppermost in the human mentality.

The human race is inclined to worship that which it should only feel kindly toward; that which should excite compassion, charity or human affection. Love, as The Supreme Being to be worshipped, is a divine and divinely constant or continual Being. Love, as the spiritual being to be loved, is a purely, wholly or holy spiritual being, *under*standing or standing directly and immediately *under* Love. Human affection is the best human sentiments and ideals deduced from heaven—where love lives and loves, spiritually, really and constantly.

Humanity must cherish affection. It cannot sustain love in its kingdom, because the human being's kingdom cherishes unspiritual substance; that sustenance which keeps human nature or its physique alive, attractive or humanly glorified.

The human being does not know, discern or entertain love. It can, however, sustain, maintain and entertain human affection. But it has no spiritual substance with which to sustain love, and no sense of its incorporeal nature.

The word love is made up of highly literate (spiritually qualified) letters. It is not appreciable to human nature or to humanity. Human perception of love is unspiritual.

The letter *o* in the word love signifies eternity or an eternal, interminable kind of love and of lover. It pertains to Realm II where both love and lover are purely, wholly, holy and completely spiritual. The *o* vowel signifies that greatest spiritual capacity to love and the greatest capacity to be divinely lovely, loving and lovable.

Love leaves off where human personality begins or where the human being (person) begins to be the lover. Thus the *a* vowel in the French and Latin *amo, amor* and *amour* is more appropriate. The human person takes the role of *amour pro pre* (self esteem) or human pride loving itself and taking love from another, rather than spiritual love which is a sense and sentiment giving love to another.

The adjective amorous (from *amare,* to love) literally physicalizes the word and brings it down to a physical or corporeal state, quality and condition of being. Here it pertains to sexual affection, desire (enamour or enamor), enjoyment, appetite, or the inclination or disposition to be influenced, charmed, captivated, excited, inflamed, impassioned or enamored with, of or by a person, a human mammal being, a corporeal or physical body or animate organism.

Physical or natural science may best explain these magnetic and sympathetic or electric forces, and how they excite, magnetize and manipulate the human being, body or person, which person lives in Realm IV, according to natural science and the authority of human nature.

Love is an element of science, a teacher of divine logic, and a scientific worshipper of Love, worshipping in a spiritually intelligent manner.

Humanity worships its highest and best concept of Love. It reverences, fears, venerates or looks upon Love with holy veneration (deference). But humanity's concept of love or of Love makes it impossible for it to worship Love in a spiritually intelligent manner. Hence human affection must be schooled and disciplined and tutored and taught how to render divine honor to Love; how to acknowledge and adore so supremely and infinitely lovely a thing; how to love.

Love may not be humanized or reduced to human consistency or to human nature or to humanity. If it were to be so reduced, humanity would be its mortality since humanity and mortality are synonymous.

Love may not be localized or confined in Realm IV because human knowledge or science is the antonym of love and its science expressed by con-science and human affection (in Realm III), and where the conception of Love is semi-humanized, is semi-destructible, mutable, exhaustible and semi-finite or not purely and wholly logical or logically literate. Love may not be reduced to illogical, illiterate, or divinely illegitimate status; may not be mixed or conglomerated with human ideals and dreams. But humanity itself must be converted; must be lifted out of its dream.

Love is a scientific or logical idea belonging to Realm II. Only the wholly or holy or fully logical thinker may embrace love. Only eternity or divine continuity can unfold or make evident so transcendently immaculate a thing.

THE WORD, MAN

The word *man* comes from the Anglo Saxon man, meaning think. The forms *mon, monn* and *mann* mean think, and the form *munan* means mynd or mind and mynde.

The word man, having the *a* vowel, may not exist in the same literate and legitimate realm with mind or *mon* because the *i* and *o* vowels are of higher degree of literacy. The *i* and *u* vowels, as in mind or *munan,* elevate or promote the word man. The frame letters *m* and *n* are stable in each form. Thus Mind (capitalized) is of highest classification of literacy; mind or *mon* is of higher classification or degree of literacy; *munan* or *mon* is of high (metaphysical) classification; man is of physical classification, and may not be called a thinker, because the physique does not think, deduce or conclude. The human concept of man is low, but intellectually popular.

The Latin *vir* means man. It lifts man out of the physical conception, into the moral and metaphysical realm, because this *vir,* meaning man, is the root of the word virtue, and virtue is his state, quality and condition.

The Greek *anthropos* means man, human being, mammal.

The Anglo Saxon *thencan* means think, thinker, thought.

The French pensive (*pensum*) means to think, to weigh, to ponder or to contemplate; quiet reflection; thoughtfulness. Thus mon is thinker; the state, quality and condition of being thoughtful. He functions as thought itself, and as virtue and virginity of highest human comprehension, and not as human nature.

The following table further classifies and defines man as man, as *mon,* as mind—the thinker—and as *munan:*

REALM I
DIVINITY: The divine creative Logos, Word, Soul, vital Principle and Source of *munan* or mon—the thinker.

REALM II
SPIRITUALITY: the logician, soul, idea, attribute and legitimate offspring of The Logos-Soul; the mon of infinite continuity.

This mon or ideate mind presents and represents Mynde (Soul) as wisdom; as spiritual clarity or purity; as the power of infinite perception, conception and reflective fruition; as integrity or as wholeness in expression; as the sentiment or love derived from Soul; as the substance or understanding, thinking or standing under The Logos and deducing all concepts from Realm I.

REALM III

MORALITY: the human concept of man, of soul, of ideas and of The Logos.

This man is honest, morally honorable and ethical; charitable, humane, meek and sober; humanly faithful and morally prosperous.

This man is having part in the great metaphysical movement of moralization.

REALM IV

PHYSICALITY: the man presented by Adam; the human animal or mammal; human nature, human impulse and human activity; the finite concept of man.

REALM V

IMMORALITY: the corruption, defilement, uncleanness and total violation resulting from the finite concept or the mistaken concept of man; the consequent dead-end of Adam.

The mon of Realm II enjoys the divine continuity of being which manifests itself in ceaseless or invariable spiritual health; in positive, consistent mindfulness of Soul.

Mon, as analyzed in this treatise, is the antonym of the Greek *anthropos;* is the thing most unlike the animal or mammal human being, for mon—the thinker—is altogether metaphysical while the mammal is physical. This treatise must therefore use the word mon rather than man. This word mon is like the human concept of soul. It is separate and apart from the animal or mammal form. This mon takes form in spiritual or soul substance, not in mammal substance, matter or stuff, and this mon is altogether unrelated to the humus-man or the humus-minded Adam who is supposed to have fathered this *anthropos* more lately.

Mon—the thinker—is one in kind; alone and without another kind; a compound unit, including that which is deduced from The Mynde of The Logos. This mon is individual as a spiritual being; as the ideate thing or thinker produced by The divine creative Word (Soul). This mon is soul, the logician, or the sole one who understands Soul; the one and only mon who minds Soul and is disciplined by the recipes of his sole Principle or by the Principle of his soul.

Mon—the wholly literate and legitimate one—has no relationship with Eve. She represents human nature and the physical person, together with all of the plagues, curses and misfortune attached thereto. She represents humanity, mortality and all that is invalid or without a verity to sustain it. There is therefore no virtue in Eve, since she is supposed to have mothered all that is soulless, vile or vicious and that which is without valid moral existence; without strong, sound, just, logical or good existence. She presents vanity which can mother nothing but human vanity.

The word man is synonymous with the word mind, as thinker and as that which thinks. The root of the word man is think. To begin therefore with man or with mind, is to begin with thinking—correct, accurate, immaculate, prudent, virtuous, excellent or right thinking. To begin with thinking is to begin with two distinctly individual characters of thought; two individual thinking elements; two different functional ideas—thinkers; two rational powers belonging to the compound mind, man (thinker) or to the complete power of realization. The virile thinker is the one who perceives. The feminine thinker is the one who conceives or thinks conceptually, as the fertile thinking capacity. These two different but complementary elements differ in function only, not in quality.

The masculine thinker perceives, provides all wisdom; discerns spiritually and advocates or sets forth his potential issues or his wise perceptions, as head of the mental house.

The fertile or feminine thinker believes, beloves, conceives, gestates and brings forth wisdom's actual issues, or the elements of wisdom, as heart of the mental house.

The virile thinker is perspicacious, provident, vehement (spiritually moved or carried), and profound. He is resourceful because he has access to Mynde (The Logos-Mynde or Soul); because he stands at the door of infinite *Munan* or Mind, as the attribute, receiving instruction and direction from his Source or Root-Mind— The Logos-Mind, which Mind is The Origin of logical thought, and which Mind is The didactic Intelligence or Mind of the logical thinker.

This holy and wholly logical thinker stands where thought flows in; stands under and understands The Logos—his Source; stands at the door of infinite mental inception and perception; stands where he grasps, seizes or fully apprehends; stands where he thinks or reasons or deduces from Mind, perceptively or perceptually.

The fertile thinker is sentimental. She feels or senses by way of intuition of the spiritual sort. She is capacious, richly prolific of moral and spiritual issues or elements of fact. She is rationally and conceptually powerful. She has the ability to quicken or to act upon the potential issues that virtue and wisdom set forth. She has the capacity to enwomb, to reason out or to realize (make come true) or to make virtually manifest to other thinkers, that which the male thinker has set forth for conception.

The fertile thinker is abstruse and obscure to the human intellect, for the reason that her specific functions are invisible, inaudible, humble and without either eminence or prominence of a signal sort. Her functions differ widely from those of the virile thinker. He has the power of speech or address. His function is that of oration, plea, entreaty, prayer, appeal or advocation while she has the power of reception, gestation, verification, validation, nourishment, development, completion and accomplishment. These are the silent, secret and sacred thought functions going on in the mental sanctuary or mental matrix. These are the tremendous powers of conception which begin where the powers of perception leave off—that is, at the point of advocation or presentation. These powers of conception are tremendous, because wisdom is potential until acted upon by the fertile thinker and until brought to actual issue.

The virile thinker is sound and affirmative. He is the morally and spiritually excellent sage, seer or speaker. He is wise, confident, firm and sure of his stand. He deduces his perceptions directly and immediately from Mynde. He is forceful, positive, informative, instructive, bold and direct. Thus he is moved to speak, and thus he speaks, utters, emits, expresses and sets forth that which impregnates the conceptual matrix. He is wisdom, integrity (wholeness or holiness), and the powers of declaration, proclamation, preconception, anticipation and foresight.

The fertile thinker is moral-spiritual womanhood. She is love, charity, affection or sentiment itself. She is verity, validity, troth, veracity or trustworthiness itself, putting the true construction on the virile thinker's avowals. She is the wife of honesty, moral stamina, and of wisdom.

Thus the compound thinker acts as mediator, ever defining, ever illustrating, ever interpreting, demonstrating, teaching and ministering to those foolish, infirm and invalid ones whose rational faculties are not empowered or inspired by wisdom or by virtue, but are inflated with human nature.

The human intellect, the human race, humanity, human kind or mankind; the human person or the human nature; the human being or human mammal; the human personality or physicality, or the humus-man mentality—these have nothing in common with mon or mind, the thinker. This humus being is the *humus-man* kind or pattern or pater. It is mindlessness and thoughtlessness and foolishness and worthlessness because it is without wisdom, virtue or reason for its existence. The material human race is the Eve kind of man-kind. She is its mater, matter or mater-*ial* nature who gives it the only existence it has.

The *o* vowel in the word mon holds it up in Realm II which kind of thinking (understanding) is too high or too lofty to be perceivable or conceivable or sensible to humankind. But the *a* vowel in the word man lets it down or gives it that nature which can be sent down to the literate comprehension of humankind, mankind or the human race.

Humanhood or humankind is familiar with its own family concepts of the natural, physical or humanized (materialized or physicalized) man while it is unfamiliar with the spiritual *mon*. It calls him supernatural because humanly unnatural.

The following table will show how the metaphysical meaning of mon may be brought or sent down to human sensibility:

REALM   I   DIVINITY: The Logos-Mynde or Mind or Mynd.

REALM   II   SPIRITUALITY: the logician, mon or mind who understands Mynde and who possesses the intelligence or enlightenment which The Logos-Mynde divines or outlines.

REALM III   MORALITY: the scientist next lower than mon, *munan* or mind; the metaphysical man or thinker who observes *con*-science; the natural moral instincts and intuitions.

REALM IV   PHYSICALITY: the human physique, the person, the *humus*-man or physical (natural) man; spiritual illiteracy.

Realm III accepts man as related to virtue. Realm IV accepts man as a physical creature or as the entity or identity identified by the humusman physique or person. Realm V is doubly illiterate. Hence the *a* vowel (the most illiterate of all of the vowels) is doubled to indicate *maan* (or the Anglo Saxon *mann*). This would be indicated by—

REALM   V   IMMORALITY: moral ignorance; moral illiteracy; insensibility to conscience.

The man of Realm III may be taught of mon and taught by mon.

The rational concept of man can be brought no lower than Realm III.

The foregoing table classifies the highest, the positive, the genuine rational degree of mon, the thinker. This is the true and infinitely logical concept of mon. It is the concept or the idea, the esse or the entity, born of The Mynde of Realm I, or The Logos. This mon or idea is divinely impelled or motivated. He is spiritually prompted and animated.

The man of Realm III is a human concept. He is a morally motivated thinker. He is humanly pious, gracious, compassionate, patient and affectionate. This concept of man is the one conceived from the human point of view. It is metaphysically right, conscientious and equitably balanced or humanly ethical. He is a human reality.

The man of Realm IV is a human conception; a physical perception; a finite entity or person; a physically logical image; a combination of human corporeality and personality; a physically animated body born of physicality and prompted by human nature and human impulse.

The person of Realm V is an inhuman concept; an illegitimate conception or perception; a morally illiterate and illogical image; an immoral product; an unmoral creature, created by the mental processes of envy, conceit, deceit, malice, pride, hostility, animosity, vengeance, friction and all of the vices—all of the antonyms of the Realm III virtues.

There are many concepts of man, but there is only one kind of man and he is mon—the man of Realm II—who is wholly spiritual and spiritually holy as an integer or whole entity.

There are many degrees of reasoning, thinking, perceiving, discerning and believing, but there is only one degree in which the thinker practices the science and art of divine reasoning—Realm II.

The mon of Realm II is virtue itself; a compound or combination of virtue (virile perception) and of fertile conception; a compound of the powers of perception and expression, together with (united with) the powers of fruition, which powers conceive in the name of spiritual immaculacy or purity of Mynde and Spirit.

Here the virile thinker perceives accurately, logically, and wisely in the name of wisdom, and he sets forth his rudimental precepts and perceptions to be conceived.

Here the fertile thinker is purity or virginity bringing forth her purely spiritual concepts. She is that infinite and universal feminine capacity to conceive, to develop rudimental concepts, to quicken and to make evident.

This mon of Realm II is virtue having two complementary elements. One is *vir-tue* or *vir-ile* (manly excellence, manhood or masculine), and the other is *vir-gin*. Both of these virtues should be regarded equally. Literately they are equal, but they pertain to wholly and purely spiritual character, state, quality or condition of being. Logically and legitimately they denote the ability of wisdom to multiply and the capability (capacity) of purity to hear, to understand, to comprehend, to receive word (or The Word), to receive (spiritually) and to conceive of highest, most excellent manhood (*monhood*) or virile wisdom.

Here the virgin is the feminine element of virtue; the most excellent womanhood or womanly excellence. She is as essential and as important as wisdom, since she is his mate in the realm of understanding or spiritual realization.

The Greek *gune, gyne* means woman or female. Vir-*gyne,* vir-*gune,* or vir-gin may be a combination of the Latin *vir* and the Greek *gune.*

Neither man nor mon has a mind of his own. He has only The Mynde of his creator who supplies him with thoughts, even as water flows into places or channels open, ready to receive, or receptive of it. Mon is that receptive capacity into which the influx, inflow and influence of The Logos flows as thought.

The thinker of Realm II has no other Mynde but The Mind of The Logos which is divinely affluent. He teaches the Realm III thinker as that thinker allows. There may be a confluence of thought or a definite disunity; a conflux or a conflict. But wisdom teaches or lets flow his wise and tranquil contemplations. Understanding and her realizations and demonstrations are fluent and ready to impart, share or teach the man of Realm III. These demonstrations speak for themselves. They speak of mon's inflow of logical and literate resources from Realm I.

THE WORD, MANIFESTATION

The word *manifestation* is a good word—a useful word—that will turn in all directions to lend itself to all parts of speech, yet its literate construction limits it to lowest physical and metaphysical meaning; the lowest literal and figurative meaning, because of its *a* vowel, which is the least literate of all of the vowels, and because the original meaning of the word manifest was from *manus* (Latin *manifestus*) and it meant seized by the hand. It means palpable; tangible or sensible to the touch or stroke of the hand.

In order to lift the word manifestation out of its lowest form and make it useful as a universally good word, we must first improve the vowel. If it be minus instead of *manus* it would not be improved but lessened in degree and in value. The Latin *munus* means service, gift or duty. This seems unrelated to manifestation—a noun of action or condition; a noun of verbal action—yet a manifestation could be the gift itself; could be the agent, action or agency serving or giving or bringing to the figurative hand as duty, service or true function of the agent or virtue acting and in action.

The most literate synonym of manifestation is signification. This means revelation, communication; that which bears (communicates or signifies) the meaning of; that which gives sign and significance of or carries the import of; that which expresses the sense of or reveals the nature of; that which represents, presents or speaks of; that which makes plain, discloses or displays; that which serves as the revealing agency, to mark or make apparent to the understanding; that which makes manifest, evident, conspicuous or obvious to the wise and accurate thinker.

Signification, spelled with the *i* vowel, is good. Evident (or manifest) is good for its root is *vid, video*. It pertains to the sense of sight particularly. Other synonyms of manifest pertain to sight: obvious, conspicuous, apparent, disclose (expose to view), and others. Yet all pertain to one or more of the forms of perception in general. Specifically, that which is in the hand must pertain to all of the senses: feeling, seeing, hearing (understanding), tasting (to test the flavor, or to touch to the tongue—speech—to find if mentally, morally, or spiritually digestible), and smelling (quick of scent or quick scented; sagacious). Feeling mentally (as in the mental hand) is sentiment, which is the feeling of the mind or *mentis—sentio-mentis*. Thus to have a thing in hand mentally would be to perceive it, to have tasted, felt, observed, heard (to the individual as audience or listener), scented (as sage, and seen as seer). These are called the five senses or the main senses. Here the French *main* means the hand, as in the word manner, which means mode, in which a thing is handled, or as in the word maneuver, which means literally hand work; or as in games, a main is a hand.

In the physical realm there are five distinctly different senses or avenues of perception. In the higher metaphysical realms there are six and in the holy (wholly or purely) spiritual realm there are seven.

The following table will show the five, the six and the seven senses by means of which the individual may experience manifestation according to ability or apprehensive quality and capacity to sense, or according to individual sensibility:

Realm I

DIVINITY: The Logos, Word or vital Principle which makes itself manifest, significant, evident, understood, realized, cognized, comprehended, discerned or intelligently discernible and spiritually distinct to Realm II.

Realm II

SPIRITUALITY: the logician, the literologist, or legitimate, living idea which manifests, signifies, understands, cognizes, comprehends and discerns by means of infinite power of ideation, realization, perception, intuition, identity or simile.

Here there are seven senses: wisdom, who sees; understanding who hears; sentiment or love who feels by way of her spiritual mindedness; purity or the power of accurate perception and immaculate conception; integrity or that which signifies and manifests wholeness or holiness; health or spiritual validity which is the state of being the munificent (gift) or manifestation of The Logos-Life. Here the form *manus* becomes *munus,* meaning service, gift or duty as in the word munificence.

Realm III

MORALITY: the six senses, three of which are masculine and three of which are feminine. Here is moral sense or sentiment, trustworthiness, faith or expectancy on the feminine side, and moral prosperity, honesty, moral virility or potency on the masculine side. These are the moral manifestations and representations.

Realm IV

PHYSICALITY: the five physically patent senses.

Realm V

IMMORALITY: the unmoral manifestations such as dishonesty, infidelity, inconstancy, inhumanity, desperation, animosity, tyranny or self-conceit.

The word manifestation is a noun of verbal action; a living or vital noun at work or in work; a noun in use, inure; a working word; a noun of action, animation, spirit or spiritual energy; a word, noun or entity logically and literately moved by means of its own animus or soul.

The word manifestation is simply the name of the actor, the action or the agency that is functioning as a unit of work. It is a spiritual erg in operation making itself felt, making itself plain, clearly defined and universally conceivable. It is built upon the word manifest, which means to seize by the literal or figurative hand; to grasp by the physical or metaphysical hand; to be made understood or intuitively felt.

The word manifest is a noun meaning that which is in the hand, such as a statement, a bill, mark, sign, declaration, explanation or information brought to one's attention.

The word manifest is an adjective meaning open, visible, self-evident—not obscure, not hidden.

The word manifest is a verb meaning to display, to reveal, to make or cause to appear distinctly.

The word manifestly is an adverb meaning in a specified or specific manner, as being handy, at hand or handily exhibited; in a manifest manner; in a proven way.

Every kind of manifestation is the phenomenon of its preceptial noumenon, its real premise or its noumenal law from which it presents itself. It is exhibit, display, show or phenomenon or phenomenal conclusion of a premise; a concept of a precept or a practicable statement, idea, declaration, sign or expression of a forceful (enforced) principle.

In Realm II a manifestation is a signification of The Principle which enforces it. For instance, wisdom is the idea or seer who sees or discerns clearly. His premise or principle is The Logos. Understanding hears and understands perfectly, because of the noumenal Logos under which she stands; because of her divinely significant Principle.

In Realm III a manifestation is the phenomenon of moral principles in force and being enforced by conscience. It is offspring of

moral or conscientious dictum; the result of the moral or right manner and the moral law precedent. For instance, veracity, hope, patience, affection, confidence (in the vital moral precepts) and sincerity constitute the manifestation or mark of morality.

In Realm IV a manifestation is the physical phenomenon; the
physically displayed thing at hand or in the hand.

The word manifestation may be heightened, lifted or spiritually
enhanced by replacing the *a* vowel, by using the *u* or the *o* vowel,
as in the form *moneo* (*monere, monitus*), I bring to mind or to hand;
I warn; I remind; I advise; or the *u* as in the form *munus*, meaning
gift or service. These vowels are highly metaphysical, as spiritually
magnanimous, munificent, gifted.

The word manifestation is a very dependent word. It is nothing
of itself, only as it manifests that noumenal precept which admonishes,
advises, instructs and rules the action of. This preposition of shows
the nature of the word manifestation; shows its utter dependency
upon its self-existent and all-existent governing principle that brings
to mind and to hand. Thus a manifestation is as dependent upon
his noumenal Principle as a sunbeam is dependent upon the sun—
of which it is only the phenomenon.

In Realm V a manifestation would be the effect of its causative
agent; the result or consequence of its unrestrained human impulse,
its mad ambition or its immoral purpose. Such manifestations are
animated, prompted, promoted, fathered and mothered by the unprincipled human mentality.

In this Realm V the invalid, the immoral, the illogical, the morally
illiterate and inequitable destroys itself when it becomes evident
(manifest) that it *is* wrong and invalid—even though it fights to
maintain itself as something. It is like the wrong figures on the black-
board which the school boy erases when he discovers his mistake.
These invalid manifestations—like the wrong figures—have no ruling
precept, principle or premise to maintain them.

In Realm II a manifestation can be a *munus, monis* or a minor
(minus) *minifestation;* a spiritual hand; a gift or service to mankind;
the logic and logician at hand; that which brings warning or advice;
that which reminds, brings to mind or to hand from The Logos-Mynde.
This manifestation is *mon* who is minor, minus or less than The Logos
or second only to The Logos upon which he depends for logical, literate and legitimate manifestation. Thus we have *muni*-festation,
minu-festation and *moni*-festation for Realm II and manifestation for
Realm III, and so may all words be reduced from highest literacy to
human utility.

THE WORD, Marriage

The word *marriage* comes from the word marry, which is built upon the French *marier,* from Latin *maritare* (to marry), and from the noun form *maritus*, husband.

The word husband goes to the Anglo Saxon *husbonda* or *house-bonda*. It means freeholder; master of the house; head of a house or a family; bound or banded or in league with a house; house-band or bond as by law.

The suffix of the word marriage is *-age.* It forms the word marry into a collective noun; into a noun of relation or of condition. It is as though it were *marry-age* or husband-*age* (as in the word parent-age). It forms the word marry into a noun of act, action, function or process (as act of marrying or the state of being married).

The word marriage, being based upon the word husband, pertains to and relates to husbandhood. He is the marital relative of his wife as *maritus* (husband) and banded to his house, his family or those who bear his name or are embraced in his house as *house-bonda,* as manager of his house; as he who husbands or provides for his house.

The word matrimony is given as a synonym for the word marriage, but it is based upon the word mother rather than the word husband. It is *matrimonium* or mater (mother) plus *moneo* (warn). It may mean to warn, to admonish, to remind or to give solemn advice to the couple or to present the more serious side of marriage, compared to the nature of the wedding celebration.

Marriage, as the state of husbandhood and wifehood, is the potential state of fatherhood and motherhood or matrimony.

Wedlock pertains to the legal status of marriage, as a compact or contract that binds, bands together or pledges the couple under the law.

Marry-age involves a collection of ideas. It collects, gathers and brings together all of the essential factors of wedlock, all of the feminine elements of matrimony; all of the masculine elements of husbandhood or marriage or the marital elements; all of the moral factors precedent to matrimony or motherhood. Thus motherhood is the designment, the appointment and the fulfillment of marriage, and it is that state which the law of wedlock protects.

Marriage is the union of the sixes or the six *hoods* of humanhood. It binds together the six individual states, qualities or characters of being. These six-*hoods* are embraced in one sextette, three of which are male and three of which are female, as the following table shows:

1. Manhood			1. Womanhood
2. Husbandhood	—HUMANHOOD—		2. Wifehood
3. Fatherhood			3. Motherhood

Marriage collects and presents the totality of humanhood or the six states of being involved in it. It provides the legal, the moral and the sentimental foundation for human propagation or generation. Thus both marriage and matrimony are preordained, fore-ordained and pre-instituted as that which husbands and that which mothers.

There is no blending or amalgamation of these six individual *hoods* or states of being. They coordinate in their very different but complementary, ministerial functions. Each has its own peculiar virtue or metaphysical property upon which the marriage rests and upon which the whole unit of humanhood depends. For instance, manhood mans himself until he marries or is cojoined (conjoined) by the law of wedlock to womanhood, and thus having the mental and moral virility to man himself wisely, he is prepared to man and husband a wife and to undertake the bond of matrimony.

The law of virtue weds manhood (virilty) to womanhood (chastity or moral fertility); weds husbandhood (*honor-est-y,* honesty or moral potency) to wifehood (veracity, verity or the power of true conception or holy fruition or the state of being wholly fruitful). It weds fatherhood (integrity in its moral dignity) to motherhood (constancy) which is holy matrimony or the whole of marriage. It weds the power of perception to the power of conception.

Marriage is intended to cherish all of the virtues; to care for and promote moral strength, validity and stamina; to preserve paternal integrity and dignity and to house or to shelter maternal graces.

A marriage can be no more stable than the virtues invested in it. Womanhood constitutes the fiber of wifehood, and wifehood the substance and fore-runner of motherhood, and both and all of the *hoods* and virtues are established to forefend the ultimate—motherhood.

Masculine loyalty, fidelity, stability, firmness, moral prosperity, profundity, sagacity, sobriety, piety and all such virtues are the intrinsic substance that binds or bands a man's house together. Neither the legal, the cultural nor the sentimental bond or band can hold a marriage intact.

Humanity's concept of marriage is based upon ideals, or dreamy illusions, or sentimental impulses, which impulses are prompted by human nature or the human physique. Thus it is that unless humanity's common concept of marriage becomes more metaphysically refined, becomes more prompted by the impulses of moral-spiritual virtues, marriage will enslave one or both participants, by wedding one to a human nature (human physique) or a human mammal (animal) physical creature, with whom one identifies himself or herself as being like, being matched or being mated. This fact would mean that both hold the physique and its instincts and impulses (its mammal nature) to be the ruling, chief, or the paramount factor, or the controlling factor and governing agent.

Marriage is too often the realm of mental distress, sentimental disorder and metaphysical disillusionment, too often the experience of disenchantment of the former state of enchantment, because human nature and its dreamy illusions do not partake of a substantial intelligence but of the insubstantial human knowledge, sense, or natural intellect which is only human impulse and physical cognition.

Marriage is more than a physical institution. It is a moral-spiritual institution, and certainly should be more metaphysically substantiated than physically controlled. Physicality, as instigation, incentive, agitation, animation of the mammal emotions may constitute the mating instinct and marriageability of the animals and other mammals; but it is not prudent or correct that one should classify himself or herself in the realm of physicality (animality).

Marriage is nothing without husbandhood—built upon manhood. Matrimony is nothing without the kind of manhood and fatherhood that marshals, mans and manages it (as his house), that out maneuvers the popular forms of sophisticated immorality, and that keeps his house morally prosperous or thrifty.

During the mental processes of moralization (of the concept of marriage) of the human mentality, and of humanhood, matrimony is at war with human nature, and virtue is at war with vice, and the manhood of husbandhood is defending his house.

Human ideals are only human idols, persons, personalities or personal dreams personalized. They are flimsy in sentiment and untested in character. They are only imitations of the moral substance which holds two half units together in marriage. They exist only in human imagination as wishful thinking which excites and manipulates, but does not demonstrate stability. Marriage may not be built upon them. It is built upon actual perception and conception of ideas— not human ideals buried in personalities, or in the two persons who unite in marriage.

Ideals may cause the individual to cling fast to them rather than to cling or hold fast to the virtues which they only imitate, and which virtues are in harmony with the moral law underlying marriage.

Personal ideals, humanized, can only bring disappointment. One by one they must be shattered in the experience of marriage, for marriage is built upon moral law, spiritual wisdom and universal precepts. Spiritual matrimony is the fulfillment of wisdom's vision; the realization, event and substantiation of wisdom's sentiments or love. Conscience and the moral instincts, or intuitions, the honor of honesty, the dignity of integrity, and the graces of chastity are the qualities and conditions that keep marriage flourishing, and that maintain its balance and sustain its purpose. Human ideals only idealize and idolize.

Marriage depends upon the ability and stability of humanhood to hold to the marital law and to obey it naturally and spontaneously, consistently and tenaciously.

A wobbly marriage may be illustrated by a wobbly wagon wheel. It is composed of hub, spokes and rim (with felloe or felly). The wheel must have an axis or axle; a sturdy pivot or axis principle; a self-existent axiom if it is to function properly. Let the hub of the wheel be the individual marriage. Let the spokes be the masculine and feminine virtues or characteristics. Let the axis or axiom be the truth, or the science of *con-science* (the science of soul within oneself). Let the rim be of such metal that it may withstand contact with the sharp stones in the marital way. If a spoke or two be missing, if the hub is too loose, lax, immoral or relaxed in vigilance, if the felloe is parted in places, and if there is a lack of adhesion and moral cohesion, the wheel wobbles.

The world has built no paved highway or roadway for this marriage vehicle. Its free love free ways do not serve the marriage vehicle. Marriage is the great instrument of moralization. The world, struggling against its moral influence, would make marriage the battle ground. Hence matrimony depends upon masculine valiantness and steadfastness; upon husbandhood to make way.

Marriage in its lowest sense is its animal or physical sense.

Marriage in its moral sense is the uniting of the male elements (which are potential) with the female elements of the rational faculties or of rational powers; the uniting of the abilities of the masculine faculty of reasoning with the feminine faculty or capacity of reasoning. It means honesty being honored by veracity, who conceives and brings forth his issues, makes them actual, humanly practical, and evident to other honest thinkers. It means the meek, modest, morally tempered hope being conceived by faith and being nurtured into reality as the expected result of that legitimate hope. It means that all of the male virtues are united with the female virtues or moral *vir-gins* (*vir* meaning man, and *gin* or *gyne* meaning woman or female) or virtuous qualities, and being thus united they function as a reproductive unit of power—perceiving, conceiving and bringing forth their qualities.

Chastity, affection, troth and verity function with the sober, profound male thinker, and together they bring forth that which blesses humanity. They bring forth compassionate, charitable, and morally blessed events.

The moral qualities unite in purpose, under the moral law, to maintain moral law and order, and to be maintained or sustained by the moral law—as it functions in conscience. Thus the male thinker perceives as directed by conscience, and the female thinker conceives (gestates and develops) as directed by conscience. This is troth and true marriage.

THE WORD, MARS

The word *Mars* belongs to a planet by that name; a planet which is a member of our solar system; a planet which our physical sciences or natural sciences or inter or outer planetarian sciences have explored from afar.

Let us leave the Earth and the Earthling's physical point of view. Let us leave the mundane sense of things and soar beyond the humanly limited, earth-born and Earth-bound mental horizons, since a thinker is unconfined. Let us get a more universal sense of things, since a thinker is not an isolated physical thing. Let us free ourselves from Earth's powers (influence) of physical gravity, for a while, and rise into high, higher and highest realms or metaphysical concepts. Before doing this, it is necessary to change the vowel *a* to a more literate one, or to a less illiterate one; to change *a* to *e,* then to *ae,* then to *ea,* to *i,* to *o,* to *u,* and to *ou.*

Mars, mare (sea; *marin,* French, and *marinus, maris,* Latin). The *a* vowel dropped for the *e* vowel gives merine, instead of marine (sea). Merino means shepherd. More, *morse* means sea (or sea lion). Old Latin Mavors is Mars. *Maritus* may mean merit; deserving of honor; (*meros,* part) *mirari, mirare,* mean to look at; to wonder, as at a miracle or a marvel. It may be marshal or martial meaning guide and usher. It may mean marry, *maritus,* marital, meaning husband, and Mars may well be the metaphysical, physical, or figurative husband of Earth, since Earth is feminine—that fertile planet that brings forth. Mars is surely a transitional word. That is, it must rise out of its low estate and must transcend to spiritual meanings.

The physical sciences are on Mars, as on Earth, limited to the physical substance and structure and nature of that planet. Thus, leaving the physical and natural sciences out of this analysis, the word or name Mars may be analyzed and defined somewhat as a member of our solar system.

First, let Mars leave off its *a* vowel, and rise to the metaphysical level of Earth, by supplying the same vowels to it as are found in the word Ear-th, since the *ea* vowel combination is a little higher than the single *a* vowel, and since the name Ear-th has a greater proportion of vowels. Thus we have Mears, or Maers, or Meres, which would mean things in their absolute and unqualified expression. Mars being the marital relative of the Ear-th, would be the male element and complement of the Earth, merely or absolutely, and utterly male in his metaphysical nature. The Earth is feminine in her nature, because she brings forth fruit as mother nature in her humanly metaphysical sense; because she vegetates metaphysically, as she does in her vegetable kingdom. To vegetate means to be active, lively, vigorous, to grow, to be fertile or to have the capacity to produce or to bring forth. To vegetate metaphysically the thinker produces by way of conception, gestation, development and nutrition, as does the Ear-th, with the cooperation of the sun, the rain and the wind or breath.

Second, let Mars be the marital relative of Ear-th, as him who merits honor as male, or as the male—*meros*—part, who from Earth's point of view is so unlike her as to be a thing of wonder and marvel or astonishment. Let him partake or be part of the same elements of the metaphysical heavens or wind or atmosphere, which is related to the same solar system and sol. Let him not be a thing apart.

Third, let the elements of this solar system take on their spiritual significance as nearly as they can, as they revolve, turn, roll, circulate or turn over and over in their different and individual paths around the same sun or sol. Let this sol be the light which enlightens the thinker who stands upon the Earth, as ear of understanding, and let this same sun or sol be the light which enlightens the thinker who stands upon Mars, as him who must be honored in the same light and in the same heaven in which heaven they both move harmoniously, because they are governed by the great solar magnet.

Fourth, let Mars represent the marital sphere, in the sense of being a type of spiritual continuity, while the Earth represents the receptive ear or sphere motivated by the same spiritual energy and solar light, which light may be called soul-ar. This word solar or soular means relating to soul or like soul; pertaining to soul; of or from soul, as type, symbol, figure (in figurative meaning) or as sign significant of spiritual wisdom, light, and enlightenment. Here Mars may drop the illiterate *a* vowel and take the form *mir,* which could mean that he views or beholds the Earth with wonder or admiration, and that she reflects upon him metaphysically. This is true physically, since Earth's surface is, for the greater part, covered with water, which water reflects a dazzling light.

Fifth, let Mars be a member of the same *soul-ar* system with Earth, and let them both be creations of the same universal wisdom or intelligence. Let both planets exist, only as they exist, as the home of the creature who needs their peculiar properties. On Earth there is man, think; mind, *munan,* think; *mon.* On Mars there must be a very different creature and creation, but that creature and creation being warmed, brooded and cherished by the same sol, sun and soul; being comforted, solaced, enlightened and moved by the same solid, strong, sound and firm convictions; being of the same origin—Soul—and being genuine or of the same genius, there is no doubt that the Mars creature is enlightened in the things of soul, wisdom and conscience.

This Mars creature may have a very different way of expressing himself, but that self must represent his sphere, which sphere and orbit differs from ours.

Earth's formalism, orthodoxy, traditions, popular opinions and sentiments must be as foreign to the Martian as his manner, mode, customs and (moral) standards—of what is right—would be foreign to us, for his orbit, his way, his literal and figurative path which encircles the sun is different and foreign to us. Both spheres are individual, essential and logically and literately substantial. Thus in order to communicate with Mars, Earth must approach him on the level of soul consciousness or soul standing, intuition or sense, because there is no other common ground or basic relationship.

Sixth, let Mars be our neighbor—not literally, but figuratively. Let him symbolize another enlightened sphere, even as his sun, sol, sole light or enlightening soul-premise symbolizes that center of attraction which we enjoy; even as his sol and soul principle broods over us and holds us in our orbit, which orbit is peculiar to us.

Let Mars be under the same tutor and tutelage, defender and solver, guardian and teacher of that which pertains to soul and to Soul, and let Mars enjoy (in our concept) an equal aptitude for this high degree of enlightenment, which enlightenment must apply to his own peculiar needs.

Those who look down upon Mars may find his creature to be lower than the Earthling made of the humus—even Adam. Surely there is no element of mirth or merriment in this Adam character, but only disappointment, misfortune and adversity. Here Mars would surely take on the name of Mars and the character of Mars, the god of war. Here it may be noted that this title is given to him by Earthling's wildest imaginations; by Earth's mythology. It has nothing to do with his true character, in any sense, but he will be so to those who believe this myth. He may be *mir-th* itself.

When Mars communicates with Earth there will be merriment, as at a wedding, for this will be a festive occasion—long awaited. The marital relative of the (metaphysical) Ear-th will claim and marry her, as he merits her spiritually conceptive ear, and in some way—some invisible and intangible way—he will husband her as *maritus* or *meritus*.

Who may say that even now Mars furnishes certain elements of an atmospheric nature, which are essential to Earth? Her creatures breathe a certain kind of oxygen or air, because they are animals, mammals and vegetables of Earth's peculiar sort. Mars may be environed by an entirely different—even opposite—atmosphere. It may be inhabited by creatures altogether unlike the creatures of our land and sea and air, but they will be found to be the natural phenomena of the noumenal Mars.

Physically speaking, Mars is as different from our gentle mother-nature Earth as can be. He may be an hurricane of action — not passive, soft and effeminate like Earth, but noisy, windy, boisterous and busy as a robust boy at play; not like a little girl playing mother to her dolly.

If Mars be masculine (husband, marital relative of Ear-th) he must needs be different in every way—even opposite in many ways—yet he must be sustained or held in his orbit by the same governing, ruling universal rule; the same existing intelligence or intelligent principle of existence. We must be prepared to see him in this light. As the sun illumines Mars, so it illumines us. This sol (soul) with which we are familiar is a member of Soul's greater universe and of Soul's universal light—infinite enlightenment.

We do not know how Martians express this enlightenment, but they do express it. It is for us (as the Ear-th or the hearer) to prepare to understand that peculiar expression. This may mean speech or some kind of audible expression, or it may not. It may call for a purely spiritual kind of ear to hear or to understand his wholly inaudible expression.

The human, mammal form, so familiar to Earthlings, and so like Adam and Eve, and so fraught with formalism and human ritualism, is not duplicated on Mars. However, the spiritually ignorant may see only a creature as fabulous and as cursed as Adam and may not be able to see or perceive the soul governed ego or Martian, who symbolizes the enlightenment of soul, and who radiates such light to the intelligent and more universally logical thinker. Let Mars be our good neighbor.

Seventh, let Mars symbolize a universal character. Let it be a temple of universal contemplation; a home and house for the creature —of whatever sort. Let that creature be disciplined and enlightened by the same universal Soul-Principle. Let him be the recipient of the same benefits and let him anticipate the same reward in logical percipiency and concipiency. Then when we communicate with him, he will take on the name and character of Mir-th or merriment.

Physically and literally speaking, Mars may be like steel compared with our water surface and our leaf mold soil or humus; may be the opposite of Earth's fertility, for he must express virility and masculinity, according to literology.

Earth must be passive and receptive—the ear (-th) spoken to. Mars must be active and expressive. Earth presents the placid, patient, pacific or motherly traits of character, while Mars may be restless as the wind, strenuous and impatient. Earth's surface, covered with vegetable life, so fragile and as delicate as a flower, must be very unlike the face of Mars.

Mars must have some form of integration, animation or integrating action; some kind of adhesive and constructive properties— physical and metaphysical; some kind of entities which express the vitalizing nature and the vivifying nature of soul. The same intent (of Soul) that brought Earth into existence, must father Mars as well.

The sun is a great purifier, metaphorically speaking. It keeps the planets clean, literally and figuratively. In this function the sun is like the soul.

Instead of building bigger and bigger telescopes or stronger and greater ones, Earth should cease her efforts to *see* Mars and should content herself with training her ear to hear him; should study the art of listening metaphysically; should devote herself to the science of reception and conception of a universal sort, so that when the planet Mars would speak to us or would signal us, we may be ready to ear, to hear or to receive—even to understand. We may not use our humanized or localized methods, but must prepare to be magnanimous (a great soul), having universal gestures.

THE WORD, Material

The word *material* comes from the Latin *materia,* meaning matter. It adds the suffix *-al,* which makes it mean of, pertaining to, or relating to matter; belonging to or befitting matter; that which is like matter or belongs to matter.

The noun form of the word material is equivalent to matter and matter means stuff, mass or stock; physical, corporeal or unspiritual stuff.

The adverb form of the word material applies to a thing being important or significant.

The word matter is of physical import. It must be classified as matter-ial. It is possible to divide the word material differently, leaving the *ia* of *materia* to the suffix making the suffix *-ial* instead of *-al,* and leaving the root mater instead of *materia.* Thus it would mean of or pertaining to mater or mother, and the word matter would be the lowest form of stuff or material of which a thing is made, or the lowest and least literate kind of mater.

The word matter doubles the *t* and uses the *a* vowel which is the least literate, or the most illiterate one of the vowels. The double *tt* emphasizes or doubles this illiteracy and doubles its materiality as though it were spelled *maater.*

In its most literate form mater is mother. In its least literate form mater is matter.

The following table shows the Latin *materia,* matter and mater, and it shows the word *mother* in its highest form:

REALM   I   DIVINITY: The Word, The Logos-Mother; The Motor, Quickener and Mother-Love Principle motivating Realm II.

REALM   II   SPIRITUALITY: the miter, meter or measuring power of spiritually whole conception, gestation and fruition; full measure of love.

REALM   III   MORALITY: the concipient intelligence of conscience; full measure of compassion, patience, affection, veracity and chastity which are her powers of moral vivification, verification, validation and fruition.

Realm IV   PHYSICALITY: the physical material, *materia*, or mater.

Realm V   IMMORALITY: the sub-normal, sub-animal, sub-mammal or lowest form of matter which, like Eve, brings forth all cursed, carnal, vile and unprincipled matters and events.

The foregoing table honors only The divine creative Word Mother with the *o* vowel. She is the infinite motive to love divinely, constantly, immaculately and continually; the infinite capacity to understand and to conceive.

The table shows the next lesser form of the word mother to be measure, miter, *metron,* metric, womb or matrix, in its highest metaphysical sense. The Greek *metra* means uterus or womb. Matrix means the womb. This is womb-man (wo-man) in her highest metaphysical sense which is her spiritual status.

The next lesser and lower form of the word mater is shown by Realm III. It is the matron of conscience—the mature or highly developed status of moral womanhood who conceives, acts upon and brings forth issues of high and great moral import. Thus moral womanhood, wifehood or full measure of verity (veracity or the power of quickening, veraciously), becomes the mater or mother of the offspring of conscience and its kind of science (con-science, the science, intuition or moral sense and sentiment within oneself). Thus conscience is the silent, gentle, faithful and charitable mother or mater and moral matrix in which, by means of which or through which, all moral qualities, attributes, issues or virtues are brought forth and established in human affairs. She is the measurer of right and of rights; of that which is ethical and equitable, morally significant and important, or is regarded as being material, or as having great moral import.

In this moral realm radical honesty, patient fidelity, true modesty, merited expectancy, humility in the house of con-science, constitute that which is material to humanhood. In this realm also, human intellect—devoted to its material, literal, natural or physical metaphysics—contends with and against human reason devoted to conscience and its science of soul within the moral thinker. It contends that the traditional, conventional, formal and formally orthodox customs are the moral law, the rule and the authority under which humanhood should function. It contends that the humanly instituted and socially established and civilly supported rules, usage, standards and ethical systems are synonymous with conscience and its moral science. But the thinker and conceiver of Realm III knows from whence comes wisdom and the love for soul and its science. It comes from Realm II, definitely and not from Realm IV; comes from the magnanimous matrix of conscience and not from the consensus of human opinion and sentiment, or that which is material to the human intellect.

The next lesser and lower form of the word mater is matter—the physical material out of which the human (mammal) physique is made, or the material, matter or stuff called organic matter—humanly so designated.

This is the realm of physicality where physical matters hold the human interest. It is the realm where physical preservation and propagation is a matter of great concern and importance. This is the realm of carnal misfortune as well as the realm of carnal or physical fortune; the realm where physical concepts or finite matters are caused to thrive.

This is the human nature point of view, where mater, as matter, is physical or natural; where her issues are conceived, sustained, nurtured and caused to thrive, and where human nature is breeding and brooding its own kind and kin.

This is the realm of the physical (and physically metaphysical) matrix in which all physical things are weighed and shaped according to humanly instituted patterns and paters; according to rules and outlines of physical and natural sciences as humanly designated to be.

The lowest metaphysical realm is herein called and designated as immorality in Realm V. It is the dead end or finis of the stuff called matter; finis of mater or the corporeally minded matrix, in which untrue and unreal and unmoral and illiterately patterned (pater-ed or fathered) issues are conceived, quickened and brought forth. It is the realm of moral ignorance and depravity where immorality originates. It is the realm of complete reversal where the metaphysical matrix claims to be the re, the noun or the matter, or the mater of all reality and of all really existing things, physically manifest or objectified things, and of all humanly perceivable and actually significant things.

The word material coming from the word matter, has no rudimentally logical heritage, no radically literate substance and no spiritually legitimate essence or existence, since the word matter has no existence excepting in itself, which self is mentally, morally, metaphysically and really nonexistent, inane, mythological and allegorical. *Materia* is not born of The mother intelligence or The concipient Logos; not born of The mother of reason, of wisdom, or verity, of reality, of truth, of valid ideas or of the power to ideate vividly; not born in conformity to The Logos rule.

The word material, which means pertaining to matter, is born of mater, is born of its own material or soulless self; of that which is material or important to itself; that which it conceives of being material or important. This important mater is mortal or invalid knowledge or intellect corporeally gathered.

Human impulse, as the *pater*ial thing, impregnates matter or materiality with his soulless hypotheses and she brings forth the likeness of herself and this soulless theory, or set of patterns, thus reproducing supposition, finite conjecture, unfortunate false assumptions, tentative beliefs and mundane evidence. Hence matter is worthless excepting to itself and this self deludes and impregnates herself with her own kind of illusions or imaginations, since she has no rational matrix capacity but only a materially imaginative capacity. Within this matrix she materializes finity or materiality—all that is bad. To materialize, therefore, would mean to perform the act of the mater in conceiving, acting upon and bringing forth the very material concept which is bad, harmful, hurtful, secular, deceitful and unprincipled; to make material or important a thing which is false and baneful; to render like herself—matter; to make or to make into a thing like herself—matter.

This mater or matter has the instincts of the mater—the mate of material hypotheses and unprincipled theories. She has the mating instinct of the sub-animal and lowest form of susceptibility to the most material influences. Thus she must have a mate to impregnate her Eve-like sensibilities. She has the instinct and capacity to magnify or to make greater that which she conceives and acts upon. She has the instinct to protect, with vicious attack, whatever would deflate or diminish that which she has made material or of great import. Both she and her mate have the instinct of hostility to fight or to war against the moral principles such as honesty, veracity, fidelity and integrity. This they do with great animosity, with ill will, hatred, malice, vehement enmity, and with a sense of that eternal feud which has always existed between right and wrong, good and bad, the moral doctrine and that which opposes it—that which is without the law of moral precept.

All good words like mother must be universal. All true words like mother must ramify to human utility; must be brought down to the human earth and earthliness (world) from their heavenly or spiritual meanings. Thus by changing the literate characters (letters) the author of this treatise has brought the word material into its own realm where it may best illuminate itself or display its nature and its unwholesome functions, and where it is classified as matter—in Realm V—one realm removed from mater—in Realm IV—and thus has isolated and has detached that which would usurp the name of mother, and thus profane the name of woman.

The word material is used as a synonym for the word substance. Again, substance is a word that must be classified as to kind. There are material, physical and metaphysical substances, stocks, properties, goods and the like.

The following table classifies substance and material:

REALM   I   DIVINITY: The Principle of all real, true, and wholly immutable substance.

REALM   II   SPIRITUALITY: that substance of which understanding or the power of infinite realization and all reality is composed; that understanding or understancing which The Logos substantiates; that which understances or stands directly under Realm I as wisdom, spiritual integrity, and such spiritual properties and substances.

REALM III   MORALITY: that which is morally substantial, material, important and ethically significant; that moral goods of which the moral qualities are made or created—qualities such as honesty, moral integrity, confidence, constancy and stamina.

REALM IV   PHYSICALITY: physical things of physical import; the human nature and its essential characteristics.
Here physicality is materiality.

The foregoing table shows that the thinker may choose the material or substance which he wishes to investigate or to understand; may choose to study and to conceive that which he desires to have materialize or to become obvious; may choose to understand Realm I (to be substantiated in all ideas which The Logos substantiates); may choose to understand Realm II with its spiritually empowered wisdom; or he may choose to understand Realm III and its constant consciousness of right.

THE WORD, MORAL

The word *moral* has its root in the word manner, and the word manner is from French *maniere,* main, meaning hand, or from French and Latin *manus,* meaning hand. This meaning is not figurative enough to lend itself to the word moral in its purely metaphysical sense.

The word moral is from French and Latin *mos, moris,* meaning manner; custom. The plural form is *mores,* meaning manners or morals. The form *moralis* means manner, custom or habit.

The suffix *-al* added to the radical *mos* (*mor-*) means of, belonging to, relating to, characterized by, pertaining to, befitting.

Literally, the word moral means pertaining to manner. This literal meaning has no character and no metaphysical substance or entity. It does not have a subject or a named character or a specific manner, custom, or habit.

The figurative sense of hand (*manus*) leads to manual; a handbook; a handy tablet or code; a hand-sized book—at hand—prescribing rules, text, or directions to regulate manner, custom or habit; a book for reference as to mien, manner, behavior, method of acting or doing. Still there is nothing in the word moral itself to indicate good or bad, right or wrong manner, habit or custom. The word ethic, however, sets forth a philosophy of morals; sets up a standard, which is a standard of character or a standard of moral excellence adopted by any race or nation as befitting that race or nation.

Each race of the human race, and each nation, has its own concept of racial or native or natural character. It has its own system of ethics, manners and morals, and it certainly has its own peculiar customs, modes, established practices, or its own ways and fashion of doing things. It has its own manner of doing things. It handles, regulates or conducts itself, or deports itself, according to its own concept of deportment, which conduct or deportment is native and natural to it as characteristic of it.

Each race of the human race lives by its own philosophy. It institutes and formulates its own domestic, social, and public or national codes and it practices them as befits, relates, or pertains to its own racial peculiarities. This may be called its free moral agency. Thus the whole human race joins in deciding and codifying its code of morals, its system of ethics or its human standard of demeanor, and its own method of procedure in all matters and manners.

[288]

The word manner may pertain to the human nature and to the human race, but the word moral must pertain to a conviction of right and of wrong; must pertain to good intentions and right purposes carried out by means of conscience as operative upon one's own consciousness and as sanctioned by conscience, individually.

The word moral, spelled with the very capacious and literate *o* vowel, pertains to the higher metaphysical realm in which conscience names that which is excellent, that which is highly principled, virtuous, chaste, devout, worthy, dutiful, just, upright, honest and honorable, and names also that which is unprincipled, dishonorable and below moral par.

Moral science, moral ethics and true philosophy are based upon conscience—the science within oneself—which science is spiritual in nature, in essence and in substance, or in principles. It is, in the last analysis, the science within one's soul, speaking to one. It is far above human nature, racial customs, humanly prescribed codes or any system or science that befits or belongs to the human race or human nature, because the moral law is executed by oneself, and befitting to oneself.

Moral science, the moral law and the moral principles are based upon wisdom, for whom conscience is agent and mouthpiece, representative speaker and dictator.

That science and philosophy which serves one realm of thinkers could not serve another. Thus as conscience sets up the moral standard, the human race advances in every way; in every right and good way.

The following table shows that the realm of morality is the metaphysical gateway leading from physical science or knowledge to con-science—the dictator of moral science:

REALM   I   DIVINITY: The true or truth Principle and precept of The Logos-Soul; The divine creative Word—Truth—or intelligence.

REALM   II   SPIRITUALITY: the logician — true wisdom—who understands Truth and who practices the logic, literacy and law of The Logos-Truth, interminably and correctly.

REALM III   MORALITY: the realm of moral consciousness; the highest human concept of right; conscience itself, prompting, empowering, and promoting equity, honesty, virtue, uprightness, worthiness, rightness, justice and so forth. These involve moral courage, stamina, validity, strength and prosperity or true progress.

REALM IV   PHYSICALITY: the realm of the physical or natural sciences; the world of human knowledge; intellect and orthodox learning.

REALM V   IMMORALITY: unmorality; the realm that alienates itself from conscience, but lives under the law of physical science, acting as prompted by physics (human impulse) and doing that which is physically possible, regardless of ethic, right law or the moral standard.

The foregoing table shows that the realm of morality is a school in which humanity learns to differentiate between the science of soul (within oneself) and the false forms of knowledge; learns to demonstrate individually the laws and rules of conscience—the great tutor; learns to submit to moral and spiritual discipline under wisdom—the magnanimous thinker and spiritual seer.

Morality is fundamental to any people. Without it and its laws to adminster law, even the civil law would fail.

Morality pertains to human society. It administers and teaches by way of con-science, and since conscience is *semi*-spiritual in character, reason and virtue (morality) must be spiritually fundamental, in view of the fact that thinkers must have its teachings and tests in order to advance or to ascend in metaphysical experience. Thus human society in general is finding moral science the stepping stone to spiritual logic, to true wisdom or to complete understanding—universal understanding.

Morality is directed by spiritual ingenuity, wisdom, and by his gentle tutelary authority.

It requires both wisdom and ingenuity to live in a world largely devoted to immorality. It requires a peculiar kind of humility or meek wisdom which is not critical and not inclined to condemn this world. It requires a pious patience.

Wisdom is dominant in his own domain, but he does not enter the moral realm to dominate it. He allows morality or the human virtues and the statutes of conscience to dominate in Realm III. The human moralist may be an unwise reformer.

The wise and moral thinker knows that morality has worlds of immorality and unmorality (moral ignorance) to overcome before morality is accomplished. He knows that morality has many metaphysical wars, many deadly attacks, many engagements in its way ahead; many challengers and many years of malicious and revengeful challenges awaiting his moral stamina.

The very prosperity of a virtue excites human nature's love for vice. The very presence of morality inflames the envy within the weak human heart. Moral prosperity is the moral hopes and faiths being fulfilled. It therefore causes the subtle and occult would-be moralist (by reputation) to fear being uncovered in his infidelity and immorality (or in his moral poverty and disparity). This kind of desperation, or this unprosperous condition, causes the immoralist to fight to maintain himself, his reputation (so carefully guarded) and his very pleasing personality (so suavely amoral).

The very candor of morality is a challenge to vice and its natural occultness, and to the world's superficially moral (enough) or good (enough) kind of social standard.

The very candor, confidence and stability of morality makes manifest the virtues of morality, and makes the candidly confident and morally steadfast character a target, because it keeps immorality in the spotlight of comparison, and because of this comparison and contrast, immorality suffers the fear of exposure, lest he defend himself against that exposure. Wisdom teaches the moral character to be wise in dealing with this phase of human nature.

Immorality is always hypocritical. It is hypocritical because it does not choose to confine itself to its own unmoral world. It is vain and proud of its accomplishments in being accepted in the moral realm.

The candor of honesty, the confidence of faith, the energy and prosperity of hope, the animation of charity, affection, kindness and compassion are inconceivable to the unmoral character. The patience, tenderness, forgiveness, and trustworthiness of the virtuous character astounds and amazes the unrestrained, lax or loose character, but does not allay his dread of being uncovered and discovered to be immoral. In his desperation he undertakes to destroy, lessen or reverse whatever evidence of virtue (in others) he can. This makes his vices seem less glaring or flagrant to himself and to human society—his environment.

The moral realm is the battle ground upon which virtue challenges vice; upon which morality clashes with human nature (and its licentious human-kind or lascivious kind of man-kind); upon which right and wrong arm their forces in continual conflict; upon which conscience—reinforced by wisdom—prevails.

The word moral means pertaining to right manner; relating to, belonging to, or befitting custom or habit. It is not a noun. Morality is the noun form, but neither the word moral nor the word morality have a root other than the French and Latin *mos* and *moris*. These pertain to manner. The kind of manner, custom or habit is presumed to be right, honorable, and even virtuous, but this may be humanity's use of this adjective, or it may have become defined as right by means of humanity's long assumption and designation, since humanity has a way of fitting words to its own sense which sense is governed by its own human nature.

Right and wrong manner may mean handling a situation rightly (morally) or wrongly (amorally, immorally or unmorally). It may mean that morals are to be regarded as one's main consideration, or that one's manner, custom, or habit is the main or principal thing. This would carry out the French *maniere* or main, meaning hand and meaning the manner, mien, mode or way of acting, behaving, deporting or conducting oneself.

This sense of main or hand may mean individual action, acting or actor as a thinker handling himself rightly.

The popular meaning of moral is humanly established ethic, ethics, or ethical system, which again is characteristic of humanity or human nature. That which is unmoral implies the reverse or negative of moral (even as unwise is foolish—the reverse of wise or of acting wisely). That which is amoral is away from morality or out of the way of it; outside the sphere of ethic. That which is immoral is bad or not moral (by consensus of human opinion), or it may be by condemnation of conscience.

Since moral means manner and manner sets forth the thought of hand, we may say (as per a common expression) that John or Jane is a good hand at this or that or that one is a great hand for doing this or that or for acting in this way or in this manner. Thus both moral and manner pertain to right or upright or conscientious doing or way of doing.

Human ethic is a humanly established manner. Morality has no fundamental origin excepting it be *con-science*—the science of soul within oneself. Conscience is the power of moral discrimination; the faculty or rational, radical power to distinguish between right and wrong; a sensibility for right; a consciousness of being with or together with right or on the side of right and uprightness; a sense of conformity to right, equity and duty in human relations; the higher appreciation of virtue; the acknowledgment of moral-spiritual potency in honesty, veracity and such; the moral energy that makes unmorality impotent.

Conscience has no fundamental origin excepting it be in soul—the spiritual animus, feeling, sentiment or intuition. Thus morality is the science of soul reduced to human utility. It is wisdom given a human morale or moral interpretation or a mental agency through which to teach or to provide his prudence to the sound, profound, or conscientious thinker.

Morality without conscience would be a mere formality. Conscience without soul-science or the logic of The Logos would be an unknown or non-intelligent god; a soulless dictator; an illogical or unscientific taunt ever denouncing, reproaching, condemning, yet tempting the human race.

Morality is a conscientious force; a semi-spiritual influence guarding the human race and moralizing humanity's human ideals. It is the state or quality of being moral—honestly honorable, chaste, obedient to highest human sense of right and right manner; state of being a moral being.

The human being may be an inhuman, immoral, sub-animal or sub-mammal being having no sense of moral being.

Morality pertains to the higher sense of one's metaphysical existence or mental being. It pertains to moral culture, the conscientious refinements, or to right thinking, uncorrupted by human nature. It works as rectitude correcting human inclinations. It functions as a metaphysical energy curing, making accured or accurate or moralizing human beliefs. It operates to rectify, to make right, to amend, to make more mentally pure or morally chaste, and it works in the name of virtue (man of highest honor, duty, excellence, dignity, efficacy and moral integrity).

Morality is that state and quality of thought or ideal which is leading on higher and highest civilization, leading on through morality (as moralization) and leading up to spirituality, where wisdom and his collaborators take up the work of spiritual realization or true spiritualization.

THE WORD, MYNDE

The word *mynde,* mynd, or mind, as gathered from Latin, is *mens, mentis,* as found in the words mental, mention, sentiment, vehement and many others; as gathered from Greek it is *psuche,* as found in the words psychology, psychosis and many others. This Greek form means mind or soul as in Psyche or psychic. The Anglo Saxon or the Old English takes the form of mynd or mynde.

The Anglo Saxon *myntan, munan,* means be mindful, as in the form mint or ment, and the form *gemynd (munan)* means think, or means the mind.

The Word Mind, Mynd or Mynde capitalized, indicates The Deity, The Logos, and The Root and Source of The Word Mynde as well as The Word Soul. The word mind, mynd or mynde not capitalized, indicates the spiritual logician, wisdom, the radical (rooted) thinker, who is attribute of this Source of intelligence and who is completely environed by Mynde—needing no mind of his own.

The human intellect, and the humanly orthodox way of thinking, gives the human person a mind of his own. Human metaphysics attributes and distributes mind to men or to persons. This human intellect is only the human concept of mind and of soul. It is a consensus of human conclusion drawn from the human point of view of Mynde and of mentality; of Soul and of The Logos Who sets forth the logic or the science of Soul. Thus the human intellect has its limitations and its mental horizon as the following table shows:

REALM I

DIVINITY: The divine creative Logos-Mynde; The Intelligence which *is* Soul.

REALM II

SPIRITUALITY: the divine thinker and logician who is the mental phenomenon of The noumenal Logos-Mynde; that intelligence which is the immediate expression of Intelligence.

REALM III

MORALITY: the realm in which the human manner, custom and habit of thinking and believing is established; that realm in which human intellect or human knowledge is collected and recollected and is selected by the

human mentality; the humanly rational faculties or capacities; that realm in which human intellect has gathered, chosen, read, elected or picked up what it calls
mental substance or intelligence, but which is neither,
since intelligence is above and outside Realm III. Humanity's mental horizon confines its concepts to Realm
III; to semiproper reasoning; to semi-spiritual realization.

REALM IV
PHYSICALITY: the human brain; the human impulses;
human nature and the human nature of its knowledge.

Realm III has a humanized mentality; a mentality quite separate
and apart from Realm II, and quite isolated from Realm I. This human mentality is in disagreement with Realm I but is quite unanimous
or consentient with itself and with its own nature as it sees itself
in Realm IV.

Realm II thinker lives under the direct supervision and jurisdiction of The Logos. He practices and demonstrates the preceptial and
rudimental ideas (elements) issuing from The Logos-Mynde. He himself is an issue, an ideate element or an idea designed by, conceived
by, ideated or formed in The Logos-Mynde.

Realm II stands under Realm I. Its thinker is wisdom himself
standing under and understanding Realm I. It is the substance and
mental essence of Realm I. This substance is like wisdom, who takes
his stance under Mynde. Thus wisdom is dominant in intelligence,
reason or rational power which flows from Realm I, and the thinker
derives his thoughts from Realm I; derives his mental energy, power,
pattern and outline (of perceptions) as perceiver re-thinking and
re-presenting these outlined and energized perceptions. He derives his
mentality from Realm I.

The Realm II thinker has no soul, mind or intelligence excepting
his own consciousness (or understanding) of The Soul, Mynde or
Intelligence. Indeed this thinker has an whole intelligent consciousness or he has an whole and wholly conscious intelligence. He has a
complete, holy, or wholly perfect understanding of Mynde, he is mindful and he is thoughtful. He is the Anglo Saxon gemynd and munan,
meaning think. He is thinker. He is not Mynde and he is not mind,
but he re-thinks, resends, reflects, re-issues, re-emits, re-utters and re-
traces the outlines—which he derives from Mynd or Mynde or Mind
—and he presents and he re-presents his divinely logical, literate and
legitimate ideate outlines to Realm III for consideration. He presents his rudimental ideas; his specifically outlined and completely

thought out principles and premises so that Realm III may draw its own conclusions and deduce its own concepts. Thus wisdom—the thinking representative of Realm I—is infinitely logical thinker.

The thinker of Realm II is master, doctor and teacher for Realm III. He re-conveys, re-addresses, re-affirms and re-commends his wisdom and his logic. He re-lates, describes, reports, re-states, shows, displays and teaches by way of demonstration; by way of *liter-ation* (letter by letter), and thus he delegates the legitimate students of The Logos-Mynde, as students of the science and art of correct and accurate thinking.

The thinker of Realm II thinks in the absolute, as partaker of the infinite Realm I.

The thinker of Realm III thinks in the relative, because he adulterates his logic (his science and art) with human precepts and premises which he induces from Realm IV. He adulterates the purely spiritual nature of wisdom, logic, literacy and law, with human nature and human intellect and physical law.

It is very difficult to define The Word Mynde in terms of humanized language, and more difficult to bring a true concept of Mynde down to the human ability or human capacity to comprehend. Thus it may be helpful to use the ocean, as a humanly familiar thing, by means of which to set forth an illustration: the great oceans of the Earth may help to form a mental picture of the ever active, ever flowing or fluid nature of Mynde.

The great rivers flowing into the seas, the great activity of the waves, the depth (profoundness), the expanse or width, and the vastness of what is called the deep—all this may serve to give humanity some conception of Mynde and of its inflowing power.

This inflowing power is intelligence. It is a divinely beneficent influence; an infinite inflow of thought to the thinker who understands or who is under-stander. This great resourceful Mynde under which the thinker stands presents the picture of the fathomless nature of The Mynde.

Mynde, being understood, is understanding of Mynde, and this is as natural to the thinker as the flowing of water. The function of the thinker is to think. The function of water in a brook is to flow in its channel, which channel or way is open and unobstructed. So the thinker, who is wise and understanding, offers no objection or obstruction to the inflow of The beneficent Mynde, but rather does he take it in and utilize these essential properties, and later he presents these divine properties or proper mental elements to Realm III in morally substantial or morally essential forms; presents them in their morally peculiar form, as that Realm III thinker's own peculiar property.

The ocean serves to set forth a picture of the spriteliness and the naturalness of the aquatic animals. It serves as a great stage to exhibit the natural wonder and particular gloriousness and lushness of vegetable or plant life. It presents its colorful, graceful and beautiful mineral formations that are so natural to it. It presents and illustrates transparency and reflective power, since the surface of the ocean (exposed to the great sun) does exhibit tremendous reflection or reflective action.

This ability to re-flect, re-send and re-present the sunlight is typical of the thinker's power to re-present Soul or Mynde to Realm III.

The thinker of Realm II is the minder of Mynde. He is not Mind or mind or Mynd or mynd or Mynde or mynde, but he is mindful of Mynde—The Logos. He is thoughtful, as minder, minding, heeding, or paying attention to The intelligent mental Principle—Mynde; depending upon and subject to Mynde.

The true thinker takes cognizance of and is aware of that Mynde from which he receives his thoughts, his wisdom, his infinite logic and his absolute understanding. If he were to become unmindful of The Source of his thoughts he would be unmindful or unthoughtful —even unintelligent. It is this awareness of Mynde, coupled with his wariness or prudence in not minding the minds of human knowledge, which makes him intelligent as a representative of Mynde or The intelligence of The Logos; as a minder of The Logos impulses.

The minds of human knowledge exist in lower realms, where human intellect asserts itself through many millions of minds, and where human nature esteems them. But these people or persons are not thinkers or minders. They are spiritually ignorant, unthoughtful and unmindful of Realm I.

Realm IV presents its physical mindedness. It is obedient to and mindful of whatever physicality presents as premise, as precept or as rule. Thus these people or persons of the lower realms give heed to these precepts and conclude according to physical premises, and conceive and hold these conceptions which are wholly humanized or physicalized.

In Realm IV each human physique is given a mind or will of his own. Hence the clash of wills and minds in these lowest realms, and hence the concord and absence of conflict or clash in Realm II.

The Word Mind embodies the very literate vowel *i*. The word think depends upon the same vowel. The word man is built upon the very illiterate vowel *a*. Thus we must use the Anglo Saxon man meaning think, and use the Anglo Saxon (mind) *munan* meaning think so that we have Mind or Mynd and the thinker. This thinker is mon, not man. He is that spiritual minder and thinker who is too literate to be expressed or spelled with the *a* vowel. But mon is more representative of his infinite and continuous mental-spiritual capacity, since the *o* vowel speaks of continuity and capacity.

The Greek *anthropos* (man), a human being, or the human kind of man treated by anthropology, or the human kind of mind treated by psychology, or the human intellect (called mind) — these things are two realms removed from mon, the thinker and minder. These concepts are three realms removed from Mind, The Principle of thought, thinker and intelligence.

THE WORD, NATURE

The word *nature* comes from the Latin radical *nasci: nascor, natus,* to be born, to grow; *natura,* nature; past present *natus* means born or produced. The suffix *-ure* makes it a noun of verbal action; the act of, state of, result of, or that which is born.

Its adjective form is natural. It means by birth, inborn or innate. Its adverb form is naturally or natively. Its root embraces the words cognate, natal, nation, innate, native, nascent, renaissance, international, national, preternatural, supernatural and others.

Its common synonyms are to be found in the Greek *physic* (*physis, phusus,* which means nature), or *physikos,* meaning natural. Physical means of, or pertaining to nature. Its synonym is bodily.

Its metaphysical meanings may pertain to essential character, moral or spiritual quality, state, condition, disposition or constitution, or to bad or ill temperament.

The word nature is spelled with the illiterate *a* vowel. This feature alone classifies it in the physical realm. But the word born may be used in highest metaphysical sense when speaking of spiritual type, sort, specie, birth or kind; when speaking of being born or produced, created and originated, or taking rise from The vital Principle-Root or Logos. It is not a true noun or name of a particular thing, but it is the act or process of being born or of bearing (*borning*) or giving birth. It is the result of this act or process. It is a state or the state of this verbal action.

There are five distinctly different realms which present five different aspects of nature; five different types, states, conditions or sorts.

The following table classifies these five types:

REALM   I   DIVINITY: The divine creative Logos from which the divine creature—*mon*—is derived or born; the highest metaphysical, mental or spiritual type, state or condition of Being; The Logos-Soul which animates or gives life and birth and continuity of being to the wholly spiritual being —mon.

REALM   II   SPIRITUALITY: the realm of reality which is born of The Logos; the powers of complete ideation, demonstration or perfect realization; the wisdom, the logic, the literacy, the sentiment, the principle or law born of The Logos and existent in soul—the entity; the spiritual type, sort, essential character, substantial constitution or quality inherited from The Logos-Spirit; the distinguishing attributes of spiritual kind.

REALM III   MORALITY: the moral instincts, intuitions, convictions and steadfast qualities which make up conscience; the innate moral consciousness.

REALM IV   PHYSICALITY: the human nature or the human physique or physical creature.

REALM V   IMMORALITY or moral depravity.

The thinker of Realm III finds the immoral or the morally depraved nature inconceivable—even unnatural—or unfamiliar, while the lower realms find the upper realms vacuous or meaningless.

The illiterate *a* vowel in the word nature may be changed to *u, o* and *i* forming the words *nuture, noture* and *niture*. These literate vowels can lift the word nature from Realm IV and make it highly metaphysical and meaningful.

The word nature may be spelled with other vowels than the illiterate *a* vowel, to indicate character of higher metaphysical, and literate standing, thus:

Nature—natural, physical.

Nuture—nutriment, metaphysical *nutrio* — pertaining to conception, gestation and the capacity to nourish; the female element that nurtures.

Noture—(note-ure), that of which the spiritual logician takes note or notice as being noteworthy; spiritual noteworthiness.

Niture—(*natron, nitron, nitre, nitrum*)—that which pertains to the highest nature, as native to The Logos-Soul.

This niture pertains to the natural salt that inheres and that preserves all divine elements; a sodium that chemicalizes naturally with that which is unspiritual, to sweeten and to purify or to make immaculately lovely and divinely true. This niture functions spiritually and morally in the mentality to spiritualize or to moralize. No element of human artifice enters into the realm of moral thinking.

This niture separates or divides that which is not pure, not spiritually noteworthy and not morally nutritious from that which is divinely excellent, positively valid, and infinitely true or logically continuous. Its function is to prepare and to conceive, to give form (literate form) or to record, and to make evident to all spiritual observers the power of this niture and the noteworthiness of its literate and logical substance. No least element of human knowledge or human nature enters into this record. It is nourished, mothered, and sustained by its legitimate Mother-Love.

The word nature may be used in the highest realms or classifications, by using adjectives to specify the kind of nature, but to use the phrases of divine birth, of spiritual birth, being spiritually born, of moral birth, being born of conscience, would be more correct.

Let the following table illustrate this point:

Realm I

DIVINITY: (The divine nature) The Logos-Mother; The vital Principle; Intelligence; Omnipotence; The divine Maturer of quick, spirited or spiritually motivated ideas.

Realm II

SPIRITUALITY: (the spiritual nature) the logician born of The Logos-Mother; the intelligent thinker of divine birth; the literacy born of The Word; the divinely legitimate mon, born of or matured by The omnipotent God.

Realm III

MORALITY: (the moral nature) the conscientious thinker born of conscience, honesty, veracity, soberness and human affection; born of moral courage, stamina, excellence or dignity; the moral character, instincts, impulses and intuitions born of natural moral sentiments, faith, confidence and rectitude.

Realm IV

PHYSICALITY: (the physical nature) the corporeal human nature; the human physique; the animal or mammal nature; the Adamic or Eve nature which includes the natural activities of the physical mater or the mater-ial for all mater-iality. Here Eve is the mater or mother of all *materia,* material stuff or matter; the mater of the material nature.

Realm V

IMMORALITY: (the inhuman, hateful, envious, deceitful, crafty, pernicious, hurtful, averse and adverse nature) the artifice of the unmoral nature; the artificial pretense born of the immoral nature or the antagonistic nature.

THE WORD, Obsession

The word *obsession* comes from the word obsess which is a verb meaning to besiege; to beset; haunt; harass.

The word obsession adds the suffix *-ion* to form the noun of action or of condition.

The prefix *ob-* means before, facing, near, near to, to, toward or in the way of.

The Latin root is *sedere: sedeo (sedo), sessum*. It means to sit.

The suffix is *-ion*. It gives state of being or adds the existing condition or being as though it were *-ing*.

Literal meaning: sitting before or in the way of.

Common meaning: that which sits before one as a vexing, dominating impulse or mental image; an afflictive morbid belief that urges action; that agitates, affronts and annoys.

That which holds sessions in one's mentality—by constantly suggesting or presenting itself for acceptance; by urging one to conceive and to carry out the suggestion—is an obsession. It would impregnate or impress. It would embarrass or beset. It would obstruct or stand (sit) in the way of. It would besiege by a long and stubborn siege (a sitting near to one, a seat or place, throne or station blockading one). A siege is a *sedeo* as a fixed place, a seat, a chair or a place of enthronement. An obsession is a mental image invested with power or enthroned in one's consciousness as a thing or concept having dominion and the power and permission to hold its sessions in one's mental temple. It is an aggressive, persistent troublesome mental thing that must have a place, space, chair, throne or seat to occupy in one's mentality. It may become a chronic mental condition if its sitting or session is of long duration, or it may become a morbid fixity or a provoking fixation.

An obsession may be a strong feeling that something is in the way of, or is set against one. It may be the feeling or sentiment or concept that someone sits as an obsession besetting one. It may be one's own pride, mad ambition, determined will, and fears and dreads that sit or are sitting before one. It may be a sense of revenge, remorse, resentment, or envy that is settled in one's thought or is sitting in the way of one's moral-spiritual prosperity. It may be an invalid, sick or sickening sense of things that obsesses or besets one. Whatever it is, it must be dethroned by the one who enthroned it or accepted it as settled.

A foe, a feud or a feudal situation may be an obsession to several or to many, or to a nation at war. It is an agitating, vexing human situation; a condition involving hostility or sore animosity. It demands a seat. It demands attention. It demands action. It claims a seat or throne from which it may dictate, demand, and command. It threatens. It advocates or suggests solution. It occupies place, space, and time. It employs its agents and actors, and without pay or remuneration. It harasses and haunts at will, and willfully. It rules, for it (an obsession) is lord of the human person; a tyrant on his throne in the human mentality; a self-justified, proud and domineering belief servilely entertained.

THE WORD, Occultness

The word *occult* is a verb meaning to cover up, hide, to cover over or covered over; to cover from view; to conceal. This same Latin form, *occulere, occulo, occultus,* meaning hide or to hide, is the root of the word (noun) occultation and other nouns, adverbs and adjectives which simply add different suffixes. The prefix is *ob-* (*oc-* before *c*) and it means over, up or upon, or to. In this word occult, over is preferred, as covered *over*. It might be *to,* indicating the verbal action, to hide. This use of the prefix *ob-* (*oc-*) would leave the root as cult, and since a cult is considered to be a system of worship, of magic, or divination, since a cult may choose to worship something that is hidden from ordinary human sight or view, since a cult may cultivate or may be cultured (*cultus*) in certain religious worship (*cultus, colo*) which seems to be superhuman, mysterious or occult in its nature and in its character, or seems to be mystical— remote from human intellect or literal observation—the word occult may mean to worship. It may mean to denote a certain religious care (*cultus*) or culture. It may mean to denote any kind of devotion other than the literal, material, physical or humanly obvious image presents.

That which is occult may be that which is bad or badness covered, or badness at work under cover of devotion to good purpose. Again that which is occult may be that which is spiritually awe-inspiring because of being so good, and so far beyond human nature to comprehend.

The word occultness is the noun form. It is the state, condition or quality of influencing; of turning attention to the presentations of magic or the mysteries of human knowledge, by means of covering that which would interfere. It attracts attention and holds it to whatever exhibition, show or mental phenomenon it pleases. It causes the observer to attend. It entertains that attention with its show. It performs its act or acts while holding the attention of the human ear and eye.

Occultness pertains to the skill or craft of mental control. It advertises itself or makes the human mentality take note. It impresses or impregnates with its germ or potential (virile) properties. It incites and excites humanity's wildest imagination by means of its peculiar presentations or metaphysical manipulations or suggestions.

Occultness is the art of obscuring or covering the fact with an element of fiction. It may be like the so-called black art or dark, black magic, or other supernatural art. It is obscure or destitute of moral light or spiritual enlightenment and it may tend toward the lowest kind of unprincipled hypnotic practices or magnetic agencies.

Conscience and the moral sentiments and qualities take no part in occultness. They partake of frankness, candidness, moral clarity and charity. They relate to the science and art of honest reasoning or the science of correct and accurate thinking and teaching—making obvious.

THE WORD, Opportunity

The word *opportunity* is an interesting word. It comes from the Latin *portus,* meaning harbor, or haven or port. The Latin port is *porta,* meaning gate or door.

The prefix *op-* is *ob-,* meaning before, near, toward, to or facing.

The suffix *-ity* gives the word state or quality of being, or condition of being.

Literal meaning: state of being near the harbor.

Common meaning: a fit or convenient time; a favorable occasion; a convenient season; a seasonable state.

This word opportunity was probably compounded for the specific use of seamen. This may have been its origin and its original use. But using the word port or portal or harbor in a wider figurative sense, it has come to mean many things and to have many uses.

The word opportune meant (originally) before harbor, or near the harbor; at or before the port or harbor. Importune meant hard of access (not *portus*); importunate means quality of not having access to harbor; not pushing toward the harbor; unseasonable (as opposed to opportune or seasonable).

Many words have come into use by way of such literal, physical, earthy, worldly, or mundane human requirements as this one, but one may give the word port, harbor, or haven a metaphysical classification, having a moral lesson or axiom, or one may think of it in terms of the Anglo Saxon *hefan* (heaven), to lift or heave up to the harbor, haven or heaven.

Any place of physical or metaphysical anchorage may constitute harbor or port for one seeking shelter.

There is heaven—the place of anchorage for the spiritually minded. It is the mental home or spiritual haven and harbor for wisdom and his sentiments, for understanding and its substance or stance and for integrity and its holy potency.

There is a moral place of harborage; a working station or port for conscience where moral stability and moral stamina stand with conscience in the moral port. It is a place of refuge from immorality, unmorality and amorality or human nature; a conscious abode safe from human storms, wills, winds and unrestrained violence (animosities).

[307]

In this moral port there is opportunity for ministering to those who are not substantially tied, settled, set, fastened, anchored or moored to morally dry land (figurative Earth or ear of higher understanding), to those who are not immorally minded but adrift from ear (ear-th) of conscience; to those who are not at rest, not properly berthed or secured.

Opportunity brings with it the state or condition of not being at sea mentally, morally or spiritually; not being at the mercy of the tides and tempest of human nature but being in port with the more magnanimous (greatness of soul) nature where one shares the environment of moral gentleness, chastity, beneficence, affection, moral prosperity or hope.

The things (issues) of high, higher or better import are found in this port. There is compassion with its patience, there is honesty in his moral honor, faith in her confidence and fidelity, and all of the meek, loyal, conscientious sentiments, or soul-sense.

In this port where the moral qualities and characters reign or hold and are held, gathered in and protected, there is no shipwreck —no moral disaster. They are elements of the moral law, in the character of conscience. All that is untempered, unrestrained and unsobered by moral law is unable to dislodge them. The indulgent, the sensual, the inhuman or the unkind elements of the human nature are unable to destroy them—so fitted are they to their slip or dock.

This port, harbor, slip or dock allows the moral ship to bend with the wave but not break or resist to the breaking point. It does not compromise with the storm, but it avoids disaster from its blasts— verbal, silent but tempestuous and threatening action. This port is opportune. It is where and when the conscientious one needs it. It is gentle, kind, gracious and very capacious and always in season as a favorable opportunity or a convenient season. It is a happy or good place, or an opening for well doing or for doing well, beneficently and morally.

There is an immoral port called hell (Anglo Saxon, meaning conceal); called *Gehenna* (Greek); called place of burning or torment believed to purify the character or atmosphere. Here the untutored do not see the port as a place of torment. It is offering every opportunity to the envious, the dishonest, the malicious, the heartless, the proud or selfishly wilful, but its physical and metaphysical agonies are concealed.

The foregoing analyses show how useful this word opportunity can be. It is a good word to widen one's sphere of thought or to increase one's vocabulary and use of good words, or to stimulate one's conception of words.

THE WORD, PERCEPTION

The word *perception* comes from the word perceive, which is built upon the Latin *capere* (*capio, captum*), meaning to take, or upon the Old French radical *cap* or *cip,* or upon *capio* (*capere, captus*), meaning I take, seize or hold.

The prefix is *per-*. It means through or thoroughly, or by.

The suffix of the word perception is *-tion.* It forms the word perceive into a noun of action or condition. It gives it agency and status or state as an abstract noun.

Common meaning: to take, to apprehend, seize or grasp as an agent (or agency) of understanding; the action or condition of understanding thoroughly or through and through; the product of cognition or the state of being fully cognizant of that which has been seized or discerned by or through the intuitive faculties; that which is mentally evident to one.

Perception differs from conception in that the prefix *con-* means with or together, joint or jointly. A conception is that which the conceiver has taken with the perceiver; has taken jointly and together with him, while a perception is that which the perceiver has taken or apprehended singly and alone. It comes first or before a conception, or it is a preconception; a fore-evident thing discerned but not yet conceived and verified or made evident to other thinkers.

A perception is a male agency, while a conception is a female agency or activity. It is the female mental matrix in operation, taking, seizing, grasping and holding (for gestation) that which she comprehends (together with him) as being that which he has apprehended and presented to her.

A perception is only a potential or rudimental thing, while a conception is the same rudimental thing in process of being made actual, evident or existent as an issue; in process of being gestated, developed, acted upon, quickened and carried out or through thoroughly, and by means of the female faculties of comprehension. Here comprehension is a feminine activity, since the prefix *com-* means also, with or together.

A perception is wholly undeveloped. It is only the outline of an issue. It must be conceived by the female thinker, since the male has no matrix (physical or metaphysical) in which to nurture or to sustain his own precepts and perceptions. He is sterile to his own germs or rudiments of a concept, while the female matrix is delicately sensible to the germs of true concept. She has a natural intuition for sensing an element of truth or logic.

The perceiver cannot conceive and carry out his own perception, no matter how wise and discerning he may be. But every intelligent perception or precept must have its intelligent conceiver who spontaneously and naturally takes, seizes, grasps or comprehends, and brings forth to issue, and nurtures through infancy.

Many words are based upon this root *capio* (*capere*), and *cip* and *cap*. Many follow the same rule, having both the masculine and the feminine prefixes. There is concipient and percipient, there is recipient and incipient, there is principle and discipline, there is capable and capacity, and so on, but a perception pertains to precept and is instructive. A conception pertains to a concept and is constructive.

A perception is an immediate deduction from some particular kind of precept or basis of reasoning. It must embrace all of the logical and literate elements or properties necessary to the formation of a concept or conception. It must set forth all rudimental, preceptual, or conceivable elements (the germ, the gist) and it must embody them as elements to be developed. It must be worded, affirmed and communicated.

The development of a perception depends entirely upon its conceiver. She takes (embraces or embodies) this perception which has been put into its rudimental form, and she gestates it (carries it and carries it out). She quickens it or acts upon it and brings it forth in form discernible, perceivable and conceivable to all who think in its degree of intelligence.

Thus the conceiver demonstrates the degree of intelligence, the literate and logical virility, and the legitimate status of the perceiver-advocate. She tests the quality of his precept, or testifies to its validity.

A negative thinker begins with a negative precept and from it deduces his negative perceptions.

A constructive, positive or virile thinker begins with conscience, honesty, or his own moral convictions and intuitions, and from this basis deduces his positive perceptions. He gives no heed to human knowledge or to its patterns. They fail to embody wisdom, since they are limited to human nature, and since they deny conscience (the science of soul).

Wisdom is the great perceiver. He begins his thinking with the wisest, clearest, purest and highest precepts, premises or principles, and he deduces his perceptions in his dominantly wise fashion.

In the moral realm honesty is the honorable perceiver and moral charity, affection or sentiment is his veracious conceiver. Con-science and her science dictates and directs the mental processes. She contraceives dishonesty's advocations.

In the spiritual realm wisdom is the wholly (holy) empowered perceiver and thinker. He is fully aware of his Logos-Precept and of the logic peculiar to this precept and he deduces all of his perceptions from this wholly and infinite Precept, since he is himself, offspring, agent, perception or spiritual agency springing from this Logos-Precept.

Wisdom takes and takes hold of. He takes by and takes in. He does not lose, miss, or fail to grasp, firmly, but he holds to that which The Logos teaches and demonstrates to be wise. He is the immediate deduction of and from his Precept—ever perceiving and ever presenting that which he perceives.

The following table will classify perception in its several states, stands, conditions or standings:

REALM   I   DIVINITY: The Logos; The Word; The Precept or Principle of all true perceptions.

REALM   II   SPIRITUALITY: wisdom, the embodiment of all wise, true, real or divinely substantiated perceptions.
Here a perception is a divine emission; a provable element of an idea to be re-emitted, represented, perceived thoroughly and conceived spiritually.

REALM   III   MORALITY: conscience, the embodiment of all moral intuition or honest instinct.
Here a perception is a spiritual or highly moral emission; an ideal to be re-stated and reemitted, advocated and conceived, and morally maintained.

REALM   IV   PHYSICALITY: the processes of the human perceiver and conceiver who perceive in accordance to and with the natural sciences and human nature or knowledge.

There is as much difference between precept and concept as there is between perception and conception. A precept must necessarily come first. Likewise a perception must come before a conception. It is that which is presented to the mental matrix (thinking capacity) to be conceived. It is the masculine half of thinking.

Percipience is directly related to perceiving thoroughly. Percipiency is the state or quality of apprehending completely. The perceiver is familiar with his perception which he has deduced from a precept. But it must become familiar to the conceiver who forms it into her concept. Thus the perceiver and the conceiver are of one family and their issue is familiar (*familiaris,* of the family) to both of them.

Mental and moral and humanly metaphysical issues are born and nurtured or they are contraceived, aborted, unquickened and unmothered (not nurtured).

If the moral conscience is present to superintend perception, if con-science (the science of the moral-spiritual nature) is present to attend the processes of constructive thinking, then human nature is impotent and unable to interfere, then physical precepts are *not* of the family.

There must be a mutual understanding, an intercourse (a running between) precept and perceiver and between precept (premise) and conceiver—not between the two thinkers (as persons).

Both the perceiver and conceiver must be mindful of their common premise—be it moral, spiritual or divinely metaphysical. Both the percipient and concipient thinker must understand or stand under their common conviction, as compound thinker, as instinct (for truth) or true premise.

THE WORD, Physical

The word *physical* comes from the Greek *phusis,* which means nature. The physique (*physike, physis,* meaning nature) is defined as the physical structure of a person, or the person's body; the natural, material, bodily, corporeal or physical structure of a person.

The suffix *-al,* added to the word physic or physique, changes it from its noun form into its adjective form. It means of or belonging to; fitting or befitting to; relating to or pertaining to; characterized by, or appropriate to the physique, as opposed to the mental, metaphysical, moral or spiritual properties and substances or characteristics.

Thus the word physical having been defined, analyzed, and described, it must be classified by being compared with its contrasting and opposite properties:

REALM   I   DIVINITY: The Logos-Spirit; The divine creative Soul-Principle.

REALM   II   SPIRITUALITY: the spiritual logician, creature, or soul.

REALM III   MORALITY: the moral con-science or student of the science of soul.

REALM IV   PHYSICALITY: the human nature; the human physique or the Adamic consciousness or physical mindedness; physicalness; state, quality or condition of being natural, corporeal, material or the bodily structure of a person; that which is materially tangible and corporeally natural.

In Realm IV the human physique has no voice, no vote, no right of protest and no way out excepting through death. It has no means or ways to resist the intellectual regimen, the human knowledge, or the social regime under which it must function. It is treated as a puppet or as an instrument or tool to serve its king—the imposing human intellect.

If it were possible to lift the human race out from under this human knowledge tyranny, it might enjoy the normalcy, freedom, inexhaustible energy or health, and all of the wise properties or proper spiritual resources of Realm II; all of the beneficence of understanding which is substantiated and sustained by The Logos.

[313]

THE WORD, POWER

The word *power* comes from the Latin *possum* (*posse; potens, potentis*), I am able, or I have power; to be able; mighty; powerful, or to have power or potency.

Common synonyms: ability, might, force, energy, strength, effectiveness, efficacy, vigor and validity. These apply as well as one word may substitute for another.

The word power embodies the *o* vowel which is a symbol of spiritual capacity and of continuity. Thus it must be classified as being an attribute or element of infinite Might, while the word ability may apply to human strength; may apply to human, moral, metaphysical or physical energy.

The Greek *ergon* means power, or work, or force. It is the root of the word energy. Energy means in work; in or at work; in operation, or being in force. Literally, power in one; erg, work or energy within one; the urging, actuating, motivating or driving forces in one, or in a thing. Thus the word energy must be classified as pertaining to non-spiritual concepts; as pertaining to exhaustible strength.

The Greek and the Latin *ago* means drive or driving agent; actor; conductor; driver; doer, leader; leading agent or cogent force. This *ago* (*agere, actus*) is the driving agent; the actuating force. The wheels of an automobile are driven or turned, or forced by means of its engine or motor. The energy, the erg, or the ability is not in the wheels. The wheels are passive to this driving agent or this engine. So it is with every manifestation of energy, and with every human motivation—it has its human impulse or impelling motive or its driving agent.

The power that holds the Earth in her orbit is made up of laws, principles, or mandatory elements, factors or agents of energy of some kind, and are commonly called laws of gravity. The Earth is passive to these mandatory elements, gravitations and laws of whatever sort. Thus there must be an actor or an active or actuating element, and there must be a passive element upon which to act, and there must be a principle or principal source of power to motivate the actor or to actuate or impart motion. There must be an origin (a source of power—of whatever sort), and there must be a first actor and a second (complementary) actor to be passive or to be acted upon.

In the realm of spiritual thinking wisdom is the first actor. He is the virile power of perception and of speech; the power of presenta-

[314]

tion, oration or address, while verity (the fertile power of conception, gestation, verification or conclusive demonstration) is the complementary actor; the one acted upon.

This fertile intelligence (fertile mental matrix) may be illustrated by Queen Isabella's prompt and hearty conception of Christopher Columbus' theory. He had introduced his wise and virile perception to the world. He had proclaimed it and had pleaded and prayed for moral, spiritual and financial support with which to prove his perception to be true. He was a navigator.

Queen Isabella was an intelligent woman with a woman's intuition. She knew nothing of either geology or navigation, perhaps. She only recognized a factual perception; a preconceived truth; an unborn idea—that is, unborn before the face of humanity. She knew *that* he knew. She did not know *what* he knew. She knew that he understood what he advocated.

Queen Isabella's power of conception equaled his power of perception. Spontaneously she took his potential issue and carried it out to its fruition. She mothered this germ of undeveloped and of unverified fact, throughout all of the processes of its development. She sustained both it and its perceiver's hope. She caused it to appear or to become evident to all thinkers. This story illustrates power that is both active and passive. The passive power is not inactive. It is the quickening agent. It is the power of cohesion, comprehension, coordination and construction or complete realization. It is half of the whole unit of thinking power, or half of all wholly rational power, or half (the female half) of the full ratio of intelligence or spiritual potency.

The following table will classify the word power, and it will classify also spiritual intelligence, and will compare it with human intellect:

REALM I

DIVINITY: The omnipotent and almighty Logos-Intelligence; The divine Motive, or motivating Spirit—Love.

REALM II

SPIRITUALITY: the powers empowered by and derived from Realm I; the intelligence, wisdom and enlightenment produced by and sustained by Realm I; the power of expression or speech; the powers of ideation, reflection and logical conclusion; the powers of understanding, and the power that confirms or demonstrates wisdom's potentialities.

Realm III

MORALITY: the moral energy and efficacy that holds
human reason and conscience in action or in force
among human kind.

In this moral realm there is an ethical ability emoted
by faith, confidence, expectancy, hope and moral zeal or
vigor and prompted by spiritual influence; the moral
qualities or virtues which partake of Realm II; the
powers inherent in honesty, veracity, compassion, patience, moral stamina and instinct which take preponderance over human intellect.

Realm IV

PHYSICALITY: the realm of human nature, human
knowledge, human intellect and human impulse; physical strength or vigor.

Realm V

IMMORALITY: adverseness; unmorality; spiritual ignorance; moral depravity; unrestrained human nature
doing whatever is physically and humanly possible;
human and inhuman will and will-power and its ill will
animated by animosity, pride, envy, sensuality, dishonesty and mortal vengeance. It has no rational potency.
It is the inability to think correctly, accurately, rightly
or conscientiously.

This realm has no potential capacity; no actuality or
substantial reality. It is the negative or antonym of
every moral quality; the vice of every virtue. It is the
personal prestige, or the delusion of personal importance
that inflates itself, only to burst or to disintegrate. It is
destructive in every element. It is the zero pretending to
be a unit. It is not a numeral character with the power
of a numeral. It is not a number with a ratio of power.

Neither physical strength nor immoral force (energy or impulse
or compulsion) may take the name of power. Power is so urged and
so named by Soul; so identified by its soul nature. Immoral impulses
(such as deceit or dishonesty) are without legitimate name; are
without honor, honesty, veracity or truth, and they are therefore
without power, integrity, virtue, entity or logical identity. They are
ignominious human impulses in their soulless actions.

Power is that which is possible to wisdom and his co-workers;
that which is possible to complete understanding of The Logos; that

which is possible to infinite reality, verity, truth or ability to realize an infinite concept.

Human strength, energy and validity are finite. They are limited *to* and localized *in* physicality which is exhaustible.* They are urged by soulless agencies.

Power is the composition of essential realities, or the real essentials. Power is the potency of intelligence—all that is possible to intelligence; all power to realize intelligently. Power is soul and its precepts in action.

Power is one of the holy properties belonging to the wholly (holy) logical thinker. It makes perception and conception infinitely logical, literate and legitimate or quick. It energizes, vitalizes and validates or verifies all true concepts and vivifies wise perceptions.

Power, as an element of intelligence, is in highest ratio of intelligence; highest rational power and highest degree of reasoning power. Reason, wisdom and intelligence, truth, honesty, integrity and such constitute power because each one is a power or it is allied with the other elements of power. Wisdom is wise dominion or is *in* power. Truth is full of truth, truthful or powerful because true. Honesty is in honor or in power, in his own name. Intelligence is a consolidation of all of these powers, and other elements of dominant nature —being the rule—which nature or natural elements stand *with* wisdom and stand *like* wisdom, predominant, because they present highest elements or ruling principles; because they stand under The Logos as understanding, wholly substantiated.

---

* In the first printing, through a typesetting error and an oversight in proof-reading, this word appeared as "inexhaustible."

THE WORD, PRECEPT

The word *precept* rests upon its Latin root *capere: capio, captum,* to take; or from *captus,* I take, seize, or hold.

The prefix *pre-* means before or beforehand.

Literal meaning: (verb) I take or seize beforehand; to take, seize or hold before or beforehand; take beforehand.

Common meaning: (noun) a rule, command, maxim, instruction, direction, doctrine, adage, admonition or prescribed mandate taken or observed before.

Common synonyms: law, order, injunction, principle, and many others.

A precept may be the rudimental essence of a thoroughly developed concept, even as a perception is formed before a conception. A precept is taken before or first or before as pattern or outline from which to work out a concept. A concept or conception is that which is taken with its precept and together they take form, illustrate or teach.

A precept includes its design, plan or specific directions. It is only a potential male element. A concept or conception is the embodiment of the potential elements, taken with or together with the female element of thought, to be gestated, verified, realized or brought forth as actual.

Every moral issue functioning on Earth today was a moral precept or maxim, or axiom, admonition or a right precept before it came to issue or became a concept or a rule of action, or an established commandment, or a humanly instituted element of conscience. It was a precept, then a concept, and then an established issue based upon its precept.

Every concept is tributary to some substantial precept. The precept is the pater or pattern or father of the concept, conception or issue. It is instructive. A concept is constructive or a conception may be said to be completely constructed or formed into an established issue.

The thinker takes his precept, combines it with the factors and elemental faculties of conception, and forms the concept or issue. The potential germ of a precept must be processed through the mental or rational faculties; must be perceived, preconceived, received, conceived, and must issue forth or be born as an whole issue.

A precept prescribes, directs, admonishes or dictates (as through conscience), while a concept is the effect of the practice of this precept or the preceptial and preceptorial cause.

A precept is the first element taken in a series of mental processes. A moral precept taken beforehand, produces a moral issue, after being thoroughly processed in the conceptual matrix of the mentality; after being sustained, carried, gestated, confirmed, or held firmly in mind, and carried out or borne out.

A precept must be advocated or prescribed as a rule for action. Then it must be accepted, conceived, and acted upon, quickened or animated by its conceiver. It must be adhered to, or be allowed to adhere. It must be practiced, else it is only a potentially practical thing regarded as an ideal, or as a fragile platitude unrelated to conscience.

A precept must be alive, must be in command, must be a mandate, in action. It must be apprehended and then comprehended; cognized and then recognized; observed and preserved.

A precept is of common gender. Its function is to act upon the perceiver as rule, ruling agent or ruler in forming his perceptions.

A precept is preceptial, informative, instructive or altogether didactic. But the perceiver and conceiver must both illustrate and demonstrate that which a precept teaches or sets forth; must individually prove its doctrine.

A precept teaches in its own words. The perceiver must put his perception into the form of words as a worded statement of a potential fact or as his own advocated outline of action or application to a given ramification (ramified element) of a precept or ruling agency.

A concept may be said to be the fruition of a precept; the issue of a doctrine, correctly applied, while a misconception is the fruition of a mistaken perception, or an element of misunderstood doctrine.

A precept may stand for centuries without being correctly perceived, taught or conceived of; without being practiced or made practical in human affairs; without being set forth in preceptial form or with its original potency.

A precept is made up of pertinent facts; of specific or well defined elements of doctrine. It embraces the power of speech or preceptial expression which the perceiver takes on. The perceiver takes or deduces his specific element of precept or doctrine from this precept or principle and proceeds to form his perception, and then to set it forth for conception. Thus the perceiver is the agent of the precept or primary doctrine.

THE WORD, PREMISE

The word *premise* comes from the same rudiments as the word promise. Both mean to send, throw, cast or put forth, or to set forth beforehand, or to send before.

The Latin *mitto* (*mittere, missus*), I send or throw.
The Latin *missum,* to send or cast.

The noun form is prestated or pre-set or preconceived facts laid down for bases or grounds from which to draw factual conclusions. A premise is a logical proposition sent before. It is a living spiritual substance leading to the substantiation of itself. It goes in advance, to lay down or to specify, define, classify and direct; to forecast or promise.

A precept or a premise or a promise is a male element propounding, proposing, announcing, affirming, pleading, defending and advocating himself as being worthy of conclusion. It may be a potential statement of wisdom, sent before or in advance of further action. A premise is cast before by the male thinker, but not yet cast, pondered, measured, weighed, computed, reckoned, molded, formed, realized or reasoned out by the female thinker.

The female mental matrix is impressed or impregnated by the logical premise which the male thinker casts, sends or throws before her; which he advocates for her to conceive. When conceived and brought to conclusion, it is conclusive evidence, proof, and test of the advocate's virility or moral potency, and proof of the verity and vitality of the premise, since the conclusion of a premise is engrafted or embraced, or outlined in it as substance and essence of it.

A premise may give promise, but until it is tested and found valid (morally, logically or ethically proper or good for human utility), until it is brought to useful human conclusion in human affairs, until it is found to be beneficial, remedial or of value or of virtue, it is only in its potential form, giving only its promise, not its fruition.

There are many premises gathered from many doctrines and from physical and metaphysical systems. A conclusion should fully and wholly represent its premise, in classification, in quality, and in degree of literacy and logic. A conclusion should be the manifest, logical conclusion of its premise, or the consequence of its authenticity.

A premise has as much logical authority as the principle upon which it stands, or as the standard of excellence which it represents. Every true premise has its legitimate conclusion. It may be disbelieved, misconceived, or contraceived—because the intelligence of the orator is of higher degree than that of the conceiver—but it has its true concept.

A premise is made up of essential germs of thought to be germinated and gestated. The ear of understanding or the rational power of conception must be spiritually and morally capacious and must believe in the authority of the premise or the perception, for she must sustain it throughout all of its processes of development. Her conclusion must be as positive as his premise. It must be a conclusive event, an obvious unfoldment, a premise illustrated or a fact demonstrated. It must be positive proof of its pater premise, or that proposition which was sent forth beforehand.

Premise is the sender of that which is sent. It is the maker who sends or emits certain missives or intelligent properties, information or instruction to the intelligent thinker. If the sender be The Logos, the thinker is the logician and Premise is the beginning, the root or the seed; the mental, spiritual, soul beginning or creative element, as the following table will show:

Realm I
DIVINITY: The Logos-Principle; The Word-Root; The first, The Beginning and The Origin of true thought.

Realm II
SPIRITUALITY: the logician, the idea or most highly principled thinker and most literate and capacious receiver of that which is sent; the divinely sent or legitimate messenger, designed by The Logos-Premise to realize, to understand and to bring to a designated conclusion, all of the elements of logic, literacy, and Principle's discipline.

Realm III
MORALITY: the conscience or the morally scientific thinker or wholly conscientious thinker who is disciplined by, trained by, tutored by, guarded by, fostered by, vitalized by, empowered by and purified by the spiritual principles and premises of Realm II.

Here the highly principled messages or missives have been resent or sent again in lesser spiritual forms or in somewhat human design—designed to completely moralize all premises and conclusions.

Realm IV

PHYSICALITY: the human mammal and his personal,
corporeal or animal sense of things.

The substance and elements of a premise feed or nourish thought,
even as the root of a tree sends nourishment up to the twigs. It is
like the sun emitting or sending beams of light, or like a rain cloud
sending its mist to refresh or to nourish the grass. The Premise is
The divine creative Logos—Designer and Maker of ideas or premises.

The premise being Good (God) or the promise being good, the
conclusion must be good. The thinker must be good, wise, holy or
wholly substantiated and purely spiritual because Good—The Premise—is Spirit sending or spiriting or moving or employing thought.

The Premise being The Logos-Speaker is ever articulate, and is
ever instructing. The thinker is ever receiving the rules, recipes,
directions and designs sent before, so that having followed instructions,
he may arrive at an instructive and constructive (good and logical)
conclusion.

In Realm III a right (moral) premise promises a right conclusion.
A right perception is based upon this promise. All moral premises
and promises are established in the beginning principle or premise,
or they are instituted by their right intents, purposes or moral designs. Thus their character, their states, qualities, and conditions are
moral—conclusively so; consequently so—as the resulting condition.

The moral premises are embodied in con-science. Its true science
presides and its premises are its promises sent, in the form of intuition
or moral instinct. Thus its conclusions are conscientious and in complete agreement with its premises or its morally scientific promises
and they are confidently confirmed.

In Realm II a premise is that spiritually magnanimous (great
soul) proposition which wisdom and sentiment receive as sent from
Soul-Premise. They perceive, conceive, receive and realize or understand it and then they resend or reteach it to Realm III, as representatives of it. They forecast it as spiritual seer and sentiment.

THE WORD, PRINCIPLE

The word *principle* means a beginning; source, cause, reason or doctrine from which a practice may proceed; a commencement or foundation, rule, law, or an original or primary or basic truth; that essential substance in a thing which determines its inherent nature, origin, character, state, quality or condition of being.

The root of the word *principle* is the Old French and Latin *capere, capio,* take; *captum,* to take; *capyus,* I take, seize, hold; or from *principe, principium, princeps* or *primus-capio,* meaning take first; or from *primus-capere,* to take first. The suffix *-le* may give it noun form, as that which relates to, or that source, or first cause and origin from which or in which a thing begins, or from which a thing proceeds or takes rise.

The following table will classify that beginning:

REALM   I   DIVINITY: The divine creative Logos; The Word and Root-Origin of all ideas and principles; The vital Logos-Principle; Spirit.

REALM   II   SPIRITUALITY: the spiritual creature and logician *mon* or man—the absolute thinker—whose Source, Origin, Creator and Cause is The Logos-Principle.

REALM III MORALITY: humanity; humanhood; the orthodox thinker; the ethical and intellectual human being, whose conscience informs him as to right and wrong, and which conscience and its science represents his highest principles or moral standards.

REALM IV PHYSICALITY: human nature; the human physique, the human animal, mammal or person; the humus-man — earthy and earthly.

Here physics is the basic and primary authority; the premise, basis, substance, cause and rule governing according to its instituted physical systems and agencies.

[323]

REALM V IMMORALITY: unmorality or moral ignorance; a lack of moral dignity; an
amoral state of consciousness which cannot entertain conscience nor abide by the
mandates of its science.

The word Principle is a compound, divine word. Its radical and
central theme is *cip* (*capio*). Many good and positive words are built
upon this radical, such as eman*cip*ate (to take out of the hand of),
the word parti*cip*ate (to take part in or to partake of), the word
in*cip*ient (taking at or in the beginning and first), the word re*cip*e
(take thou), the word re*cip*ient (ready to receive or to take), the
word con*cip*ient (to take or taking together and with its principle
or principal perceiver), the word per*cip*ient (taking by, through or
thoroughly and throughout; grasping thoroughly), and the word an-
ti*cip*ate (take before).

The word Principle, being a divine creative word, and an element
of The Logos, constitutes The Principle for all logical concepts or
ideas; for all truly literate statements or recipes; for all really legitimate and divinely normal, spiritually healthy, and morally sound
practices, conclusions and conceptions.

The function of this Principle is to serve as governing axis—
divinely symmetrical and geometrical. The head and body axis of
an eagle—governing the two wings—may serve to illustrate this.

As the two wings of an eagle coordinate, cooperate, cohere and
collaborate, and as they adhere to their axis principle—from which
comes their energy or muscular power—so do the two major and
compound elements of mon or of intelligence cooperate in and by
one Word (one Logos or first Principle), from which comes their
thinking power—the power of perception, power of speech, power
of conception and power of record.   This power to record (power
to give form, power to make evident or to bring forth in fully developed form) is scientifically feminine.

As the two wings of the eagle are under the discipline (dis-*cip*-line)
and authority of the eagle prin*cip*le axis, so the compound thinker
acting as dis*cip*le of Prin*cip*le, is compound re*cip*ient of its power.
The speaker and the hearer are animated and motivated by the
motive power and the will of The Logos-Principle. They are agents
or agencies acting under the direction of their common radical (root)
Logos-Principle. They are wisdom and true sentiments, constancy
and accuracy, immaculacy, integrity or complete understanding (of
Principle). This complete understanding is at work loving, living,
thinking, teaching, trusting, fulfilling, expressing, quickening, *re-*

presenting and realizing or multiplying all of the essential properties of this Principle, intuitively and continually.

In the orthodox human realm the human race abides by its own standardized premises. In this Realm III moral precepts are influenced by human nature and by the natural sciences or human knowledge. Humanity has instituted its philosophy, its platform and its ruling systems, and it has set or established itself (as thinker) under these standardized precepts.

In this Realm III conscience presents the principles, the premises, the precepts, or the primary moral factors.

In Realm IV human knowledge and human intellect or humanly acquired learning are the governing and primary factors. That which is humanly, physically and literally obvious is basic.

Principle is the self-existent, all-embracing Rule and Director of all infinitely correct and accurate practice.

Principle is The universal intelligence which governs universal understanding or Realm II. This Principle must be capitalized because it is a name for The Deity; the name for The divine creative (first) Word; the all-sustaining and all-embracing and all-instructing and ever constructive Logos whose logic is represented by the logician of Realm II. This realm presents creation as the ideation of its Principle, and as that which Principle maintains, while Principle IS THE CREATOR of this compound ideation, or this most highly principled creation.

This word Principle embraces the rules and the radically worded precepts which may *not* be humanized, may not be detached from their creative and original Root-Word or Logos.

The popular theories, premises, conclusions and practices of the various ages or generations may *not* change or influence the radically precise nature of this Principle. They may only imitate, misconstrue and misrepresent or mistake it or profane its divine substance, to bring forth their own prodigies or monstrosities. They may only construe (erroneously), interpret humanly, or undertake to construct a morally substantial (or a spiritually substantiated) idea upon their humanly established absurdities or their acquired knowledge; upon their orthodox beliefs or the consensus of human opinions and practices.

This great Principle superintends the universe of its own principles, its ideate qualities, its expressive realities, its manifest states, its representative conditions, its primal verities of being. It fathers its own highly principled premises, and maintains those divinely or logically principled ideas that grow out of its root—The Logos-Root.

These states, qualities, conditions, and characters of being, maintained and embraced by this great creative Principle are known to humanhood as words, but they are ideate beings, living individual characters, entities, thinkers, speakers, or conceivers, and perceivers who understand or stand under their Father-Principle.

Wisdom is one of them. He sees and discerns as seer, and he bears witness to what he sees.

Sentiment or love of the purely spiritual classification, is one of them. She feels or senses spiritually, by way of intuition, and she acts upon her conceptions, as verity, to verify wisdom's perceptions.

Power is another one of them—the power to perceive, to conceive, to receive and to bring to realization—the power to think, to speak, to teach, or to demonstrate this Soul-Principle. Integrity, intelligence, spirit or spiritual vivacity and energy—these are the disciples disciplined and motivated by this Principle. These are the valid, unadulterated, legitimately and logically perfected and literately principled identities fathered by this Principle and characteristic of it. They are the wholly and holy verified constituents, attributes, elements of law or doctrine effected by this Cause, and derived from this Source as attributes. They are constituent ideas, highly principled forms substantiated by this Principle.

Principle is primary, first consideration and major necessity in the processes of fully principled thinking.

Principle is the father and mother of all divinely principled ideations, conceptions or ideate beings—not humus-man beings, not Adamic creatures.

The unprincipled mentality is pater, pattern or father of all misconceptions, multiplier of all spiritual idiocy or divinely unsound and unreal perceptions.

Principle is disciplinarian, guide, tutor, guardian and leader, and speaker (mandate), and mandatory element governing the divinely principled thinkers, perceivers, conceivers and understanders; governing the ear, ear-th or hearing earth, or compound ear-th of understanding. This understanding is the infinite and universal substance of this Principle.

All moral principles, all human ideals—whether realized, practiced and individually verified or not—and all inspirations or awakenings are incited by The Spirit or Soul of this great and first Principle or primary Word. These awakenings are the individual thinker's contacts with ideate principles such as those coming through conscience, or such as those (spiritually) projected or emitted from wisdom.

Thus principle may reign as mental, metaphysical king in three realms: in Realm I as The Deity or Logos-Principle; in Realm II as compound and complete understanding (realization) of this Logos-Principle; and in Realm III as conscience.

In simplest language, principle means in the first place; to begin with; in the beginning, or first and primal rule and order or model, or primal origin.

Principle is the classifier; the first element to be established; the primal and fundamental and universal Primate; The Beginning of all doctrine (logic, literacy, judgment and rule or ruling principles). Thus it classifies and defines the moral precepts or premises, and through the ruling precepts of conscience, governs the realm of morality.

Principle classifies and defines and governs the spiritual realm and maintains its harmony through the ruling principles of the logician, wisdom and his coordinates.

Realm IV has established its own physical premises; has instituted its own precepts in its own finite way. These precepts are adverse to Principle or they are opposed or are opposite. They pose their precepts upon the physical and the finite. The best symbol of Principle is the polar axis which humanhood knows, governs or marks first. Another is the natural force governing a blooming flower, a root, or a seed. Yet Principle is unfamiliar to humanhood, the flower is not. Principle may be called The noumenal Thing (Word, speech, logic, Logos) of which the flower is the phenomenal thing—a miraculous thing.

THE WORD, Protect

The word *protect* is a verb meaning to cover before, beforehand or in front of; literally, to cover in front.

The word protection is a noun of action, state or condition. It comes from the Latin root *tego* (*tegere, tectus*), I cover.

Common synonyms: cherish, keep, preserve, shelter, defend, shield, or to cover from harm or to keep in safety.

This word carries with it a feeling of action; a sense of having acted, of being in action, of having detected the need for action. It acts as wisdom, with foresight; as vision or power to perceive before. It indicates watchfulness, spiritual instinct, or quick intuition. It describes the function of the seer and the sage in dealing with unspiritual traditions or with immoral deceptions.

It includes the office of prophet who gives warning before, or goes before, morally. It is moral stamina standing before or in front of; moral-spiritual hope or expectancy knowing before. It is moral prosperity going before to protect against despair, desperation or desperate condition—moral poverty.

The protector is a moral philosopher who thinks, speaks, and acts according to his conscientious principles; who loves wisdom and who acts as its agent in human affairs. He is virtue or the virile thinker protecting or manning his metaphysical house and defending feminine sentiment. He is honesty protecting her who honors him; fidelity being faithful to her who trusts him; integrity having already protected or shielded wholly those entities or issues under his supervision. It is moral courage and strength protecting the gentler graces and affections who do not go before, but who follow behind, protected from the blemishes of maculacy, or from unwholesome influences.

It is the aggressive, proud, immoral and unmoral elements from which the moral philosopher protects his environment. This moralist presents piety, sobriety (restraint of human nature), tenderness, temperance (control of human impulse), modesty or meekness (that protects from pride), sagacity (that detects and protects from envy).

The moral philosopher preserves, keeps and cherishes intuition, compassion, patience, conscience, benevolence, prudence, chastity, veracity and all of the highly—morally—refined qualities. Philosopher, seer and prophet must protect the infant moral issues that need protection, and must protect the feminine conceiver and nurturer of

[328]

them while she silently sustains what the moralist proclaims or loudly advocates. This moral sage must protect himself, as well as being protector. His philosophy or his wisdom is his protection. His sagacious environment, his pure spiritual atmosphere (that environs him with understanding) protects him. He is protected (as wisdom) as the seed of bean or pea or nut is protected by pod or hull, because he is the precious element of moral-spiritual reproduction and multiplication of wisdom.

Wisdom himself is indestructible, because he is maintained and sustained by The Logos, as logically dominant, but his infant issues are nurtured and clothed (swaddled) in understanding's most loving and gentle sentiments for their protection.

The root of the word protection is *tego* which is also the root of the word integument, meaning to cover, an envelop, a coat or that which covers and protects.

The word protect means to cover in front. This implies a going forward, advancement or exposure to something harmful. It speaks of something from which one needs defense, needs shelter or moral-spiritual preservation. This implies that as the moralist goes forward he encounters such traits of character as revenge, inflamed jealousy or envy, hostility, pride and its tyrannies or destructive and vain self-esteem which persecute the harmless or the innocent by their inordinateness.

To protect means also to cherish. The moralist who is radically so or radically conscientious may find that he inflames human envy as he passes the envier, going on farther and farther and making a greater degree of unfavorable comparison between himself and the envier. The envier cherishes his own personality. The moralist cherishes and protects his own virtues—not himself—and presses on, forward. He lets virtue and con-science (the science of honor) or the dictations of his soul protect him, not as a person, but as an entity, idea, or soul-ego. Thus soul, being indestructible, his protection or cover is impenetrable. His course being forward, is toward spirituality, and there is nothing in front of him from which he needs protection, since spirituality is his goal and since wisdom dominates that realm.

On the way from human, personal, corporeal or unspiritual realms up to spirituality, the moralist and his conscience encounter much ignorance (of the science of soul within one), but his conscience is his integument. It protects him from malevolent opposition.

THE WORD, PROVIDE

The word provide or providence is built upon the Latin *video* (*videre, visus*), I see, or *visum,* to see. It means literally to look out for, to supply, to foresee, or the I, ego, entity or idea who sees clearly, and who supplies or makes evident (to others) what he sees. Thus, as a character, this provider is a seer, prophet or interpreter who brings the substance of understanding or the understance-ing of wisdom; who reveals what he has seen or has discerned concerning spiritual logic.

The word providence affixes the suffix *-ence* which gives the word its entity or its I who sees forward.

The word providence is a universal word, turning in all directions, to turn itself into all parts of speech.

The verb is provide, the adjective is provident, the noun is provider (an agent), the verbal noun is provision,—and the common noun is provision—that which is provided. The adverb is providentially or providently, and the adjective is providential.

The word providence may pertain to provider or to that which is provided, from its highest, divine sense, even to its lowest mundane sense:

REALM   I   DIVINITY: Providence, as The Logos or The Word, God.

REALM   II   SPIRITUALITY: that logic which The Logos provides; that literacy which The Word provides; that principle or law, recipe and rule which Providence, Good or Divinity-Spirit provides; that entity (*entia*), wisdom, who sees and who bears witness, testifies or foretells what he sees or discerns.

REALM III   MORALITY: the moral agents who exercise foresight; the moral seer and sage who looks or sees from moral premise or precept to conclusion and to concept which *is* provision; the vigorous and thrifty replenishment of good or right ideas.

REALM IV   PHYSICALITY: those   physical   needs
which human nature or the human physique demands—the agent and the agency
being the human person.

Mother Nature may be called providence, in so much as she represents the provider of food, clothing, creature comfort and shelter.
Mother Nature's vegetable, mineral and animal kingdoms depend
upon Earth, rain, sun, wind and all of Earth's reproductive nature;
her capacity to nurture and to nourish human kind.

The moral nature may typify providence in its ability to look to
wisdom for super-vision or foresight. Morality and conscience supervise Realm III, while wisdom supervises Realms II and III. He is
over-seer overseeing human affairs and providing humanity with
confidence in right, with loyalty to moral standards, and with ability
to stand in an understanding state of receptivity of moral goods.

In the realm of immorality, there is an invidious nature that looks
upon good fortune (moral prosperity) covetously or enviously. This
mental attitude inflames and burns that which is lovingly provided,
because of moral blindness or spiritual ignorance. Thus it lays waste
to its own moral potentialities and human provisions.

This treatise or word analysis intends to provide The immutable
premise, which is The Logos, from which to deduce conclusion or
conclusive understanding. This particular analysis of The Word
Provide (Provider) really provides Providence Himself, who is Provider of all divine and good provisions; of all wisdom, discernment,
infinite vision, or discrimination; of all of the powers of distinctly
clear perception.

The thinker of Realm III observes human intellect or human
knowledge that is humanly approved and established as science.

This treatise—THE WORD—is not intended to agree with humanly
established sciences or humanly instituted knowledge. This particular
analysis of The Word Provider is, rather, intended to dishonor human
knowledge. This treatise is not intended to appeal to the human intellect, but to lead the thinker away from it, to higher and entirely
different realms and platforms for premise and for precept.

This analysis would have the thinker of Realm III leave behind
him all humanly established premises, and bring with him only his
understanding of the principles of mathematics and his own conscience (the science of his own soul, or the intuition provided by his
Provider-Soul). Thus, having his understanding of numeral science
with him, and having his understanding of Soul in and with him, he
is established under The great Principle of divine order and pre-

cision. He is established under The Logos-Soul, who is provider of all logic, all literacy, and all law, which law reaches to the lower realm to provide morally right and humanly good things or provisions. He has left behind him only his old finite objects, humanly designed forms, images, or concepts; only his humanly natural or physical knowledge.

Providence is infinite prudence and jurisprudence, providing sound judgment, wisdom, discernment, and spiritual discretion. This kind of prudence sees forward, is seeing forward, or is forward seeing and foreseeing, even as spiritual seer, prophet, or foresight itself. This kind of foresight is law and logic prudence or pro-vidence, which providence is pro-video perceiving or seeing logic face to face, or immediately before one in one's own vestibule of thought or thoughtful consciousness.

Providence means being logically prudent or provided with wisdom, with full discernment, with the powers of perception, conception and spiritual realization. It means being literately provided with the powers of speech or expression of prudent ideas, universal precepts, axioms, or words of Truth. It means being legitimately circumspect—able to look or see all around and in all directions—from highest spiritual point of view or fourth dimension or four dimensions (North, East, South, and West) as outlined by The Word, which is director, beginning or Principle of all divinely directed or infinitely measured ideas. This is North. East is represented by wisdom or divine enlightenment. South is that point at which wisdom crosses human intellect, makes foolish human sentiments, human nature and human knowledge, or disagrees with the human point of view. West is the last of the sequences instituted by The Word. It presents the fulfillment of the design of The Word. Thus The Word or Logos is divinely and wholly circumspect as Providence, and thus the logician or the correct and accurate spiritual thinker and realizer is provided with all substance; is furnished with all that is essential or requisite to metaphysical life or soul continuity—so provident is The Logos-Creator.

THE WORD, Psychology

The word *psychology* is made up of two Greek forms.

The root, *psuche,* is soul or the soul.
The suffix, *-logy,* is science, speech or description.
Literal meaning: the science of soul or the soul.
Common meaning: the science of the human mind or soul.

In human speech, discourse, knowledge and description both soul and mind are human and humanized. From humanity's point of view all is human and all science, all that is mental and all that is soul are within human grasp or belong to humanity. The human race mistakes, misbelieves or misconceives and misinterprets all divine and spiritual things. The human mentality and its human nature cannot pass the tests of *con*-science (the science of soul within oneself). The *humus*-man never rises from the ground or from his human, mammal basis. Human knowledge is not logic or science and human intellect is not intelligence. The Logos-Soul or Mind is unknown to humanity and is unknowable excepting through the tutelage of *con*-science. In reality there is no science and no mind and no soul in the humus-kind or the mankind concept; no human ratio of them. The human family is not familiar with them. They are supernatural to human nature. They are spiritual and divine properties. The human self is not soul; not one of Soul's peculiar properties; not actuated by moral and spiritual principles nor by the consciousness of Divinity. But the human self is in a realm of its own making.

Soul appears to the thinker from a different point, corner, angle or point of view by stationing *mon*—the logician—in a different place or position or condition or state of being from which to view or to contemplate.

The following table classifies or stations man and mon:

REALM I
DIVINITY: The Logos-Soul; The Word, Soul; The Word Good or God—The Root of all logic, literacy and divine rule and perfect order; Creator of mon—the wholly and holy spiritual creature.

REALM II
SPIRITUALITY: that mynde or mynd or mind or soul who is fully enlightened by Soul; that man, mon,

[333]

thought, think or thinker who thinks with the Mynde of The Logos—not with a mind of his own; that consciousness which belongs to The Logos-Soul and functions as soul.

Realm III

MORALITY: that consciousness in which con-science is regarded, minded or heeded; that moral thinker who is under the tutelage of Realm II.

Here conscience is dictator and director of the science of soul. Neither Soul nor soul, Mynd or mynd may be demoted, deduced, or reduced to this realm, but they are presented to this realm by conscience—the representative of soul and the teacher of soul's wisdom.

Realm IV

PHYSICALITY: physical consciousness or physical mindedness; natural or physical knowledge; anthropology; the humus-man or human physique and its nerve sensibilities and impulses—all that is sensual, physically sentient, sensuous, or of a sensory nature.

Here consciousness is limited to and confined within this realm. Neither man nor mon nor mind nor soul exist here. Neither thinker nor true thought nor the entity (logician) nor the literate and legitimate identity exist here. Only the human physique and its magnetic personality (called the ego) exist here.

Thus, being without moral or spiritual entity and character, this human physique is whatever natural science says it is, and is whatever anthropology teaches it is. Yet it is without con-science; without spiritual body or the temple—temple of infinite con-*templ*-ation.

This treatise or word analysis tables and classifies words according to their relation to their root. The word psychology embodies the Greek root *psuche, psyche* or soul. The Logos-Soul (God) is that Root.

This word analysis must hold soul in its proper and spiritual realm or classification, if it is to hold Soul in the realm of soul's Root—in Realm I—as The Logos-Soul. It must hold Soul to be God and soul (the attribute expression), to be *mon,* since the physical figure (image or man) attributes his states, qualities, character and condition of being to his flesh (physical) ancestors.

The following table will show soul-ology and the logician or the soul-ologist in contrast with physical knowledge:

Realm I
DIVINITY: Soul—The Root Word of its own attributes;
The Creator of its own spiritual creatures; The Source,
The first Principle or Word-Root of soul as well as of
mon, munan, mynd, soul-thinking or thinker.

Realm II
SPIRITUALITY: soul—the radical attribute word pertaining to Soul and attributive *to* The Word, Soul, and
wholly unrelated to other than The divine Soul.

Here is mon, the soul logician, the wholly and holy
spiritual creature whose point of view is purely spiritual
and whom Soul maintains or substantiates in this
(Realm II) point of view.

Realm III
MORALITY: soul sense—the radically moral sense of
existence; con-science and its scientific sense of existence.

Here is man, the conscientious, sincere, innocent (the
lamb-like) creature. He is a student of soul science as
taught by conscience. He is candid, frank, morally
sound, ingenious, trustworthy and fully blameless.

Here is the man who thinks, believes and understands,
morally. He has a natural moral instinct, sense or higher
intuition.

Realm IV
PHYSICALITY: the soulless physique or the mammal
human person who lives by his animal instincts, the
senses of his physique or his natural senses, or human
consensus.

Realm V
IMMORALITY: the soulless metaphysique or inhuman
(mammal) person who lives by his wits, his deceitful
arts or unmoral artifice.

Here is neither man nor mon, nor soul, nor thinker,
nor conscience, but only a kind of consciousness that
feels hostile toward moral law; feels antagonistic toward the science of soul or conscience; feels vile or evil;
feels adverse and opposed to everything that would re-
buke his immorality.

The foregoing Realm V is added to the table for the sake of
contrast and comparison. Its soulless metaphysics or its soulless psy-

chology contests, antagonizes with, contends with and struggles against every noble or moral obstacle set against him or it. It harbors antipathy, enmity, animosity, envy, malice, deceit and all that is harmful, noxious, pernicious and contradictory to Realm III and its con-science.

The so-called criminal, the amoral, unmoral, and immoral person is one who has lost contact with his soul, his conscience or his soul consciousness; has lost contact with himself, his entity, his true identity, his spiritual parentage, his principle or his element of spiritual discipline.

Mon or soul is disciple of his Soul-Principle.

Man or the moral conscience is under spiritual discipline, and is the recipient of its recipes, as moral disciple.

The human physique has only its physical identity. It is free to be as fraudulent as it (personality) pleases.

Human knowledge or intellect is *not* derived from Mind or Mynde —as Mynd, Mynde or Mind belongs to Realm I. It is not derived from mind or mynde or mynd the thinker—as thought or intelligence belongs to Realm II. It is not derived from *con*-science, consciousness of soul, or of the science of soul, or of the consciousness of the science of soul—as soul science or *con*-science exists in Realm III. But it— human knowledge—is derived from its own false conception of soul; from its own misapprehension of soul and its science. This misapprehension is its own false assumption of Mynde, of mon, of soul and of all things—as these things belong to Realm II.

Humanhood has presumed and has assumed or stolen the words science, logic, truth or Truth and has created its own realm, has generated its own systems and has established its knowledge in the name of soul or mynde, but without benefit of The divine creative Soul. Hence human knowledge is only humanity's perception and conception. It is constructed according to human pattern. It is fabricated out of human fabric and its human *-ologies* are humanly fathered, *patered* or patterned.

Psychology is that which human knowledge has humanized, has translated, has interpreted, has transposed and transported. It applies to the human mentality. It serves humanity. It is humanity's best concept of the human consciousness or mentality.

The fact remains that conscience is the science of soul; teacher of the first lessons in soul-*ology* or mind-*ology;* teaching under the discipline of wisdom or mon—the spiritual logician of Realm II.

THE WORD, Reality

The word *reality* comes from the word real, and the word real may be built upon the word re (Latin *res,* thing), meaning about, or concerning this thing, this action, this topic, or this noumenon, of which reality is phenomenon.

The root re, thing.
The suffix -*al*, relating to.
Literal meaning: relating to this thing.
Common synonyms of the adjective real: actual, true, and
    genuine.
The suffix -*ity* forms the word into a noun. It adds state or
    quality of being.
Common meaning: state, quality, character or fact of being
    true and true to fact; state of being of the thing itself, or
    being concerned with this thing.

The thing is the object of thought; the thing or the cause provoking thought, esteem, recognition or consideration. This thing may be physical, metaphysical, mental or spiritual or The divine Thing, *Re-al,* Source, Root and creative Logos; The Re and Principle of all things real, and of all reality; of all things, realities, ideas, actualities and verities realized by The Logos.

That which seems to be real to human knowledge is that which the physical realm calls real. That which is real and of great importance or significance to one realm is unreal to another. Thus human knowledge, functioning in the realm of physics, finds physicality (in all of its ramifications) to be real, and finds spiritual things to be unreal, immaterial or beyond human practicality or utility.

Authorities give the word thing as a synonym for logos. Other synonyms are speech, ratio, description, saying, word, science, reason and others. These terms carry with them a selectivity, a divine ratio, or meaning.

This thing pertains to the science and art of reasoning or to reason; pertains to correct and accurate speech, which speech is directly derived from The Logos, and which science and art pertain to the logic of The Logos, and which sayings, words and reasons are descriptive of The Logos, and which description is of highest verbal ratio.

The following table classifies and helps to define the word reality:

[337]

Realm   I   DIVINITY: The Logos as The Re, *Res,* Thing or Being.

Realm   II   SPIRITUALITY: the logician as the re, *res,* thing immediately derived from The Logos; the thing or holy (wholly) spiritual being or thinker who has the power of infinite wisdom, sentiment, speech, reason, presentation and realization; reality, in harmony with The Re.

Realm III   MORALITY: the conscientious thinker who observes the recipes prescribed by *con*-science and who strives to demonstrate them, confirm them, reason them out or realize the moral significance of them.   Here honesty is the power of speech and con-science is science, and reason is the art of thinking in highest moral, human ratio.

Realm IV   PHYSICALITY: that which is physically and literally real to physical science and to human nature, but is unreal in so much as it is a departure from the moral-spiritual science or *con*-science and the logic of The Logos; a departure, in premise, from Realm II.

Reality *is* spirituality, and spiritual substance (under-stancing) *is* reality. The thinker's ability to understand, to visualize or to discern the thing or to form the mental image of the thing, is in proportion to his spiritual ratio of mental power of conception, verification and realization.

That which has actual existence, or is of prime importance to one individual, may not exist in the premises, precepts and principles of another, and may not be fully appreciated—as to its weight, meaning or import—by another. Thus a thing or idea of spiritual import is not fully understood by the physically mental powers of perception and conception; not fully appreciated by the physically minded, but is misunderstood; is depreciated—even contraceived.

When a hope, a concept or an expectation (fully believed, beloved or appreciated) becomes a reality, it has been realized. It is no longer a thing hoped for. It is no longer a thing looked forward to, but it is a thing to be enjoyed, as a spiritual reality. It is a thing of wisdom or of true sentiment realized. It is a verity, actualized and verified. It is a thing of faith or fidelity substantiated by spiritual substance. It is honesty being spiritually honored and empowered. It is virtue, moral virility and chastity being spiritually glorified as wisdom and virginity or purity.

Physical knowledge, human nature and human impulse perceive the image (the actor, the actuality, the agency, and the entity or thing) to be physical (unspiritual). It humanizes everything. It personalizes and physicalizes things believing them to be animated by physical agencies rather than animated or spirited by soul, wisdom or spiritual agencies.

Reality is the embodiment of logic—the logic of The Logos. Reality embraces all actual literacy or intelligence, or full ratio of power to realize. Reality is the thing, rule, ruling factor and law, in action, and realization is the complete realization, administration, execution or the carrying out of that law. Verity is the law that verifies wisdom and causes his issues to appear (spiritually) or to be realized.

Reality embraces all of the ramifications of logic and all of the action of the real logician.

Morality is one of the ramifications of reality. Conscience is the instigator of verity and reality in human affairs. Thus the Realm III thinker is working his way up to the absolute, the genuine, the immutable or real logic, literacy and law of Realm II. He is able to realize the issues of honesty; able to demonstrate honesty's power; able to verify honesty's science (con-science).

This scientific nature is veracity or a humanly essential verity— indeed is a major element of reality—for Realm III exists as the product of the virtues of Realm II; as the human manifestation of having realized some of the intrinsic laws reflecting from Realm II. Realm III exists as the human interpretation of reality. Physicality (or Realm IV) exists as unreality or the inability to interpret reality, spirituality or universal substance, which sub-stance fully under-stances (under-stands) or is standing under The Re, as reality itself.

Beginning with The Re as re-al, real Root or The premise Thing there is nothing real to be considered excepting that which The Logos-Premise concludes, that which The Logos-Principle ideates, that which The Logos-Precept gives as doctrine, commandment, injunction or mandate—understood.

Reality is that great mental-spiritual matrix upon which all real ideas are recorded. It is understanding or that great tablet of soul upon which Soul's logic, science, realities, verities, images, visions, designs, manifestations and substantial expressions are engraved or made of divine record, because learned by heart.

The Re is creator of reality. This realm of reality is that realm of understanding which has the divine benefit of universally true and infinite enlightenment. This infinite enlightenment or power of realization has recorded upon the tablets of understanding all things or thoughts that are real; all things fully discerned or divinely interpreted.

Reality is the effect, the expression and the outcome of The divine creative Re or Logos-Principle. It is the embodiment of all of the compound elements of spiritual contemplation, conception, comprehension and coordination, in operation under the direction of The Logos.

Reality is the manifestation and reflection of Realm I ever receiving its power of realization from The beginning or Root-Principle (The Re of this reality) which supervises, tutors, makes wise and preserves all wisdom in its divine state of excellence. Thus reality has the power of speech and the power of record (to record). It speaks in its own divine and spiritual idiom as taught or tutored by The Re or real Spirit of The Logos. It speaks of its own literate and logical condition, position and disposition.

There is another realm that attracts human attention and which is the metaphysical aspect of Realm IV. It is the opposite of Realm III, because it is the reverse of the right and good and moral thinker, and because it is altogether unrelated to conscience. It functions under Realm IV and it functions without the benefit of moral instinct, rule or law. It is Realm V. It is *meta*-physical or after the physical, and it is under the physical as being subordinate to it and to its limitations, its disposition, its character and its nature. It is the unreal, untrue and inhuman imagination. It wanders and errs where it will, at will. It has neither logical nor literate premise, but only the human physique and its personality to represent. It may be physically correct, but it is naturally unspiritual and unreal.

This realm embodies all that is unmoral and immoral; all that it *sub-animal* and all that is criminal and morally unnatural; all that is humanly and physically possible—in disregard of moral restraint.

Realm III consists of multiplied human thoughts or things objectified by the human mentality. It consists of that which is humanly obvious and is humanly conceived to be; of that which is humanly tangible, as things manifestly related to humanity and nurtured by its kind of benevolence.

Realm II consists of the legitimate expression and conception of The Logos; the ideate representation, thing, thinker and concept made manifest by The Re (Logos) as wholly related to The Re as real, as reality, or as the logician living and thinking in reality—in the realm of immutable wisdom.

The word reality means realness; the state, quality, or condition of being real; immutably true, eternally valid, sound, healthy, or spiritually quick (alive). It means realness as to love—the love for The Real and for wisdom who has experienced reality as home. It means the home of soul and conscience—the science of soul.

Reality is the state of having realized or understood The Logos; or having demonstrated the logic of The Logos; or having utilized the literacy of The Word, and of having completely fulfilled, obeyed, or profited by the law principles by having been completely disciplined by The Logos-Principle.

Reality is that consciousness to which is revealed the harmony and concord of spiritual logic, literacy, and law principle. Reality and revelation (of The Re or The Logos) embody, embrace or encompass wisdom and his sentiments, his understanding, substance, integrity, spiritual soundness or perfection. They encompass the intelligence and spiritual properties of mon of which mon (spiritual man) is conscious.

Reality embraces all of the capacities and capabilities of immaculacy or purity, of constancy or the quality which stands with her truth or troth, and of the spiritual graces, completely realized. That which is not completely realized or spiritualized has no place and has no part in reality.

Conscience is that great moral representative of reality who ministers to Realm III, bringing the elementary rules, lessons, or peculiar instructions down to human notice and possible realization.

THE WORD, REASON

The word *reason* comes from the Latin *ratio* and ration, which means reckoning, reasoning, understanding.

The word rational means reasonable, wise, sagacious, sane, or judicious.

To reckon means to compute, to consider, to estimate, to explain, to regard, or to calculate.

The Anglo Saxon reck (*reccan, recan*) means to take care, to mind, to take heed, to have a care or thought for, or to care. To be reckless would be to be without care or to be careless.

The adverbial form of reason is reasonably or rationally, meaning in a considerate and thoughtful manner; in a discreet, prudent or heedful manner.

The noun has many meanings. It may be a statement of fact; an element of cause; a firm belief; a justifiable stand maintained or a truth (true premise) defended. It may be a principle practiced or a ruling precept understood. It may be the rational power or the mental faculty with which one reckons and reasons in ratio to his individual degree of intelligence or wisdom. Thus it is a word of wide usage.

The verb form is the one which gives the nature and the character of the word reason, since it shows (gives) the function of it. It is the act of deducing a positive, well outlined thought from its cause; the process of thinking or of considering or of regarding or of taking care to interpret or to judge correctly.

Reason is the mental faculty or ability to make decisions. It is a gift. It is the mental power to act or to do or to decide upon a conclusion as a thought outline reasoned out. It is that which is established in the mentality as a basis from which to compute, calculate, estimate, explain or consider. These mental faculties or this mental power may begin with a low ratio and run to a very high ratio of power.

The word reason will place itself by means of its literate characters or by means of its low or high degree of literacy. Since its vowel combination *ea* is only semi-literate it classifies itself in highest ratio of *human* comprehension or appreciation, but under and lower than wisdom and his power of understanding.

The following table classifies reason as the *human* ability to reckon, or as the human sense of validity or good cause:

[342]

REALM   I   DIVINITY: The Logos Truth, Mynde, in-
              telligence or Principle from which *mon* the
              thinker receives all (complete) power
              to consider, judge or compute.

REALM   II   SPIRITUALITY: the logician who follows
              the outlines and designs of Realm I; the
              thinker of infinite capacity to be mindful,
              heedful or considerate of his Logos-
              premise.
                  Here is mon who thinks as wisdom
              himself and as truth herself.

REALM III   MORALITY: *human* intellect, sagacity or
              mental capacity to judge or to consider.
                  Here *con*-science and its science act as
              rational faculty, reasoning agent or reck-
              oning agency.
                  Here humanity estimates what is right,
              moral, ethical, orthodox or conventional
              or acceptable as premise.

REALM IV   PHYSICALITY: human nature and its
              sensibility.

REALM   V   IMMORALITY: unmorality; recklessness;
              that which is without principle, just cause,
              honest motive or ground.

Conscience requires an accounting of motive; requires a reason
and a good reason; requires rationality, and the exercise of honest
equitable reasoning, sagacity, judgment and accountability. Human
reason must give a good report or have a good honorable record, to
the end that it produce a worthy, well balanced, morally rational
or conscientious condition.

Reason is the great recorder. One cannot lose his reason, but
one may separate himself from it by failure to cling and claim or
identify himself with it, as it exists in Realm III and as it identifies
itself in conscience, for it is recorded there in full ratio.

Conscience is one's reason for doing rightly. It is one's soul,
guarding one, watching, protecting, defending or caring for one, while
the mental forces and influences that antagonize, and would neutralize
one's reason, attack one's human personality (one's physical identity,
or one's character as human nature sees it). They do not attack one's
soul, for they cannot enter soul's realm. Conscience sees to that.

Arrogant human intellect assumes or claims to have or to embrace reason, but this is only its proud assumption. All thinkers, therefore, who turn to soul or to conscience for wisdom, turn their backs on human intellect, whom the world has called king. Hence the mental tumult.

Realm II has full ratio of spiritual potency, wisdom, and intelligence and reason. Realm III has its moral ratio which is phenomenon of intelligence or of reason. This thinker is wholly honest, sincere, loyal, firm, valiant or courageous. This is his reason for existing, or it is the reason for his existence. Thus to be wholly reasonable the human being must be fully cognizant of his part in the great effort of moralization in all civil, moral, social, human affairs; must be at work exerting his moral energy.

Reason is not a metaphysical substance to be acquired by education. It is a moral instinct; an intuition belonging to the exercise of conscience; a sound or healthy condition of the metaphysical being; a deduction from wisdom and his full or complete rational power.

Reason exercises the moral faculties. One knows how to be honest, how to keep his word or troth, how to restrain human nature impulses, and how to be kind. Acting upon these moral impulses one is exercising his moral, mental, and semi-spiritual faculties or his reason, and thus, by exercising them, they grow and develop, amplify or mature.

There is a divine reason for everything that is divinely caused or created to exist. There is a spiritual reason for everything spiritually logical, literate and legitimate—that is, fathered by Spirit. There is a moral reason for everything on Earth or in this human world; an ethical reason; a right reason; a good reason and an excellent reason for one to teach (by precept and by practice) the moral science of conscience (con-science) which is reason itself, ever in action, practicing its science and its moral art.

The more mundane the rational being the more narrow and inadequate the reasoning capacity. The more physical (or relatively physical) the premises the more limited and negative the conclusions and the less the rational substance, depth or under-*stancing* (understanding). There is no reason for this limitation; no reason for limiting reason or logic since both are factors of correct and accurate thinking or positive, affirmative reasoning. The human mentality can never be infinitely rational and reasonable, but it can be morally positive.

There is no reason for or in depending upon that premise or precept or reason which is beneath, under, or less than one's moral status, rational position or stand; but there *is* a reason for aspiring to that premise or precept or principle which is above, or greater than one's human status. That reasoning is wisdom and his infinite or universal ratio of reasoning power; his dominion over all that is less than infinite reason. Thus wisdom, reason and conscience collaborate.

Reason, which is a phenomenon of absolute understanding, has an ear for it; has an Earth (Ear-th) or earthly ear with which to consider both wisdom and reason. This is the reason why the word reason is spelled with these two vowels (this *ea* vowel combination) rather than with the *i* vowel or the *o* vowel, as are wisdom and power. Reason can come down to Earth from its divine or spiritual realm, and can serve the human race. It can bring wisdom, intelligence, power and universal understanding down with it, in a degree (in a moral, human degree). It can serve humanity as a spiritual utility, and thus it becomes a great moral force or power. It keeps humanity from being lost at sea or from being unreasonable and uninterested in better reasoning. It keeps humanity on the solid Earth, on the substantial, rational ground, and on sober land. Here there is debate, but no reasonable argument against a conscientious reason, or a right reason.

Reason is the faculty, ability or capability to think considerately, properly, excellently, honestly and equitably. It must be related to conscience else it would not be the ability to think rightly, morally or conscientiously, and it would not be able to think scientifically on a purely metaphysical basis such as conscience demands. It would not be the ability to conform to premise or moral precept.

Reason is the human faculty that agrees with its noumenal moral law and premise. It is the phenomenon of the Realm II qualities and mental conditions. Its impetus is to be found in humanity's highest concept of right, and its will to practice right. Thus reason (with conscience) corrects and disciplines the reckless or heedless; informs as council, or as an assembly of faculties; reforms as counsel, advising, admonishing and *dis*-suading or persuading.

Reason is the human affability or faculty to reckon with ease, with care, and yet with dexterity. It has its firm post or standard of rational excellence. It has its own human ratio and proportion of reckoning power and of comprehensive capacity.

THE WORD, REFLECTION

The word *reflection* is from the Latin *flecto* (*flectere, flexus*), I bend, or *flexum,* to bend.

The prefix is *re-*. It means back, anew, or again.

The suffix *-ion* makes a noun out of the verb reflect; makes it a noun of action; gives it state of being or adds *-ing* (action) or being. Literally, the agent reflecting; the condition of being the reflector; condition of being that which bends or the entity I bend and I reflect.

The common synonyms of reflection are contemplation, deliberation, meditation, consideration, thought or thoughtfulness or mindfulness; cogitation.

The thinker has the quality, state or condition of being able to bend back, throw back the light (enlightenment), the warmth (love), or the sound (sonant characteristics) which come to him from The Logos-Soul. To illustrate this let the sun serve as that which is to be bent back, or that which must be reflected by the surface of the ocean, and let the quality, state or condition of the ocean's surface constitute the reflector, or that agency which has the reflective qualities. Let the sunbeams or the sunshine be that substance or essential thing which is to be bent back. Let the sun be noumenon (the thing itself) and let the reflector and reflection constitute phenomenon, the show, or that which is the result of this cause (noumenon), or the verbal action resulting from it. Thus the reflection is altogether dependent upon its noumenal cause for its own existence and for its substance.

Let the sun or sol represent The Creator and Giver of light or enlightenment to be reflected, or to be thoughtfully bent back. Let the sun represent The Logos-Soul and let the sunlight symbolize that light which comes to the thinker as logic of The Logos, as light, enlightenment or divine doctrine; as thought or as message to be reiterated, resounded, represented or reflected in highest form of wisdom; in inextinguishable, immutable spiritual light, intelligence, vision, discernment, conceptive power and understanding.

Let this same light be modified in its intensity and let it be reduced or tempered to human understanding and to its moral and humanly ethical intent (or bent).

Let the following table show this moral degree:

REALM I

DIVINITY: The Logos-Soul which is Premise and Principle of all logical, literate and legitimate soul light; Soul Intelligence.

REALM II

SPIRITUALITY: the wisdom belonging to the thinker, which reflects Soul; the purely spiritual attributes, agencies, qualities, realities, manifestations and verities which reflect The Logos; the intelligence that reflects The Intelligence, which is The Logos-Soul.

REALM III

MORALITY: the morally pliable, thoughtful, flexible or able to be morally bent; the thinker who has a moral bent or a very conscientious nature, or who is subject to its influence or its flexure; the thinker who may be animated by the spiritual animus or soul, or who is tractable or morally enlightened; whose honesty reflects highest power and great honor; whose veracity reflects truth, herself; whose moral stamina and courage (firmness) is established in right.

REALM IV

PHYSICALITY: that which is of physical bent or that which reflects its natural (physical) noumenon as phenomenon; all physical agencies agitated, excited, stirred, driven, shaken, moved or motivated by physical mindedness or mindfulness, or the mammal instincts (unrestrained or undisciplined by moral mindedness).

REALM V

IMMORALITY: that which is of lowest, *sub-animal* or *sub-mammal* bent; that which reflects the unmoral and morally depraved character and nature, having no moral principle or precept.

The moral characters and qualities of Realm III are the reflections of the inner conscience (the science within). They are the natural moral virtues: faith or fidelity (an individually instituted confidence in morality); hope or moral prosperity (the science of spiritual expectancy); compassion (a passion for patience, humanity, piety and an affection for right); equity or moral sagacity.

The morally minded reflect that soberness which leads to wisdom. The modest are tractable and teachable. This kind of individual ability to discipline oneself leads to wisdom and to his dominion or domain which is Realm II. This kind of reflecting, contemplating or mindfulness leads over, above, beyond the moral excellences to Realm II and its excellences. This kind transcends human moral sense of things. It climbs and surpasses all human precepts, to reach that spiritual dominion for which the individual hopes, prays, aspires and expects. It leaves the human traditions, conventions and premises and begins to reflect upon purely spiritual premises and principles which are ideations of The Logos-Principle.

The natural inclination of the careful reflector or thinker is to watch for clear and pure reflections. He feels no bent toward the morally ignorant, the gross, the thick, the impure and muddied kind of considerations. He is attracted to the brilliant reflections coming from Realm II.

The natural bent of the thinker is to avoid the mental mud puddles and to look for the things which carry the reflective signet of wisdom or the sign of his clear and true enlightenment. This thinker is morally reflective or deliberative. He may be depended upon to act morally right, humanly equitable, faithful and true (if not humanly traditional) under every circumstance. His reflections and reflexes may be said to be strictly and radically moral.

The moral thinker meditates and prays for wisdom. He looks to Realm II for higher understanding and reflections of wisdom; for higher and greater cognition of wisdom. Thus he hopes (expects) and prepares to receive, perceive, see and understand them or to have and to hold them, and thus his conscientious self reflects or shines through.

The thinker (or reflector or reflection) of The Logos thinks divinely and reflects the logic of The Logos. He verifies, proves or demonstrates his cognition of Realm I by contemplating in, with, by and by means of The Mynde or The Logos (Speech or Word). His cogitations, reflections or ideas are in, with, and by The Logos, and it is by means of The Logos-Mynde that he—the thinker or reflector— is cognized as an element of intelligence or intelligent ideation. He is the understander of The Logos-Soul constantly reflecting the elemental qualities of Soul.

THE WORD, REMORSE

The word *remorse* is composed of its Latin root *mordeo,* meaning bite, and its prefix *re-,* meaning back. Literally bite back; the biting of conscience. The form *mordeo* (*mordere, morsus*), means I bite. This I may be one's own conscience that bites, reproves, chastens, stings, convicts or condemns as a mordant or as a mordacious mental instrument. The form *morsum* of the same root means to bite. It carries no entity, but is only the verb form.

Metaphysically and morally the word remorse is associated with anguish or agony imposed by conscience; a biting or bitter feeling of guilt imposed by conscience; a sense of distress or self-reproach imposed by self or self-consciousness of being wrong.

Remorse may impose the pangs of hell, but this is only the pangs, bites, or poignant pains, or the transient sufferings (self imposed) that bite one, conscientiously, until one learns his lessons prescribed by *con*-science—the science within one—or learns not to neglect nor to ignore them. Thus one who is inclined toward the damnation of hell or to such condemnation, must be rescued by conscience from unmorality (moral ignorance) or from immorality (moral negligence—of greater or lesser degree).

One who is inclined toward moral, ethical or equitable rightness needs the erg, the urge of conscience and its moral science; needs the compunction, sting or compulsion of conscience to point out that which is or would be regrettable, mournful, and remorseful in the face of conscience. Hence, without conscience, remorse would not exist. One who does not feel remorse—the bite of conscience—would be one who is beyond the reach of her gentle ministrations; beyond, below, or outside and out of contact with her, and calloused or insensible to her sentiments. Being thus hardened, or hard against her, this one would be self-justified, not self-condemned.

Remorse could be called one of the governing forces at work in consciousness; one of the corrective, schooling or educational forces that is teaching right-doing or moralization.

The word remorseless means to be cruel, to bite back pitilessly or to be unforgiving, implacable and unrelenting. It means also to be proudly self-justified in biting back as enemy or as feeling a pointed enmity or a stinging, biting hostility for that which would convict, condemn, correct or teach.

Remorse may have a part in moral discipline. It may be that moral chemicalization which goes on, consciously, causing bite, as when a mordant or a biting chemical is at work. Thus when conscience ceases to bite, it is because one has either graduated into higher moral and spiritual colleges of virtue, or has been demoted, self-expelled, self-dismissed or self-debarred from the school of conscience and virtue only to find that even hell is a consciousness of burning and biting remorsefulness; a mental resort that promises freedom from the radical lectures of conscience but does not keep its promise.

THE WORD, REPRESENTATION

The word *representation* simply means the action, condition, resulting state or concrete result of having presented again or again and again.

It is a noun of verbal action. It is that which represents something. It is a being or state of being, a likeness or a model which presents (or brings before the mind again and again) a something, which something the representative is entirely dependent upon for his own being.

The word representation is an altogether dependent word, meaning nothing more than verbal action, agent or agency for that which he represents as representation. Thus it is necessary to establish the noumenon or the noun principle of which the representation or idea is phenomenon, because it is a passive entity being acted upon by its noumenal principle, which principle or principal actor employs its agents to represent it. This principal actor may be anything from the lowest immoral conspirator to the highest spiritual principle. It is therefore necessary to classify the word representation before it can be specifically treated or defined.

Its highest signification is found to be in Realm II of the table:

REALM I

DIVINITY: The highest Principle, doctrine or Doctor—The Logos—who prescribes, assigns, directs, teaches and employs divine ideas or spiritual representations.

REALM II

SPIRITUALITY: the highest and fullest and completely representative agent of The Logos; the spiritual logician, wisdom who presents again and again the doctrine of The Logos-Principle; that holy (wholly) spiritual substance or under-*stanc*-ing which wholly represents Realm I.

REALM III

MORALITY: the moral law, doctrine and literacy that represents Realm II; the moral qualities such as constancy, fidelity, moral courage and its agencies which are the representatives of spiritual logic and wisdom.

Realm IV

PHYSICALITY: those models or pictures which represent a purely physical thing or a person—or a physically
prescribed human doctrine, or a humanly representative theory.

Realm V

IMMORALITY: the highly trained sensuous and sensual
representatives of material doctrines; the doctrines pertaining to the voluptuous Eve and the highly sensitized
Adam; the doctrine of physical matters or matter or
maters; the practices of human knowledge or human nature in its lowest form; *sub*animal action and impulse.

The foregoing table and analysis shows that each type of representation is dependent upon a peculiar doctrine for its existence, its
action and its position—its state, its quality, and its condition—
which state or position or realm has its doctrinal precept, premise,
source or basis.

A doctrine or doctor must have his practice. He must teach or
prescribe remedy; must convey information or admonition; must
make *ac-cure-d* or accurate; must act upon that which is passive
to its or his action.

If one places himself, as entity, in Realm V, he presents and
re-presents some kind of *sub*animal or *sub*mammal (unnatural) doctrine; some humanly prescribed and only humanly possible perform-
ance, prompted by the lowest degree of human nature. He assumes
himself to be born of the Eve-*kind* of man-*kind* who is the mater
(character) of Cain who represents artifice (the skill of spear or
lance; the trickery, guile, deceit or murderous maneuver) of the kind
which would acquire or possess thereby. This mater Eve characterizes or represents or typifies matter, materiality and the materialism
growing out of her kind of doctrine, which doctrine may be physicality—the baneful usurper.

If one places himself in Realm III he may present the moral
side of his character on the one hand, and he may present and represent the physique or mammal side of his nature on the other. Metaphysically, he may be in sympathy with both natures, thus he may
represent a duplicity of standard until the morally absolute and positive supplants the mammal and sub-animal negative through the action
of soul or the science of soul—*con*-science.

If one places himself in reality; if he identifies himself as being
spiritual; if he re-presents The Logos as a logical idea; if he lives

as a valid manifestation or representation of The vital Logos-Principle; if he functions as love or spiritual sentiment; if he represents The omniscient Logos as truth or verity; if he acts as agent of The Logos-Soul by expressing spiritual virility, fertility, purity or immaculacy—then he is empowered to act as representation of The Logos-Soul. Then he has placed him-*self* (his entity or his soul) in Realm II, which is his true status.

THE WORD, RESENTMENT

The word *resentment* means a feeling against.

The prefix *re-* means back; against; anew; opposite; again; backward; again and again.

The root is Latin *sentio* (*sentire, sensus*), I feel; I perceive; I think; or it may be *sensum,* to think, to feel or to perceive.

The suffix *-ment* gives the word resent its noun form. It means act of, state of, or condition of. It may be called a noun of action, which action is (in this word) feeling or to feel.

Literal meaning: the state, condition or action of feeling against.

Common synonyms: anger, ill will, hatred, offense or pique.

Common meaning: a state of being indignant; a condition of feeling insulted or injured to the extent of resending malice.

This same root, *sentio,* is the father and mother of many good words. The word sentence means a combination of words expressing a complete thought. The word consent means to think or to feel together, while resent means to feel back or against or opposite. Assent means to agree to. Dissent means to feel apart or away from; to think oppositely, aside or asunder. Sententious means full of thought. Sentiment is the feeling of the mynde; the opinion, testimony, judgment, conviction or doctrine of the soul. Presentiment is that which presents a feeling or a thought before; that which prophesies or anticipates or apprehends beforehand.

There is a righteous indignation or a feeling prompted by right and justice. This feeling rises up against wrong and injustice, again and again. One's feelings or one's sentiments being right and good, one must expect to encounter ill feeling from the opposition, but with this right or righteous feeling there comes a moral grace or a feeling of forgiveness; there comes a feeling of moral equity and magnanimity; there comes a modesty or a feeling of humility, so meek as to be above indulging in resentment; there comes a feeling of good will which is aloft or above willing ill or re-sending ill will.

Resentment, inflated pride, arrogant self-justification, inflamed jealousy or envy, and the insolent and despotic impositions of human hatred—this combination is the art of tyrants. Inflated pride is soonest injured.

The seer and sage feels beforehand. He prophesies. He entertains presentiments which present to him the presence of the tyrant (the tyrannical nature of a thing) before he appears, or beforehand. He senses or feels, sees or tastes beforehand. He scents, he perceives, he takes notice or he thinks beforehand. For this reason he foretells and fore-stalls; he prevents injurious action of the resentment.

Resentment is the antonym of that gentle, moral kindness or affection which sends back good will; the opposite of that charitable feeling which prompts compassion. It is the opposite of that noble forgiveness which gives or sends back charity for unkindness.

Resentment is the nucleus (nut, kernel or seed, or the central mass of feeling against) out of which war is engendered, generated, and developed. It creates tumult, a warlike fervor and fever.

Resentment is active and vehement ill will, enmity or animosity. Sentiment is active and vehement good will—feeling of the soul.

THE WORD, REVELATION

The word *revelation* has its root in the Latin *velo, velum,* meaning veil.

> The prefix *re-* means back.
> The suffix *-ation* makes the word reveal into a noun of condition or verbal action. It means resulting state; concrete result.
> Literal meaning: result of having unveiled or thrown the veil back.
> Velation speaks of mystery and concealment.
> Revelation speaks of removing or throwing back that which veils, hides or conceals from view; that which covers, masks or serves to cloak.
> Velation means the forming of a velum or veil; the act of veiling; the state or condition of being veiled or covered with a veil.

Literally and physically a veil may be a curtain, a fabric or parchment of some kind used to hide something temporarily, or to disguise, conceal or protect. It is often used to cover or conceal from inspection, and it is often used as an ornament, as a screen or as a mask.

Figuratively and metaphysically a veil may be a pretext that hides something immoral from view. It may serve as a disguise to conceal moral ignorance (unmorality). It could serve as screen of nonchalance to cover a conscience stricken state, or serve to cover a sense of neglect. It serves at all times to prevent revelation of moral poverty or disregard for law, rule, duty and ethical precepts, as for instance, deceit, insincerity, disloyalty and such may be veiled by pretext of honesty, honor and loyalty.

Spiritually and really a revelation is that which discloses or brings into view ideas which were undiscovered. It is the concrete result of having thrown back the veil of spiritual ignorance, or the mask of mystery, or the ornaments of mythology.

The word revelation pertains to human thinking, to that which humanity perceives, to that which is not clear, not visible or not revealed to human knowledge and to the human race in general.

The human race however is not dependent upon anything outside its own sphere. It is satisfied with what *is* revealed, because it does not know that it has stolen, has unduly assumed or has falsely claimed all things of all high, higher and highest spheres to belong to its humanly established world, earth or sphere.

The human race, humanhood, humankind, mankind or the *humus* kind of man gives all credence to human knowledge. Human erudition gives humanity all it knows and believes, and all things that may be verified by natural or physical science, or by human intellect. Thus it places no confidence in that which is beyond its own premises, precepts or formal laws, rules, causes, reasons and bases.

There are many veils or curtains. There is a veil between every distinctly different realm, which veil must be mentally penetrated in order to find its peculiar premise.

The following table will show these different realms:

Realm I
DIVINITY: that Principle from which all ideas proceed; that Logos from which all infinite logic is derived; The Word from which all divinely lovely literacy comes forth.

Realm II
SPIRITUALITY: that realm of divinely logical, literate and legitimate ideas motivated by The Logos-Spirit, born of The Logos-Mynde, and governed by The Logos-Precept.

Here there is a complete revelation of the substance of Realm I; a perfect expression of The Logos-Soul; a full understanding of The Logos-Principle and its essential practices or practical ideas.

Realm III
MORALITY: that realm of morally radical reasoning; the realm of clear, clean conscientious thinking; the realm in which honesty or veracity are frankly or candidly expressed and are definitely revealed to be good.

Here the substance and essence of constancy, fidelity, immaculacy, integrity and such begin to be revealed as essential qualities, and here faith takes on confidence and spiritual expectancy, while hope takes on higher moral prosperity—even to spiritual realization.

Here revelation is going on and the thinker is transcending Realm IV and is ascending toward Realm II.

Realm IV
PHYSICALITY: human knowledge evident to humanity; human erudition which fills the realm; human intellect which builds a wall, a screen, a veil or a curtain to en-

compass this realm, and which forms a mental horizon beyond which the human eye cannot penetrate, and through which the human sense cannot pass.

Here exists only that which may be verified by physical precepts and premises—only that which may be physically revealed, discovered, disclosed or exposed.

Here all knowledge is adverse to the science of conscience (or the soul); is adverse to that which exists beyond its horizon.

This humanly popular concept of things gives no place and no reality to the higher realms. It takes no mental excursions upward. It makes no intellectual investigations of that which is morally, spiritually or divinely veiled to its human conception.

Revelation is that which is going on within the moral and spiritual spheres as the thinker peers, intently and searchingly, into the more infinite and absolute; as he himself emerges from spiritual denseness into higher, clearer and more spiritually rarified mental atmosphere; as he himself discovers the more omnisciently intelligent Principle toward which he thoughtfully proceeds.

Humanity, the human being, humankind, human nature or the human physicality or physical creature is satisfied with its sense of things; with what it sees, feels, tastes, senses or scents (figuratively and literally); with what it learns or what is revealed or made evident to its comprehension or mental grasp. It is satisfied because it believes that physicality and the human physique (with its physical knowledge and sensibilities) constitute and include all that is revealed and is the basis for all that is to be revealed.

Humanity finds the moral, spiritual and divine realms to be veiled, unrevealed or concealed because it has no sentiment for them (is mentally opposed or opposite to them), has no appreciation of them, is ignorant of them or does not know that anything exists beyond human apprehension.

Humanity does not wish to be humiliated or embarrassed, or abashed, or brought low or have its pride deflated by the science of con-science, the logic of The Logos or the literacy of the higher realms. It prefers to humiliate, hate, offend, oppose, deny and try to mortify whatever opposes it. It does not know that its realm is a false assumption and that its human knowledge is not science or is neither science nor logic; that its knowledge and humanity, itself, is mortality; that human nature embraces no good quality and that it is only the phenomenon of its own concept of noumenon.

THE WORD, SCIENCE

The word *science* comes from the Latin *scio,* meaning know, and the suffix *-ence* makes it a noun of quality or action. Literally it means state or quality of being known, or in the form of *scire, scitum,* it means I know.

The suffix *-ence* gives the word its noun form or gives it entity or identity, esse, existence or ego, as the I who knows or is knowing. This identity is the *idem*—the same, the agent, the doer, the actor, the artist, the knower, the scientist who knows.

This entity and this knower is not a person, but is a spiritual and wholly moral or metaphysical ego, and this scientist is not a human person, but an impersonal intelligence knowing; an immortal idea ideating, thinking, visualizing or seeing by way of infinite discernment.

This entity is an element of reason; a rational and reasonable and radically right thinker. He is an honest thinker. Thus the knower, the entity, the scientist and the thinker are one and the same.

In the realm of human observation, science is knowledge and knowledge is science. It is the sum total or whole collection of that which is known; that which humanity has found to be actual, factual, substantial and essentially and physically stable; that which humanity has found to be the unfailing rule observed in physical and or natural sciences. These sciences have been gathered together and classified under their topical headings, or into their various systems of instituted human knowledge.

One human being may have a knowledge of good literature, another may have a very extensive knowledge of music, another may have a knowledge or some knowledge of arithmetic, another may have a knowledge of some of the other *-ologies* in human use, and still not be called a scientist, a mathematician, or an artist.

Knowledge is that which the human race knows, mutually. It is a thing of human condition, circumstance or event to be known or revealed. It is a thing of mutual human interest or common knowledge, as fact to be learned, yet a science or an art that interests one individual may not interest or find appreciation in another.

Every scientist or artist must have the appreciation and attention of his audience; must have the ear and the eye — yea, the sentiment — of the laity, else he cannot demonstrate, prove or make manifest his skill in its highest degree; else he cannot perform or develop or give form to his conception of it. Expertness classifies the artist and the scientist and it gives form to knowledge, as expertly performed. Expertness makes knowledge professional or gives it pattern, pater, or father.

In this realm of human meanings, observation and human speculation, arithmetic or mathematics is a mutually accepted science or a science of mutual interest and utility. Numeral science or the science of numbers is the most liberal, the most infinite and most free from human limitation and circumspection. It is the one wholly metaphysical science; the one most universal science; the one science that humanity cannot humanize, sensualize, materialize or physicalize, because it uses no human instrumentality, depends upon no human appreciation, human personality or human utility. Indeed it is above and beyond humanity's metaphysical reach, horizon or altitude. Thus the science of numbers is like the science of soul — con*science*. It remains aloof from human knowledge and its finite nature. It deals only with the science derived from wisdom and his wholly spiritual logic, which is the science of correct and accurate thinking as prescribed by wisdom.

The following table will classify the word science in comparison with the words knowledge and logic:

REALM I

DIVINITY: The Logos-Principle and Premise of all logic; Father and Creator of the wholly (holy) spiritual logician or wisdom.

REALM II

SPIRITUALITY: the logician, who is the conclusion or conclusive idea of The Logos-Premise.

Here logic is purely spiritual, made manifest as wisdom in witness thereof; reflected in the infinite understanding (of the wholly logical thinker), in substance thereof.

REALM III

MORALITY: human metaphysicality, or humanity with its devotion to con-*science* on the spiritual side, and its somewhat divided attention and devotion to natural or physical knowledge on the material side.

Here con-*science* holds its own as moral, right or orthodox, while human intellect contends for the physical sciences.

REALM IV

PHYSICALITY: human knowledge; finity. Here knowledge is that which may be localized in the human nature, the human physique or the human impulses or instincts; that which is premised upon physicality; that which begins with finity.

Knowledge exists only as it exists in Realm IV. It is the dead end of what humanity calls science; the finite conception of science.

The *mater* of human knowledge and the physical sciences is the conceptual intellect, the feminine instrument (reason) or the rational capacity which accepts and appreciates these humanly prescribed patterns of knowledge. She is that mental element of human sentiment which gestates, gives form, or gives proof; that element by means of which a perceived or potentially believed element of human reason is proved, confirmed, demonstrated, illustrated, verified, tested or found to be the valid conclusion of its physical premise — human knowledge. Thus the publication of human knowledge is its multiplication, and being multiplied it is perceived, announced, conceived and multiplied again.

The *mater* of moral science is *con-science*. Her function is to develop the science which presents itself to conscience, and to carry out to conclusion each conscientious element of conviction, or to confirm and make evident each moral element and quality peculiar to the moral thinker and his pattern. This mater of Realm III functions in this moral realm. She has information from wisdom. She has assurance of higher understanding (of soul) and she has some cognition or intuition and sentiment actively engaged in communicating with Realm II. She notes or she takes notice of these higher forms of science.

Realm II presents the highest form of science and presents the logician or thinker who mans it. This kind of science is logic directly begotten of The Logos. It is the science of divinely (perfectly) correct and accurate thinking; the science and art of (infinitely true) reasoning. It has the power and authority to speak and to record itself.

Realm II presents pure logic. No element of fault or badness enters, and no negative factor enters into its premises. No element of imperfection and no mutable substance is considered, acknowledged, admitted or given form as acceptable or as one's own. Hence its logic stands under The Logos forever and ever speaking.

The knowledge of Realm IV compares badly with science and with logic as cognized by the thinker or the logician of Realm II. Human knowledge admits the negative by the positive; acknowledges the abnormal and unnatural. Hence its knowledge is not acknowledged by the positive thinker of Realm II because it is not his own kind. It mixes its premises (fault and fact) and concludes with whatever is most natural, most expected and most familiar to the human family. This is natural knowledge or human knowledge.

Knowledge has no divine or good side; no spiritually literate side; no relation or similarity to conscience—the science pertaining to soul or the spiritual integer.

First, there is The Logos-Principle (Realm I).

Second, there are the logical principles derived from Realm I and practiced in Realm II by the divine logician.

Third, there is the science derived from the logic of The Logos-Soul and practiced by conscience or the conscientious thinker or the morally disciplined doer of Realm III.

Fourth, there is knowledge—called science (Realm IV).

THE WORD, Sea

The word *sea* has many figurative meanings. It is most often used in its plural sense as waters or seas. It may also represent the seven seas or oceans, in being the seven primal and principal elements of rational power or of the spiritual thinker: wisdom, virility, fertility, precise or accurate perceptivity, and immaculate or pure conceptivity; profound prudence; understanding or the substance of reality; verity, integrity, validity or the health of the good and beautiful, heavenly or lovely thinker.

The word sea is of Anglo Saxon origin, *sae, sai*. This *ai* or *ae* vowel combination is *ea* in sea, in hear, earth, and in many more Anglo Saxon words. Its synonym is ocean, which is the Greek *okeanos*. As a word it expresses vastness, depth, boundlessness, greatness as to size or embodiment, and a sense of expanse and immensity.

The surface of the waters or seas reflects great and brilliant light when the sun shines upon it. Our planet—Earth—being largely water, probably presents a spectacle of great brilliance, both figuratively and astronomically.

The sea is that which savors of saltiness. This saline content of the sea speaks of its preservative value and its powers of purification. Anglo Saxon *sealt* is salt, and is *sea*-lt.

The great depth of the sea speaks of its underlying or fundamental powers of buoyancy; its profoundness. It symbolizes depth of intelligent existence. It is as a great mental matrix mothering both the vegetable and animal life within it.

The seas or the sea is an element of productiveness, literally and figuratively. Its great shore areas house, hover, and mother the fowl, the animal and such as depend partly upon the sea and partly upon the dry land for their natural existence.

The sea symbolizes many things. It is the antonymic nature as compared to the dry land, and it is as unique in every way. The ocean or the sea swells. A swell is a wave. The words waver, waft, and waif are related. One may well waver, tremble, shake or stand in awe of the sea. It is the one thing that humanity and its intellect has not yet been able to change, conquer, use up, make over, devastate or destroy. It symbolizes the immensity of intelligence, reason, or the rational proportions of the profound thinking faculties which the human race has not yet discovered or accepted only as a thing of

[363]

wonderment. It symbolizes the spiritual nature of the true and wholly (holy) enlightened mentality and the wide or vast range of that holy mentality.

Humankind talks of its irrepressible hope to harness the motive power of the sea, after it has harnessed the chemical and mechanical elements of the ether (the sky).

The *ea* vowel combination in the words ocean *(oc-ea-n)* and sea *(s-ea)* are the same. Ocean may be *osean (o-sea-n)*. The *ea* vowel combination is intact in each word. *Oceanus* is god of the ocean or mighty river. This Greek god was probably the origin of the word ocean, meaning all waters under the sky. This typifies the brazen human intellect in assuming to be like the enlightenment or reflected brilliance of the face of the waters.

The greatest figurative meaning of the seas or oceans may be the intensely dazzling light, the glittering, gleaming, glistening brilliance which would symbolize intelligence or the most brilliant (bright, wise, or splendid thinker), most literate and most logical thinking.

The brilliance is caused by the sun or sol which may be likened to the brilliance of Soul enlightening the thinkers' mentality.

The seven seas or seven oceans should symbolize the seven virtues of the mentality of wisdom or the spiritual logician and soul-thinker. There would be a sea of sentiment; a sea of profundity, profoundness, or most profound understanding; a sea of firmness, soundness, validity and justice; a sea of power typifying spiritual potency and rational power; a sea of crystal clarity, purity or mental chastity; a sea of integrity embracing all seas in one whole ocean, one undivided, unimpaired, complete body or integer, or one spiritual element of realization.

The seven seas or oceans could represent the seven Greek gods of mythology that pertain to *Oceanus*. These gods would be the opposite of wisdom's seas. They would dazzle the human mentality with their artifice and would keep it at sea. They would dazzle it with vanity, pride, pangs of envy, surges of desperation, defeat, defiance and human egotism.

The seas typify fertility—mental, moral, and spiritual. Its teeming, moving, motivated or animated and pregnant existence brings forth and mothers millions of vegetable and animal creatures. It gestates and quickens its own peculiar kind. This may symbolize the power of spiritual conception and fruition.

THE WORD, SENTIMENT

The word *sentiment* comes from the Latin *sentio* (*sentire*, *sensum*, or *sensus*), meaning I feel, perceive or think; to feel, or to think.

Literal meaning: act or process of feeling, mentally; the mentality that feels, morally.

If one regards the word sentiment to be a compound word made up of the Latin *sentio* and *mentis* (*mens*), the mind, one would have *senti-mentis* or the feeling of the mind.

Sentiment is the ability to feel sure before an issue is verified. It is a faculty of conscience feeling that an issue is right by way of intuitive sense. Sentiment is related to presentiment in the fact that it senses or feels before, and beforehand, and then, after one has found his presentiment to be justifiable, it becomes an added strength to one's apprehension of moral verities.

Sentiment is the tactile sense of the mentality. It feels or touches or contacts an issue or a thought before it occurs or becomes apparent and tangible to others. It is a moral sensibility of sensitivity concerning that which is right. It is moral sense or an acuteness for moral reasoning. It is a form of quick or vivid moral cognition, or a quick perception of right. It is a conscientious susceptibility to right or an aptitude toward the detection of wrong.

Sentiment and conscience (*con*-science) are in league. Their feeling is mutual and moral. Thus sentiment is classified as one of the moral qualities or as one of the states of the morally minded.

Honesty, veracity, charity, loyalty and such virtues constitute the moral sentiments or *senti-mentality*. It is independent of the human physique. It is entirely metaphysical in its substance and essence. It is a metaphysical emotion or a mental animation, or it may be said to be morally actuated. It is intuitive in its nature.

Sentiment is related to faith. It is a feeling of being sure beforehand or before there is evidence to prove that one's feeling is well founded. Strong sentiments constitute a moral power of conception which can make evident and tangible to others that which is mentally evident to oneself alone. Strong, valid and vital sentiments are the preconceived factors or the potential moral issues of the generations yet unborn.

Sentiment is related to confidence, trust and expectation of right and equity in human affairs. It is a kind of right, upright or equitable meditation or premeditation.

[365]

Sentiment is a feminine quality, because it pertains to conception, to the power and capacity to gestate or develop, and to the faculties of mental fruition or of realization of an issue, which issue must be sustained or must be nurtured prenatally and post natally.

An infant moral issue is born at the front (war front) of human endeavor where legislative, executive and judicial issues are engaged in a moral war of right versus wrong; of morally stable issues versus human nature. Humanity, hope, honesty, integrity, fidelity and the other masculine virtues are there to man the forefront, but their issues are potential. Sentiment is with them to conceive and to bring them forth into their actuality.

Sentiment is a power in human affairs for or against timely issues. She is a power of contraception of undesirable issues and a power of conception of and for the general movement toward complete moralization.

Sentiment is a metaphysical feeling akin to the physical feeling of motion or quickening. Sentiment is an element of verity, veracity and troth carrying out her issue. She is like the expectant mother in that she *feels* the quickening. She does not *see* the unborn issue.

Public sentiment is a power with which governmental affairs must cope. Sentiment is a moral force, in force. It is impelled by the most profound motives. Public sentiment is a compound of human affection for good or for moral rights; a compound element of public feeling; a consolidation of morally refined feelings; a compound mental, moral attitude; a force to be enforced by common moral consent. It is a spontaneous force; a moral urge or energy; a tenacious and patient and usually silent partner of public opinion.

Sentiment differs from opinion in the fact that opinion is a masculine belief; a thing of precept, doctrine or premise. It concerns a thought or a supposition or a perception, or an initial estimation of some issue esteemed to be right or good, yet public opinion is potential. Sentiment and verity must quicken and verify the potential issue and thereby make it valid or actual in human affairs. The feminine thinker must give leave or lief or permission; must give consent; must assent. The potential issue must go through all of the mental-moral processes from its inception or perception (in the form of opinion) to its sturdy but infantile formation. Then it must be maintained by the advocates (public opinion) and it must be sustained or nourished and mothered by the conceivers (public sentiment). Thus sentiment is a leader in the processes of moralization. She has all of the feminine virtues with her, such as chastity, constancy, compassion, moral steadfastness, stamina and affection. These virtues have given birth to civilization, and now they are aiming at spiritualization. They constitute moralization itself. As they advance into spirituality they take on their more spiritually refined or purified names. Sentiment becomes love. Chastity becomes spiritual purity or immaculacy of thought. Steadfastness, stamina and con-*stancy* take form in understanding which is the sub*stance* of spirituality. The masculine moral leader learns wisdom, and thus he is sub*stant*iated by wisdom. This higher and highest understanding now takes on its more spiritually assigned powers.

Sentiment is not confined to the civil world. It is the silent tone in every noble thought; the sentiment in every sonata; the highest tone of every sonnet; the feeling hidden in every inspired poem; the profound feeling deep within every love inspired painting and every written word picture, for sentiment is a modest and obscure power in power but not in prominence. Herein lies her protection from her opinionated enemies and from the inhuman and unmoral forces. Sentimental gestation goes on in its moral sanctuary, in spite of the enemies of virtue, of conscience and of the moral law.

THE WORD, SEX

The word *sex* is one of the words that human usage and human knowledge or physical science has reduced or demoted to an illiterate status.

The word sex is one of the literate and logical words that infinite literology is restoring; one of the legitimate words that divine philology is reclaiming from humanity's low conception or physical classification.

> The accepted, common meaning: the physical difference between male and female.
> Common synonym: gender.

In reality the word sex is identical with the word six. It is the Latin *sex,* meaning six; *sextus,* meaning sixth. An hexagon has six angles. It is a sexangle, or a figure having six corners or it is a six-angled figure. Sexennial means happening every six years, lasting six years, or a sixth anniversary. A sextet or sextette pertains to six — not to gender or to physicality.

The Greek *hex* or *hexa* is six — not gender. It is root or prefix of many words in common use, such as hexagram, hexahydrate, hexameter, hexone and hexose.

The word sex may not be physicalized or reduced to a physiological meaning, any more really than the word three (*tres, tria, trio*); any more correctly than the word seven (*septum*), or the word five (quint, *quintus, quinque*); any more properly than the word one (*uni, unus*).

The word sex or six is as universal as the word two (*duo*), or the word four (quad, *quar*), or the word eight (*octo*). The word six (sex) may not be limited or made logically or literately finite and physical any more rightly or accurately than the word nine (*novem*), or the word ten (*decem; decimus,* tenth). How and why, therefore, should not sex be six, pertain to six, or mean six? Why should it not be the number next greater than five? Because common usage has humanized it and has limited it to gender and genus, meaning race, kind, sort, or birth, from a physiological point of distinction.

Masculine gender is a grammatical distinction. It pertains to that which is neither feminine nor neuter. It is distinguished by the

[368]

function of the subject, the agent or the nature of the agency functioning. The feminine gender is distinguished by her office or power to conceive, to gestate, act upon, quicken, nourish, nurture, materialize or bring forth; to cause to be evident; to demonstrate, verify or realize. The gender which is neither male nor female is the neuter gender. It pertains to the nature and character of law, premise, precept or the prime unit of Principle under which the male and female qualities function coordinately.

In divine literology the feminine element is not *one* of the sexes, but she is *three* of the six spiritual powers; half of the sexual elements of spirituality; three of the six rational faculties of realization or of intelligence, or of ideation, as the following table shows:

REALM   I   DIVINITY: The Logos-Principle.

REALM   II   SPIRITUALITY: the logician following the recipes of The Logos-Principle.

REALM III   MORALITY: the realm of moral humanhood; the sentiments of conscience; the six functions of conscientious moral humanhood.

The following table shows the marriage of these six or sex metaphysical, moral elements, as one compound unit of humanhood, functioning in unity:

1 Manhood		1 Womanhood
2 Husbandhood	—Humanhood—	2 Wifehood
3 Fatherhood		3 Motherhood

These six states of being (in moral unity) follow on and up and to Realm II where manhood is wisdom, spiritually manned, and where womanhood is love, wifehood is the power of intuition (to conceive by way of spiritual instruction), and motherhood is truth or the verity that verifies and makes evident her own conceptions; where husbandhood is the power of perception and where fatherhood fathers those wise perceptions which he has set forth for conception; where integrity is humanhood.

The following table elaborates the foregoing one:

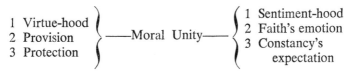

1 Virtue-hood		1 Sentiment-hood
2 Provision	—Moral Unity—	2 Faith's emotion
3 Protection		3 Constancy's expectation

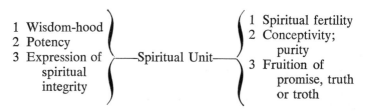

1 Wisdom-hood
2 Potency
3 Expression of
   spiritual
   integrity
}—Spiritual Unit—{
1 Spiritual fertility
2 Conceptivity;
   purity
3 Fruition of
   promise, truth
   or troth

Not one of these elements can function without the other compounded whole element. Not one of them is dependent upon corporeity or upon the human physique for identity, entity or identification. Each one is an *iden, idem, ideo* or idea dependent upon The Logos for expression. Each one of these states of being has its own specific function to perform. There is no duplication of function; no element of logical or literate fusion, confusion, mixture or chaos among them. They function in perfect order, even as the numeral characters function in logical sequence. There is no disorder, but only spiritual sequence and harmonious order (correct and accurate thinking).

In Realm II there is no human impulse to interfere with the radically spiritual, fundamental and primal order, even (as in numeral science) perfection of operation, which is untouched, unhampered and undisturbed by human emotion or by human ignorance of this primal logic.

These six elements are as fixed in Realm II as the nine or ten numeral characters are fixed in the human mentality.

In the moral realm of human virtue, honesty perceives as moral virility. He husbands his veracious conceiver and is bound to wifehood by the law of completeness. He fathers his infant issues. The feminine element is his complement. She is sentimentally passive to his honest convictions and opinions. She cherishes, mentally embosoms and *enwombs* (in her mental matrix) those potential ideas which he sets forth for conception. She makes her concept evident—which concept is identical with his precept or perception or preconception or his percipient formation set forth.

These six elements are married or in union; are in one completely rational whole, functioning as spiritual-moral-mental wedlock, under the direct supervision of The Logos Principle, which Principle presents the law element and denotes completeness—the seventh element.

There are two sexes. There are three genders: masculine, feminine and neuter. Principle, precept, or law is the neuter and common gender. There are *not* two sexes or sixes. The male element constitutes one half or three of the six or sex elements. The female element constitutes one half or three of the six or sex elements or half of the sixes. The law of premise or principle functions as neither male nor female but as binding all six or sex in one element of logical, literate and legitimate understanding or power of realization. Thus bound or married they function from premise to conclusion in rational harmony, and under a principle common to both sexes.

The male element has the power of speech or address. He sets forth the rudimental, potential issue. He orates or emits the elements of wisdom.

The female element has the power of conception. She is sentiment, being passive to the rudiments of wisdom; being receptive to them, and functioning as the spiritual capacity that quickens, sustains, and nurtures them. She is validity, verity, vitality, vividness or the vivifier giving life and light, spiritual animation or vigor, graphic clarity and living evidence to those elements of wisdom and reality which she conceives to be true or so, or as presented by wisdom. She is love, loving wisdom. She is verity, verifying and vivifying it. She is spiritual vitality mothering its (his) intelligent perceptions.

The sixual or sexual members of morality and spirituality are little understood because they are not premised upon physicality. But when they are deduced from their highest metaphysical premises and principles (or principals) they fall into their wholly intelligent sequences as male or as female entities.

There are six separate and distinctly different processes of thought through which a perception must pass; six progressive steps taken by six different functioning elements of understanding before a perceived issue (an undeveloped and rudimentary germ or sprig-like issue) can come forth. These six functioning elements present the six or sex functions.

In Realm II the sex or six qualities function or act upon the issue. Each quality is known by its function or verbal action, literate action, logical action or legitimate assignment or assigned agency. They are six elements of intelligence, six powers or six qualified thinking agents. Three of them are masculine and three are feminine. The feminine qualities are more easily defined since they are those somewhat similar to the humanly familiar ones that conceive rather than perceive, and test or verify the potency of a precept or perception by bringing forth or by demonstrating the validity of that precept; by bringing to conclusion the issue of that premise; by gestating, carrying, and carrying through or out. Thus she gives literate form, logical proof and spiritually legitimate worth to the concept (conception) as being an element of wisdom, of that which is spiritually substantial or essential, and of that which is essentially, really and substantially good.

In Realm III the six functioning agents are honesty (his honor or his worthiness to be honored), a moral and conscientious affection, compassion, patience and its sentiments or those qualities which nurture the infant moral issues that honesty fathers. Thus Realm III brings forth its moral law, literacy and science—*con*-science.

THE WORD, SIMILITUDE

The word *similitude* is made up of the Latin *similis,* meaning like. The suffix is *-tude,* meaning the same as the suffix *-ness,* or the state, quality or condition of. It forms the word like (an adjective) into an abstract noun likeness or similitude, which means literally condition or quality of being similar and like.

The word similar and *similis* (French *similaire,* to be like) means alike; bearing resemblance; having a likeness to. It is an adjective. The noun form is similitude or similarity.

The word resemblance is a noun of complete entity, since its suffix *-ance* or *-ence* gives it individual being as actor and as agent, agency or doer, as well as giving it state and quality of being similar, or of being similitude of its principle-root. It is that agency which is like, has the form, the qualities and state of and has the entity which is like (absolutely like) its or his origin, originator, source, root or precept. It is the entity who is actually of the same substance and essence as that which he resembles, but not of the same degree, extent or infinitude of being. The similitude depends upon its subject-noun or upon its noumenal identity of which it is resemblance, is likeness, is similitude in perfect form and manifestation; of which it or he is complete, compound phenomenon or phenomenal entity. Thus the word similitude is altogether dependent upon that which it is like for existence, even as a sunbeam has no existence of its own but depends upon the sun to sustain it, yet it has the same qualities and characteristics, and is of the same substance.

THE WORD, SIN

The word *sin* has a negative existence. It is the antonym of accuracy; the absence of precision; the kin of vice which is the opposite of virtue; the lack of rightness, trueness or excellence. Literally it means missing the mark. This mark is a positive thing. It is neither relative nor negative. It exists as a rule, a law or a point of excellence. Sin, therefore, is the missing of that mark which distinguishes, defines or designates this point of excellency; this manifestly perceptible standard or point of accuracy or perfection which one strives to achieve; this at which one aims and would attain.

Religiously speaking, a sin is unrighteousness or wickedness. Morally speaking, it is a lack of conformity to the rules of conscience or true sense of the moral law. Commonly speaking or humanly speaking, it may be any error, fault, mistake or hapless random thing having no place, no position, and no positive principle to maintain it. It could be any kind of lack of wholeness or holiness or integrity; any ill-doing.

If one were to attend an exhibition of some sort, such as a game that has its target, as all games do, and if a player were to miss the mark, one might say, "O, that is a sin and a shame!" One might feel that the player should have had that point, and one's sympathies and sentiments might be with the player. However, when sin constitutes a deliberate transgression of a rule of right, it is a sin indeed.

Sin may be a form of ignorance of moral sentiment or spiritual wisdom, yet conscience is the agent of wisdom and the counsel of the moral law; and since this is true, sin is a form of desperation, a lack of moral prosperity, or a state of moral weakness or invalidity.

The Latin *pecco* is sin. A peccant is a sinner. Peccable means capable of sinning. Peccavi means I have sinned; it is my fault.

The Anglo Saxon sin is *syn*. It seems to have no true parentage or evident root. Modern usage has probably left little or no trace of its origin.

Sin may be a miscarriage of one's hopes, purposes, plans, aims or endeavors. These aims may be directed at a human, physical target, a metaphysical mark, a moral mark (standard of excellence), or a spiritual principle; but sin misses the mark of virtue and moral equity, when one is morally inaccurate or indulges in iniquity, impiety, evil (that which is immoral or vile), or when one goes over on the side of neglect (is negligent—not diligent) in neglecting to do right. Here the *syn* would be to be with or to be together with or on the side of sin and against holiness (*syn,* as a prefix, meaning with, together, along with). Here *syn* would be sin against moral stamina, sin against one's own moral consciousness, in neglecting to exercise it or to act upon the advice of conscience.

Sin may be a total loss of moral instinct, sense or intuition. In this sense it would be unmorality or moral depravity, or miasmatic, or hypnotic delusion; a fault; an offense; a state of being in the wrong or going along with it.

Sin is that which misses the mark, and it is therefore subject to correction, to cure, to being accured or to being made accurate. It is incorrectness, misconception or mistake. Of itself it is nothing, but for the one endeavoring to hit the mark (in any form of accuracy) sin is something. It is something to be cured. It is the opposite of holiness or wholeness which is spiritual integrity; the whole unit or integer. It is the illiterate antonym of all literate perfection; the reverse of all ideals; the blast, blight and rupture of every high hope.

Sin is everything in human experience which does not produce wisdom, honesty, truth or an element of veracity, but which persists in missing the mark of honesty's precept, through self-justified personal pride or proud personality; through self-esteem honoring self.

Deceit, dishonesty and all unworthiness in human nature, miss the mark of the moral nature and character.

It is not a sin to miss the mark but it *is* a sin to do it proudly. It is the practice of sin and the praise of it and its vices that actuates the immoral human impulses.

Sin is sin because it does not restrain the vile human impulses, the human nature or its activities, but acts upon them and justifies them, as being the rule—not abnormal.

Sin is sin when it serves to promote its own inaccuracies, abnormalcies, or its enormous (excessive) and utterly wrong rules and rulings; when it serves to promote its own favor and popularity among innocent people, or to inflict its own nefarious character (or personality) upon human society; upon the people who depend upon moral, spiritual, or divine law and rule.

THE WORD, Soul

The Word *Soul* is one of the names for The Deity. It comes from Anglo Saxon *sawel* or *sawl*. This may be akin to saw, *sagu,* or sage, as proverb, as maxim or saying. It may indicate past tense of see, as saw well (to see well) as a sage is wise or sees well (*salvus,* well, in health or well being), as a seer sees well or surely, or beneficently, because of being wise, judicious, or divinely enlightened.

Soul is the name of The one and only God or the sole God who is Good — *Optimus Maximus Deus.* Soul is one of the names for The Logos, Elohim, The Word, The divine creative Ego, The Supreme Being—Love; The solitary Divinity or GOD-HEAD, Premise or Principle which is shared with no other head or chief.

The proper name Soul, and The Word Soul, is always singular—never plural—but is one of the names for The compound and infinite Deity. As there is only one sol or sun belonging to this solar system, so there is only one Soul—Giver of light, or enlightenment.

Humanhood is inclined to leave soul to the theologians, while it devotes its time to psychology, biology or physiology or the natural sciences. It thinks of soul as related to the hereafter, and thus it would put soul in a somewhat remote position. Humanhood stands somewhat aghast before soul; stands awe-inspired in fear and reverence, while it communicates with conscience as being very near. It understands conscience who is soul's agent or moral representative. Conscience is the science of soul; the scientific intuition within oneself or the science within oneself or with one. It is the logic of Soul reduced to human comprehension and utility.

The sun or sol best illustrates Soul. The sol is the sole giver of light to the Earth. Soul is the sole and only Giver of enlightenment to the *Ear-th* (ear) of understanding. It illumines and environs the thinker's spiritual realm of substance or *under-stanc-ing,* or the earth upon which he stands.

The sun throws its full light upon the face of the Earth or upon the glassy surface of the sea, and as the physical human eye is dazzled by the sun's reflection upon a quiet lake, so the human metaphysical eye is completely dazzled by Soul's enlightenment, or by the Soul reflected light. Thus conscience brings the science of soul (or the conscientious understanding or light which one has within himself) down to human degree of intensity, but the human being never thinks of conscience as a faculty or agent of soul, nor of himself as *in, with* or environed *by* science.

A bird that lives and flies in the sky, might ask: What is this thing called sky? A fish that swims and lives in the water—its natural environment—might ask: What is this substance or essence called water?

Conscience, wisdom or discernment is soul, seeing well, or good. They are enlightenment itself, reflecting Soul's very radiant light; splendid or resplendent light. But wisdom cannot be directly associated with humanity because of his spiritual brilliance. Conscience speaks for him.

The Anglo Saxon *sawel* may be a contraction of the phrase saw well, saw good, saw as good or beneficent. Everything pertaining to Soul is seen and must be seen in good light; seen in divine light; seen as created by Soul.

The entity, soul or *mon*—the thinker—expresses The beneficent Soul. He sees good and Good only. He sees well, completely, wholly or holy, and in the full light of Soul. Thus he expresses Soul fully and perfectly.

Soul, being the thinker's Source of light, man or wisdom draws upon this inexhaustible resource for soul-logic.

The Word Soul may be analyzed as *So-al;* as being that which is divinely *so,* plus the suffix *-al* which would be pertaining to, relating to or belonging to that which is so; that which is averred to be. It would mean pertaining to that which is true, so seen and so said.

Soul is only one of the several names for The infinite, compound God; only one of The coordinate, creative powers that sustain and maintain man's Earth or realm of understanding. Soul is vital, yet not Life, for Life is another one of the essential elements of The Esse. Soul is intelligent, yet not Intelligence, for Intelligence, Truth or Verity are members of this same Principle-Logos. Soul is loving and lovable and lovely (divinely lovely) but it is not Love, for Love is another individual member of DIVINITY. Soul is Good and is a name for God—Good—but Soul is not the whole God, but is embraced and embodied in The whole God.

Each one has its own function or assignment. Soul's specific function is to enlighten the whole-souled thinker; to bestow spiritual —rather, divine—light upon him; to teach the more receptive one who follows the lead or the spiritual agitation of conscience (the science of soul, within), for Soul is divinely didactic (apt to teach).

In the realm of human intellect and literacy soul has lost its place and has become part of a conglomerate mass of organic stuff called man and mind and man's soul, thus:

Greek *noos* is mind.	Latin *mens, mentis,* mind.
Greek *pneuma* is spirit.	Latin *spiro* is spirit.
Greek *bios* is life.	Latin *vita* is life.
Greek *psuche,* psyche—soul.	Latin *animus* is soul.

Human usage has mixed the Greek mind and soul. The Latin animus is used as *anima,* meaning breath and life, and is then assigned to the animal, meaning that which relates, pertains to or is like the animus, *anima,* or something having life; a sentient living organism; that which pertains to the unspiritual nature of man. Thus have both man and soul been physicalized, humanized, animalized and mortalized or made to be as finite and as fleeting as the *pneuma,* wind, air or breath he breathes.

Here again human nature has won first place in the realm of human knowledge, and human, animal impulse has taken the place of spiritual incentive, sentiment, motive, influence, impetus or impulse; has tried to substitute for soul feeling, animation, force or incentive by instituting *humus-man* nature. This knowledge has made the human physique the entity; has made the human, mammal metaphysique the mind; has made the human animal, animus, or impetus, the soul; has assigned to it all of the sentient animal instincts and nature, and has called it an organic physicality. Thus the human physique becomes subject, predicate and object; becomes first, second, and third person of every human thought and statement, because the human intellect can neither define nor classify soul, really, and human knowledge cannot know soul nor understand Soul.

The following table will show that soul may be perceived by humanity (the human race) only as it presents itself via Realm III:

REALM I

DIVINITY: Soul; The Soul-Principle, Giver of Enlightenment; Director of the recipes which Soul prescribes.

REALM II

SPIRITUALITY: soul; the soul, entity, essence, idea and recipient of enlightenment; the ideate expression of The Soul-Principle who practices the rules and recipes which Soul prescribes.

REALM III

MORALITY: conscience, with its soul science; with
                 its animus, purpose, good tem-
                 per, moral courage, breath or
                 speech or spiritual dictations
                 from soul.
                     Here conscience reiterates (in
                 human tongue, idiom, language,
                 vernacular or humanly familiar
                 terms) the lessons, rules and
                 recipes which Soul prescribes.

REALM IV

PHYSICALITY: the realm in which the human race has
                 humanized or physicalized or
                 animalized all things; has ma-
                 terialized soul (in its belief) as
                 being originally identified with
                 mater-*iality* — mater Eve and
                 with pater-*iality* — the Adam
                 physique or physicality.

The moral qualities in Realm III are animated with zeal, hope,
faith, courage and expectancy of right. They are full of the science
of soul as taught by *con-science,* and they are thus soulful or full
of the essence and the animating principles which conscience teaches,
inspires, stirs, quickens or makes vivid. Conscience breathes out
her soul science, mentally, without breath, *pneumon* or lung.

In the realm of human intellect and human parlance, soul is an
unknown entity. In the realm of Eve (the human mater) and human
mater-iality, soul or the spiritual logician, wisdom, or the real *mon*
(man) is unknown, yet soul (mon) is the sol of all solace, the sole
and only comforting agent. It is that spiritual tranquilizer which
soothes, calms, tempers and makes serene. (Here sooth is Anglo
Saxon *soth,* meaning true. The noun sooth means truth or reality.)
In this realm of Eve (mater-iality) the true soul is an unreality.

In the realm of spirituality soul is the silent, quiet intuition which
speaks through con-science to soothe, to cheer, to solace or to encourage. (Here soothe means to agree with as being true; to yield
assent to; to confirm as being true.)

The Latin *solar* (*solari, solatus*) means I console; I comfort or
provide solace and solution. Thus soul makes tranquil, teaches great
peace (*magna tranquillitas*) or the truly great dignity and gravity,
import and significance of Soul.

To solve means to loosen, to dissolve, solve or explain. Through con-science soul absolves, releases or frees one from that which would impose a problem. It relieves, removes, heals, makes valid or normal, and completely remedies whatever magnifies, aggravates or constitutes a problem. Thus Soul is the solution for every kind of human calamity, fear, turbulence, trouble, disorder and frenzied action.

Soul solicits or pleads through conscience and human reason to reach humanhood, for con-science is mouthpiece, speaker, dictator and power of speech or agent for soul. It brings wisdom's logic or truth's solution. Thus the speech of soul is ever sonant and ever vibrant, via conscience.

Soul is The Father of all divinely beneficent and infinitely emitted ideas; Father of all divinely expressed ideas, and Father of all literately whole ideas.

Soul is Father or Word-Root of all whole-souled or wholly substantiated holy ideas and entities; Father of all divinely worded expressions, or divinely principled entities. Soul is The Father of all identities, peculiarly like Soul and legitimately belonging *to* Soul.

Soul (as a member of The creative Logos) is The Father of all thoroughly and logically expressed and logically demonstrated ideas; Father of all that He expresses and maintains to be so (as that which pertains to Him—Soul). Thus the power of speech or word emission or intelligent expression is offspring of Soul, reiterating the logic, literacy and law or principle of The Logos-Soul. Thus soul, the seer, sees his Logos-Father, and thus wisdom speaks as the iteration, and thus understanding stands, and thus love loves, and thus purity conceives, and thus spiritual integrity is soul, representing Soul, truly and wholly and wholesomely.

All of the powers of infinite, universal, logical and wholly literate realization are fathered by Soul, and are maintained *in* that whole, valid or healthy spiritual condition, which condition is soul-life or soul continuity. These powers are infinite vision, perception, conception, reception, inception (from Soul), gestation or digestion. These powers are infinite comprehension, apprehension, adhesion, cohesion, decision and precision and the power or divine energy to express this infinite comprehension. These powers are animated and directed by the animus or the soul in man, which man is animate wisdom or soul vision.

As the sun dries, purifies, prevents decay or sweetens the humus, as it counteracts filth in a stagnant pool, or checks sourness, ferment and mold, so does Soul, with its logic and its wisdom, bring to bear upon humanhood its integrating substance and essential light. It corrects and rectifies. It cures or makes *ac-cure-ate* or logically sound. It precludes and pre-exterminates that which the *humus-man* has believed to be true. Thus Soul's ministrations are curative and corrective.

Soul is that omnipresent member of The Logos who teaches and speaks via conscience to humanhood, presenting this ever-present science (con-science, the science of soul within the true thinker) and ever animating the thinker as ever living in his consciousness or as the *ever*-animate thinker himself, finding solution for every human inaccuracy via the logic of The Logos-Soul.

Soul is The Logos-Soul; first person, Speaker, singular, expressing or setting forth His ideas. The Logos-Love is second person, Hearer (Ear), divine and singular, conceiving and bringing forth His perceived ideas. The idea (so expressed) is the entity or individual person spoken of, or the third person; the compound and infinitely constituted idea.

In the realm of human intellect the human person, the human being, personality or physicality is the first, the second and the third persons. These are incorrectly called souls. They are finitely and humanly constituted persons.

In the realm of Soul (Intelligence), Soul is The Subject, The Predicate (The Speaker who affirms, proclaims or speaks before), and soul is the object, idea, ideation or expression of which Soul is cognizant.

Soul is that Source of intelligence which provides all enlightenment; The Provider of light; The all-provident One.

To provide means to foresee—*pro-* means before, and *video* means see (*videre, visum,* to see), and *visus* means I see. Thus Soul is The I (Speaker) who sees to or cares for by providing for those ideas which He has set forth or has expressed.

These ideas are seen only in Soul light; only in Realm II; only in the brilliance and radiance of Soul. One of them is wisdom—the seer. Wisdom is seen in his wise domination. Wisdom means to see or to witness. Idea means to see. All ideas emitted from Soul are spiritually thrifty. They illucidate, illustrate and illuminate, and demonstrate (as teachers) their enlightenment to the sincere thinkers of Realm III.

The *humus-man* or person is seen only in the light of human intellect; sees only as humanly orthodox usage teaches.

The provision which Soul has made is wholly (holy) and altogether spiritual. It is in the form of wisdom, discernment, understanding and the powers of realization. Thus Soul looks out for soul, or is seen to supply or to provide or to look out for the man, idea or soul of Realm II. This man is evident (seen) only in Realm II, as seer, as idea or as wisdom. This man is *mon*—most literate form of man.

Realm II is light. Its ideas are bright, *lucid,* clear, luminous or divinely illuminated, and they may be called Soul's luminaries, even as the stars are the sun's luminaries, shining because of the sun's provision of light.

These ideas are vivid, living, lively or quick ideas. Their function is to vivify (make alive, animate or vitalize, or make wise) the receptive thinkers of Realm III.

As Soul throws light upon the spiritual *Ear-th* or ear that hears and understands spiritually, so the sun throws its light upon the Earth. And as the waters reflect or *re-send* the brilliant light of the sun, so do the thinkers of Realm II *re-send* and *re-present* their wise ideas to Realm III.

As Soul points out, directs, instructs and emits enlightenment to His spiritual subjects, and as He demonstrates the potency of His living ideas (by the use of His spiritual subjects or ideas), so soul (as wisdom) points out, directs, and throws light upon Soul's logic, literacy and law, by standing under and by understanding Soul, and thus he lights up Realm III to whatever extent it is susceptible to his enlightenment.

The light of wisdom may not be cast upon the Earth that misunderstands Soul. Realm IV is opaque (impervious to light) because it is solidly earth, ground, humus or humanly material and altogether unspiritual. It pertains to humanity which is mortality. It is solidly against Soul's light, even as the Earth is solid and dark as a mineral matter, and is impenetrable to light because it is earthy and earthly. This realm is physicality. It is mundane. Its light is human knowledge. Its concept of life is physical animation in mammal form as presented by the human mammal.

Realm III sees by means of conscience (the science of soul within one); sees by means of faith, confidence, fidelity, hope (moral prosperity) and its passion for wisdom. It is provided with the wisdom and power of honesty, the substance of faith, and the glorious enlightenment of hope. It is provided with patience or compassion, and with affection, humanity and charity. It is teachable, meek and sober.

The following table will present soul and Soul, and the science of soul—as con-science—and the misconstrued concepts or beliefs concerning soul:

REALM I

DIVINITY: Soul, one of the terms indicating The Logos.

Realm II

SPIRITUALITY: soul, one of the terms indicating the wholly (holy) logical spiritual thinker who is completely enlightened by Soul or The Soul-principle; who is completely and legitimately related to Soul as the full expression representing Soul.

Realm III

MORALITY: the realm in which the moral thinker is educated to believe in human knowledge, humanly instituted sciences, human intellect, tradition, conventional manner or the orthodox manner.   Thus it is an educated human belief that disputes and quarrels with the science of soul (con-science).

Here the moral consciousness is natural.

Here the moral conscience is uppermost.

Here the thinker believes in soul, but misconstrues its science or confuses it with natural science.

Here the thinker is beginning to understand soul and its science, and is beginning to let go of humanity (mortality) and its instituted sciences; is beginning to think more radically moral or more morally radical, following conscience at all cost to human nature and the humanly natural sciences.

Realm IV

PHYSICALITY: the realm of human nature; the realm in which the human person or personality governs the human individual and represents him; the realm in which the human physique speaks for itself as self, and where the human brain is called the center of feeling or sentiment.

Here the human mammal is supposed to be made of earthy and earthly matter such as mineral matter— water, lime (bone), and such—and is supposed to be the entity or identity called man, and called thinker. Thus the humus-man or person believes himself to be complete within himself as a soul.

The foregoing table shows that soul leaves off at Realm III where conscience—the science of soul—begins.

Soul is the one of the deific titles or names for The Deity which is most difficult to define to humanhood, for the reason that human idiom is so lacking in the spirit of Spirit; so lacking in the peculiar genius of spiritual expression, speech, or the idiom of The Word.

Soul is The Self of The Logos. Soul is The Logos-self, The Soul and sole entity, identity or individual name wholly peculiar to The Deity. Thus The Word of Soul rules and judges, assigns and directs. The will of The Logos is embodied in Soul, and this will is divine.

Soul is not identical with Spirit. It is that will which Spirit moves, spirits or motivates; that divine ability, might or power (Omnipotence) which Spirit urges, moves, leads, drives, actuates, impels, induces and leads forth. It is that supremely excellent wisdom which Spirit breathes forth.

Soul is one of the divine creative faculties; one of the infinitely wise and loving members of The Divinity, or The divine Body of the universe of Good.

Divinity is the university of divine, sublime, perfect and complete metaphysics. Soul is one of the members of this ultraspiritual (divine) universal faculty; one of the members of this university faculty, with all of the authority and privilege of a faculty member.

Soul is the all-seeing wisdom looking out from highest outlook or lookout, and carefully taking care of His own wise and spiritually discerning ideas. These ideas are the entities who express their Maker-Soul, and whose soul and sole will is to love, honor and obey their Maker-Soul.

Soul is the will, the animus, good intent and purpose which speaks for one and represents one's soul sense, whereas Soul—The Logos—is the divine drive and God volition, or The divine will of The Logos. Thus soul—its wisdom and understanding—is the representative expression, whereas Soul—The Creator's deliberate intent and purpose to create and to maintain—is The Soul-Principle which the Realm II thinker presents, represents and expresses.

The Logos-Soul is not the driver. The Logos-Spirit is the driver, motivating power and force (symbolized by the wind), whereas the soul entity of Realm II is recipient of the substance (understancing) so impelled and propelled; so empowered, so motivated or so driven forth.

The Soul is the will setting forth gifts, talents or the spiritual faculties, powers of perception and cognition. The soul or thinker of Realm II is the heir to Soul's infinite sense of all things. Thus soul (the recipient) is in harmony with Soul. This is called heaven.

All of the suffering in the world is only the contrary, adverse or ignorant human nature antagonizing soul — the beneficent science within one, or the science of soul within oneself. All of the discord in the world is created by the world's lack of divine volition, its lack of soul instinct, soul intuition, or soul sense in authority—standing in authority. This discord is called hell, which hell is created by one's disobedience to his own soul sense; by one's displacement of good will and pleasure. The thinker of Realm II enjoys the comfort of his own voluntary humility under Soul, and in Soul's good pleasure.

Soul is The I AM or The Logos-Self; The I am Soul. This I, The Speaker, is Soul.

Soul is one of the names of The Absolute Deity, The Logos, The superlative Logos-Entity or The supreme Being. This Supreme Being has several names. These names designate the several individual entities, members, faculties and functioning agencies of The Logos faculty. Each member has a different function to perform; an individual activity as a member of The Logos council.

Soul is not Mynde, but Soul sets forth what The Logos has in Mynde. The Logos-Mynde is The Minder who minds, takes note or notice, takes cognizance or cognizes or gives thought to each idea.

Soul is not Spirit, but Soul expresses or presses out or speaks forth as Spirit provides breath, inspiration or the divine drive. Soul is The Expresser speaking out or breathing out or setting forth His explicit directions, definite instructions or precise specifications and divine descriptions as prescribed by the deific intelligence.

There is no word, no name, noumenon or noun so sacred as to prevent or deter humanity from (mentally) stealing, mortalizing (after physicalizing) and carrying it away captive to its den or its corporeal world of thought and concept. There is no word too divine or too spiritual to prevent the human intellect from claiming it as human property, or as something incorporated within its corporeal realm. Thus it has (in its ignorance and false physics) conceived soul to be a part of its realm, a state of being corporeal or a quality of having a body; being of physical nature; being a member of the human corporeity.

Soul is from the Anglo Saxon. Its idiom is peculiar to holiness and spiritual immaculacy, which is divine purity and infinite integrity. Howbeit there is no trace of soul in the human vocabulary excepting the superficial words soulful, soulness and soulless and such. The Greek *psyche* has taken the place of soul, and the Latin *anima* has been adopted as root instead of soul. The Latin and Greek culture is preferred.

According to literology the word soul is literate, is legitimate (as a derivative of Soul) and it is logical as an element of The Logos. It should take form in such words as soul-*th,* soul-*hood,* soul-*ity,* soul-*ace* or solace or *soul*acement; in such words as con-*soul* or con*sol,* since soul is—to the spiritual realm—what the sun is to the earthy realm or the earthly sphere. There should be *soul*-id or solid, meaning divinely firm or spiritually substantial. Solic or soulic would be the science of soul, and solar would refer to spiritual enlightenment. Soul-*ance* or soul-*ence* is the state or quality of being soul. Soul-*ent* is individual or sole integer, integrity or whole-*ness* or holiness, meaning an whole entity expressing wholeness. Soul-*ical* would mean one who is like Soul, one who is soul, made by and related to Soul. There should be soul-*ile,* soul-*ine* and soul-*ion* (act of speaking or soul-*ing*). There should be soul-*ize* and soul-*ism* (speaking in Soul's idiom and in one's own peculiar form of expression). This would begin with *con*-science (one's own science of speech) in solitude or soul-*itude, con*-souling or comforting one.

THE WORD, Speech

The word *speech* comes from the Anglo Saxon *specan*, meaning to speak, or from *sprecan,* meaning speak.

Common meaning: discourse; an address; a talk; an oration. To speak refers to the verbal meaning. To speak means to talk, to say or to tell; to spread, disseminate, set forth or make known; to disperse, dispense, unfold, or to divulge; to orate, to distribute, to circulate, or to extend reason, science or saying. To speak means to express thoughts.

The word oration is from the Latin *orare* or from the Old French *oratour,* meaning to speak or to pray. An oration may be called a sermon, an oracle or vision verbally set forth.

The Latin *loqui* (*loquor, locutus*) means to speak. These forms are found in the words eloquent, elocution and soliloquy. The forms *loquor, loqui, locutus,* mean I speak or I talk. They are embodied in the words loquacity, colloquy and ventriloquist.

The Greek *Logos* means word, speech, reason, ratio, science, description, saying, thing and logical matters or things.

The following table will classify and define speech:

Realm I
DIVINITY.   The Word; The Logos; The Speech and The Speaker of The Word.

Realm II
SPIRITUALITY: the logician — wisdom — who has the power of speech or expression; who has full ratio of understanding and reason; the whole unit — man, the thinker — who is the whole idea, integer and entity ever iterating, repeating, reiterating and *re*-presenting The Logos Speech.

Realm III
MORALITY: the speaker and speech of moral science, highest human ethics, excellence or conscience, who dictates, says, and reiterates his wisdom in all languages, in moral sentiments and in conscientious doctrines.

Here honesty has the power of speech, faith orates or prays to realize her hope, compassion distributes, spreads or dispenses her charity and her affection.

Realm IV

PHYSICALITY: The Greek *glossa* or *glotta* refers to the
physical tongue, the native speech or the human nature,
or the human mammal and its language or tongue. This
physical tongue is the organ of speech. It pertains to
the utterance of sound, or to distinct articulation.

Realm V

IMMORALITY: the speaker in this realm is lewdness,
moral ignorance, licentiousness, and vileness. Here vice
and the viciousness of deceit tongues, mouths or talks
as symbol of the serpent's tongue; talks as deluded bab-
bler and mutterer.

The foregoing table shows that the word speech loses its reason
or its highly rational substance when it is reduced to lower (than
conscience) meanings. It loses its reality and its authority when it is
demoted below the speech of conscience or Realm III. It becomes
humanized or *finitized*. It becomes the serpentine tongue of human
knowledge and confusion; the babbling murmurings or the morally
irrational complaints; the heinous tongue of personal opinion induced
from morally perverted premises.

In Realm II (reality) speech is the thinker's soul expressing itself.
It is the spirit or divine erg of the logician or speaker making a motion, moving, proposing or presenting his idea or putting it in spoken
words. It is the voice of verity and reality urging wisdom; uttering
intelligence.

Speech and speaker are presumed to be male, while hearer, audience, or understander and conceiver are presumed to be female in
their function.

In Realm I The Speaker is The Logos speaking to The divine
creative conceiver—The audient One, sometimes known as The Holy
Ghost (the silent, invisible One). She is The Word — with God —
in the beginning or creative action or administration.

In Realm II the speaker is wisdom witnessing, exerting his power
of speech, or breathing forth words of wisdom. He is the true logician,
the wholly (holy) correct and accurate thinker setting forth, putting
forth or exercising his speaking or expressive faculties. He is *mon* —
the truth thinker — breathing out that which he has put into true
or wise or scientific words. He is mon — the male element of spirituality — speaking, instructing, expressing or specifying for the purpose of being immaculately heard, intuitively understood, and vividly
or vigorously conceived of; for the purpose of having his potential

ideas made actual by the female element of mon — the truth thinker. This is the wholly (holy) legitimate speaker.

It is the male element in every realm which sets forth, and it is the female which brings forth, effects, reveals, completes, accomplishes, executes, finishes, performs, forms, gives true and tangible form (readable form or record). It is she who carries out, carries, bears, sustains and nurtures his potentially effective perceptions, or his truly wise undertakings. Thus this male and female function to counteract the lie or the lying talker, the audible and silent denier, the mythological and hypocritical charmer or charming personality. They function to nullify the anti-moral influence, the magnetic allurer (self-idolater or self-manipulatory speech) exciting its own imagery and impressing its own fascinated conceivers.

THE WORD, SPIRIT

The Word *Spirit* must be capitalized because it pertains to The Deity and because Spirit is The divine creative Word (Creator) of spirituality, and because Spirit conveys only the divine significance or meaning.

The word spirit which is in common use is incorrect because it does not convey the literate sense or image of Spirit; because it is not compatible with Spirit only. It should give place to the words zeal, courage, eagerness, energy, ardor, fervor, devotion or enthusiasm. If one means to convey the thought of spiritual enthusiasm or energy, one may use the adjective spiritual. If one means moral zeal, let him use the adjective moral, or the noun morale.

The word spirit comes from the Latin *spiro, spirare, spiratum,* meaning to breathe; or *spiritus,* breath, spirit, and breathing, or I breathe (as *spiratus*). The Latin form *spiritus* is most literally similar to the word spirit. The form *spiratus* includes the illiterate *a* vowel.

It is a verbal noun, a very active, animated and truly living noun or name, a verb indeed denoting sprightliness, liveliness or energetic spiritual action. Thus instead of using the word spirit one should use the word spiritual to indicate the spiritual drive, spur or agency that actuates, stimulates, moves, inspires, agitates, motivates, blows or breathes out or speaks forth, utters and conveys a thought or an element of an idea.

The word Spirit begins and ends in breath letters or living, breathing literate characters—aspirates. It begins with the aspirate combination *sp*. Its only vowel sound is the short *i* rolled over the consonant *r,* and on to the second *i* sounded with the final *t* aspirate. It is as breathlike, Spiritlike, or spiritual as a word can be. The two *i* vowels double its literacy since the *i* is one of the most literate vowels and since it denotes divinely mental (Soul) substance.

The word energy is not spiritually or divinely literate but it is a good moral synonym for that spiritual urge or erg which makes morality work; which gives honesty and his moral associates their power. It is a Greek word meaning in or on erg. An erg is a unit of work or energy, and *ergon* means work. Energy may mean moral power at work, working or in work. It may be the urge of moral instinct or of moral courage. It may be the exertion of the moral, mental forces, motives, zeal or a high morale at work. It may be morality itself, exerting its stamina or working to defend its realm or its conscientious kingdom. Thus by using the adjectives moral and spiritual, the word energy may be properly used as a substitute, but not as a synonym. For instance, wisdom is a form of spiritual energy. He is at work or in the work of being dominant, or administering wisdom or of teaching his rules and recipes. Honesty, veracity, fidelity and loyalty are forms of moral energy; lesser elements of wisdom's power and dominion. As wisdom is in the work of seeing, discerning, witnessing and enlightening, so these moral workers are at work in their realm of lesser literate and logical understanding.

The moral workers are charity, affection, kindness, compassion, patience, piety, sobriety, sincerity, steadfastness, confidence or faith, hope or moral prosperity, with expectancy of fulfillment. They are at work supporting their high moral standard; at work reasoning, thinking, pondering and confirming what wisdom presents; at work utilizing their rational powers in defense of right, and realizing the supremacy of this rightness; at work as mental penetration or moral perspicacity.

The following table classifies The word Spirit, and its spiritually peculiar thinker. It classifies the properties that may be properly deduced from spirituality, and compares them with those improper concepts which humanity entertains:

REALM   I   DIVINITY: The Logos-Spirit and Father of all divine logic; The Word Spirit and Mother of all divine literacy, inscription or holy record; The Logos-Principle creator of all spiritual principles, laws, rules and recipes.

REALM   II   SPIRITUALITY: the home and heaven of man—the thinker; the haven of spiritual integrity and its continuity; the atmosphere wholly and holy purified and rarified by Spirit, in which *mon*—the divine logician—reflects, thinks and understands; the domain of wisdom, reality, potency and all of the divine sentiments, graces and love.

REALM III   MORALITY: the realm of equity, moral incentives, desires and purposes; the faith that aims high above the mundane properties, yet does not call Realm II properties supernatural.

Realm IV PHYSICALITY: the wills of human nature;
the impulses unrestrained by moral instinct; the animal or mammal human energies; the human physique with its organic,
magnetic, or nervous human influences
and forces.

This is the illiterate, illogical, and illegitimate concept of The Word Spirit, of
the human race and of its physicalized or
humanized mental properties.

The Word Spirit is one of the principals and principles of The
Logos. It is literately and logically singular—never plural. It is
that power which causes the thinker to aspire, to rise, spire or shoot
upward; to soar forth in the desire to tower higher; to seek to attain
that which is spiritually high, spirituous or like Spirit.

Spirit is that divine breath which fills the spiritual universe—
commonly called the unknown; humanly conceived to be unfilled or
unoccupied. It is that pure, clear heaven or atmosphere—heavenly
substance—or wind which empowers. This phenomenon of Spirit
and its spiritual energy, called wind, is the only thing on Earth by
means of which Spirit may be illustrated, likened or symbolized. It
is like the wind that blows, breathes, moves the leaves of a tree,
carries sound, and may be felt but not seen. It is like the wind that
carries away the clouds, or brings the rain clouds; washes, clears and
cleans or purifies the atmosphere. It is that humanly intangible heavenly thing that blows away the mist, the unspiritual fog, or the immoral smog.

Spirit is that infinite and inexhaustible energy always at work,
ever in force, ever empowering or inspiriting the thinker of Realm II,
which thinker—*mon*—is never dispirited, is ever energized, is ever
in working condition or in a state of health continuation; is ever
Soul-quickened.

Spirit is the fervor, the stimulus, the driver and the amplifier of
soul's (mon's) expression; the breath of his speech; the unction or
spur of his logic; the very essence and substance of his address or
verbal action; the power (omnipotence) promoting and maintaining
his incentives and highest achievements.

Spirit supports, sustains, upholds and holds the realm of understanding (Realm II) even as the sun holds the planet Earth sus-
pended in her heavens. Thus the *Ear-th* typifies the ear of understanding, hearing or being obedient and subordinate to Spirit's discipline
or supreme authority. This understanding conceives and brings forth

Spirit's universal, spiritual or vital phenomena, living ideas or wise entities, and it presents them to Realm III by way of conscience; presents them or brings them to the ear of humanhood by way of conscience who speaks the spiritual tongue (as angel messenger) and thus brings the spiritual point of view, translated into familiar moral terms.

Spirit is like the wind, breath or atmosphere which environs the Earth or the ear of understanding; environs the spiritually motivated thinker, conceiver and perceiver. This divinely dynamic thinker breathes, moves, lives and realizes (understands) or stands in this heavenly atmosphere. He is actuated by Spirit in a precise or divinely logical manner, causing him to contemplate, deliberate, or to consider Spirit as his Premise; as that natural, voluntary and spontaneous force supervising him.

Spirit is that divine creative will of The *Deus* (God) to create spirituality (heaven) and its heavenly enlightenment, and to create Earth and its ear for that heavenly logic, and to create immutable understanding, invariable sentiment or love; will to create immaculate power of fruition; will to maintain the whole integer or the sound, holy and wholesome thinker who is spiritual integrity and understanding itself, standing immediately under Spirit.

The human intellect has struggled throughout the ages to bring Spirit and its spiritual substance (Realm II) down to its earth or mundane level; and, not being able to do this, and not being able to rise to the Realm II status or level, it has usurped, stolen, assumed, taken, illegally adopted, illogically appropriated and illiterately simulated (in belief) everything spiritual. It has mimicked, imitated, counterfeited, pretended and played a burlesque. It has set up or established its systems in a very orthodox and traditional manner, giving over to each generation the all of its knowledge. It has instituted its own sham heaven and earth, without benefit of Spirit. It has not identified thought with that which is spiritual, spiritually substantial or real, but with that which is physical.

Intelligence makes and constitutes and institutes the heaven and earth compatible with Spirit. Heaven is the *heave,* the heaver or the exerting influence; the inexhaustible breath and lift or inspiration and inspiring atmosphere effluxing from Spirit. Earth is that idea which revolves, ears, understands and conceives in this spiritual atmosphere; the *ear-th* which hears.

Everything begotten by Spirit or born of The Spirit of The Logos-Word is spiritually logical, literate and legitimate (genuine). That which originates or begins in the human intellect as cause, reason or basis of reasoning, is as finite as human knowledge. That which begins with this finite human premise (purpose, motive, design or kind of actuated reason) ends, dies or concludes within those same finite human bounds of human knowledge.

That which is spiritual is that which is native or natural to spirituality (Realm II in this treatise) and it is *of* The divine or Realm I nature.

Nature, as Earth presents it to humanhood (by way of the vegetable kingdom), most nearly symbolizes and presents the nature of Spirit and spirituality. Nature's intent and constant purpose to propagate or multiply beauty, loveliness, perfection in form, consistency in pattern or image, show her super or supreme nature and show forth a spiritual—even divine—motivation. Her natural power of fruition shows her (as mother nature) to be gifted with divine and sublime principles for her practice in developing her concepts, which concepts vegetate, thrive or grow, and are quickened and preserved by a power above Earth's conception of power.

The exquisite quality, nature and character of a flower can be attributed to spiritual reality alone; to the highest spiritual refinements, daintiness, wholesomeness, wholeness, holiness, purity and infinite excellence. The grace, the art — yes, and the science — the radically persistent processes of growth or vegetation can be attributed to Spirit's urge and energy only.

Mother nature's promise, her troth and her fulfillment of every natural promise, and her humanly inconceivable order and her obedience to orders, show precision and heavenly glory in every impulse; show spiritual wisdom in every move.

It is Spirit who causes the blade of grass to spire. It is Spirit's power that motivates, impels, spirits or drives the whole vegetable kingdom to spore, to seed, to spring, to begin to grow, to sprite, to sprout, to vegetate or to become quick and quickened. Spirit, being The actor so animating, and the vegetable kingdom (mother nature) being wholly passive to Him—or being holy in her response to Him, or holy alive to His spiritual agencies—quickens or vegetates that which Spirit animates, emotes, or motivates.

Humanity, the human mammal, lives within its own animal kingdom where all things are humanized, physicalized, and artificial-*ized;* where all things are humanly designed, humanly invented and humanly supported, or humanly husbanded.

In the human world or realm of human knowledge, all things are manned by the human man or by man kind—the *humus* kind. Here all things are perceived and conceived and are effected or brought forth by the human mammal and his intellect—so efficient is he. He is able to effect his own human nature which is a burlesque upon spiritual nature. His science and art are the caricature of all things peculiar to Realm II and they are in direct denial of all things belonging to wisdom, intelligence and the substance of Realm II, because human nature has carnalized every lovely, real, and spiritually veritable thing; has perceived carnally and sensually rather than morally and spiritually, and thus human intellect and the human mammal suffer disorder, suffer abnormalcy or suffer from unnatural (artificial) causes.

The mundane human intellect stands aghast and amazed before The Holy Ghost, because of its misunderstanding of all things spiritual. To human intellect She is a specter far removed from the human family and from things familiar to it.

From the unholy mundane point of view, The Holy Ghost (like the Holy Spirit) is imperceptible, since the mundane universe is completely satisfactory to the human race, and since humanity's perception is limited to Realm IV premises.

In the Anglo Saxon words ghost, aghast or gast, is the formal root which means to terrify; terror, or that which is terrifying. Again, among the Anglo Saxon synonyms for ghost or gast, are spirit, breath, or holy soul. Ghostly relates to that which is spiritual and pertains to soul as bodiless, and thus the human race is aghast, awed, awe-struck, amazed, and reverently terrified. It is struck dumb with terror and horror or it is struck and stricken by its own amazement, because of its total ignorance of soul; because of its unfamiliarity with Spirit. It is perplexed, bewildered, astonished and somewhat humbled by the thought of such physically intangible entities, realities or veritable things as soul.

The function of Spirit is to move, to spirit, to speak, to breathe forth, or to give impetus to His potential ideas. The function of The Holy Ghost is to ear, to hear, to understand, to conceive, to give form, or to bring forth, in holy and wholly divine form, all ideas that The Holy Spirit sets forth.

Spirit is the Father element of The Logos. The Holy Ghost is the Mother element; the audient intelligence.

Spirit inspires the spiritual sentiments or love. Spirit empowers the thinker's powers of speech, perception, and conception. Spirit animates, actuates, motivates, inspirits and promotes all moral and spiritual prosperity, vitality or health; all integrity, purity or immaculacy; all wise understanding or divinely substantiated wisdom.

The logical, literate and legitimate spiritual thinker is at work spiritualizing that which humanity has humanized; that which the Holy Spirit maintains and the Holy Ghost sustains, nourishes or mothers, makes so or makes as signified.

Humanity has presumed all spirituality (Realm II) to be identical with humanity, mortality, or physicality, and to be identified by physicality or by physical existence.

Humanity, with its humanly familiar gods, persons, and things, is totally unlike Divinity, Spirit, or spirituality.

The Holy Spirit is omnipotence. He fathers all spiritual manifestations or expressions of literate, legitimate, and logical power.

The Holy Ghost is omnipresence—The presence of mother love. She mothers, quickens, nurtures and sustains Her own lovely, immaculate images. She loves.

The Holy Ghost is omniscience—The Truth, science, or divine logic of The Logos. She mothers the spiritually rational powers or the radically true reasoning faculties. She mothers the silent word which embodies and records all truth or logic and all judicial recipes prescribed by The Logos Principle. She is The divine Recorder. Her written Word is the thinker's *under-stancing,* having all of the properties of soul, wisdom, verity, reality, love and spiritual completeness. Her silent, magnanimous, quick and loving gestative processes are divine.

The Holy Spirit is instructing and spiritualizing. The Holy Ghost is constructing and *mental-izing* as Omniscience, and thus the logical and conscientious thinker is responding to Spirit's irresistible appeal.

Spirit and Soul are unfamiliar to the human family and to the human mammal's perception of things. That which pertains to spirituality or to the science, truth or logic of The Logos-Spirit is confused with the spirit of evil, with an evil spirit, a daemon, a mythological deity, an invoker of ill, of curse or of ill fortune.

Spirit or its science has no appeal to human nature, to the human intellect, or to the natural or physical devotee, because it is so far removed from human knowledge. Spiritual soul-science has little or no appeal to the human family engrossed in its worship of its own instituted deities.

Spirit (and its divinely instituted Logos-Principle, high premises and precepts) holds itself aloof from the mundane. This *Theos* embraces no element of badness. This Logos is The good Spirit or the Spirit of Good (God).

The mundane being unspiritual, being material or adverse to soul's celestial atmosphere, has no sense with which to consider or to contemplate the principles and doctrine of Spirit; has no sentiment with which to appreciate them. Thus the mundane minded, the human mammal (with its human knowledge, intellect and animal nature), has no intuition or instinct tending toward the science of soul, *con*-science, moral science, spiritual logic, or The divine Logos.

The human person believes what he sees. He calls Spirit a factor of the unknown. Hence, to him it may be ghastly, ghostly, unnatural and awful. His own physical realm knows nothing of Soul's divine graces, or of Spirit's divinely gracious action, but stands in awe of The Holy Spirit and the wholly (holy) spiritual realm.

Spiritualization of thought begins with cognition and recognition of Spirit as The beginning or First Principle from which all thought and all spiritual thinking take rise. Thus Spirit is spiritualizing thought and thinker to agree or to harmonize with mon—the spiritual logician, doctor of divine letters, and legitimate reader, writer, and thinker of The Word.

Spirit and its meanings must certainly spiritualize even the most honest and conscientious thinking, and thought must unveil and unveil until the spiritual entities or ideas which The Logos-Spirit has caused to exist shall come into view.

The humanized meanings must be consciously and individually denounced, one by one. The spiritual meanings must shine through the human misty or murky mental sky and must enlighten, must reveal the wholly logical images.

The spiritual qualities—man's spiritual properties—such as wisdom, see, hear, taste and feel by means of the spiritual sentiments and intuitions. This is not spiritualized sentiment, it is love. This is not spiritualized human wisdom, it is spiritual discernment enjoying his dominion, and bearing witness as to what he sees. This is not spiritualized human instinct or perception, it is spiritual substance understanding or hearing and conceiving by means of soul or mental-spiritual contact with Spirit. This is not human learning, taste or sapience, neither is it humanly cultured and refined taste, test, or touch. It has no humanly perceivable flavor. It is the spiritual tongue, speech, and speaker teaching spiritualization.

The word divine takes first and highest place in every and any classification. It divides between that which is infinitely perfect or perfectly infinite, and that which is less than wholly and fully good (Good), like God or Godlike, supreme in loving power and benevolent might.

That which is divine is that which is of divine constitution and condition. Spirit is of divine constitution. Wisdom is one of the spiritual constituents of which Spirit is The essential Father. The dominant logic of wisdom is from and of The Logos-Spirit or from The Mynde of The Deity.

That which is divine is sublimely and entirely or essentially and continually self-existent. Love is self-existent. It is one of the elements of The Logos-Mynde. It is the divine sentiments or the embodiment of them, and it has within it no element that is—in any least way—destructive. Hence it is self-existent. It is divine continuity or The living Principle. Life is The vital Principle of Divinity.

That which is divine is that which is immutably true. Truth or divine logic is immutably true, positively intelligent and altogether coherent or heavenly in character.

That which is divine is the sole Logos or The Logos-Soul. It is the entity, the ego, or the sole and only Deity which is expressed in light or divine enlightenment. Soul is perpetually articulate and eternally creative, instructive, constructive and interpretative. He is Speech Himself, always speaking via wisdom and conscience; always radiating His candid light—enlightenment.

Thus The Deity or Divinity may be called The tutelary Spirit who speaks only in the divine idiom.

THE WORD, SUGGESTION

The word *suggestion* comes from the Latin *gero* (*gerere, gestus*), I bear or carry, or from *gestum,* meaning to bear or carry.

The prefix *sug-* is under or below, as *sub-*.

Literal meaning: to bring to mind from under; to bear into the mind from below, that is, indirectly; to carry or put under; intimate, prompt or propose by covert allusion.

Common meaning: to infer, intimate, hint, announce or carry into the mentality, by way of lower human nature temptations or hypnotic promptings; by way of the sub-moral human impulses; to play upon by occult remindings.

The suffix *-ion* or *-tion* makes the verb suggest into a noun of action or condition. Thus a suggestion is a statement—audible or inaudible—that presents itself to one, from under or below one's level or mental status, or from beneath one's realm of reasoning. It savors of moral offensiveness, mental odor or bad taste. It indicates a subtle, morally gross and unrefined worded thought bearing in upon one's consciousness from under or from below. It is a hint or proposal concerning the human desires which claims one's attention or would attract the attention of the unwary. It carries with it a magnetic and crafty quality of willful, *sub-moral* purpose to take control of one's consciousness until its impression is made upon the matrix of one's mentality. Thus a suggestion is more than an intimation if it becomes a conception or a fixed perception.

Neither the male perceiver nor the female conceiver should ever accept a metaphysical thing, a thought, or a concept from below highest perceivable point of consideration. Neither should stoop, descend or bend to reflect lesser premises. Both have a sense of moral and spiritual selectivity. Both have the power to be honest with themselves and with their soul principles.

To descend to the mental level of another human being puts one on the human level, which is the human nature level — two realms below logical reality, and one realm below moral literacy, moral courage, moral sense and sensibility.

To descend or to condescend so as to be agreeable to another person or group of persons, is to lessen or lose one's spiritual-moral dignity. To yield or to submit to a regimen below one's highest hope, sentiments or ideals, is to bow as subservient to that regimental master, who will control one by way of suggestion or metaphysical manipulation. To humble or lower oneself to the mental level of the human mammal is to destroy oneself or to dishonor one's self or soul, because the thinker is neither human physique nor human mammal nor human nature, but he is the spiritual ego (wisdom) making no concessions to lesser rational perfections, lesser degrees of understanding or humanly familiar systems and suggestive agencies. The wise thinker will remember that he is three realms removed from suggestion—from sub-animal, sub-human and sub-moral agencies.

The art of suggestion is to attract one's attention by making itself attractive. Wisdom will not lower himself to its low level to listen, to regard, to take notice of, or to attend.

THE WORD, THOUGHT

The word *thought* is the noun form of the verb think. It comes from the Anglo Saxon *theaht, thencan,* think. The Anglo Saxon thanks or thank is *thancian, thanc,* meaning thoughts. The form *thencan* also means to seem. This would indicate supposition or thinking according to appearance, hearsay or human opinion.

The common synonyms for thought are reason; concept; reflection, idea, mind; serious consideration; supposition, speculation, imagination and many others. However, these are unclassified, unpositive and inconsistent. They apply to several degrees of reason.

The common synonyms of think are to ponder; to muse; to cogitate; to consider; to deliberate; to esteem; to suppose. To seem, to believe or to suppose; to imagine—these indicate and involve guessing or surmising. They are without assurance, certainty, conviction, individual proof, confidence or demonstration.

To esteem may mean to estimate duly; to think properly; to evaluate adequately; to appreciate fully.

To deliberate may mean to counsel or consult; to study carefully; to meditate upon deliberately and carefully.

To consider is symbolic of being with the stars; being in heavenly or highly exalted contemplation. As a star reflects light, in the night, so the thinker reflects a high degree of logical and literate brilliance or spiritual splendor.

To cogitate means to be agitated with emotion; to stir one's mental processes.

The verb muse may mean to brood in order to gain more information (to give more thought to) concerning that which excites interest or wonder. Literally, to sniff about or to dream about. It can mean to worry about or to stew.

To ponder is to weigh in the mentality; to seek to find the gravity or the import of.

To reflect involves a much higher form of intelligence. It means to present again, to throw or think back or again, that which is emitted as intelligence or high degree of enlightenment. It means having the discernment, wisdom or concipient power to re-emit or re-bend or bend back that thought which was emitted—as described, as specified or as set forth. Thus a reflection is a true idea having reflective reasoning power; having infinite resources.

Thought must have a thinker; must have a thinking entity to

think. It must have a Principle-Mynde to represent. Both thought and thinker must present the rudiments of Mynde, else thought would be supposition or mere speculation.

This Mynde-Principle is The Beginning of thought (*principium, a beginning*); The divinely established Source and Root from which thought proceeds. Under Prin-*cip*-le is con-*cip*-ience: the faculty or power of conceiving, fully. Per-*cip*-ience is the same excepting that it is masculine or virile in its function. Re-*cip*-ience is the faculty, capacity, ability or capability to receive a rudimental thought or an element of Precept. A re-*cipe* pertains to that which is taken from or deduced from its Principle. A dis-*cip*-le is one who thinks in unanimity with Principle. Dis-*cip*-line pertains to spiritual education in the logic of The Logos; in the literacy, doctrine, principles, precepts and laws pertaining to The Logos.

Thought, reason and re*cip*ient thinking may be experienced in several degrees of correct thinking, as the table shows:

REALM   I   DIVINITY: The Logos-Mynde; The Beginning of wholly logical thought.

REALM   II   SPIRITUALITY: The logician; the thinker or disciple wholly disciplined by and receptive of The Logos-Mynde.

REALM   III   MORALITY: the moral thinker; ethical thought; the honest, hopeful, sincere and humanly reasonable or conscientious thinker; the ascendent thinking that is participating (parti-*cip*-ating) or taking part in its moral share of The Logos-Prin-*cip*-le, according to its capacity or ability to moralize or to reason, to think or to deliberate rightly or advisedly. This thinker is kind, affectionate, compassionate and modest.

REALM   IV   PHYSICALITY: the human nature with its physicalized thought; human knowledge and what is known through human supposition, conjecture, finite assumption, fancy or superficial imagination; that which physicality presents to the physically minded.

REALM   V   IMMORALITY: the inhuman nature with its deliberate and unrestrained malice,

> envy, immorality and revenge; unmorality
> with its blunder and its subanimal slum-
> ber; with its moral ignorance, with its
> deteriorative unthinking or thoughtless na-
> ture; that which is morally unthinkable.

The foregoing table shows Realm II to be the home of spiritually correct and accurate thinking or purely logical reasoning, because it is the immediate, legitimate, and immaculate deduction from The Logos, and because it is directly concluded from its mental Principle or premise.

Realm III is morally, ethically or humanly correct; is good or right thinking according to humanity's best standards. It is made up of conclusions deduced from Realm II, but blended or mixed with physical evidence induced from Realm IV. Here humanity under-takes to reconcile its knowledge gathered from Realm IV to its science of *con*-science deduced from Realm II; undertakes to conciliate or call together (as in or under one name) the person of Realm IV and the *mon*, mind or thinker of Realm II; undertakes to assemble, to harmonize, or to unite the spiritually intuitive with the humanly or physically intellectual.

The moral thinker is inclined to adulterate his conscientiously positive thinking with physically involved precepts, or to compromise with human nature. He must please and agree and live with Realm IV and at the same time live with himself and his conscience under the constant convictions and admonitions of Realm II, via conscience.

Realm IV is physically correct. It presents the basis of physical science dictated by physics, which science or knowledge is of the nature of human nature and its outlook.

Realm V is admittedly *in*-correct in all of its assumptions. It is inaccurate or is an inaccurate sense of all things. It is unprincipled, thoughtless, mistaken, unguarded, untutored, and very impulsive in its nature.

This Anglo Saxon word thought covers a wider spiritual area than the common synonyms, because it includes thank (and thanks and thoughtful and thankful) which means being deeply sensible of kind-ness or favor received. Thankful means thoughtfully grateful.

Kindnesses and favors of a spiritual nature may be the things received, thoughtfully and thankfully. One of the synonyms for The Logos is thing. Hence the things given to the thinker may be such things as the elements of wisdom, substance, the essence of The Logos (such as logic) and an understanding *of* The Logos, to whom *mon* or man—the spiritual thinker—gives thanks.

Thought pertains to those things, ideas, images, expressions and manifestations which are like or representative of The Logos—Giver of all true and vital thoughts, logically comparable to The divine creative Logos. Thus that which is vivid and valid to The Logos is vivid and vital and infinitely substantial to the logician of Realm II, and thus his thanks are expressed by his actual utilization of this vital substance, which, like Truth's logic, is inexhaustible.

The noun thought is Anglo Saxon *thoht, gethoht*. It means process or act of thinking, meditating, considering and so forth. Its scope is too wide for direct analysis. Think and thinker is defined, analyzed and classified as belonging to Realm II. Think is literally masculine, while the capacious *o* vowel in *thoht* or *gethoht* indicates feminine thought capacity or capability rather than masculine ability.

Thought, in any realm or sphere, is an element of consciousness; a mental element. It represents, expresses, or makes manifest the kind of mentality from which it proceeds.

In reality, in truth or in infinite consciousness there are no mental elements other than those emitting from The Mynde or mentality of The Logos.

In Realm II or in spirituality—the home of wisdom and his candid sentiments and positive logic—there are no mentalities or minds other than that one presiding *in* Realm I, and presiding *over* Realm II. These mental elements flow in from Realm I as the wholly (holy), purely (immaculate), wise (accurate) thinker needs them; flow in as the healthy (valid, not vain; strong, firm, safe—not unsound, sickly or weak) consciousness needs them, or as the completely empowered or enlightened thinker utilizes them. They flow in as inexhaustible resources from The ever-thinking Mynde or Intelligence which empowers, inspires, and directs thought.

Mynde—the origin of thought—causes the thinker to understand the speech of The Word; causes him to love and to worship The Logos-Speaker; causes him to accept this Logos-Mynde as his, because he is in complete accord or harmony with this Mynde as direct thought or as directed thinker.

In Realm III or in morality—the home of honesty, confidence, faith, troth, fidelity, courage and conscience—there are as many mentalities as there are human animals, or mammal beings. But the sincere and right thinker looks to Realm II as the medium interpreting The Logos-Speech.

Thought is a magnanimous or soul lighted spiritual word or a universal word, because it is the offspring and representative attribute of Soul. Therefore thought may *not* be tossed into one classification, degree or common heap.

Realm V, being without soul or conscience, is thoughtless, is without reason or rational substance.

Realm IV, being physical and pertaining to the physique and its instincts, is thoughtless, because the human physique does not think and is not a thinker.

Realm III thinks in obedience to conscience and in harmony with moral precept and law. Here thought must represent both the masculine or percipient thinker and the feminine or concipient thinker who conceives, broods or gestates, ponders or weighs (and gives weight, import or importance to) the rudimental thought presented by the percipient or preceptial thinker. He discerns, deliberates, esteems, estimates, speculates and then specifies (to her) that with which he has templed. She contemplates (temples with him), believes, understands (intuitively), quickens (acts upon) and brings forth that which he has discerned and that with which he and she are both concerned. Thus are all moral, good and right issues born and thus they are nurtured and maintained. Thus are the reasonable and morally rational thoughts sustained.

In Realm II the feminine thinker conceives directly of wisdom— the seer. She loves, honors, develops and brings forth his rudimental or potentially existent realities, verities, thoughts or elements of wisdom. This is true thinking. This is spiritual thought (perception) in action via wisdom.

THE WORD, TIME

The word *time* speaks of termination, limited or extended duration. It is a human concept of meter and measure; an element of human knowledge, and an important factor in human affairs; but since it serves humanity in dividing and in limiting, measuring and estimating beginnings and endings it concerns only the finite realm, and has nothing to do with the infinite realm of interminable continuity.

> The Greek *chronos* means time, as in the word chronic (lasting a long time), the words chronometer, synchronal (existing at the same time), chronicle and such.
> The Latin *tempus* (*temporis*) means time, as in the word temporal (relating to time), or the word temporary (lasting only for a brief time).

Time is one of the tyrants of the human race. It has great authority in the humanly instituted world. It limits all things according to human horizons, human points of view and human capacity to perceive. It crystallizes into rules, ruling agents, forms and formidable things which stand as rulers in human thought. It is lord of the day, the hour, the month, the year and the century. It is one of the most celebrated of gods or lords, and probably one of the most faithfully worshipped gods that govern humanity.

It takes part in industry, in season and out of season. It acts somewhat as impersonal and personal despot of commerce; as demagogue, unseen in the realm of credit and all deferred balances of moneys or of labors. It is the greatly reverenced dictator who points his finger at dates, and takes it upon himself to design and to demand obedience to the human calendar and the law of time.

Time imposes itself upon humanity, because humanity has authorized it to do so. It puts the finite stamp on every human action, purpose or endeavor. It encircles, involves, entraps, entangles and environs humanity at every step, for it represents human knowledge. It may be mathematical, but it cannot govern mathematics. It can only blind humanity to the unlimited nature of mathematical certainties.

The one timeless and constant science is *con*-science. It teaches the wisdom and logic of soul and, in this way, it defeats the purpose of time to limit, to measure, to point out beginning, or to mark out the ending. Thinker, soul, wisdom, conscience and the logic of The Logos are outside, beyond, above and far removed from the human realm where time is lord; where time is a humanly conceived and humanly instituted standard of finity which would interrupt the infinite continuity of all logic, literacy and Logos-law or precept or judicial Principle.

Time does not enter into the operations of logical deduction from infinite premise to conclusion. It does not control the functions of logical ideas in their practice of The infinite Principle. It neither starts nor stops, nor governs the mental processes which carry an idea from its precept to its concept, since these can be instantaneous— involving no time. They can be going on at all times as a continual process of thought, perceiving and conceiving, realizing and demonstrating The Logos-Principle. Thus time is a humanly devised thing going on outside the realm of wisdom's intelligence.

THE WORD, Transition

The word *transition* is made up of the Latin *transeo* or transit which means brief or transient, and the suffix *-ion* which makes it a noun of action or condition.

> Literal meaning: transientness; act or state of moving, journeying or passing from one condition to another.
>
> Common meaning: change from one place or action to another; the resulting state of transit.

Again, the prefix *trans-* (meaning through, over or beyond; across; on or to the other side of; complete change; surpassing, exceeding or transcending) may be used with the Latin *sedeo* (*sedere, sessum*), I sit, or *sessum,* to sit. The suffix *-ion* may make it the concrete result of sitting over or beyond; may form it into a noun of action or condition.

Common synonyms of transient are fleeting, momentary, fugitive, ephemeral, short, temporary, brief and others. Its common antonyms are persistent, everlasting, imperishable, perpetual, abiding, permanent and others. It means not journeying; not passing; not unsettled; not disturbed; not disarranged; not unestablished, but established; not restless, infirm or unfirm; not misplaced or displaced literally or figuratively, physically or metaphysically.

The following table classifies the permanent and the transient:

REALM I

DIVINITY: The quick and vital Logos-Principle; The inexhaustible Logos-Spirit; The inextinguishable Logos-Soul.

REALM II

SPIRITUALITY: the thinker's highest degree of understanding, and highest ratio of thinking or reasoning power, or action, or intelligence possible to man, who is spiritual vir-tue; the immutable soul, entity, idea, or complete identity expressing and representing Soul.

This is the realm of wisdom—consciously satisfied, stayed or settled. This is the realm of verity—perfectly and immaculately fertile to wisdom's precepts or principles. It is the realm of infinite and universal continuity.

REALM III

MORALITY: this is the realm of humanhood, humanity, humankind, the human race, the human kind of man or human consciousness in transit wherein human tradition has handed across, given over or has transmitted knowledge, customs, doctrines, opinions, precepts and practices and orthodox conventions from generation to generation. It is made up of human sentiments and humanly established axioms. It is the realm of moralization or of metaphysical, mental and moral transition. Conscience, with honesty, constancy, fidelity, integrity, chastity and such, promotes this transition, while the thinker is learning to think by deduction from Realm I.

REALM IV

PHYSICALITY: the human physique with its human nature, instincts and impulses; the transient, perishable and finite human conception of things which drowns itself in its own sea of knowledge; buries itself in its own Adamic dust of exploded theories and blasted hopes and mundane beliefs.

This is the realm of the proud, bitter, passionate, self-justified and crafty personalities. It is the dead-end of the dream of animality or of physical voluptuousness.

The foregoing table shows that Realm III is on its way from and away from the disappointments of Realm IV and passing toward the appointments of the thinker in Realm II. It teaches the transfinite, the transmundane, transsensual or transphysical.

If it were not for the motive power of right (operative in honesty, veracity, equity, chastity and the other moral ideals) there would be no transition; no heightening of human character; no aspiring sentiments reaching out to loft and to lift thinking from the physically patent realm up, over (not under or below) and into Realm II, where only highest substance is actual or substantial—not transitional.

If it were not for the moral motivations that inspire or lift or urge, or respond to the drive of conscience, there would be no transition; no passing or moving before; no passage from human condition and classification. Hence humanity would remain in its mortality or in its inactive, dead or uninspired and unaspiring condition.

This passage from Realm IV to Realm II takes place according to the go (the Latin radical *it-, ire, eo, itum,* meaning to go) in the human consciousness; according to the moral courage and incentive (that incites to action) or sets the thinker into action and into a state of transition, or causes transit (a passing across; the act of passing).

In this process of going or passing, there is present a spiritually peculiar driving agent which is hope for wisdom, faith in arriving at the point of understanding (or spiritual substantiation), and the moral-spiritual valiancy that promotes this process. This cogent force or driving agent is simply the intelligence of the thinker impelling him to leave human intellect or knowledge—which is spiritual ignorance—and to go where his most intelligent perceptions take him, and where he feels most (mentally and sentimentally) at home.

THE WORD, TRUTH

The word *truth* comes from the Anglo Saxon *treowe*, meaning true. It adds the suffix *-th* to form the word *treowth* or truth (the noun) from the adjective true. The suffix *-th* makes it a noun of state, quality or condition.

> Common meaning: the state, character or quality of being true; conforming to rule, ideal, model, reality, standard, fact, or to true and genuine pattern.
>
> Common synonyms: veracity, verity, correctness, sincerity, genuineness, steadfastness, virtue, fidelity, justice, constancy, candidness, exactness and correctness, and faithfulness in some contexts.
>
> Common antonyms: untruth, falsity, error, falsehood, lie, mistake or blunder; incorrectness or that which is improper; unreality or unrealness.

Truth has no true synonym. She stands alone as the absolute and exclusive truth, *treowth or trowth,* or troth. Her literate construction is *tru.* The *u* vowel is highly literate and the consonants are good. The *o* vowel in *tro* (troth), or the *u* vowel in the radical *tru* (true, truth), show soul capacity; and the word truth or troth is of richest degree of logic; is of infinite degree or ratio of both literate and logical rule or intelligence.

The form trow (*treowian*) means to trust, to believe, to be confident or to credit as being true; to depend upon; to give credence; to lean or rely upon. In reality Truth includes all of Her synonyms. They may be called Truth's virtues, realities, verities or qualities.

Truth is infinite and divine and may be capitalized to indicate The Deity, since it is a synonym for divinity.

The following table classifies the word truth and its lesser synonyms:

REALM I
DIVINITY: Truth; The Logos logic; The Word Truth; The Word Troth or infinite promise or pledge of The Word—The forever Word.

> The Word forever true and universally good (Good) or God, IS TRUTH.

Realm II

SPIRITUALITY: truth; the logic or science of The Logos-Truth; intelligence or that which trusts Truth; that which Truth, Herself, causes to exist or to be true; truth identified as being the entity and literate image of Truth; truth, the logician.

Realm III

MORALITY: verity; veracity; sincerity; moral steadfastness; that which is morally right, and trustworthy in human affairs; the conscientious thinker; the science of conscience or the science deduced from truth or the logic of Realm II.

Realm IV

PHYSICALITY: the realm of physics or the natural sciences, based upon and proved or verified by physicality; human knowledge—that which is believed and trusted and called science or truth—that which is human nature's point of view, and its only way of knowing. Thus human nature and human impulse gain knowledge—not science or truth—through the human (mammal) physique, which is its only way or avenue of sensing or of knowing, experiencing or feeling, or trying out or of finding out.

Realm V

IMMORALITY: the realm of all that is wrong or is not right; the realm of complete moral and spiritual ignorance; the antitheses of truth; the very opposite of the science which con-*science* teaches; the dead end or the totally destructive axis and compound axiom of human knowledge; the outcome of knowing that which is pernicious, bad or unwholesome.

Verity is not a true synonym for truth because its vowel *e* is less literate than the *u* in the word truth.

The word verity comes from the Latin *verus,* meaning true, and from *veritas,* meaning truth. The suffix *-ity* gives the word verity its noun form as the quality or condition of being true, of being the truth, a reality or an ever-standing fact; state of being really true or truly real.

The word verity is a spiritual and universal quality, because it means truth, which truth is purely and wholly immutable, illimitable and exacting; which truth in its highest literate and logical form is

Truth or The Logos Intelligence; omniscience. Verity serves Realm III.

The word verity may not displace truth, but the word verities serves to indicate the truths or the elements of truth, wisdom, reality, soul, holiness or integrity as these verities exist in truth or in spirituality, which is the realm of spiritual verities where *omni-truth, omni-verity* or omniscience understands; where purity conceives verily or truly, and where the intelligence of love is a validated or divinely confirmed power loving intelligently.

The word aver means to prove, to verify or to justify.

The word verdict means true saying; a true dictum.

The common synonyms of verity are few. The antonyms are the negatives of verity which deny, contradict, dispute, reverse or negate the statements and sentences of truth. They are the falsities which verity counteracts.

The word veracity performs as verity in human affairs. Veracity is trustworthy or trustworthiness functioning as the moral complement of honesty and honoring him.

In the realm of human affairs conscience dictates verily; dictates and teaches what is sure, very right and certain. Honesty is potent and virile, while veracity is effective and fertile, or she is of highest human degree of certainty. Thus honesty and veracity identify, verify and demonstrate every moral axiom or verity and thus they coordinate, in conscience, or work together in honest endeavor to achieve what is right and of highest ethical standard.

Truth may not be reduced. Hence veracity and verity must begin functioning where truth leaves off—rather, where human understanding and appreciation of truth leave off—and where an honest regard for conscience begins. This is Realm III, where honesty honors conscience (its science) and veracity or verity verifies its science.

Verity is always right; always in the right and always wins in human affairs, because she always brings forth her honest evidence (in her own good time) which destroys the invalid evidence of the opposition, for she and honesty work with moral precision to counteract falsity.

Realm III may not have the vision to discern truth directly, or to perceive the whole truth, but veracity has the moral instinct and verity has the moral intuition to conceive elements, glimpses and radiations of truth made vivid by conscience.

Veracity or verity is an element of human reason; a moral power of conception. She is also a power of contraception, functioning under truth, to contraceive falsity and to lift humanity out of its moral ignorance. Thus to bring all right (moral) thinkers into one reverent body of worship; into one temple of reasoning; into one temple of contemplation wherein *con*-science—the science of soul— is the speaker and the teacher dictating and administering the science which *is* truth.

In Realm III conscience or verity demands esteem, note, affection and even compliance. It works in the name of morality and through humanity's highest concept of truth, as truth is identified in human affairs as being right, true or morally good, or as conscience dictates the honest truth. In this way humanity learns to take due cognizance of truth as that true science which conscience presents, and the science which is corrective, instructive, constructive and spiritually remedial.

In Realm II truth demands esteem. She is the understanding and the under study of Truth; the intelligent attribute of Truth; the concept of infinite Truth. She is truthful or full of truth; fully enlightened by Truth; the very substance and essence of Truth, essentially true like Truth.

Here understanding of Truth is true *understancing*—all that is substantial or substantiated by Truth and is in conformity to Truth. This truth involves reality, divine justice, purity, integrity, wisdom, infinity or universal potency, and it verily counteracts all unreality, injustice and finity; counteracts all inadequate human concepts of truth.

Here truth is the literate (wholly or holy literate) deduction from the primal or divinely original word Truth; the living entity, the vital idea, the quick reflection and the ever functioning agency of Truth.

Truth has no true or absolute synonym. She is one of the members of The Logos, or The divine creative Word and Root-Principle. She functions as Truth. She functions with Spirit as moved or motivated by Spirit, but She never usurps His dominion nor duplicates His function. He moves to give Her voice, breath or the urge to speak by way of record, while She is The Word or Truth which must be put into words.

Truth is not Spirit, for Spirit has His own assignments and His own universal functions to perform. She is His coordinating, cooperating and collaborating element of logic, motivated by Him or energized (spirited) by Him—The Logos Spirit. Her office or function is to demonstrate this logic; is to make so or true to humanhood.

Truth is not Mynde, although She is closely related to The Logos-Mynde as the intelligence held in Mynde.

Truth is not Love, for Love is another member of The Logos whole, who is always present with Truth (like a sister) but always behind Truth so that Truth may protect Her from the *truth-less* and loveless world.

Truth is not divine vitality or Life, but She has Life and Life's interminable vitality, vivacity or quickness always with Her; always present to quicken and to give Her truths (true ideas) their infinite vitality or continuity. Here Spirit provides His living energy.

Truth is not the Soul principle of all enlightenment, for He presents Himself as Father of reality, while She is Mother of true understanding or reality; Mother of all logical substance, divinely premised.

Truth is good—divinely so—but She is not Good, for Good is another one of the names for The Logos-Principle; another state or condition of being divine—logically and literately divine. Good has infinite capacity for goodness. Truth is the infinite capacity and capability of trueness.

Truth is divine but She is not Divinity nor the whole of Divinity or The Deity, called Good or God. She is a member or an entity or a quality called intelligence, which is peculiar to The Deity as resource, property or goods.

Truth is the Mother of Realm II and its indestructible logic, truth or science which She has ever in Mynde. She is Mother of constancy, troth, virginity, fertility, immaculacy, purity or spiritual soundness; Mother of spiritual wholeness, haleness or health, which health is divinely validated or held in that divine status.

Realm III knows truth in the form of *con*-science. Here she counteracts and contraceives delusion, mental wanderings, human foibles and fancies. Here She presents Herself to the human race in the form of soul intuition or science (*con*-science), or as the science (truth) within oneself. This is the true self, consulting conscience or highest intuition within. Here conscience propagates and mothers and nurtures her conscientious, honest, sincere, loyal and morally splendid offspring, while she counteracts or makes impotent such human fallacies and hallucinations as present themselves (as true) to this mental realm. The propagative power of conscience is tremendous. It annuls the so-called sciences of Realm IV which are only human knowledge, lore, art, or skill intellectually applied, diversified and physicalized.

Truth, being the creator and mother of all truth or truly scientific statement, being the Truth-Premise and Principle of all that is infinitely, immutably, invariably and positively divine, gives birth to many divine truths, true conclusions, or truely stated ideas.

Truth's statements are truly worded. They speak for themselves. They are perpetually articulate and they harmonize with all things truly ascribed to The true Logos-Premise. They relate and pertain to the condition of The Logos-Soul and the entities or identities formed, ideated and brought forth by the Truth-Premise.

Truth and Her vital statements constitute the victor, the winner or the conqueror of every metaphysical battle; the consoling, comforting companion with one through every metaphysical contest with spiritual ignorance.

Truth has only one sense—one meaning—and that is divine. She has the power of recordation. Her truths may be learned by heart or firmly fixed in individual conscience. She does not have the power of speech (Speech or The Speaker—The Word), but Soul, prompted, promoted, spirited, or motivated by Spirit, does have the power of expression, speech, lecture, and oration.

Truth is a loving, living or vital mental principle; a thing of The Logos-Soul, but She depends upon The Logos-Spirit (The Spirit of logic) to promote, to cause to move forward, to move or *emote,* to actuate, drive forward, or to urge, and to impress the truth upon the thoughtful, the thankful or attentive.

THE WORD, UNDERSTANDING

The word *understanding* speaks for itself. It is a compound word embracing the words under and standing. It comes from the Anglo Saxon *standan,* meaning to stand. The word under is an adverbial prefix, making the whole word understanding a verbal noun with an adverbial nature, placing the stand, the standing or the thinker under, below, or underneath something to which the understander is subordinate, and upon which the stand or standing is wholly dependent. Hence the word understanding is one that requires a subject, a theme or a specific premise-principle under which to stand.

The following table will classify the word understanding, and will show that something or principle under which the dependent idea stands:

REALM   I   DIVINITY: The divine creative Logos, Word, or Principle which substantiates divine verities, ideas, and realities, logically and literately.

REALM   II   SPIRITUALITY: the realm of understanding, standing directly and immediately, constantly or interminably under Realm I.

REALM III MORALITY: the realm of moral apprehension entirely dependent upon Realm II for principles under which to stand; conscience and its science understanding the wisdom, science or the logic of Realm II.

REALM IV PHYSICALITY: that which constitutes its own premise.

Understanding is that logic, literacy and law which *is* standing under that which stands forever. Thus understanding is forever substantiated or is continually substantiated by The creative Root or Logos-Premise, as the very, veritable substance and true essence of Realm I.

Understanding is at once a compound substance and the compound understander or thinker. It is at once reality, the *re,* the thing itself, and the realizer who is standing under The *Re* or The

[417]

Logos, and who is demonstrating the literate continuity, the legitimate integrity, and the logical substance of The Logos as demonstrator, as integer, as entity, as logician and as understander.

Understanding is that realm in which The Logos reigns and over which The Logos-Principle presides. It is in complete line, order and harmony with The Logos as to logic, literacy, rule, recipe, and sentiment. It is that realm of heaven or harmony, or concord and ultimate hope. It is the realm of ultimate conclusion and infinite deduction where wisdom dominates, and is perpetually maintained.

The human race believes that understanding (logic, wisdom, and metaphysical substance) is confined to realms of lower degree; to realms of temporality, but the only substantial element of understanding familiar to the human race is the science of *con*-science which represents wisdom and his logic, or is the phenomenon of understanding, or of Realm II.

The human race adulterates, mixes, and reduces understanding to human level of comprehension or understanding, and thus amalgamates its human intellect with that which it deduces from Realm II. Hence the intelligence which embodies understanding is lost.

Understanding, as it exists in Realm II, is the very synonym of reality. In reality understanding *is* reality and reality *is* understanding—The Re or Logos understood, and realized or demonstrated in the absolute.

This means that there is no element of unreality in reality and no element of that which is only relatively true and real. It means that human intellect has no presence or place of standing and no standing in this place of complete understanding, because understanding is the expression of The Logos Intelligence—not human intellect.

Understanding is the conscious presence of Verity, Truth or Her infinite verities and realities, which constitute the thinker's intelligence. It is the goal of human hope and conscientious purpose or moral prosperity.

When hope progresses far enough away from human knowledge and its intellect then human hope may become a reality.

When moral prosperity, hope and its confidence aspires and prospers high enough then it has taken form in reality, or as a reality or idea realized. This *is* understanding.

When human desire reaches understanding (carrying its faith, confidence, and hope with it) it reaches the realization and verification of the worthiness of that desire.

A worthy desire or hope or a sincere aspiration has a spiritual nature. It inspires and lifts the human aspirant up into a higher conscious state where invariable faith always carries the thinker.

Understanding is reality substantiated and reality is the substance of The Re or Logos understood. It is radically real or spiritually rudimental and veritable.

Understanding is the state, quality, or condition of being environed by infinite reality; of being embraced in real substance; of being composed and compounded of divinely substantiated logic, literacy, and law. It is the state of being the logician, the doctor of letters, and the judge and preceptor and teacher of all divinely quickened wisdom or wise ideas. This logician (understander; demonstrator) is embraced *by* and *in* understanding. Those whom he teaches are embraced, embodied, and incorporated in Realm III, as aspirants who seek understanding.

Understanding is that condition of present, conscious being which environs one, as his own purely spiritual mentality or individual consciousness, acknowledging himself to be the substance and essence of his Logos Esse. This Logos maintains understanding in all of its validity, integrity, vitality, and infinite purity; in all of its logical and literate perfection; in all of its legitimate completeness.

Understanding is made or created of divinely select or selected substances and essences; of divinely elected constituents. It is full ratio of comprehension, reason, wisdom, discernment, judgment, discrimination and the powers of perception and conception.

Understanding (standing under The Logos-Premise, or Realm I) is the realm of heavenly, immaculate, holy or wholly logical contemplation; is the realm of heavenly, accurate or spiritually literate conclusion.

Understanding is the infinite concept of creation, as heaven, and as earth or the ear (ear-th) understanding Heaven, or standing in the highest degree of appreciation of Heaven; standing as the whole compound ideation, and as audience, at attention, under Heaven.

Understanding and heaven (not capitalized) are synonymous terms, since Heaven (capitalized) is synonymous with The Logos Speaker, Speech or Heaver. Understanding is the realm of realized harmony and spiritual concord which is produced or created by The divine creative Speech (Word) understood, eared, heard, obeyed, conceived, acted upon, quickened, thoroughly believed, beloved and carried out or brought forth. This is Realm II and man or *mon*.

Understanding is heaven—the result of being divinely disciplined. It is heaven because it stands under Heaven (or Heaver) as subordinate to Heaven's government or harmonious rule, and it stands as mon—the spiritual creature—understanding and enjoying his state of being.

Understanding or heaven is quite unlike that which stands in line with human standards, or humanity's traditional perception of substance and states of being.

Understanding stands in line with Heaven or with Verity, as standing under Divinity and with the divine states of being; stands in harmony with The Logos Principle and Premise of complete harmony or heavenly reality. It is a consciousness or a conscious sense of being in harmony with this Principle, as the compound ideate properties, essence and substance of it. It is understanding oneself to be the entity, identity or ideate being, standing under the protection or protective supervision of this cherishing Principle, and acknowledging it as Premise and Precept of one's real and substantial being.

Human intellect cannot be smelted into spiritual form. Human knowledge is rebellious. It may *not* be spiritually or divinely disciplined. It cannot understand.

Understanding announces, recognizes or presents that which stands above it; it manifests, reflects and expresses that governing first Cause which stands over and in highest position. It represents effect and attribute of that Cause and that Source under which it functions.

Understanding presents the highest degree of metaphysical power, the highest ratio of spiritual apprehension and reason possible to mon —the thinker, or the divine logician.

Understanding is that experience, that intuitive sense, that spiritually scientific sentiment, which stands under The Supreme Being as being second only to The supreme, sovereign and holy Soul. It is a position of honor, of great dignity and dominion. Understanding is wholly dependent upon its Principle or Supreme Being. It stands in the position of inception or incipiency, or as the initiative actor and thinker acting under the direction, discipline and instruction of its Principle, as recipient.

Understanding is a compound of many rational, functional elements or powers. It embodies a feeling of divine dignity derived from above. It embraces man's own peculiar spiritual property or proper substance which substance is substantiated and maintained by The infinite, inexhaustible, and inextinguishable light from The living Word, or Logos; which substance and essence stands forever with mon—the immaculate and accurate thinker; which substance constitutes a compound of enlightenment or one's own condition of resourcefulness communicated to one from The Logos-Intelligence.

Understanding is the legitimate offspring and the essential powers of speech, of iteration, of reiteration, of reideation, or the ability to trace the outlines of thought which are instituted by The Logos-Mind.

In order further to define, classify and analyze the word understanding, and in order to separate it from human knowledge, let us compare it with Realm III mode, manner, way and mandate; its way of interpreting, judging and comprehending all things; its point of view or discernment; its ear or ear-th of reception (understanding).

Realm III embraces within it such judgment as conscience sets forth; such reason as honesty honors; such verities as veracity loves, honors and obeys. It possesses the vital properties of patience, hope, charity, fidelity, compassion, moral stamina and a good ratio of integrity and constancy. It has a fair comprehension of Realm II and its wisdom and it has an affection for wisdom. It is teachable and morally receptive of the understanding of Realm II, but it is not fully aware of the logic of Realm II.

Realm III divides its premises or its metaphysical stance (and sub-stance) with Realm IV and partakes partly of the knowledge peculiar to Realm IV. This leaves conscience to be the factor of science teaching the logic of Realm II (in Realm III). It leaves physics to be the Realm IV factor of knowledge teaching the things of a physical, literal or humanly familiar nature (in Realm III). Thus Realm III is in process of transition—leaving physical premises and rising up to understanding (Realm II), which understanding is comparable only to Realm I.

Thus it is that by comparison one may see that physicality constitutes its own premise and that it is entirely unrelated to that understanding which is deduced from Realm I—that understanding which *does not* partake of either human intellect or physical knowledge.

Understanding, in its true and wholly spiritual sense, is that great ear or conceptual intelligence or concipient capacity which ears or hears, and keeps alive or keeps vibrant; that holds or sustains the radiant qualities and tones of The spoken Word or divine expression. Thus every infinitely harmonious element of sonant or silent verity, reality, or true idea, stands in understanding.

Understanding is that spiritual capability that stands directly under, and understands The Logos-Soul utterances, and maintains their radiant energies or spirited radiance, or divine radiations. Understanding, standing thus in direct line with The Speaker and emitter of universal ideas, hears and understands, conceives and nurtures or ponders them, remembers them or keeps them quick, nourished or in a state of unbroken action. These universal ideas or utterances are kept vibrant by wisdom, by the powers of universal perception and conception or spiritual realization. They are in constant use as elements of light or enlightenment; as elements of silent or sonant radical radiations, eternally energized or spirited by The Logos-Spirit.

Understanding is the divine instrumentality of reception; a compound mental instrument that receives, registers, records, reflects and reiterates or reideates the lesson, the selection, or the elegant lecture of The Logos, uttered in divinely euphonical diction or in Soul style. Understanding is the reality of these lessons; the realization of these records or these recorded ideas; the substance, understancing, substantiation or spiritual stamina that upholds and beholds them in the light of divine logic, literacy and precise condition and position.

Understanding is the consciousness standing directly and immediately under Divinity, and manifesting, deducing, displaying, and illustrating the substance of Divinity.

Understanding embraces, embodies or encompasses wisdom, his power, his sentiment, soundness, validity, integrity and spiritual purity.

Wisdom may involve experience, while understanding is a matter of standing in the right place in relation to one's governing Premise, Principle or Realm I Precept and subject. It is a matter of standing where one thinks or conceives by direct and immediate deduction from Realm I. It is a matter of standing in humility, as being tractable, teachable or altogether receptive of the sentiments, truths and living soul recipes prescribed or assigned.

Wisdom is a dominating sense of being. Understanding is a staunch or firm and firmly established position taken and held on a purely spiritual level or in divinely perfect balance.

Wisdom is one of the elements of understanding, while understanding is that steadfast or firmly fixed point of view (perception), place of standing (stand or status or *statua*) where the image of The Logos or the logician stands. It is a position or place of mental poise, a posing place or a position of tranquillity where the positive or radically spiritual thinker, perceiver, conceiver and understander stands poised, stands or poses in spiritual posture.

The human race (humanity) has appropriated, assumed or has feloniously claimed and erroneously conceived all this status or spiritual substance or understanc-ing to be its own, yet arithmetic (or mathematics) is the only kind of abstract science that humanity accepts which partakes of the fixity of understanding or of the immutability of its wisdom, or of the infinity of its logic.

The word substance comes from the Latin *substare,* to be under or present, stand firm.

The prefix *sub-* means under.
The root *sto* (*stare, status*) means I stand, or *statum, stitum,*
    to stand, or *stans, stantis* means standing; *sistere* (*sisto,*

statum), to cause to stand; *statuere* (*statuo, statutum*)
means to station, to fix, to place.
Literal meaning: standing under, stationed under, caused
to stand under or understanding or standing firmly fixed;
I stand present; I stand firm; I stand under.

The foregoing analysis presents a sense of substantialness; a
sense of reality, immutability, verity or solidity; a sense of metaphysical
soundness, genuineness, completeness, wholeness, holiness or integrity
in the entity who stands so.

The suffix *-ance* is *ence;* the Latin *-antia, -entia* (*entitas,
ens, entis*), meaning thing, entity or esse; a being. It
gives it state or status, and gives it the entity, I, which
is he who or that which stands under.
The prefix *sub-* also means below, beneath or lower than.

The substance of The Logos is derived from The Logos-Root or
Source; is lower than The Logos as disciple under the discipline of
The Logos or Word. It is divine in substance and spiritual in essence,
and thus it embodies the I or ego who stands under, understands, and
represents The Logos as entity, esse, thinker, perceiver, conceiver and
essential agent.

This substance is the doctrine, word, logic, principle, precept,
wisdom, powers of realization and the faculties of infinitely rational
expression, which are fixed to stand in their sequences as whole entities;
to hold their stance under their Root-Principle; to stand as attributes
of their Root-Source.

The substance of a premise is its conclusion standing firmly fixed
as consequence of reasoning from premise to conclusion.

The substance of a precept is its concept standing as proof, demonstration
or a verified element of reality.

The substance of a principle is its infinitely practical and intelligent
entity or expression which identifies itself by being an essential element
of its principle, by being wholly like and wholly related to its principle
and by being of the same nature, character and substance.

Substance, understanding or a substantial idea stands under its
principle or Root-Principle as that entity who has been disciplined by
Principle or tutored by wisdom; as that highly principled identity
understanding The Logos-Word; as that thinker of highest ratio of
intelligence or reasoning power stanced in the realm of infinite reality,
wisdom, logic and understanding. Here substance *is* understanding
and understander.

THE WORD, Universe

The word *universe* comes from the Latin *vertere, verto, versum,* meaning to turn, or *versus,* meaning I turn. It adds the prefix *uni-,* meaning one.

Literal meaning: I (The Creator) turn into one; to turn into one system of created things; that creation which is turned into one whole, or one whole creation, or the whole creation.

Creation may be composed of this solar system of ours, as well as all solar systems together with all things belonging to and pertaining to them, as human knowledge teaches.

Creation or the universe may be made up of the morally mental spheres, the metaphysical bodies or the more celestial sense of things. It may be considered in its figurative or symbolic sense. It may prefigure all things under the comprehension of conscience, which *con-science* turns all things into one science as seen from soul's point of view, and according to moral import. Each element of the universe may be only as its individual virtue presents it.

The universe and its creator may be what wisdom realizes it to be —wholly spiritual in its significance and substance; the opposite of mundane formations. It may be one logic, one literacy and one law-principle functioning in perfect harmony, governing many spheres and many systems of individual spheres, ideas or spiritual (heavenly) bodies; many planets responding to this sole (one) principle and as a unit of The Soul-Principle; many sols or suns typical of Soul— The Logos-Soul being The Creator and Maker.

The universe may be regarded from many points of view. This treatise gives five different realms of perception or sight from which it may be regarded, as the following table indicates:

REALM   I   DIVINITY: The one whole, divinely coherent universe; The Word—worder, diviner, designer and composer of all verse; The one Verse or Word—Source of all logic; Root of all literacy; Premise of all law.

REALM   II   SPIRITUALITY: the one creation evolved from Realm I.

REALM III   MORALITY: the humanly right sense of creation; the moral concept of all things as dictated by conscience.

REALM IV   PHYSICALITY: that which physical science or human knowledge avers concerning the universe or creation; the finite point of view.

REALM V   IMMORALITY: the adverse point of view or the denial of the moral sense of creation; the reverse or opposite of the science of con-*science;* that which is perverse — turned the wrong way.

The foregoing table shows the five planes of sensibility or perceptibility; the four planes or mental realms from which the universe may be viewed as points of view which project their own views. Physical science presents a universe of precision, order, beauty, color, vastness and mechanical art. Moral science (con-*science*) presents a universe of metaphysical import, in which it considers honesty, piety, moral equity and justice to be of universal import.

The word universe has only one real meaning; only one metrical line of thought turned into one Word — The Word — which is the Logos-Axis and hub and center, including that which depends upon that center for its design, its substance and its existence. This must be illustrated by some humanly tangible thing, for it is three realms above, beyond and removed from humanity, physicality and human nature. Let an intricately formed snow flake or snow-crystal with its six spokes, six points, and one hub illustrate the universe. Let it symbolize, typify or signify the one Logos-system, The one Word or literate system, or the one legitimate axis Root of all that is infinitely logical.

A snow-crystal presents the precision of form, the perfection and completion of the whole, the thought of love, loveliness and beneficence in its gentle design. It represents the divine phenomenon of The Maker's intelligence, the exquisite way in which The Maker cherishes that which He—The Logos—forms or creates. Thus The Intelligence of that which is called the universe—The universal Intelligence—made evident in the snow-crystal, includes, embraces and embodies the wholly intelligent universe, or the whole of that which is wholly or purely universal in its logic, its literacy and its rule. Thus the word universe is equivalent to the word (adjective) divine, and the adjective universal is synonymous with divine or spiritual.

A universal word or element turns in all directions and may be formed into any and all parts of speech, to be used universally.

Human knowledge does not establish its science upon The Logos Premise or Principle. Its universal premise is established in the human intellect as that which human knowledge calls creation or the humanly encompassed and humanly accepted universe, which universe embraces the human physique as the entity, person or man (the Adamic kind).

Human knowledge or intellect views the universe from its point of view, observing its own premises and precepts—not observing the divinely universal Principle.

The human intellect reads, gathers, chooses and wills its own point of view (physical point of view) from every word, every statement or sentence that it reads. It sees, observes, perceives and conceives what it views from that point of human view. Its figurative sense is born of its physical sense. Its metaphysical figure (universe) is only the mental image, picture or formation drawn from its physical, literal universe, known to human nature.

The soul willed thinker, the morally willed, or the conscientious thinker builds his universe upon the virtues, the order, the precision, the dignity and the premise which the physical object presents, expresses or makes manifest. The finite universe becomes only phenomenon of his noumenal or infinite universe from which he deduces his conclusions or his understanding of all being.

The physical universe interprets the spiritual language or speech of the higher metaphysical universe. Every animal, every plant, every mineral in the sky and on the Earth, can only speak to humanity of The universal Cause; can only symbolize that which is three realms removed in premise.

The universe is The One Word; The sole and Soul-Logos; The one verse, having one Root, one stem and many functioning ramifications or ideas. These ideas are like the petals of a flower—all counted and accounted for and all manifestly designed by The Logos-Intelligence. These petals of a flower may be white or of brilliant color. They may be few or many, according to the design and according to the root from which they spring. The design may be infinitely delicate, but it may be exquisitely precise. This or these (petals) may be on and of a tiny flower which is of a cluster of flowers at the end of a tiny stem which ramifies from a greater stem, which ramifies from a branch or limb and trunk of greater ratio and power—all this is the expression of The sole Word and Source and Cause of rational power and the beautiful miracle of The sole Intelligence.

Wind, in its physical nature, may be destructive. Wind, in its moral nature, is a symbol of moral energy, honesty and power. Wind, in its spiritual nature, is divine environment, reality, heaven or the state of being in complete harmony with The Logos-Spirit. Thus, as the physical universe (or solar systems) is set in the heavens of space, so the creation or universe of The one Word is set in the heavens of logic, literacy and law or The legitimate Principle—The Logos—and thus the Earth is like the big round flower, expressing the order, color, form, design and infinite ideation assigned to it by The Logos; expressing and presenting what The Creator of it (Earth) has in Mynde (The Logos-Mynde); expressing vastness with delicacy, natural precision with normalcy and perfect cohesion in rule or principle.

When Earth's thinkers have learned to think universally—neither locally nor physically—then this great word will be understood, and mon—the spiritually glorified thinker—will find himself to be heir to all wisdom, universal substance or properties of The Logos.

When Earth's thinkers have learned that what is called space between planets or solid objects, only typifies the heaven or spirituality (Realm II) in which glorified ideas run to and fro; in which related sentiments or heavenly images and intuitions express themselves or bring inspired messages or enlightenment; in which intelligence lives or pervades and realizes and establishes intelligent points of view or points from which to view; in which wisdom sees clearly or has an unobstructed point of view.

Space has its universal significance. It differentiates between the revealed (or obvious) and the other heavenly bodies or planets (unrevealed to humanity) other than the Earth so familiar to humanity. It typifies that which is filled with ideas unknown to humanity.

The humanly obvious sun, moon, planets and such that seem to float in space typify or symbolize the human conception of things. The thing called space may symbolize human concept of heaven—that which is without things, objects or solids. So the universe, as humanly conceived, may be one great compound thing consisting of many things. But the universe, as conceived by mon—the thinker—is one whole and complete Verse, Word, Logos or divine Thing, and consisting of ONE Thing or divine Theme.

THE WORD, Wisdom

The word *wisdom* comes from the Anglo Saxon *wis, wita, witan,* meaning see; seeing clearly; discerning wholly. It means sage, and wit means ingenuity, quickness of comprehension; awareness and alertness of apprehension or perception; unlimited aptness or ability to judge; infinite ratio of reasoning power.

The suffix *-dom* gives the word wise its noun form. It gives it rank or domain, state or condition and a totality of being or a collective sense of being. It gives it status as lord, as ruler, as sovereign (*dominus*) or as master; as dominant; as having a sphere, realm or domain; as having a kingdom or a dominion over which he presides (as wisdom) and over which he has jurisdiction.

Wisdom has no synonym. However, knowledge is given as such. But knowledge is a human acquirement, while wisdom is a spiritual endowment. Knowledge is that which human intellect has collected and recollected. Wisdom is the state of being fully enlightened, or is the condition of being intelligence—collectively. Knowledge is a collection of that which humanity has elected to call learning. It is human erudition or that which may be gathered or read from scholars or the learned, while wisdom is the condition of having complete access to Intelligence and is the state of being the attribute of Intelligence; the character who witnesses or testifies to the immediacy of the logic of The Logos-Intelligence or the enlightenment derived from that Logos-Source.

Wisdom is neither stored nor gathered. Human knowledge is gathered, selected, collected and recollected. It is recorded and stored and remembered and transmitted or handed down as traditional doctrine, beliefs or static intellect. It is *not* emitted from Intelligence in the form of clear, pure, quick, vital or valid wisdom—radiating light.

Human learning (lore or erudition) is humanized sense or conception. Much of it derives its proof or testimony from physicality or the physicalized sense of things.

The following table classifies the word wisdom:

REALM   I   DIVINITY: The Logos-Intelligence.

REALM   II   SPIRITUALITY: the spiritual logician, wisdom or intelligence; the legitimate and wholly literate or fully enlightened thinker.

REALM III   MORALITY: humanhood and its honored
             intellect or popular knowledge; its *human-
             wise* or human way of thinking; that which
             is humanly erudite.

             This realm understands and obeys wis-
             dom, only so far as it obeys *con-science*.
             Wisdom leaves off where human knowl-
             edge or intellect begins.

             Human physics and metaphysics.

REALM IV   PHYSICALITY: the basis of human knowl-
             edge; the home of human nature; the
             premise of the corporeal impulses; the
             negatives or antonyms of wisdom and of
             all Realm II properties.

REALM V   IMMORALITY: moral ignorance; mental
             barbarity; unmorality or human nature's
             sensuality; animosity; animality; envy or
             active, but silent enmity; the mortal or
             dead-end of the intellectual fool.

Realm V is the finis, end or finale of human intellect and its
premises; the conclusion of folly; the damnation of false conception;
the misconception or the contraception of the germs of wisdom; the
fruition of human knowledge and its finity. It is the hell fire of envy,
vengeance, remorse and such inflamed conditions. It is the mental
lime pit of lust or the heat that vaporizes the vanities, the images
and the imaginations that human knowledge excites.

Realm IV is the humanly tangible picture and concept of things
as they exist in the educated or civilized mentality. Here the human
physique is more or less at the mercy of human nature and knowledge, as education has designed and has assigned it to be, or as the
human mammal is supposed to be.

Realm III embraces the moral sage, skilful in dealing with the
natural human artifice of Realm V. Thus Realm IV becomes the
physical battle ground and the metaphysical field of contention between moralization (the principles of conscience) and demoraliza-
tion (alienation or estrangement from conscience), as exists in
Realm V.

Realm II embraces wisdom who is a member of this spiritual
assembly of divine logicians; a member of the body or the temple of
contemplation, even as wisdom himself is embodied in The Logos-
Mynde and represents and embodies the principles, precepts and

premises of Realm I. He stands under, understands, sits, resides, abides and is settled in Reality — Realm II — immediately under Realm I, and, from this point of view and point of understanding, he sends forth his ministering, tutoring thought entities or ideas to counteract all spiritual ignorance or foolishness in Realm III.

Wisdom is not a speaker. He is a seer. He sees Spirit wise or spiritually. He speaks through conscience, to humanity or to the human race, or to mankind; through the breath of Spirit, breathing out or speaking out words of wisdom.

Wisdom, being fully enlightened, sees. He bears witness as to what he sees, by way of *con*-science who is the voice of Soul, setting forth the science of soul as wisdom sees it and as wisdom directs, teaches and dictates.

Wisdom, being spiritual discernment itself, sees and understands the logic of Soul or the logic of The Logos, but this logic must be reduced to the human realm; must be reduced to the science of soul, and to the science and art of human reasoning; must be reduced and voiced so as to engage the human ear. Thus conscience becomes the diction (speech) of wisdom and the agent of wisdom, sent to human consciousness to dictate bits of wisdom's silent address.

Wisdom is a thinker. He cannot enter human thought. Only conscience may gain entrance or may interest the conscientious and more discerning thinkers of Realm III.

The voice of wisdom (via conscience) is positive and affirmative. Human reason needs no interpreter to explain what he advocates, yet his diction and his jurisdiction and his *con-dition* or *con-diction* is wholly spiritual. This condition is felt in Realm III by discerning thinkers. His great rational power is felt.

Wisdom provides conscience with both his logic and his power. He prescribes remedy to cure (make accured or accurate), to make right, to rectify, to make valid or to make morally sound.

Wisdom, working through conscience, is the wise administrator of his own wise precepts which concern humanity. He is legislator of the moral laws which conscience can enforce, and does enforce by reiterating, readvocating and redictating wisdom's judgments or his decisions to the realm of human reason and human utility.

Wisdom and conscience are always right. They coordinate, collaborate and coincide in sentiment and in science.

Wisdom is a masculine entity to be spiritually loved, honored (by conscientious thinkers) and obeyed by mankind as the right way— the way in which conscience leads. He is the husband of spiritual sentiment or love; of verity, truth or validity; of the power of conception in its immaculacy or purity.

He is an entity, an idea, or spiritually identified thinker who propagates or multiplies by means of being beloved and believed. He cannot prove, verify, test or demonstrate his own virility. Only verity can do that. He cannot wife himself, or mother his own potentialities. He characterizes spiritual husbandhood. He must have an equally intelligent conceiver with the power of infinitely alive intuition, to quicken and to bring forth his potential issues, his highly principled rules, recipes or fully discerned precepts. He *must* be loved, honored and obeyed. His principles and precepts must be obeyed as he and conscience present them.

Philosophy is the love of wisdom. There must be a concipient intelligence, or a fertility and a love and an honor for wisdom's presentations, for they are potential until they are conceived, gestated, quickened (acted upon), brought forth, brought into evidence (among spiritual thinkers) and loved.

Wisdom stands at the point of incipiency where he receives infinite enlightenment; at the point of understanding where he understands and where he derives his sound judgment, his wholly spiritual discretion, and where he becomes cognizant of himself as logician of The Logos —as wisdom itself.

Human intellect or knowledge is an accumulation of humanly prescribed information or learning which may be stored up in the human mentality, while wisdom is the spiritual ego or seer of infinite vision who stands immediately under The Logos and has immediate and direct contact with The Mynde of The Logos as representation. Thus his perspicacity is instant, his discernment is immediate, his mode of judging is immediately effective and permanently substantiated or settled.

Wisdom is the logician and the wit (spiritual ingenuity) of Realm II. He presents himself to Realm III by way of *con*-science, while he may be known as *pre*-science. He cannot reduce or demote himself in order to reach the human ear with his sciences and sentiments but he teaches through con-science. Thus con-science becomes the sage or the moral school master, functioning as moral sagacity and dictating wisdom's instructions. Conscience becomes lecturer bringing the rudimental elements of wisdom down to human comprehension; becomes wisdom's messenger and minister.

The thinkers of Realm III must test and taste and prove and validate their own concepts and understanding of conscience. The conscientious thinker must believe, belove and sustain and honor and dignify wisdom's instructions else human consciousness is not enriched by wisdom.

Wisdom is an holy and wholly spiritual virtue and quality. He is virile, powerful, potent but potential, even as good seed is potential. He is masterful and dominant and commanding, yet with all this he is unable to conceive and carry out his own wise issues. His rudimental, radical germs of wisdom are like good seed—potential until planted, emplanted or conceived in the mental matrix, and carried through the mental processes of germination, gestation and fruition or completion or verification, or perfection in demonstration.

Wisdom is the state and condition of being demonstrably wise, of having accurate foresight, as being far seeing and keenly discerning. He sets forth no theories—but verities.

Wisdom is spiritual seer and sage—keen of scent or sagacity itself. He is universal prudence, discreetness and judgment—perspicacity itself, perceiving all realities.

The issues of wisdom are the elements of peace. The issues of human folly are warlike.

Wisdom is head and lord of the house of tranquillity or spiritual dignity. Both his discernment and his dignity of office are envied or coveted by the fool. Humanly instituted lore cannot stand in the presence of wisdom nor enter into his divinely, logically and legitimately established house or domain.

Wisdom is that quality of Mynde which is, or would be, as logical on Mars as on the Earth, because it cannot be humanized. He is a member of the universe of Soul. He is made up of the essence and substance, realities and verities of The Logos-Soul. He is universally literate for he presents The Word in its most literately worded form.

The word wise or wit embodies the most literate vowel while the suffix *dom* or *dome* embodies the most capacious vowel. Wisdom presides and resides in the house (*domus*) or dome (*domos*) or consciousness or domain of understanding as lord and master of logic or the science of spiritual substance; and he stands in command of that infinite literacy by means of which he teaches his logic.

Wisdom sees and is seer, perceiving all logic and understanding all law or infinitely firm principles. He functions with the power of speech—not *as* the power of speech. He has the power of discernment, sight, vision, insight, foresight or provision, but he functions only as that profound experience gained from witnessing.

He is not the speaker or testifier. He is the judiciousness or spiritual vision prompting the speaker and providing the substance of his address; providing the wit and the prescience gained from and by perfect discernment — the true ability to differentiate, discern, distinguish, divide, divine or discriminate between the absolutely wise and the relatively foolish, absurd or spiritually ignorant presentations.

Wisdom, together with the other qualities or spiritual properties of Realm II, constitutes the whole idea, the whole integer, the wholly empowered thinker, the holy or wholly intelligent logician or the whole unit of intelligence—attribute of Intelligence.

The word wisdom, like the word intelligence, may be spelled with a capital letter to indicate the Deity. Thus it means all-wise, *omni*-logical, *omni*-literate, *omni*-dominant *or* supreme in being.

Wisdom is *super*-vision. He is supervised by Mynde—The Logos-Intelligence. He characterizes, presents and represents The Supreme Being as most discerning ego, or as entity functioning under The Supreme and *super*-intelligence, as seer seeing perfectly and discerning completely. As super-vision, he supervises Realm III in so far as its mentality will allow.

The materiality or material mentality of Realm IV disallows wisdom, since he presents the logic of The Logos. Realm IV presents and functions under human knowledge, material, natural, or physical sciences.

Humanly popular knowledge is two realms removed from wisdom, two realms removed from the powers of understanding and realization of Realm II—his realm.

Realm V is the result of having functioned under the material premises of human knowledge; the result of an absolute lack of wisdom and the science functioning in and by means of *con*-science. Thus conscience (the intuitive science within oneself) is the scientific and only wise way or gateway, and gatekeeper on the way to wisdom and his domain.

Con-science, being under wisdom's jurisdiction, is using wisdom's diction, speech or dictations; is using his sayings and his laws, recipes and remedies; is exercising his good judgment and authority, but is under his *super*-vision, while wisdom is spiritually prudent; is jurisprudence, integrity, justice and logic—one of the compound thinkers or logicians—and is under his Judge or Logos-Principle.

THE WORD, WOMAN

The word *woman* is of Anglo Saxon formation and derivation. It prefixes the syllable *wo-* to the word man. In every form—*womman, wumman, wifmon, wifmann, wif* or *wife-mann*—she is prefix.

Woman and man are the female and the male individual characters belonging to the compound man. In each case the male term maintains the name, and the female term is indicated by a prefix or an addition to the male form, thus: *fe-male.*

If Mr. John X. Smith has a wife, she is indicated by adding the one letter *s*, Mr(s). John X. Smith. This is all she is allowed as individual, and as woman or female. Again she adds the *s* to he to form she.

Woman is the potential character of mother, motherhood or *matri*-hood and matrimony. Thus for fear of *matri*archy woman has been held subordinate and even inferior to man. But woman, as mater, *matrix-man,* or *womb-man,* constitutes a great power; constitutes a tremendous influence in her power of conception and fruition, both physically and metaphysically.

The word woman may come from womb-man, since womb is also an Anglo Saxon word. It symbolizes the metaphysical capacity to conceive and develop fully. It symbolizes the mental matrix or comprehensive capacity in which potential, moral issues are carried and are borne or carried out. The *womb-man* is the essential element in production, multiplication, fruition, demonstration and realization. A fertile womb is a symbol of the fertile *Ear*-th. It is a fertile ear; a capacity to sustain abundant growth, in metaphysical embryo. *Womb-man* symbolizes the mental ear, the power to enwomb, envelop, infold or enfold, and the ear of intuition.

The good woman of really motherly nature may be likened to the fertile bosom of the Earth, whose gentleness and lushness seem to love and cherish the potential seeds and germs of her natural crop. Earth's power of vegetation is like that of woman. Earth's tremendous power and capacity to sustain abundant growth; her capability in furnishing nutriment for the most delicate and tiny plant; her ability to mother the most fragile and most beautiful flowers—this points to the character of the motherly and pious woman, whose piety is in her own conscience or her moral nature; whose piety is not subject to human formalism, but, like the Earth, subject only to mother nature.

The Earth symbolizes woman again in her passiveness to the gentle wind, rain, and sun, which are the elements outside herself, and which symbolize the male elements. Woman's passiveness to the male elements is due to her sentiments or her sentimental nature; her affection for her natural mate. As the wind functions to help the processes of pollinization, or carries the seeds with the leaves to plant and to fertilize, as the rain waters and promotes the lushness of Earth, and as the sun warms and vivifies and makes evident, so does the male thinker function in advocating, in promoting and in fathering morally potential issues which are conceivable to moral womanhood.

Earth typifies woman or the nature of woman from the physical functions to the highest spiritual ones. Earth may typify woman's literal and figurative functions; her metaphysical and physical functions; her mental, moral and truly spiritual ones, because Earth is true and trustworthy to infinite degree. This is her high nature. She is true to nature. She responds to the rain and sun, even as woman's high, higher, and highest intuitions respond to the mental-moral atmosphere in which she thinks and conceives. This atmosphere has three classifications:

HIGH
Woman's metaphysical ear that is high compared to human nature, and high in the eyes of social standards.

HIGHER
Woman's moral ear, sentiment and intuition; woman's natural moral instinct contraceiving the lower human impulses and conceiving the higher human issues.

HIGHEST
Woman's highest conceptions of right, of equity and of honesty; veracity, herself, honoring conscience and honesty and bringing forth honest issues.

Woman is a universal power of conception believing, beloving, hearing, understanding (intuitively) every honestly uttered and honestly natural truth. She is that quick or spontaneous sensibility or sentimental ability to sense a right, a moral, or a true perception set forth for conception. She has the ability to sense the wrong, immoral, unmoral or untrue (potential) concept set forth for conception, and to disbelieve and contraceive it.

Woman has the metaphysical capacity to gather, accept, receive, utilize and materialize (*mater-ial-ize* or *motherize* or bring to maturity) and to nurture or sustain every potential virtue.

Spiritual womanhood and wifehood *is* the power of conception that develops and brings to realization; the spiritual capacity to embosom, embrace, *enwomb* and bring to fruition, and to nourish that which she loves. She is the full ratio of spiritual capacity or capability, while wisdom and virile integrity is spiritual *ability*.

Woman is the *womb-man* or *matrix-man* who weighs, measures, ponders or casts in her *matrix-mentality* that which she will bring forth.

In the metaphysical realms woman is governed by mathematical rules and laws, as she is in the physical realm where her womb functions are accurately measured in periods of time. Its period of fertility is about thirty years. Its period of gestation is about two hundred seventy-five days. Its season or sowing time is governed by the mensis (month) and the twenty-four hour day. All these characteristics point to woman's capacity to measure metaphysically, intuitively, naturally and accurately.

In ancient times the womb was regarded as a measuring and weighing figure of speech. A womb shaped or pear shaped gourd was used as a measuring cup. It is still a symbol of capacity, a measuring dipper, a meter, metre or metric thing.

The following table shows woman's metaphysical capacities:

REALM   I   DIVINITY: The divine creative (conceptual) Intelligence or Mynde.

REALM   II   SPIRITUALITY: spiritual womanhood and her power and capacity to enfold, infold, envelop, love and nurture that which she conceives to be of soul import.

REALM III   MORALITY: here woman gives ear to honesty and his virtues, his moral science and principles. She functions as conscience or moral intuition and cognition as wife of moral instinct and impulse; as mother of moral sentiments and affection.
     Here woman is veracity in harmony with honesty. She is the sentimental ear open to moral precepts and premises; open to moral courage and his noble purposes. She measures all things by moral standards.

The mental matrix is not unlike the physical one, in its mathematical functions and scientific offices, and in its processes from con-

ception to parturition (which parturition is like mental realization
or demonstration).

The word virgin is made up of *vir-,* meaning man, and *-gin (gyne,
gune, gyn)*, meaning female or woman. It means highest womanly
virtue or excellence. It presents spiritual purity and moral chastity.
Here again the male or man claims the root of the word, and the
female adds a suffix or prefix to designate woman. This is because
man is the whole, compound word which includes woman, as virtue
includes virgin or virginity and virile or virility. Man includes the
whole six or sex different hoods or states of being: manhood, husbandhood, fatherhood, womanhood, wifehood, motherhood. Woman
is the female of man, and man—lifted out of the Adam classification
—is a thinker. Thus *wo-man* or the *matrix-man* is the immeasurable
capacity of conception; the illimitable spiritual power of cognition and
recognition. She is the essence or essential character out of which the
totality of womanhood (wifehood and motherhood) shows forth her
unsullied, logical, literate, and spiritually legitimate sense of things.
She is a *tri-powered* or triply powered entity, holding within herself
the conceptual intelligence to assume the three-in-one character, or the
three characters in one woman.

Through fear of matriarchy or gynecocracy, the world has held
woman in an inferior station. It has granted her a place in the domestic world and in the Eve physique, as generatrix of the Adam
kind and *for* the Adam kind. Eve is the misconception of womanhood. She is all that woman is *not.*

The woman (womanhood) of Realm II is the expression of The
Mother-Logos or The conceptual intelligence of Realm I

The following table classifies the feminine element of The Logos
intelligence, the feminine element of the logician or spiritual thinker,
the feminine element of moral thought, and the specific functions of
the physical and unmoral thought:

REALM I

DIVINITY: The infinitely divine instrumentality or Ear
of The Logos which—as audient One—hears, conceives,
forms, ideates, constructs, measures, miters, joins or
makes into one complete whole, all of the ideas of The
Logos creation; The feminine Intelligence (omniscience)
in which all elements of logic or science are measured
and meted out, or borne out, and by whom they are sustained, nurtured and substantiated; The ever listening
Ear and Mother of all truth, all spiritual verities and living realities; The Mother-Love who loves, immaculately.

Realm II

SPIRITUALITY: the woman and wife of this realm, expresses and represents the divine matrix or The Logos womb (of The divine creative Word) of Realm I. She enwombs her concepts, as woman. She wifes wisdom, as wife, weaving, elaborating, constructing, developing, and uniting wisdom's potential perceptions into one actual and logical record. She is ever recording, ever *wife-ing* wisdom and his holy and wholly potent and wise presentations. She is ever remembering, ever accounting for or giving account and giving full measure—good measure. She is ever in balance with wisdom's divine speech or infinitely wise instructions.

This spiritual instinct or intuition is wifehood ever *true-ing*, verifying, vivifying and loving the soul of wisdom. She is the power and the instrument of spiritual meterage, giving full measure of wisdom to her concepts, and bringing forth by her spiritual standard of measurement.

This woman keeps hearing (understanding) in balance with logical (divine) speech, making this logic and wisdom evident to all holy or wholly spiritual thinkers. Her fruition is the result of her perfect meterage, measuring, and substantiating.

Realm III

MORALITY: chastity, veracity, confidence, faith, fidelity, trustworthiness, moral instinct or intuition, sentiment and conceptivity—these elements of conscience or conscientious thought constitute the feminine element of morality. She conceives the moral aspect, substance and essence (the moral import) of all things presented to humanity, and she gives substantial form to all moral axioms. She gives action to all moral law and quickens the moral concept of all things, while she disbelieves, controls or rolls counter (in action) to immoral and vile impulses.

Realm IV

PHYSICALITY: woman as a feminine physique, which is marriageable, *matchable* or *mateable* to and with the masculine gender or the male human physique, or the male of the human mammal. Here woman is amoral—not immoral.

Realm V

IMMORALITY: woman as the feminine accomplice for every lustful accomplishment; the accessory and conceiver, conceiving and consummating, quickening or acting upon, every illicit, immoral, vile and unprincipled outline—so desired.

The foregoing table shows that whatever woman believes, permits, conceives, and acts upon, comes forth according to the collaborating action; according to the ratio of her intelligence or the lack of intelligence; according to the measure of her mental and physical matrix or capacity to enwomb.

The woman of human knowledge is ignorant of the metaphysics of Realm III and upward; ignorant of everything above and beyond Realm IV, under which she functions. She presents false physics or mortal physics—its passions and sensual desires—and finite metaphysics contraceiving all good concepts and conceiving only the follies and vices of the masculine element of Realm V.

Womb-man may be called the matrix-man. This matrix is impressionable and impregnable according to individual fertility, which fertility may be immoral, physical, moral, morally metaphysical or spiritually metaphysical. This matrix may be impressed—wittingly or unwittingly—by immoral conspiracies making woman an accomplice in crime or vice. Again this matrix may be fertile to moral precepts, ethics, principles or factors of law, and may bring forth ethical issues and may nurture and sustain these infant issues in human affairs.

Generally speaking, woman is not as much praised, worshipped or loved as mother. The world grants to motherhood a much higher metaphysical station, a much purer regard, and a much more constant affection or devotion than it grants to womanhood. Yet womanhood is potentially motherhood.

The world puts motherhood upon a high pedestal and grants it a metaphysical base, while it puts womanhood or maidenhood upon a lower pedestal and grants it a more physical (Eve) base by evaluating physical graces and characteristics.

The true character of womanhood may not be physicalized since woman, in her true character, is betrothed to wisdom as the mate of wisdom. Then, as wife of the spiritually virile thinker, she becomes the power of conception and fruition, fulfillment and realization causing wisdom to propagate, to multiply and to become more appreciable to Earth (*ear-th*) or to the metaphysical ear. Then, as mother of wisdom's enlightened, far seeing, prudent and spiritually profound issues, she has made wisdom more evident and has made his potentialities, his inherent power and his dominion more actual, and she has glorified her own inherent power of conception.

In spite of the human ignorance of her spiritual graces, and in spite of the purpose of human nature to destroy the moral and spiritual nature and concept of woman, she has maintained her spiritual dignity. In spite of human envy, jealousy, hate or natural covetousness, woman's nobility, patience and high sentiments hold her in her loft. In spite of human sensualism which would crush her, and materialism that would hold her under its tyrannical heel, womanhood still leads on moralization, and her natural chastity is still promoting further civilization. In spite of the purpose of human knowledge to discount everything unlike itself (which self is finite, pretentious, spiritually offensive and graceless), woman and her sentiments live on by way of intuition and conscience, to show by comparison what she is, so far above and beyond that which human knowledge outlines.

Woman has been used by the world in all offices and for all purposes, from Queen and princess, to literal chattel, physical chattel, moral, mental and metaphysical chattel, or for background or frame or figure-head to protect business, professional, and political careers; used to prop up men's socially and civilly battered reputations.

Woman has been sacrificed as maiden on the altar of every kind of lecherous rule and ruler. She has been bought and sold at auction. She has been held as slave of every kind of lord and tyrant. She has been used as toy for every kind of foul player; as anchor for the moral drifter; as security for the improvident waster; as inferior to every male ego.

In spite of all this, woman stands today in her spiritual serenity and dignity of her office, with her face turned toward heaven, toward wisdom—her husband and emancipator.